Introduction to Therapeutic Recreation

U.S. and Canadian Perspectives

Introduction to Therapeutic Recreation

U.S. and Canadian Perspectives

Kenneth E. Mobily
and
Lisa J. Ostiguy

Venture Publishing, Inc.
State College, PA

Production Manager: Richard Yocum
Manuscript Editing: Valerie Fowler, Richard Yocum

Library of Congress Catalogue Card Number 2004103847
ISBN 1-892132-49-4

Acknowledgments

I could not have accomplished this work without the love and support of my family. Thank you Paula, love of my life, and my children, Michelle and Matthew, the promise of a better future. You are all my inspiration.

—Ken Mobily

I could not have completed this book without the love, encouragement, assistance, and support of my amazing husband Robert, who is my biggest fan, fact finder, and toughest critic, and my daughters Hannah Feiyan and Maya Yunfang, who keep my life balanced and give me new perspectives.

I would also like to thank my colleagues in Applied Human Sciences at Concordia University for their continuous encouragement and advice during the completion of this book. I feel so lucky to have such a great team of friends and colleagues. Thanks to Randy, Robert, Marty, Nancy, Kate, Peter, Fern, Varda, Hilary, and Sandra for the support, edits, excitement, and suggestions.

In addition, I would like to acknowledge Richard Yocum at Venture Publishing for his feedback, his great communication, and his creative ideas in putting this book together.

—Lisa Ostiguy

Table of Contents

List of Tables and Figures

Section 1

Introduction

Chapter One

Defining Therapeutic Recreation (TR)

Learning Objectives

1. Summarize the definitions of TR for each of the three professional organizations: NTRS, ATRA, and CTRA. Speculate on the advantages and disadvantages of having different definitions for the field.

2. Provide a rationale for including health promotion as part of a contemporary definition of TR.

3. Provide an argument for why TR practice requires a separate certification (CTRS) from that of the general recreation profession (CPRP).

4. Identify and briefly define each of the components of the TR process.

5. Explain how the TR Change Model avoids some of the problems associated with most other models of practice for the TR profession.

6. Select your preferred TR setting from those introduced in this chapter. Explain why you would like to work in this type of setting.

7. Explain why it is important to take an international perspective (worldview) of TR.

Why Study TR?

No doubt if you tell people you have selected therapeutic recreation (TR) as a field of study you get blank stares from family and friends when asked to explain it. However, all people regardless of career choice will work with individuals with disabilities, either as consumers or colleagues. For those planning careers in recreation it is important to develop an understanding of TR and the needs of disadvantaged populations in recreation.

The study of therapeutic recreation may appeal to those in a variety of social sciences, because it puts so many theories into practice. According to the American Therapeutic Recreation Association (n.d.), TR is one of the fastest growing professions in healthcare, and the demand for therapeutic recreation professionals is likely to increase given the expansion of long-term care and physical and psychiatric rehabilitation services for people with disabilities. The nature of healthcare is changing (treating the whole client) and looking at prevention and the link between social, psychological, and physical health is becoming more common. TR can play a significant role. With deinstitutionalization, shorter hospital stays, and greater advocacy on the part of people with disabilities, there is a need for the development of TR services in communities.

Why Study International TR?

This book introduces the role of TR for disadvantaged populations from primarily U.S. and Canadian perspectives. Most of the current literature focuses on the TR profession as it has evolved in the United States. It is important to understand different approaches to TR and to recognize benefits of other systems. Often criticized and dismissed as being underdeveloped, the approaches and services in countries other than the United States can educate and guide those practicing in TR. There can be great advantages in understanding innovations in approaches and in solving issues and problems in the field. New and different techniques can emerge through a dialogue between TR practitioners with different backgrounds and training.

The world is now a much smaller place with e-mail, the Internet, and other forms of information technology. Indeed, information may be the most valuable resource any practitioner can possess. Innovation, research, and theory can now be shared almost instantly. This makes for much better practice.

What Is TR?

The definition of therapeutic recreation lends itself to either brief discussion or endless debate, depending on who is having the conversation. Definitions range from the practical (implementing recreation activities for persons with disabilities) to the more sublime (a profession which helps persons with disabilities find meaning in life, or using recreation as a tool to empower people who are disadvantaged). On the surface, defining TR for practical use seems like an easy enough task. But this chapter offers more than just an expedient solution to the definition dilemma. Rather, it presents a compromise, an analysis of definitions of TR that lies between succinct practicality and endless conceptual discourse.

One of the easiest definitions of TR to understand is that it is the implementation of recreation activities for persons with disabilities and impairments. This definition suggests TR is simply a matter of supplying basic recreation service in a way similar to the manner in which it is implemented by community and municipal recreation. The difference between TR and community recreation under this definition lies in the population served.

Equally practical and straightforward are definitions that maintain recreation is to be supplied for reasons of therapeutic change. In this case, recreation participation is a tool or method to bring about functional changes or other favorable changes (e.g., improvement in balance, decrease in depressive symptoms, increase in self-esteem).

Other definitions suggest TR is not as much about the recreation activity as it is about the process. TR is not the casual or random use of recreation activities with persons with disabilities. At minimum, TR is a systematic process that involves assessment, planning, implementation, and evaluation. Further, the systematic process intends to bring about some change, although opinions among TR professionals vary widely on what that change should be.

One of the earliest and most instructive definitions of TR to receive widespread attention was crafted by the Southern Regional Institute on TR (1969; cited in Peterson & Gunn, 1984, p. 2):

> a *process* [italics added] which utilizes recreation services for the purposive intervention in some physical, emotional, and/or social behavior to bring about a desired *change* [italics added] in that behavior and to promote growth and development of the individual.

Certainly, definitions forwarded by professional organizations reflect the influences of the definition proposed at the Southern Regional Institute.

Definitions of TR by Professional Organizations

In North America, three professional organizations represent TR—two in the United States and one in Canada. The National Therapeutic Recreation Society (NTRS) is a branch of the National Recreation and Parks Association (NRPA). It is the oldest of the professional organizations, formed in 1966 from a merger of the Hospital Recreation Section of the American Recreation Society and the National Association of Recreation Therapists. The NTRS represented a tenuous compromise between two polar opposites in philosophy, a compromise that did not last.

In 1984, the American Therapeutic Recreation Association (ATRA) was formed, initially for the purpose of translating a greater percentage of member dues into services for the members (Peterson, 1984). However, ATRA was soon seen as an alternative to NTRS, based on definition and philosophy.

In Canada, the Canadian Therapeutic Recreation Association (CTRA) was formed in 1996 to meet the needs of TR practitioners in Canada. The association was formed through representatives from different regions and was developed to be inclusive of both clinical and community TR service delivery providers.

The similarities and differences in definitions of TR among the three organizations are presented in this chapter. The variability in the definitions lends considerable insight into contrasts in philosophies as well.

The NTRS definition of TR:

> Practiced in clinical, residential, and community settings, the profession of therapeutic recreation uses treatment, education, and recreation services to help people with illnesses, disabilities, and other conditions to develop and use their leisure in ways that enhance their health, independence, and well-being. (NTRS, 1995, p. 1)

The ATRA definition of TR:

> Therapeutic Recreation is the provision of Treatment Services and the provision of Recreation Services to persons with illnesses or disabling conditions. The primary purposes of Treatment Services, often referred to as Recreation Therapy, are to restore, remediate or rehabilitate in order to improve functioning and independence as well as reduce or eliminate the effects of the illness or disability. The primary purposes of Recreation Services are to provide recreation resources and opportunities in order to improve health and well-being. Therapeutic Recreation is provided by professionals who are trained and certified, registered, and/or licensed to provide Therapeutic Recreation. (ATRA, 1993, p. 8)

The CTRA definition of TR:

> Therapeutic Recreation is a profession that recognizes leisure, recreation and play as integral components of quality of life. Service is provided to individuals who have physical, mental, social, or emotional limitations which impact their ability to engage in meaningful leisure experiences. Therapeutic Recreation interventions are directed toward treatment, leisure education, and participation opportunities. These interventions support the goal of assisting the individual to maximize independence in leisure, optimal health, and the highest possible quality of life. (CTRA, 1999)

Similarities

The variety of different definitions by professional associations and by authors of TR texts can be overwhelming to someone entering the field looking for a clear explanation. While differences exist, TR professionals do have general agreement in certain areas. Most definitions of TR include the following components: a focus on health and well-being, a description of service to persons with disabilities, and a reference to TR being a profession.

Health and Well-Being

The definitions presented by the three professional associations do share some features in common. Each is concerned with well-being and health. Certainly, all allied health professions are concerned with the health of their clients. In this sense, the three professional association definitions reflect a heritage of care common to medicine, nursing, physical/physio therapy, and the like. However, recently more attention has been directed toward health promotion and prevention efforts. Most allied health professions recognized it is easier to keep people healthy instead of caring for them after they become ill. In particular, the focus of health promotion within TR is on the prevention of secondary disabilities and comorbid conditions in people who already have some disability or impairment (e.g., a person with alcoholism).

Three recently constructed service models of TR have integrated health promotion and prevention: Austin's (1998) Health Protection/Health Promotion Model, Van Andel's (1998) TR Service and TR Outcome Models, and Wilhite, Keller, and Caldwell's (1999) Optimal Lifelong Heath Model. (TR service models are discussed in more detail in Chapter 9.) As a result, TR practitioners may find themselves in new territory, using exercise modalities more often than in the past. Educating patients about topics such as nutrition, diabetes, and exercise compliance, or teaching stress reduction classes to persons recovering from heart attacks are but a few examples of the new approach to service provisions.

Keeping people well is one of the new priorities in modern healthcare. Several historical developments in healthcare have produced this new "preventive attitude." In the United States, there is no universal healthcare coverage, and the healthcare system relies on a combination of private (insurance) and public (Medicaid/Medicare) support. During the 1970s, healthcare costs spiraled out of control in the United States. Healthcare insurers paid whatever the treatment cost. By the mid-1980s, a more austere attitude toward healthcare spending and concern over inflation (healthcare cost is the single most expensive item in the U.S. budget) motivated legislation intended to bring healthcare costs under control. The result is that prospective payment systems and preapproval of treatments have been in place since the mid-1980s in most areas of the United States. Cost control and cost containment measures produced an environment in which the patient and healthcare provider were required to show why a particular intervention was necessary. This served to restrict access and use of some (expensive) procedures or treatments that have doubtful chances of success.

In Canada, healthcare costs are publicly funded through taxes. The socialized healthcare system relies on both federal and provincial support. Different provinces approach healthcare in different ways, but for all Canadians the primary costs of healthcare are absorbed by those paying taxes. This system demands high accountability to the public in terms of managing the increasing costs of healthcare services. Prevention and health promotion are essential in keeping costs down. As early as the late 1960s and early 1970s, the Canadian government began programs such as "Participation," a campaign to get people to be more active in their leisure, and introduced the "Canadian Fitness Test" in schools to put an emphasis on developing physical health at a young age.

The second key development that fueled the health promotion mentality was that the character of illness changed subtlety over the last 40 years or so. Instead of the typical client in rehabilitation being a young person who had sustained a serious injury, or a middle-age person with a heart attack, the typical client is now older, and afflicted with a new malady—the chronic condition. Chronic conditions are disorders that cause the person to make significant changes in lifestyle, decrease the person's ability to care for himself, and may contribute to the person's eventual demise. In short, instead of seeing clients who are acutely ill (e.g., a battle wound, an infectious disease), healthcare professionals are now seeing clients who do not recover quickly, patients who cannot be cured, and persons who cannot care for themselves after they have completed rehabilitation.

Clients with chronic conditions need a lifetime of "treatment" simply to maintain the functional abilities that remain and to prevent impairments secondary to the original illness. For example, persons who sustain a spinal cord injury are at risk for bladder and kidney infections because of incontinence. They are at risk for substance abuse as a result of boredom. They may develop postural abnormalities (e.g., scoliosis) because of prolonged sitting and loss of tone in the postural muscles of the trunk. They frequently have problems with skin care because of pressure sores (decubitus ulcers) that may become infected. And psychologically, they are too often found to exhibit depressive symptoms because of an absence of meaning in their lives.

Spinal cord injuries are only one example of the complexity of addressing the breadth of chronic conditions. With the aging of society has come a host of illnesses that require ongoing attention just to prevent the afflicted from getting worse. Arthritis is the most common chronic condition in North America. But persons with arthritis are not cured by the treatments they receive. Rather, treatment focuses on pain management and maintenance of the ability to conduct the activities of daily living. The "cure" associated with chronic conditions has more to do with quality of life than eradication of a disease.

Healthcare reform and the rise of the chronic condition have implications for TR insofar as the type of client the TR specialist is apt to see is older, sicker, and in the hospital for a shorter period of time. Much of the intervention effort on the part of the TR practitioner today is directed toward enhancing quality of life through health promotion and prevention efforts. Today rehabilitation efforts focus on advancing the person's capacity to care for himself or herself, to live independently, and to avoid or delay complications and secondary impairments. The brave new world of rehabilitation today cannot be judged in terms of the classic marker for successful treatment that prevailed in the past—remediation of the cause of the illness. Chronic conditions usually cannot be cured. The best we can hope for is to extend the number of high quality years the person has available, where "high quality" refers to self-respect, personal control of some of life's important tasks, finding meaning in life, and self-determination of one's life course.

Service to Persons With Disabilities

Another similarity in the three professional association definitions of TR is services are to be offered to persons with disabilities and illnesses. At first glance, this seems an unremarkable and self-evident statement. Perhaps even a declaration that need not be made explicit. But who are the persons with disabilities and illnesses, and are they always the same? Who is disabled changes over time; hence, who should receive TR services changes over time. Peterson and Gunn (1984) offer one of the most liberal interpretations of whom TR should serve: "Any individual with a physical, mental, social, or emotional condition that limits leisure functioning is eligible and could benefit from therapeutic recreation services" (p. 5). Though a laudable aspiration, we probably need to be a bit more precise than "anyone in need."

First of all, we suggested a new class of afflictions is seen in health-care today: the chronic condition. Professionals in rehabilitation settings will accordingly have to settle for more modest signs of progress in their clients. In addition, once discharged from acute rehabilitation, the patient with a chronic condition will likely need lifelong attention to maintain or enhance his or her capacity to take care of personal needs and to preserve quality of life. Few healthcare professions attend to the postdischarge needs of the person with a chronic condition. Few community-based services and facilities are available for this type of client. Into this void steps recreation services and community-based TR services, if the person with a chronic illness is fortunate. Hence, because of the changing nature of who is disabled and ill, healthcare professions in general and TR specifically are experiencing a shift in service delivery scenarios from traditional inpatient services to outpatient and/or community-based services.

Second, nontraditional groups are in need of TR services. Persons with HIV/AIDS (Grossman & Coreleo, 2001), youth at risk (Baldwin, McAvoy & Schleien, 1989), and the homeless (Kunstler, 1991) have all been suggested in the TR literature as groups the profession might serve. Certainly, TR services for these groups will require new initiatives because of the client's capabilities (HIV positive patients until a setback), because of social stigmas, (clients with HIV/AIDS and homeless persons) and because of prevalence of the problem (homeless persons and at youth at risk). Many are physically well for the moment and many are without symptoms for a long time. Accordingly, the sort of services needed by these "new" groups have more of a health promotion flavor than a rehabilitation theme. (Chapter 5 further discusses services for people with disabilities.)

TR Is a Profession

Most definitions suggest TR is a profession. This declaration is significant insofar as fairly stringent criteria exist for determining whether a particular field qualifies as a profession or not. The criteria to satisfy for a profession include the following: (a) skill is based on theoretical knowledge, (b) acquisition of skill requires training and education, (c) competence must be demonstrated, (d) integrity is maintained by way of a code of conduct, (e) members of the profession are organized, and (f) service is provided for the "public good" and welfare (Millerson, 1978).

The question is: Does TR satisfy the criteria for a profession? Actually, this very question fueled an active dialog in the 1970s and 1980s that never completely resolved itself. Much of the work during that time focused on "status studies" designed to determine whether certain of the criteria for a profession were satisfied or not by the TR field. Some of the findings prompted actions calculated to move the TR field closer to satisfying some of the criteria for a profession. For example, in 1982 the first philosophical position statement for the profession was adopted by NTRS. This action suggested members of TR were of one mind when it came to the imperative for practice of TR. That is, parts of the first position statement reflected TR's interpretation of how it acted on behalf of the "public good."

Reynolds and O'Morrow (1985) evaluated TR according to the criteria for a profession and they concluded TR was a semi-profession (met some but not all of the criteria for a profession). They struggled most with the notion of whether or not TR acted on behalf of the "public good." More plainly, professions ought to have public sanction and the trust of a public to act. This has sometimes been referred to as a "calling" to act in the interest of public welfare (Sylvester, 1998). More specifically: Is a calling or demand for TR services evident? Is TR precipitated by an outcry for the service? Does a social crisis exist that TR responds to? This criterion among all of the criteria for a profession has proven to be the most troublesome of all for TR.

The concept of a calling, which serves as a basis for the founding of a profession, has religious origins. Reforming Protestants like Martin Luther maintained God elected people for salvation and those elected were "called" when that salvation revealed itself to them. This principle was expanded by some religious leaders to include a life plan for the "elect"—"God has a plan for you." And that plan included not only one's spiritual life, but also everyday life, including vocation. In this way, the reformers brought religion, with all of its implications for conduct, into contact with the secular world. It was the duty of the elect to behave in a manner consistent with being saved, to conduct his or her family life in a manner consistent with God's plan. And last but not least, the called individual is duty bound to fulfill the vocation God has chosen for him or her. This ennobled work, and in particular dignified vocations as callings from God. Of course, the religious overtones associated with work did not persist in most cases, but the idea of a calling did (Sylvester, 1998). The more honorable forms of work were those that benefited from their deified roots. Hence, the idea of a profession as not just work but a religious obligation, and later a moral duty, evolved. Above any of the other attributes of a profession, it is the moral imperative of a calling that separates professions from other forms of work and segregates them into a special class of vocation. A more thorough overview of the development of the TR profession can be found in Chapter 6.

Differences

While similarities exist in the definitions of TR, there are also unique distinctions, including the emphasis on therapy, services used in TR, the use of leisure as an outcome, and credentials necessary for practice.

Therapeutic Recreation or Recreational Therapy

ATRA divides its definition of TR into two parts: recreation therapy and recreation services. According to ATRA, the recreation therapy refers to the use of recreation as a method for bringing about change in some other entity that is a marker for health (e.g., decrease in depressive symptoms in patients with mental illness) or a functional outcome (e.g., improved balance to avoid falls in older adults). Conversely, ATRA separates recreation services from recreation therapy, maintaining that the provision of recreation without the intent or design to remedy or restore function does not qualify as recreation therapy.

NTRS and CTRA do not draw this distinction. Based on its previous (1982) philosophical position statement and its more recent (1996) position statement, NTRS continues to argue that TR distinguishes itself from closely related fields (e.g., occupational therapy) by its association with leisure. ATRA would argue that the NTRS and CTRA definitions are equivalent to the recreation services portion of the ATRA definition only. However, a second difference between the definitions serves to clarify this point.

Services Used in TR

Based on the inclusion of leisure in the CTRA and NTRS definitions, some might insist it is the equivalent of the recreation services portion of the ATRA definition. But this would ignore the specification of services offered by TR according to both the CTRA and NTRS definition. Specification of treatment, education, and recreation services in the definitions suggests the intent of TR is to include all three types of service. A distinction between recreation therapy and recreation services is not made within the text of the CTRA or NTRS definitions—each type of service qualifies as a different dimension of TR.

In the United States, the difference in the definitions resurrects the disagreement between professional organizations that predate NTRS and ATRA. The Hospital Recreation Section (HRS) of the American Recreation Society (ARS) and National Association of Recreational Therapists (NART) differed along the same lines as NTRS and ATRA, with the former organization defining TR more broadly, and the latter organization rallying those who believed for recreation to qualify as therapy it had to maintain an instrumental posture—that is, to bring about improvement in health or function.

In Canada, the association representing TR is quite young. Incorporated in 1996, CTRA developed from the parks and recreation movement. With no representation of TR specifically, CTRA was formed to promote and to facilitate communication between and among TR professionals. TR is defined broadly to include all TR professionals regardless of setting (clinical or community) or service orientation.

Leisure as an Outcome

Another difference related to recreational therapy versus recreational services is the centrality of leisure to the NTRS position—that is, leisure is an outcome as well as a modality for the NTRS. This means the point of TR for those ascribing to the NTRS definition is not only to bring about changes in health and well-being, but also to do so through leisure. Although this position is less stringent than the Leisure Ability Model of practice (Stumbo & Peterson, 1998), it does urge TR practitioners to focus on leisure-related outcomes. The CTRA definition highlights the emphasis on leisure, recreation, and play as "integral components of quality of life" (CTRA, 1999). In contrast, the ATRA definition makes no mention of leisure as a legitimate outcome for TR intervention.

What the presence or absence of "leisure" in a definition of TR amounts to is yet another version of the means/ends controversy in the TR profession. By legitimizing leisure outcomes, some who ascribe to the strictly recreational therapy approach fear that TR will not be able to live up to expectations and norms common in the allied health profession culture, a culture that places a premium on health-related, functional outcomes.

More contemporary approaches to reconciling leisure outcomes (Sylvester, 1992) maintained that leisure is a part of a life well lived—what is commonly regarded as usual and normal. Every person has a right to leisure regardless of limitations or impairments. This sentiment is made explicit in both the original NTRS position statement (1982) and its subsequent revision (1996). The emphasis on leisure as a right prompted one author to integrate leisure into a functional model of TR practice.

Van Andel's (1998) Leisure Service/Leisure Outcome Model includes leisure function as one of several functional outcomes expected as a result of intervention. Van Andel maintains leisure is a functional outcome. This line of reasoning holds some promise of easing the tension between recreational therapy approaches in opposition to recreational services distinctions in TR.

Credentials for Practice

Although the definitions supplied by all three professional organizations maintain TR is a profession, some distinctions exist with respect to the credentials needed to practice TR. ATRA points to a more specific credential for practice, the Certified Therapeutic Recreation Specialist (CTRS) document. Although they do mention licensure and registration, the former exists in only two states, and the latter is obsolete in TR. The NTRS and CTRA definitions do not state that a credential is necessary for the practice of TR.

Left unsaid, review of other NTRS documents may reveal which if any credential for practice is recommended by NTRS. Examination of the NTRS Standards of Practice (1995) demonstrates the CTRS document is endorsed for the practice of treatment and leisure education, but not for the provision of recreation services to persons with disabilities. For the latter category of practice, the NTRS Standards of Practice indicate that either a CTRS or Certified Park and Recreation Professional (CPRP; previously Certified Leisure Professional) credential is needed in the United States.

The CPRP credential is designed for the general practitioner and is not specific to TR. Although the certification examination for the CPRP credential does include a section on TR, it is not as concerned with TR practice as much as it pertains to the practice and management of recreation services in municipalities, parks, and commercial operations. This should come as no surprise because the NTRS is a branch of the NRPA, and the NRPA is a professional organization that represents recreation practitioners in general. In contrast, ATRA is a professional organization that focuses solely on TR practice.

Hence, the CPRP credential or the CTRS credential would both be acceptable for the practice of some or all aspects of TR from the NTRS point of view. Again, the difference probably relates most to the contrasting visions of what TR is and what it is to become in the future: recreational therapy versus recreational services.

In Canada, currently no formal certification exists for professionals working in TR. The focus on professionalism in TR is addressed through the promotion and adoption of professional standards for the delivery of TR services. One mission of the CTRA is to develop and implement a plan that will lead to the certification of TR professionals in the near future. Certification and the different professional issues are discussed further in Chapter 6.

In sum, the differences between the definitions seem to be fewer but more pronounced than the similarities. Furthermore, the definitions express one or more deep philosophical divisions that have plagued the profession for many years. Briefly, the flash point of the philosophical differences, like the definitions, focuses on the purpose of recreation and leisure activities within the context of TR. This matter is taken up in more detail in Chapter 7.

Before bringing closure to the present chapter, however, a working definition of TR will be presented. The definition that follows represents a combination of the definitions discussed here and takes into consideration the implications a definition of TR has for the practice of TR.

Toward a Working Definition of TR

For purposes of this text, TR will be defined as follows (see Carter, Van Andel & Robb, 1995):

> TR is a systematic process that uses recreation and leisure activities to bring about favorable changes in the persons served.

This definition contains four key elements: systematic process, favorable changes, use of recreation and leisure modalities, and population served.

Systematic Process

By systematic process, the definition implies TR is planned and not casual. The proposed standards of TR practice outlined by CTRA suggest a planned systematic process, which includes assessment, planning, implementation, and evaluation. In the United States, TR has long been concerned about justifying reimbursement from health insurers. To justify reimbursement for services, TR must be able to demonstrate that it qualifies as "active treatment." Carter et al. (1995, pp. 168–169) remind readers active treatment requires the service must be (a) supervised by a physician, (b) planned and based on assessment, and (c) likely to lead to improvement in the client's condition.

But active treatment is only one way to look at the systematic process. For others, process means something else, something akin to a job description that sets forth duties the TR specialist is expected to perform on a routine and customary basis. For instance, the National Council for Therapeutic Recreation Certification (NCTRC) requires students majoring in TR complete a professional internship that includes the TR process. By *process* NCTRC means

> ...establishment of a therapeutic relationship, individualized assessment, goal setting and the design of an individual treatment/program plan, implementing TR services with selected interventions, evaluating progress toward the plan, developing a discharge/transition plan, coordination of services, and documenting the outcome of service. (Luken & Rios, 1998, p. 3)

In Canada, accountability in a socialized medical system has become increasingly important. Following a systematic process allows for accountability and justification of the need for TR services in clinical and community agencies.

Favorable Changes

Another derivation of the TR process is illustrated in the TR Change Model (**Figure 1.1**). Here the process is seen as a series of steps and duties a TR specialist performs to bring about a favorable change in the client. The advantage of a process model is it avoids ideological and philosophical disagreements and focuses instead on the "doing" of TR practice. This is not intended to minimize the importance or need for philosophical and theoretical foundations for the practice of TR. Rather, the Change Model serves to illustrate the responsibilities that most TR practitioners share in common and routinely perform. In a sense, the model is intended to illuminate the common ground occupied by most TR practitioners.

Insofar as most practitioners will perform most of the activities represented in the model in some fashion, most are also seeking to *change* the client in some manner. Some will call the change therapy, some education, some wellness, some quality of life, some functional improvement, and some recreation participation. Nonetheless, all TRS practitioners intend to change the client in some favorable manner.

Likewise, the TR specialist who does not use some sort of assessment prior to intervention is rare today. Although the variable assessed may differ dramatically according to setting, agency mission, philosophy, and the like, all TR specialists conduct assessments. The assessed variable may be perceived pain or muscle strength for those more inclined toward medical model, or perceived competence in leisure or acquisition of activity skills for those with a more leisure outcome bent, the act of assessment is something

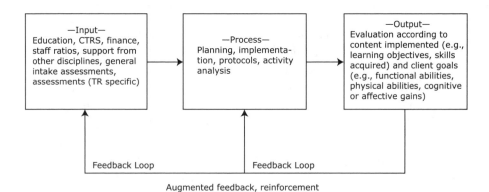

Figure 1.1   TR Change Model

all TR specialists do. Otherwise, one could hardly be in a position to maintain that TR is a systematic process, when a systematic process includes planning and implementation based on data gathered about the participant.

Use of Recreation and Leisure Modalities

In the process (planning and implementation) of TR, recreation and leisure *modalities* are also recognized across ideological boundaries. One practitioner may use aquatic therapy to bring about functional improvements (e.g., improved range of motion) in a client. Another practitioner may implement exercise in the water for a group of adults with developmental disabilities adults to "teach" them how to exercise independently (leisure education). A third practitioner in a health promotion setting may immerse elderly participants with arthritis in the water to reduce the risk of a secondary impairment (e.g., cardiovascular disease). Note that the modality is the same from one scenario to the next. Hence, many of the modalities commonly employed in TR appear to be similar regardless of philosophical or theoretical inclination. The Change Model may be applied in virtually any setting that implements a TR program.

Population Served

Accordingly, the constituencies served by TR and this particular model are not limited to those afflictions normally seen in a rehabilitation setting (e.g., head injuries, spinal cord injuries). Likewise, the participants are not restricted to only those seen in a community-based setting (e.g., developmental disabilities, arthritis). This latitude embraces acute and chronic disorders, conspicuous and hidden impairments, manifest and latent conditions. This flexible concept of "client served" maximizes adaptability of the TR profession in the future, preventing premature closure on the nature and type of impairment served.

TR on the Job: Settings and Responsibilities

The field of TR offers diverse employment and career opportunities. The nature of the field is diverse. TR specialists work in many different settings, including traditional settings, such as hospitals, rehabilitation centers, nursing homes, and community and municipal centers, as well as nontraditional settings, such as outdoor centers, the travel and tourism industry, and the nonprofit sector. In addition to the multitude of settings, the populations served are also incredibly diverse. Abilities of clients range from highly functional to people with great limitations. Clients come from different backgrounds, environments, and countries.

The broad complexity of setting and population gives future TR specialist a lot to choose from in the current job market. The purpose of this section is to provide the student with descriptions of several different work settings and to describe the typical job responsibilities associated with each. The scenarios give some examples of employment of recent TR graduates and introduce some of the settings where you would find TR specialists. The reader should appreciate this is only a sampling of the many varied work situations in which a TR specialist may find himself or herself.

Clinical-Based TR Setting

Meet Ashley

Ashley is a TR specialist at a large geriatric hospital in Canada. Following the completion of her degree specializing in TR, she was offered a full-time position as a "Recreologue" (a Quebec designation for a TR specialist with a degree in recreation). As a TR specialist, she is responsible for all recreation services on one unit at the hospital with 40 beds. Clients on the unit are categorized as heavy care, and many clients have some form of dementia.

Ashley works with a team of TR specialists in the TR department at the hospital. She follows the standards of practice set out by the hospital (adopted from provincial standards of practice). Ashley's focus of TR service delivery is on maintaining quality of life and developing and maintaining health, social networks, and functional skills. Her programs are designed for small groups or one-on-one interventions.

Meet Jason

Jason is the head of recreation therapy at an acute care hospital. Jason works on a unit of 16–20 adolescents with brain and spinal cord injuries. Jason works with clients who are stable following trauma and who stay on the unit less than three months. Jason designs TR services based on a multidisciplinary team approach. Programs (treatment) focus on developing skills and awareness of leisure and recreation, which will ultimately aim at reintegration into client homes, community, and schools. Jason completed an undergraduate TR program and obtained his CTRS certification. Jason is a member of ATRA and closely adheres to protocols set out by ATRA in designing his programs.

Meet Jenny

Jenny is a TR specialist in a private palliative care setting. Jenny works with adults in the last stages of life due to illness or disease. Jenny works from 1:00 p.m. to 10:00 p.m. each day, providing recreation and leisure opportunities to minimize the impact of institutionalization, to alleviate boredom, and to ease the transition in accepting death.

Jenny offers TR services to both clients in palliative care and to the family and friends who visit the center. Jenny offers TR services in the form of family programs, one-on-one programming with clients, and programming for young children visiting the center. Jenny describes her approach to TR as individualized with a strong focus on understanding the needs of clients and their families to design recreation services to give support during a period of terminal illness.

As demonstrated by the examples of Ashley, Jason, and Jenny, TR positions in clinical TR can be varied. The TR specialist in this setting would likely be working on a treatment (or multidisciplinary) team that includes several of the following allied health professionals: physical/physio therapist, occupational therapist, speech pathologist, nurse, social worker, psychologist, and physician. The team meets on a regular basis to assess, to plan, and to direct interventions for specific clients. There are common goals the team shares and goals specific to each discipline. Regardless of the discipline, in clinical environments, the TR specialist would be expected to focus on functional outcomes for the client. However, the mission of the agency would dictate different approaches and emphasis with the clientele.

Hours of work may vary depending on the setting. Inpatient psychiatric would be most likely to provide the TR professional with regular working hours (e.g., 8:00 a.m. or 9:00 a.m. to 5:00 p.m.), whereas physical rehabilitation settings, brain injury, or spinal cord injury units might well expect a more varied schedule (e.g., 3:00 p.m. to 11:00 p.m.). This is because of the competing demand for the client's time (for therapy) during regular working hours.

Assessment and planning (for intervention and discharge) take up a considerable part of the TR specialist's time in the clinical environment. Implementation (time working directly with the client) is often restricted to a small part of the total workday. Time with the client is also at a premium because of the changing nature of healthcare. Since the mid-1980s, a variety of mechanisms have been put into to place to contain healthcare costs. The net result has been to decrease the amount of time clients are able to remain as inpatients in rehabilitation. Much more service today is provided through an outpatient, clinic, or community-based setting.

In the United States, professional credentialing in TR is very important in clinical settings to legitimize practice and to support credibility among the allied health professions. Along with that, continuing education is an absolute necessity, though it is required to maintain professional certification anyway. In Canada, most TR clinical settings require a minimum of an undergraduate degree with some specific TR course work and clinical experience.

Community-Based TR Setting

Meet Ross

Ross received an undergraduate TR degree. Upon graduation, he was offered a full-time position as the executive director of the Boys and Girls Club. This nonprofit organization offers programs and services to primarily low income families in a large urban inner-city area. The Boys and Girls Club has limited funding to support programs and services. Ross's main role is to develop partnerships with community agencies. Ross designs programs and services to meet the needs of children and families in the community. He carries out both community and individual assessments to develop quality services. Ross meets regularly with the university to secure volunteers for specific children or programs. Ross also develops formal relationships with the community, including law enforcement, social service and municipal and community recreation providers, to create a network of support for the children in his programs. Ross is a member of two professional associations: CTRA and CPRA.

Meet Maria

Maria is the special programs co-coordinator for a large city recreation department. Maria completed an undergraduate program in TR, and has both CTRS and CPRP certifications. She is also a certified Aquatic Instructor with the Red Cross. In her role as the co-coordinator of special programs, Maria is responsible for meeting the recreation programming needs of people with disabilities in the city. Maria offers specialized recreational programs (e.g., wheelchair sport programs and Special Olympics) and adapted programs (where equipment or instructions are modified), and provides support for integrated participation in all city programs. Maria works with a team of recreation service providers. Her role is to assess leisure and recreation community needs and the needs of clientele with disabilities in her district, to advocate for integration of all community recreation services, and to promote accessibility of services. Her professional associations include NPRA with affiliations to the NTRS and Aquatics branches.

Meet Chloe

For the past 10 years, Chloe has worked for a nonprofit association that promotes programs and services for adults with cognitive disabilities. The nonprofit organization supports adults living independently in the community in supported living (group homes) and with families. The organization provides recreation and leisure opportunities for those who are not employed and offers recreational programming and social opportunities in the evenings and on weekends. Chloe offers services based on client interests, skills, and abilities. Chloe offers programs to develop specific leisure skills, such as arts and crafts, sport programs, and outdoor pursuits, as well as social opportunities, such as dating clubs, dances, picnics, and outings. Chloe works with the municipality (borough) to ensure opportunities are available for her clients in the recreation department. Chloe works with new clients on a referral basis from social services or religion-based family services. Chloe looks at leisure as a tool for empowering adults with cognitive limitations. All services in her organization focus on independence, creating social support networks, skill building, and advocacy. Chloe is a member of CTRA and an association of Recreation Administrators in her province.

Chloe, Maria, and Ross demonstrate the different roles a TRS can play in the community. In theory the antithesis of clinically based TR is the community setting. In many circles community-based TR amounted to nothing more than the provision of leisure services and programs to persons with disabilities in much the same way as services were provided for the general public. This perception is incorrect on several counts, not the least of which is the "mere" provision of leisure services.

The importance of recreation and leisure experiences for persons with impairments residing in the community should not be minimized. Data suggest many persons with disabilities will not have the opportunity to pursue a vocation full-time or even part-time. This leaves the individual with a significant identity challenge. The fact that many adults ascribe considerable weight to their jobs as a source of identity and meaning suggests that the person with a disability who does not have access to a job is at risk for experiencing identity crisis and a loss of meaning in life. As an alternative, a "leisure career" has been offered by some authors as a substitute for identity and meaning through traditional association with employment. (This concept is explored in more detail in Chapter 2.)

A second more practical reason to question the negative view of community-based TR is that significant changes in the healthcare field have driven many therapies, including TR, into outpatient and community-based service settings. Shorter stays as an inpatient, service delivery that does not require hospitalization, and cost-containment measures have caused a monumental shift in healthcare provision.

Related to the shift in service delivery is the recognition by many health-care professionals that the types of disorders that most commonly afflict people today cannot be completely cured, but only managed. This means after discharge from an inpatient rehabilitation setting the patient will still have to deal with his or her primary impairment and associated comorbid conditions for the foreseeable future. For instance, the person discharged from rehabilitation following a hip fracture (and subsequent repair) will have to cope with pain, the increased risk of another fall, immobility, and complications associated with less mobility (e.g., osteoporosis, postural deformity, depression). Clearly, inpatient rehabilitation only sets in motion a program of ongoing rehabilitation, prevention, and health maintenance. More directly stated, many persons discharged from rehabilitation will need preventive and maintenance programs the remainder of their lives to prevent deterioration and to maintain quality of life. Therein lies the role of the community-based TR specialist.

Child Life Setting

Meet June

June received an undergraduate degree in TR and is a certified family life and child life specialist. As a student June worked as a volunteer at a large children's hospital in an urban area. June was responsible for working with children who had extended stays at the hospital due to illness, or who were in isolation due to the nature of illness or treatment. Upon graduation, June was hired as a child life specialist on a long-term unit with children with severe and multiple disabilities.

Working with a treatment team, June designed programs and services to increase and to develop functional skills for her clients. Because of the long-term stays of children on the unit, June focused efforts on providing integrated social opportunities with other children in the hospital and with children in the community. June manages the child life center on the unit and ensures the hospital environment is home-like with many opportunities for stimulation. June is a member of CTRA and the Canadian Association of Child Life.

Many therapeutic recreation specialists acquire an additional credential, such as Certified Child Life Specialist. Among the chief responsibilities of the child life therapist are to help the child to adjust to a hospital environment, to assist the child in coping with painful procedures, and to decrease the anxiety associated with procedures the child may have to endure during his or her stay as an inpatient.

Child life therapy is highly correlated with TR in both the duties performed on the job and the necessary professional preparation. As of this printing, many TR courses may be used to satisfy requirements for qualifying to become a child life specialist. Child life therapy should continue to grow as a specialization that evolved from TR, and it may soon develop a professional identity independent from TR. In the meantime, many TR specialists working on pediatric units are dual credentialed in TR and in child life therapy.

Respite Care Setting

Meet Nathalie

Nathalie is a TR specialist at a small private day center catering to clients with various forms of dementia. The center where she works provides quality care and age-appropriate programming for adults living with family members. At the respite center, Nathalie works with older adults ranging in age from 75–95 with differing levels of abilities. The center provides recreation and leisure opportunities for clients, a hot lunch, and other health services. Nathalie offers a small group program on specific themes related to client interest in the morning and one-on-one services to clients in the afternoons. In her role as a TRS Nathalie works closely with family members and with members of the day center staff (volunteers, social workers, physicians, nurses, program assistants, and psychologists). Nathalie offers TR services aimed at maintaining physical, social, and cognitive skills and acts as a resource for family members looking for activities to engage in on the weekends. Nathalie is a member of the NPRA, NTRS, and a local group of professionals who meet to share programming ideas monthly.

A hybrid of community-based TR programming experiencing exponential growth is the respite care concept. Persons with severe physical and cognitive impairments are commonly served in this community-based setting. Presently in North America there are a growing number of respite care centers for older adults with various forms of dementia. These adult day centers can be private, organization supported, or affiliated with a day hospital or community center. The idea of respite care programs is expanding to include children and adults with severe, multiple disabilities. The idea behind the respite care concept is to provide quality care in a noninstitutional setting during the day so that the primary caregiver can work, complete routine chores, and get a break from the rigors of caregiving. Husbands, wives, brothers, sisters, parents, and children stand to benefit from the temporary respite from caregiving. Being given a break from caregiving may be the advantage the caregiver needs to sustain the person with the impairment in the home for a longer period during the duration of their illness. This provides a direct benefit to the patient, too, because they normally prefer to remain in their own homes and not in an institutional setting. Society benefits as well, because the higher costs of institutional care are avoided or postponed.

The role of the TR specialist in a respite care setting would naturally be to provide recreational services. But the professional's duties would likely be expanded to include preventive health and maintenance programs as well. For instance, fall prevention, nutrition, and self-care may be included among the expanded duties delivered by the TR specialist, because most respite care settings do not employ their own physical therapists, occupational therapists, and social workers. Hence, the job of the TR professional in respite care is to help the client remain as healthy as possible within the constraints presented by the impairment. Preventive efforts translate into a better quality of life for the client and caregiver and the capacity to maintain the client as independently as possible for as long as possible.

Transition Specialist

Meet Bruno

Bruno works for youth and family services as a TR specialist. Bruno works with youth on probation following a conviction of criminal activity by the courts. The clientele in youth and family protected services are clients who have spent time in institutional settings and often have difficult family dynamics and relationships. For youth leaving institutions to return to school and community, the transition can be difficult. One of the biggest problem areas is the constructive, positive use of free time. As a TR specialist Bruno is responsible for developing leisure-related skills and offering exposure to community recreational opportunities. Bruno works with community TR service providers, university students (as mentors and support for the youth), and TR service providers in the institutions to ensure transition and continuity of skills and attitudes. Bruno offers no structured programs, but often attends community offerings with this clients. Based on a comprehensive assessment of clients, which looks at needs and community environment, Bruno assists in the development of hobbies and links to important social networks. Bruno looks to two professional associations for support in his area, CTRA and a professional association representing child and youth care workers.

Another area of increasing interest for the TR profession is that of a transition specialist. This individual facilitates the adaptation of the client to a new living situation. The traditional transition has been from inpatient rehabilitation into a community living environment where the client assumes all or part of the responsibility for his own care. The rationale for using a TR professional as a transition specialist is that much of the adjustment to an independent or semi-independent living situation involves the use of free time, either as a means to stake out a new meaning to life or for the purpose of avoiding problems associated with an excess of free time (e.g., substance abuse, boredom, depression, isolation, deviant behavior, poor nutrition).

In addition, TR is often involved in the teaching and development of social skills through leisure experiences. Tasks as simple as how to make friends, how to start conversations, and when to say please and thank you can be taught, practiced, and refined through leisure experiences. Acquisition of these skills eases the transition of the client from institutional to community living circumstances.

Educational Setting

The role of the TR specialist working with the school system is to use leisure education to prepare the student to live as independently as possible. This may involve social skills training, learning how to use public transportation to reach one's favorite recreational activity, or acquiring new leisure skills to use free time more wisely.

Although unusual, school systems may also employ TR specialists to help with students' adjustment and transition from a school-centered world to a community-centered living situation. For as many as 21 years the young person with a developmental disability has focused on school as a central part of his or her life. Lessons are learned there, skills are acquired there, and friends are made there. In the United States, following the student's 21st year, he or she is expected to graduate and transition into an independent to semi-independent living situation. This is a daunting task for the student to successfully negotiate because the person's social world is oriented around the school setting and integrated with school activities.

An Organizing Framework for This Book

The authors of this textbook endeavored to approach the introduction to TR in a manner distinct from that of the conventional text. Whereas most introductory books dedicate about one half of the chapters to TR-focused material and the remaining chapters to TR and this or that disability, we have taken a different path in two respects.

First, we are convinced that there is enough conceptual material to dedicate an entire introductory book to defining, dissecting, and discussing fundamental ideas that serve as a foundation for the profession. We were not satisfied to fill one half of a text with a description of various disabilities one may work with as a TR specialist. While there certainly is a place for the presentation and thorough examination of TR intervention with specific disability groups, we maintain that topic constitutes separate coursework in a TR curriculum.

Second, to the greatest extent possible at this time, we take an international approach to TR. Little in the way of TR was found outside of North America 25 years ago. Slowly but steadily, TR has found an international following in countries outside North America. To ignore the globalization of TR would be both parochial and isolationist. The world has become a small place indeed, and to ignore the voices of an international community of TR practitioners would mean we would miss a considerable amount of innovation, creativity, and new solutions to old problems.

The previous discussion of the definitions, the profession, and the types of jobs associated with the TR discipline serve as the organizing framework for the most of this textbook. Accordingly, most of the remaining chapters are directed toward topics introduced in this chapter.

Summary

Definitions of TR from the three leading organizations show similarities and differences, indicating both how far TR has come and how much more the profession still needs to mature. The profession has focused too much on differences rather than shared principles, so most of the history of TR has caused a schism between clinicians and community-based practitioners.

The TR profession needs to find common ground and shared interests to adapt and to respond to future changes in healthcare. The contention that TR remains a systematic process must be correlated with a dynamic vision of the future to maintain TR's responsiveness to the inevitable changes in healthcare, the increase in incidence of chronic conditions (e.g., osteoporosis, arthritis, diabetes, high blood pressure), and the expansion of advocacy for persons with disabilities. The future will require TR professionals to think outside of the box, and to invent new ways to define TR.

References

American Therapeutic Recreation Association. (1993). *Standards for the practice of therapeutic recreation.* Hattiesburg, MS: Author.

American Therapeutic Recreation Association. (n.d.). Career information. Retrieved from http://www.atra-tr.org/careerinfo.htm

Austin, D. R. (1998). The health protection/health promotion model. *Therapeutic Recreation Journal, 32,* 109–117.

Baldwin, C., McAvoy, L., and Schleien. S. (1989). Best professional practice: Persons with severe multiple disabilities. *Therapeutic Recreation Journal, 23,* 27–40.

Canadian Therapeutic Recreation Association. (1999). About CTRA. Retrieved from http://www.canadian-tr.org/about_ctra.htm

Carter, M. J., Van Andel, G. E., and Robb, G. E. (1995). *Therapeutic recreation: A practical approach* (2nd ed.). Prospect Heights, IL: Waveland Press.

Grossman, A. and Coreleo, O. (2001). Acquired immunodeficiency syndrome (AIDS). In D. R. Austin and M. E. Crawford (Eds.), *Therapeutic recreation: An introduction* (3rd ed.; pp. 247–317). Boston, MA: Allyn & Bacon.

Kunstler, R. (1991). There but for fortune: A therapeutic recreation perspective on homelessness in America. *Therapeutic Recreation Journal, 25,* 31–40.

Luken, K. and Rios, D. (1998, Fall). Clinical is NOT a place: The TR process. *NCTRC Newsletter,* 3.

Millerson, G. (1978). Professional, managerial, and technical occupations. In W. E. Hopke (Ed.), *Encyclopedia of careers and vocational guidance* (4th ed.). Chicago, IL: Doubleday & Co.

National Therapeutic Recreation Society. (1995). *Standards of practice for therapeutic recreation services and annotated bibliography.* Arlington, VA: National Recreation and Park Association.

Peterson, C. A. (1984). A matter of priorities and loyalties. *Therapeutic Recreation Journal, 18,* 11–16.

Peterson, C. A. and Gunn, S. L. (1984). *Therapeutic recreation program design: Principles and procedures* (2nd ed.). Englewood Cliffs, NJ: Prentice Hall.

Reynolds, R. P. and O'Morrow, G. S. (1985). *Problems, issues, and concepts in therapeutic recreation.* Englewood Cliffs, NJ: Prentice Hall.

Stumbo, N. J. and Peterson, C. A. (1998). The leisure ability model. *Therapeutic Recreation Journal, 32,* 82–96.

Sylvester, C. (1992). Therapeutic recreation and the end of leisure. *Therapeutic Recreation Journal, 26,* 9–20.

Sylvester, C. (1998). Careers, callings, and the professionalization of therapeutic recreation. *Journal of Leisurability, 25,* 3–13.

Van Andel, G. E. (1998). TR service delivery and outcome models. *Therapeutic Recreation Journal, 32,* 180–193.

Wilhite, B., Keller, M. J., and Caldwell, L. (1999). Optimizing lifelong health and well-being: A health enhancing model of therapeutic recreation. *Therapeutic Recreation Journal, 33,* 98–108.

Chapter 2

Existentialism
Stream of Consciousness Through TR

Learning Objectives

1. Define the three basic schools of philosophy discussed in this chapter: rationalism, empiricism, and existentialism.

2. Explain how a person can discover meaning in life's inevitable suffering, especially in illness. In particular, relate suffering, intensity, and meaning to disability and impairment.

3. Define life scheme and explain its relationship to existentialism and disability.

4. Define reconstruction following a significant traumatic event, such as a spinal cord injury (SCI).

5. Explain how existentialism relates to the leisure theory of flow.

6. Define existential vacuum. Define boredom from a social psychological point of view. How do these two concepts relate to one another?

7. Using the work of Lee, identify the three ways in which patients can transition from preinjury to postinjury leisure lifestyle following a significant trauma. Next, define each of the three typologies for transition from preinjury to postinjury.

8. Identify aspects of TR practice models thought to be based on existential principles.

9. Explain TR intervention techniques that may be used to help the person with a disability "come to terms" with impairment. Give examples of expressive activities that may assist in the adjustment to disability.

10. Provide two examples of TR case studies that implemented interventions that capitalized on existential principles.

Recently the nature and tone of research in therapeutic recreation (TR) has shifted. The shift from quantitative to qualitative research has been subtle and certainly not complete. There will continue to be a need for quantitative research. But the reason for the shift underscores the importance of existentialism in TR, and how much a part of the nature of TR is reflected in existentialism. This revelation serves as a primary motive for this chapter.

What Is Philosophy?

If a *theory* is an explanation offered for some phenomenon (e.g., Why is competence an important motive for leisure behavior?), then *philosophy* is about the prerequisites to theory. Philosophy deals with the assumptions, "truths," and fundamental principles used as a foundation for building a theoretical explanation. Perhaps this is why philosophy in general, and philosophy of TR specifically, often proves to be upsetting to people—it is hard and sometimes painful to think about the fundamental assumptions of the field, to question the very foundation for TR. It may mean rejecting some of those assumptions, revealing weaknesses in a theory, or calling into question most of what the TR profession does and why the profession even exists.

Philosophy is difficult, too, because most philosophical questions cannot be conclusively answered. That is, most of the time the best a philosophy can hope for is to arrive at logical reasons for believing certain assumptions to be true. But the aggravating fact that remains is we can never really be 100% certain the assumptions are correct. Assumptions and beliefs can seem to be true, have an intuitive appeal, and be useful in solving problems. But intuitive appeal and usefulness do not prove assumptions and beliefs are true all of the time.

This chapter introduces the reader to a very different brand of philosophy—existentialism—and demonstrates how it has interwoven itself into TR history and practice. Although the reader may not be convinced that the assumptions of existentialism are true or that existentialism is useful, the goal is for the reader to become aware of a different way to think about the assumptions that serve as a foundation for TR besides the popular notions of TR as a means, an end, or an outcome.

Types of Philosophy

Chapter 7 discusses whether TR (and leisure activities in general) is valuable as the "means" to bring about beneficial change or valuable as an "end" in itself. The first position is commonly known as an *instrumental view*—TR is the instrument that produces some health outcome, such as a decrease in depressive symptoms. The second position is most often recognized as the *intrinsic view*—TR cultivates leisure participation that is an end in itself. This chapter does not present competing philosophies at length; however, each is mentioned because they reflect one of two leading philosophical schools of thought: rationalism and empiricism.

Rationalism, the older of the two, traces its roots to the ancient Greek philosophers, such as Plato and Aristotle. Rationalism assumes that knowledge and knowing are exclusively matters of the mind—only mental entities (e.g., ideas) count. This is because the physical world and our perceptions of that world may deceive us. The senses deceive us and cannot be trusted as reliable sources of knowledge. At the very least we "see" things through our own filters of biases and prejudices that distort the physical world.

Rationalism maintains that people should trust only the things of the mind, for our own ideas cannot deceive us. Through contemplation and thought the person is able to know universal truths that have permanence and do not vary with bias and whim. For example, people who ascribe to rationalism tend to hold absolute ethical principles. They might believe that confidentiality between therapist and patient is an ethical principle always (universally) true that should always be respected. People who follow rationalism tend to "stick to their guns" when it comes to ethical principles—matters of right and wrong. The problem is exceptions usually force compromise. A patient may reveal he has been abused or plans suicide, and therapists may have to report any case of abuse or potential harm, thus violating confidentiality.

In contrast, *empiricism* suggests knowledge can only be gained through direct experience—the senses can be trusted to inform us accurately. ("What you see is what you get.") Empiricism's most serious advocate was philosopher and scientist Descartes ("I think, therefore I am."). Because knowledge according to empiricism is a result of experience with the environment, its value is also connected to the sensible world. Knowledge is valued to the extent that it can be used to create a better world, and for its instrumental usefulness.

Applying empiricism to ethics results in a set of relative ethics. No ethical principle is universally true; it depends on the circumstances. As with the absolute ethics associated with rationalism, the relative ethics of empiricism have problems, too. Can anything be counted on? Are there any rules to live by, or do right and wrong always depend on the circumstances and the whims of the person interpreting the situation?

A client reveals that he plans to kill himself. Should this be reported or is it privileged information to be held in confidence between client and therapist? One therapist may believe euthanasia is warranted in cases where the client is in severe pain and knows the illness is terminal. But a second therapist might believe there is always hope, however unlikely, and the circumstances do not warrant suicide. It would be very difficult to know what to do if there were not any relatively fixed rules for ethical behavior. Both schools of thought have problems not only with ethics and matters or right and wrong, but also with issues related to understanding the world around us and the ideas we hold.

Existentialism

Existentialism can be thought of as a combination of aspects of both rationalism and empiricism. Existentialists reject the cold, sterile world of quantitative facts of the empiricist. But existentialism does weight direct experience as very important to the understanding of the human condition. Only through direct experience can the fate of mankind be understood. Borrowing from the rationalists, existentialists maintain that knowledge of the human condition is worth knowing for its own sake. Mental entities or ideal forms are drawn from direct experience for the existentialist.

By combining these two principles of existentialism, one arrives at the position where knowledge is a result of insight/intuition (valuing mental entities like the rationalist) based on direct experience (like the empiricist). Experience confirms what we already "know." But existentialists have something unique in mind when they talk about experience, quite different from a simple matter of perception of the physical world. Experience for the existentialist includes passion, intensity, suffering, and anguish.

Existentialism embraces some aspects of rationalism and empiricism and rejects other features of these two traditional philosophical approaches. It considers experience vital to understanding, but it rejects the inclination of empiricism to ground understanding and a meaning in life exclusively in direct (often pleasure-driven) experience. It places a great deal of emphasis on mental entities, such as attitude, but rejects the distance rationalism tends to place between thought and experience.

Existentialism espouses a pessimistic and tragic view of the world, and this frequently discourages further investigation of its basic principles. But existentialism is founded on the principle there is unavoidable tragedy and suffering in human existence, and the well-adjusted person is one who accepts this as fact.

From this rather dismal beginning, existentialist writers attempted to convince skeptics that acknowledging pain and suffering in the world is part of finding whether there is any meaning to life. Olson (1962) stated freedom of choice is one of the fundamental values of existentialism. Freedom of choice is not simply the fact that we *have choices*, but that we *must choose*. Choosing is unavoidable and often the cause of anguish, because in many cases none of the choices are desirable. Furthermore, not only must you choose (and you have no choice except to choose), but also you are ultimately responsible for the choice you make. For the cancer patient, it may be that he must choose between unpleasant chemotherapy or treating only symptoms. Neither choice is guaranteed to produce cure or relief of discomfort. You can see that this choice scenario laid out by the existentialists is likely to produce apathy, resignation, and a sense of hopelessness.

The challenge of life for the existentialist, then, is to overcome this sort of desperation—to find meaning in spite of the inevitable suffering that occurs. Herein lies the key to existentialism in general and its application to TR specifically: a meaningful life is not possible without a certain amount of suffering and an understanding of that suffering.

The fact that suffering exists imparts a sense of intensity or passion to living if the individual is paying close attention. The fact that people get sick and everyone must face death lends a sense of urgency to life. In other words, knowing that health (and life) are limited in time makes us live better, intensifying immediate experience—"living large" to borrow the cliche. This passion imparted to living that is a function of suffering (or the inevitability of suffering) is what is meant by intensity.

For the purpose of this chapter we can assume ill persons experience a certain amount of suffering, perhaps even confronting death. Existentialists such as Olson (1962) maintain that the challenge for the client is to overcome suffering not necessarily by securing a cure, but by accepting the past (suffering) and looking to determine the future by exercising choice. In this way the afflicted person should always recognize choices do exist and can never be taken away by illness or disability. There always remains the future potential to reinvent oneself. It is this combination of (stoic) acceptance of suffering and recognition of future (choice-driven) possibility that translates into an indomitable spirit or attitude.

Based on existential principles then, the task that lies before therapeutic recreation specialists (TRS) is to assist clients in living with intensity despite illness and disability. The following sections expand on this hypothesis and translate it into concrete practice.

Existentialism, Illness, and Disability

One would be hard-pressed to find many other examples of suffering more common than illness or disability. Physical and mental maladies are the most universally shared type of suffering among humans. Hence, most readers can relate to suffering because almost everyone has been sick and had a glimpse of the depths to which human suffering can fall—even though most bouts of illness are temporary.

But the kind of illness we are concerned about here is not just a temporary round of nausea associated with the flu. Rather, the clients the TRS will encounter in practice are more likely to have a serious illness that presents the person with more than unpleasant physical and/or mental symptoms that must be endured. The illness we are most apt to see in practice is the kind that causes a major upheaval in the person's life, to the extent they question whether there is any meaning to life. "Major traumatic events initiate a search for meaning" (Thompson & Janigian, 1988, p. 261).

Noted psychiatrist Viktor Frankl wrote at length about his experience as a prisoner in a Nazi concentration camp during the Second World War. He argued that the prisoners who survived were those who could find meaning in their desperate circumstances. He saw the experience of being a prisoner as an opportunity to show character, to prove that he was "worthy of his suffering" (Frankl, 1984, p. 76). In much the same way, clients most apt to adjust to their disability and the disruption it causes are able to rise above the din of desperation and to find meaning to life.

Several authors talk about the crisis (in meaning) precipitated by significant illness or injury. Though their words differ, the message is the same: the key is to retain or to reinvent meaning following the traumatic life event. Fife (1994) asserted that serious illness causes the person to redefine or reconstruct meaning in life.

Similarly, Brock and Kleiber (1994) maintained that illness puts the imagined future in doubt and is likely to lead to identity confusion and loss of self-esteem. This is because the illness affects the person's ability to portray roles and duties consistent with identity. For instance, the athlete who can no longer participate in his or her sport because of a career ending injury faces a significant threat to identity. Self-esteem would surely suffer because of the loss in ability to perform the role needed to support one's athletic identity. Even though most clients are not athletes, the threat to identity associated with illness can be manifested in many ways (e.g., loss of employment identity, inability to perform a role as a parent or friend).

Like Brock and Kleiber, Lee, Dattilo, Kleiber, and Caldwell (1996) suggested that injury causes a discontinuity in life and may bring about loss of meaning. They studied people who had sustained a recent spinal cord injury (SCI) and found the loss of ability to participate in physical (embodied) activities was a very difficult psychological hurdle to overcome. This is because most people who have an SCI are young adults and embodied activities are often a significant part of their identity.

Life Schemes

The phrase *life scheme* or *life story* is frequently used to label the mental picture each of us has for our life (Thompson & Janigian, 1988). The life scheme ties together past, present, and future events into a logical whole oriented around one's life goals. Understandably, if a traumatic event occurs, such as a significant physical or mental illness, then the person's scheme is likely altered because goals may now be in doubt.

The life scheme establishes meaning because it provides a sense of order (stability, predictability) and purpose (identification of achievable goals). But the traumatic life event now places order and purpose in jeopardy—goals may no longer be achievable and chaos and unpredictability may reign. In a word, serious illness or injury shakes the person's very foundation. Thompson and Janigian (1988) submit that this event then precipitates a crisis and motivates a search for meaning.

Illness signals vulnerability and makes goals difficult to achieve (Thompson & Janigian, 1988). Restoring order and purpose is the same as finding meaning. Thompson and Janigian suggested finding meaning may occur in two ways. First, the person may come to adjust his or her perception of the illness or traumatic life event. He or she may recognize the illness will change some things, but he or she can still attain life goals, though perhaps in some modified form.

While adjusting perception of the event sounds very existential (finding meaning in suffering), another method of confronting the crisis in meaning is to change the life scheme. Finding meaning by accommodating one's life scheme to the traumatic event (suffering) often means changing goals. Again, the attitude one takes is most important: Are the new goals accepted grudgingly, or with the attitude of "one door opens when another closes"?

By changing perception of the event and/or by changing one's life goals, the person is better able to find meaning in life. The life scheme/life story may then be adjusted to provide continuity between the past, present, and future. Purpose and order are restored and meaning to life is rediscovered.

Finding meaning in suffering was a theme in the preceding discussion of existentialism and illness, and it is also a key to TR effectiveness. The life scheme approach to understanding the impact of illness on the person, the subsequent search for meaning, and the mechanisms available for reconstructing meaning to life are the psychological equivalents to existential principles. The challenge to TR remains to help the person rise above the illness and use the illness experience to live an intense, full, and meaningful life. The next sections address how TR might serve to makes the search for meaning a successful one.

Existentialism in TR History

We have already established a link between suffering and existentialism. The most obvious relationship is with illness, perhaps the most frequent type of suffering almost everyone will have to endure. Coming to terms with and understanding the suffering associated with illness is essential to beginning the task of reconstructing one's life—to finding meaning in life.

The next step in the process of developing an argument for the relationship between existentialism and TR is to provide evidence that existential ideas are part of TR's history. Many existential principles lie at the heart of what some authors conceive of TR. Some TR authors are naïve existentialists—much of what they say about TR (theoretically) and much of their research on TR reflects clear existential themes. A return to Frankl to make clear the potential links between existentialism and TR is needed. Those links are intensity, meaning, and existential vacuum.

Intensity

The "will to meaning"—the search for meaning following illness—is to be encouraged by the therapist, according to Frankl (1984). But the urging of the therapist serves to create a certain amount of tension or intensity within the client. It takes energy to rebuild an identity; it takes intense effort to reconstruct meaning. It is not always a pleasant task, because reconstruction of meaning may require abandoning the hopes, dreams, and aspirations of the preinjury life.

This is why Frankl (1984) contended that tension is necessary, and a certain amount of intensity is a sure sign the process of reconstruction of meaning has begun in earnest. Frankl worked primarily in the arena of mental illness, and for him mental health was not a tensionless state. Rather, the mentally healthy person imparts a certain amount of intensity to the business of living a meaningful life.

One leisure theory bears a resemblance to the intensity that Frankl and other existentialists talk about: *flow*. Developed by Csikszentmihalyi (1975), the theory of flow explains peak experiences, many of which are leisure, in terms of matching one's skills with a particular challenge. The idea is to match the skill and the challenge closely, so the person must focus, concentrate, and put forth maximal effort to achieve success. Hence, flow amounts to an intense experience, such as mountain climbing, where the climber cannot afford to lose focus and intensity as he "flows" up the mountain.

Lee (1999) further suggested leisure can be thought of as a continuum running from flow (intense experience) to relaxation. Using Lee's framework, not all leisure can be thought of as an intense flow experience, but intense leisure may not be for everyone, or for that matter anyone all of the time.

Meaning

Following his ordeal in a Nazi concentration camp, Viktor Frankl (1984) developed a practice in psychiatry based on existentialism. He called his approach *logotherapy* (*logus* is Greek for "meaning"). A logotherapist is future oriented. The patient is encouraged to focus on the future and the potential meanings to be fulfilled. Frankl further maintained that the search for meaning provided motivational force to the client's active efforts to come to terms with his illness.

Lee also wrote about and researched extensively the effects of SCI on the individual, and worked to build a theoretical framework for understanding adjustment to SCI using leisure. Using an approach similar to that of the life scheme described previously, Lee suggested that the injured person who is actively (intensely) adjusting to his injury uses leisure to negotiate meaning and to reconstruct identity (Lee, Brock, Dattilo & Kleiber, 1993; Lee et al., 1996).

In theory, leisure is part of a person's life scheme/life story and it stands to reason that it should be involved in any adjustment caused by a significant event, such as an SCI (Lee et al., 1993). The rehabilitation of the person is then a matter of weaving leisure into the reconstruction of the life scheme. Lee believes leisure plays an important role in reconstruction of the life scheme because it offers a mechanism for the client to experience competence despite a debilitating injury. For example, the person with an SCI may experience success while participating in a preinjury activity in an adapted manner, or he may experience the success that comes with learning a new activity altogether. In either case, the focus is on ability, success, and what the person *can* do, not what the client is no longer able to do. This is especially vital for the person with an SCI, because it is well-documented that the prospects for securing meaningful employment after a significant physical injury is rather low (Coyle & Kinney, 1990).

Often deprived of a meaningful identity through employment, the person with an SCI is challenged to carve out a meaningful life scheme without one of the usual measures of worth available to him or her—a job. The task for the therapeutic recreation specialist is to assist the person in building a sense of continuity from preinjury lifestyle to postinjury lifestyle. The extent to which preinjury leisure activities can be used in complete or modified form to aid in the reconstruction of the person's life scheme is the place where many clients begin the rebuilding process, especially early in rehabilitation.

Lee et al. (1996) researched the extent to which continuity in the meaning of leisure could be used to understand the way in which 20 clients adjusted early in SCI rehabilitation. The purpose of the study was to understand how clients sought out preinjury leisure activities and how the meanings of those activities were altered to establish continuity between preinjury leisure and postinjury leisure.

"Participants reported actively seeking previous activities and negotiating the meaning of the activities to continue participation" (Lee et al., 1996, p. 222). More specifically, they found patients with SCI resorted to three methods of defining the meaning of continuity of leisure.

1. Some clients reported *seeking continuity* as an aspiration. They expressed an intention to return to some or all of their preinjury leisure activities. This reflects a motive or aspiration, an intent to try, a seeing of future goals within reach. In terms of life scheme adjustment, seeking continuity may represent the expression of a goal or goals, essential to restoring a sense of meaning to life.

2. Some clients tried preinjury leisure activities and found them about the same as before the SCI. This experience with one or more preinjury leisure activities served to encourage patients and to make them aware of the (future) possibilities. The activities were different in some ways but nearly like before the injury in other ways. The actual experiencing of leisure activities served *to establish a sense of continuity* between preinjury and postinjury leisure, serving to "jump start" the process of rebuilding one's life scheme. Again, consistent with existential principles is the call of "potential meaning" that Frankl talks about as part of the rehabilitation process.

3. The third method of finding meaning in continuity of leisure was labeled *accommodating for continuity*. Here the client comes to terms with the nature of participation and the fact that some adjustments in the way participation took place were necessary. The activity might have to be adjusted, or adaptive equipment might be

necessary. Also, the individual might have to alter his or her own perceptions of the activity to continue participation.

What is not clear from Lee's research is whether the types of continuity derived from leisure represented three distinct methods of finding meaning or whether each type represented a step in a process that begins with an aspiration (to seek continuity as a goal), transitions into an awareness (to establish continuity as an awareness of potential), and comes to rest on a reconstructed life scheme (to accommodate for continuity). Regardless of whether each method of finding continuity is distinct or part of a process, the point is Lee's theoretical and empirical work demonstrated clear and unmistakable themes of existentialism. Equally important, his work demonstrated that philosophical principles of existentialism can be translated into theoretical understanding as well as practice.

Existential Vacuum

According to Frankl (1984) the alternative to finding meaning is existential vacuum. If the client fails in his or her attempt to reconstruct meaning, or struggles for a time in the search for meaning, then an existential vacuum ensues, characterized by identity crisis, loss of order, and purposelessness.

The attributes of existential vacuum bear a close resemblance to the concept of boredom or leisure-based boredom. There is ample reason to be bored in leisure and in life after a traumatic life event, such as an SCI. Half or more are unemployed, and postdischarge leisure is characterized as passive, homebound, and isolated (Caldwell, Adolph & Gilbert, 1989; Caldwell & Weissinger, 1994; Coyle & Kinney, 1990; Lee et al., 1993).

The problem of boredom amplifies when the consequences of a lack of order and purpose in life is made clear. For persons who sustain an SCI, problems secondary to their injury are frequent and often more devastating than the SCI itself. They are at risk for development of skin lesions and infections, bladder and kidney infections, and substance abuse problems.

Coming from a social psychological perspective, Caldwell and Weissinger (1994) maintained that boredom ensues when the person is not optimally stimulated through leisure and other life activities. The stimulus array becomes predictable and repetitive, offering little new stimuli to induce participation. But reinterpretation of this social psychological premise tethers the social psychology of boredom to existential vacuum.

If flow/peak experiences occur when the person is pressed to perform up to his or her maximum ability, then a situation that requires less than near maximal effort may lead to a boring environment. This is so because the environment becomes predictable and redundant, and does not force a near maximum mental and physical effort. Further, if access to the more stimulating and challenging (favorite) activity is lost, and remaining activities are too easy, then boredom (and redundant environment) is the result.

Existentialism relates in two ways. First, favorite (challenging) activities likely serve as a part of the person's identity, providing order and purpose to life. Second, the fact that boring activities are by definition repetitive and predictable means the person does not have to try as hard, and thereby deprives the person of that vital intensity that characterizes impairment and meaningful things that people invest their lives in. The net result of boredom, the deprivation of meaningful and intense activities, is existential vacuum—meaninglessness.

Research suggests boredom is the very epitome of postinjury life for many persons with SCI. Caldwell et al. (1989) found SCI patients who participated in leisure counseling and other TR programs during rehabilitation were disappointed and bored after discharge. This rather surprising development is explained by the fact that the person who did actively pursue meaningful leisure during rehabilitation saw the potential of leisure. But soon after discharge they found the real world did not support a meaningful leisure lifestyle in the same manner as acute rehabilitation.

This expression of disappointment, boredom, or relapse (as Caldwell called it) was also found to be the case when SCI patients were interviewed after discharge in a second study completed in the mid-1990s (Caldwell, Dattilo, Kleiber & Lee, 1994/95). In short, the positive experience many recovering SCI patients had in rehabilitation raised expectations for a meaningful leisure lifestyle after discharge. When that lifestyle did not materialize, the subjects reported being bored, a more down-to-earth expression of existential vacuum.

Research has only started to investigate the solutions to boredom and existential vacuum. Lee, Mittelstaedt, and Askins (1999) tried to predict boredom in 206 persons who had sustained an SCI. They found the single best predictor of boredom (or the lack thereof) was lifeview. The more optimistic the person's lifeview, the less likely he or she was to report being bored. While this does not directly suggest solutions to boredom, it does raise a couple of important points.

First, it registers a link back to existentialism. Frankl (1984) said the vital part to living is to face adversity and inevitable suffering with a indomitable attitude—to find meaning in suffering. Second, maintaining an optimistic attitude toward living, despite the inevitable anguish humans endure, points to TR techniques that pertain more to bringing about changes in mental entities, such as attitudes and values. The second point is further translated into practical activity programs in the next section.

An earlier study published by Caldwell et al. (1994/95) provided more in the way of practical and theoretical validation of the importance of an existential approach to TR. While investigating SCI patients, they found the probability for boredom to be high, but they discovered a different predictor for boredom. Instead of lifeview, they found perceived competence was the best predictor of boredom (or its absence). The reason they discovered a different predictor than the Lee at al. (1999) study is likely because they approached the problem from a social psychological point of view. Hence, perceived competence, the subject's belief in his proficiency in a particular leisure skill, emerged as the best predictor. Lifeview is not commonly used as a predictor in social psychological research.

Nevertheless, the reader should again note the ample latitude for relating perceived competence to existentialism. The competent person is more likely to challenge himself or herself to the utmost, because he or she is convinced of his or her skill. This brings an (existential) intensity to the leisure experience. The competent person is also apt to take an affirmative attitude into the leisure experience, and not to give into the difficulties and challenges of the activity or his or her affliction.

Existentialism in TR Practice

Yoshioka (2001) maintained existential principles are found in some TR practice models, specifically the following:

- Leisure Ability Model (Stumbo & Peterson, 1998)

- Self-Determination and Enjoyment Enhancement Model (Dattilo, Kleiber & Williams, 1998)

- Aristotelian Good Life Model (Widmer & Ellis, 1998)

She concluded that although none of these models directly references existential philosophy, all have fundamental principles that prove to be consistent with existentialism.

The *Leisure Ability Model* includes some aspects of service that capitalize on existential assumptions. In particular, the leisure education area of service includes two subcomponents existential in character: leisure skill acquisition and leisure awareness.

Acquisition of competence in leisure skills is consistent with ideas of freedom, responsibility, and life meaning. That is, if one is competent at an activity, one is more likely to see that activity as a genuine choice for free time activity—we do often what we do well and do well what we do often (Mobily, Lemke & Gisin, 1991). The competent person is more apt to take responsibility for accessing the activity. Furthermore, if a person is competent in an activity, chances are he or she would participate in the activity more often and integrate that activity into his or her identity. In sum, the activity becomes a part of the meaning the person ascribes to his or her life.

Leisure awareness is the second subcomponent of leisure education that contains an existential bias. It means the client is involved in exercises that modify his or her leisure attitude and values in a more positive direction. In light of the fact that Lee and colleagues (1996) discovered leisure plays an important role in the transition and adjustment of individuals with traumatic injury, leisure awareness experiences seem vital to complete rehabilitation. Certainly, there is a good chance the injured person will have ample amounts of free time available following the injury and inpatient rehabilitation. If a negative attitude toward leisure is apparent, then the person's prospects of seeing leisure as an avenue for the reconstruction of life meaning are less probable.

According to Yoshioka (2001), another practice model that subtly relies on existential principles is the *Self-Determination and Enjoyment Enhancement Model*. This model builds its foundation on the concept of flow, which has already been mentioned as a leisure-based theory consistent with the existential principle of intensity of experience. Dattilo et al. (1998) rest their service delivery model on the goal of having fun. They argue for a very specific kind of fun, however. Unlike the joyful and carefree characteristics of fun that we normally associate with the experience of enjoyment, they argue that people with disabilities have fun when they are challenged—when their abilities in a leisure activity are tested. In sum, fun for Dattilo et al. means the client is having a flow experience.

The *Aristotelian Good Life Model* is more an ethical position than a direct TR practice model (Widmer & Ellis, 1998). It has more to say about how persons with disabilities should live and the goals professionals should seek when working with clients. The authors state the purpose of the model is to point practitioners toward ways in which they can help the person to recover from suffering and to reassert control over his or her own life. Freedom, responsibility, and suffering are the existential themes to be found in the Aristotelian Good Life Model.

Following her analysis of the TR practice models, Yoshioka (2001) concluded, "...although many of the TR practice models do not explicitly stress existentialism or logotherapy, many of them have some tacit or possible implications of the concepts of existentialism and logotherapy" (p. 59).

In addition, an analysis of one TR practice model by Murray (1998) provided a compelling focus on an important goal for TR service. Murray argued that because many people have chronic conditions nowadays, it is unrealistic to believe most clients will be cured (relieved of their suffering) by rehabilitation. Rather, she urged clients to "...learn to live with debilitation and must reintegrate it into daily life in a positive fashion" (p. 273). Murray voiced concern that TR practice models must come to terms with the reality of chronic conditions and the fact that many people seen by TR specialists will not be cured, but rather have to learn to live with their "suffering" the rest of their lives.

One primary implication that comes with the reality imposed by a chronic condition is that to be most effective the whole person must be treated. Mind–body dualism needs to be jettisoned, and to really be effective TR needs to consider the emotional and existential concomitants of chronic conditions. TR is in a unique position to address the fallout that accompanies illness, such as perceived incompetence, identity crisis, existential vacuum, boredom, and a lack of meaning to life.

Attitude Is Everything

Murray (1999) reminded readers of the existential heritage left to the rehabilitation community by Viktor Frankl in her review of *Man's Search for Meaning*. Frankl (1984) maintained that one freedom can never be taken away: the freedom to choose one's attitude. The character with which one faces adversity, whether it is a concentration camp or an SCI, cannot be taken away. It is a internal decision according to Frankl.

More recently, Murray (2000) developed an approach to TR based on existentialism. Like Lee et al. (1993), she asserted that the point of rehabilitation and TR's participation in the rehabilitation process is to help the client to "re-create" himself or herself. Although Lee prefers the word "reconstruction," the point is the same: TR should seek existential outcomes in its clients.

Murray (2000) further developed a list of existential outcomes for TR. Practice applications have been added by the authors in parentheses following each of Murray's suggestions. TR should aspire to help clients:

1. to discover what is at stake in living; to find a purpose.
   (leisure awareness)

2. to make sense of a situation.
   (interpreting through leisure counseling, developing a therapeutic relationship with the client)

3. to make meaning and to discover intentionality and struggle in living.
   (leisure skill education, increasing activity competence, facilitating genuine leisure choices)

4. to make sense of suffering.
   (activities that help the person express feeling about his or her illness and the implications of the disability for his or her life, providing "supportive witnessing" through introspective activities such as journaling)

5. to make sense of being human.
   (putting it all together—mind and body, work and leisure, finding the place of and for leisure as part of a meaningful life, developing a therapeutic relationship with the client, helping the person to find continuity in leisure from preinjury to postinjury)

In the end we must ask: What are we rehabilitating the client for? This is an especially important question given the reality of many chronic conditions—most people will continue to experience the suffering associated with their disability throughout their lives.

Richter and Kaschalk (1996) opted for the making of meaning as one of the primary roles to be played by TR practitioners. The unique place of TR in the rehabilitation process is that it attunes itself to the whole person, a point not lost to even the clinical focus of the medical profession. Physicians remind us the unique contribution of TR is it does not act exclusively to bring about functional change, but rather to facilitate expressive activities that provide meaning (Haun, 1966). TR embodies the unified mind–body relationship that Haun talked about over 30 years ago and represented in the following quote: "Suffering is experienced by persons, not merely bodies, and has its source in challenges that threaten the intactness of the person as a complex social and psychological entity" (Cassel, 1982, p. 639).

The following sections explore some practical programs designed to change attitude in a favorable manner and to help the person work through his or her suffering using leisure activities. They also identify some case studies that have used existentially based activities or found existential outcomes following intervention.

Changing Attitude Through Leisure

The first step in rehabilitation from an existential point of view is to change the person's attitude toward his or her disability. To find meaning to life one must first come to terms with the meaning the impairment presents and the associated suffering. Murray (1997) synthesized a program of activities that holds considerable promise in realizing existential outcomes for TR.

For Murray (1997) journaling provides an avenue that allows the client to work through his or her illness and to come to terms with his or her suffering.

The advantage of journaling in TR is that it is offered as an activity along with traditional leisure pursuits. It "...makes sense of living. It offers promise as a unique benefit that enlarges medicine's focus on 'fixing the broken part' to whole-person healing" (Murray, 1997, p. 70).

As Murray envisions it, journaling represents not just one activity, but a number of activity options that allow the patient to act expressively. Writing is not the only option—art, film, literature, tapes, as well as other creative modalities can find their way into the client's "journal." The important aspect to the activity is that it is generative—it arises from the person's own creative approach to resolving the situation.

To facilitate the journaling process, the TR specialist may act as a witness. A *witness* in the case of journaling helps the writer to uncover hidden meanings that generate insight into the person's illness experience. At the same time, it is essential that the therapist not be judgmental and not psychoanalyze the client's expression of his or her illness experience. There is an art to facilitating and allowing the person's story to emerge without interfering in the telling of the story. Everyone has a unique story to tell, and the journaling activity provides a series of options for contemplating clinical issues associated with the impairment. At its best the journaling activity should also help the client to process feelings associated with the impairment.

In sum, Murray (1997) may be the first author in TR to explicitly design an intervention based on existential principles and outcomes. The case studies in the following section demonstrate that several TR authors have unintentionally engendered or documented existential outcomes in clients. What ties the case studies together is meaning making and coming to terms with the impairment.

Meaning Through Leisure

Blake's (1991) work predated the findings of Lee et al. (1996), but his results bear a remarkable resemblance to the Lee's strategies for finding continuity through leisure while transitioning from preinjury to postinjury.

Blake reported on a 24-year-old male readmitted to a hospital for several problems secondary to SCI (e.g., substance abuse, skin lesions). Following leisure assessments, the therapist identified activity preferences and found that one preinjury leisure activity was of particular importance—skiing. Once the treatment team involved the client in an adapted skiing program, the client was more responsive to the entire therapy effort. In other words, his attitude toward his impairment changed and he took responsibility for important aspects of his life (e.g., his bladder program).

Participation in a sit-ski program is consistent with one or two of Lee's (Lee et al., 1996) typologies of continuity of leisure—establishing continuity (through approximating a preinjury leisure activity) and/or accommodating for continuity (through an adapted preinjury leisure activity). Clearly, this is a case where existential outcomes are abundant.

1. The client came to terms with his illness and the suffering he endured and would continue to endure.

2. Despite his suffering, he chose to assume a positive attitude toward his therapy and toward his life with a disability.

3. It [TR] had a positive impact on his willingness to participate in other therapies, increased self-esteem and positive affect, and improved his overall attitude toward the possibility of a *genuine quality of life* [italics added] in spite of his severe disability. (Blake, 1991, p. 75)

Activity, rather than outcomes, provided the initial link to existentialism for the next case study. Negley (1994) reported on a 25-year-old female with conversion disorder, major depression, and suicidal ideations. Negley's case study documented the effectiveness of using journaling and physical activity with this psychiatric patient to express her feelings. Existential outcomes emerged gradually and were less obvious than those seen in Blake report. Nevertheless, by the end of two years of TR intervention, this client was better able to come to terms with her illness by expressing emotions she was not allowed to express as a child (e.g., anger, rage). Furthermore, as a result of the TR interventions, she began to make choices, and more importantly to take responsibility for those choices.

Geiger and Miko (1995) were more direct in their investigation of meaning among nursing home residents. They simply asked the residents what leisure activities meant to them. During their conversations with the residents, the authors identified a considerable number of perceived meanings for activities. But the relationship to existentialism became evident after Geiger and Miko's review of the meanings provided by the residents. They identified four emergent themes that gave a sense of purpose to living. Linkages to existentialism have been added in parentheses following each of the themes identified.

1. Sense of continuity and security
   (similar to Lee's continuity of leisure from preinjury to postinjury)

2. Desire to learn and to be mentally challenged
   (to seek competence that may translate into choice and responsibility)

3. Desire to interact with others
   (to get on with living despite the limitations imposed by illness)

4. Sense of helping others
   (to come to terms with suffering associated with illness and disability)

Like Negley (1994), Mobily, Mobily, Lessard, and Berkenpas (2000) reported on a client with a mental illness—schizophrenia. However, the subject's main problem for the purpose of the TR intervention was rheumatoid arthritis, a painful, inflammatory condition that affected the client's knee. The main intent of an aquatic therapy intervention was to bring about relief of pain and to improve functional ability at the affected knee. The functional outcomes proved to be acceptable but not remarkable.

Existentialism came in to play in the Mobily et al. (2000) case report when the client became very involved in lap swimming as part of her therapy program. Usually swimming is not a featured part of aquatic therapy because most clients do not have the stamina for it. This 33-year-old female, however, proved to be a very proficient swimmer. Further, the authors learned that the client was very active in competitive swimming during her youth and was quite accomplished at it. She had not participated regularly in swimming for many years because of arthritis, but took to the swimming part of the intervention with great enthusiasm.

Mobily et al. (2000) pursued interviews with the client in an effort to evoke the meanings that swimming held for her, with little success. However, a writing activity did provide considerable insight, and the subject's response reminds us once again of Lee's typologies for continuity of leisure from preinjury to postinjury: "I have always loved to swim...Ever since I was a kid swimming has been for me..." (Mobily et al., 2000, p. 116).

Following this testimony from the client, the authors concluded aquatic activities provided a sense of meaningful involvement missing in her life for quite some time. Though unexpected and not the initial intent of this case intervention, the emergence of meaning through leisure and the connection from preinjury to postinjury is once again evident. Reconstruction of meaning may also be implied if the client's narrative is interpreted as her expression of a self-defined, meaningful role expressed through leisure—a "good [competent] swimmer."

Mobily and Verburg (2001) examined the effects of aquatic therapy on a person with an arthritis-related impairment, *fibromyalgia*, characterized by debilitating pain in muscles and tendons (instead of joints like the more usual forms of arthritis). Symptoms of fibromyalgia include tender points at various anatomical landmarks, malaise, fatigue, nonrestorative sleep, and depressive symptoms.

This client was also involved in a aquatic therapy program designed to address the primary symptom of fibromyalgia—pain. After several months of participation the results showed a significant decrease in acute and chronic pain. Moreover, the extent to which pain interfered with her important life activities was greatly diminished, to the extent that she was able to return to work on a half-time basis.

Like the client in Mobily et al. (2000) this client asked to add lap swimming to her therapy program. Although she was not as proficient as the client in the earlier study, she seemed to obtain a sense of competence and control when she found she could swim a short distance initially. Her perceived competence may have been augmented by the improvement in swimming capability evident throughout the intervention.

Again, the results of the aquatic therapy program indicated functional improvement in control of both acute and chronic pain. But the more interesting findings for the purposes of this chapter relate to comments volunteered by the patient herself (existential principles in parentheses).

1. She expressed appreciation for the frequent feedback given by the therapists, noting that it provided encouragement during activities that were painful.
    (coming to terms with pain/suffering)

2. She noted she could "... have fun and participate in my own treatment."
    (taking responsibility, attitude toward illness; Mobily & Verburg, 2001, p. 65)

3. She added later "...circled ratings [of pain] indicated lack of stamina and fear of pain more than actual, ever present pain."
    (attitude toward disability, coming to terms with pain/suffering; Mobily & Verburg, 2001, p. 65)

Finally, the client started to take responsibility for her therapy program by going to the pool on her own on weekends for additional workouts. Eventually, she was discharged from the aquatic therapy program and continued to participate in aquatic therapy on her own.

Summary

This chapter introduced philosophy and how it relates to TR's body of knowledge and practice. Specifically, the chapter endeavored to establish a connection between existentialism and TR, arguing that an existential stream of consciousness is interwoven throughout the TR literature. The TR field is not intentionally using existential principles as a basis for theory development and practice. Nevertheless, linkages between existentialism and leisure theory and TR research were established. The chapter provided practical examples through the identification of case studies, practices, and techniques consistent with existential principles. Hopefully, the chapter served to make these links more obvious and to advance understanding of the fundamental assumptions that run through TR literature and practice.

References

Blake, J. G. (1991). Therapeutic recreation assessment and intervention with a patient with quadriplegia. *Therapeutic Recreation Journal, 25*, 71–75.

Brock, S. C. and Kleiber, D. A. (1994). Narration in medicine: The stories of elite college athletes' career-ending injuries. *Qualitative Health Research, 4*, 411–430.

Caldwell, L. L., Adolph, S., and Gilbert, A. (1989). Caution! Leisure counselors at work: Long term effects of leisure counseling. *Therapeutic Recreation Journal, 23*, 41–49.

Caldwell, L. L., Dattilo, J., Kleiber, D. A., and Lee, Y. (1994/95). Perceptions of therapeutic recreation among people with spinal cord injury. *Annual in Therapeutic Recreation, 5*, 13–25.

Caldwell, L. L. and Weissinger, E. (1994). Factors influencing free time boredom in a sample of persons with spinal cord injuries. *Therapeutic Recreation Journal 28*, 18–24.

Cassel, E. J. (1982). The nature of suffering and the goals of medicine. *New England Journal of Medicine, 306,* 639–645.

Coyle, C. P. and Kinney, W. B. (1990). Leisure characteristics of adults with physical disabilities. *Therapeutic Recreation Journal, 24*, 64–73.

Csikszentmihalyi, M. (1975). *Beyond boredom and anxiety: The experience of play in work and games*. San Francisco, CA: Jossey-Bass.

Dattilo J., Kleiber, D., and Williams, R. (1998). Self-determination and enjoyment enhancement: A psychologically based service model for therapeutic recreation. *Therapeutic Recreation Journal, 32*, 258–271.

Fife, B. L. (1994). The conceptualization of meaning in illness. *Social Science in Medicine, 38,* 309–316.

Frankl, V. E. (1984). *Man's search for meaning* (3rd ed.). New York, NY: Simon & Schuster.

Geiger, G. W. and Miko, P. S. (1995). Meaning of recreation/leisure activities to elderly nursing home residents: A qualitative study. *Therapeutic Recreation Journal, 29*, 131–138.

Haun, P. (1966). *Recreation: A medical viewpoint*. New York, NY: Teacher's College Press.

Lee, Y. (1999). How do individuals experience leisure? *Parks and Recreation, 34*, 40–46.

Lee, Y., Brock, S., Dattilo, J., and Kleiber, D. (1993). Leisure and adjustment to spinal cord injury: Conceptual and methodological suggestions. *Therapeutic Recreation Journal, 28*, 200–211.

Lee , Y., Dattilo, J., Kleiber, D., and Caldwell, L. (1996). Exploring the meaning of continuity of recreation activity in the early stage of adjustment for people with spinal cord injury. *Leisure Sciences, 18*, 209–225.

Lee, Y., Mittelstaedt, R., and Askins, J. (1999). Predicting free time boredom of people with spinal cord injury. *Therapeutic Recreation Journal, 33,* 122–134.

Mobily, K. E., Lemke, J. H., and Gisin, G. J. (1991). The idea of leisure repertoire. *Journal of Applied Gerontology, 10,* 208–223.

Mobily, K. E., Mobily, P. R., Lessard, K. A., and Berkenpas, M. S. (2000). Case comparison of response to aquatic exercise: Acute versus chronic conditions. *Therapeutic Recreation Journal, 34,* 103–119.

Mobily, K. E. and Verburg, M. D. (2001). Aquatic therapy in community-based therapeutic recreation: Pain management in a case of fibromyalgia. *Therapeutic Recreation Journal, 35,* 57–69.

Murray, S. (1997). The benefits of journaling. *Parks and Recreation, 32,* 68–75.

Murray, S. (1998). A practitioner critique of the self-determination and enjoyment enhancement model. *Therapeutic Recreation Journal, 32,* 272–282.

Murray, S. (1999). Man's search for meaning: An introduction to logotherapy [Review of the book *Man's search for meaning*]. *Therapeutic Recreation Journal, 33,* 61–62.

Murray, S. (2000, May). *Our calling/our future: Functional or existential outcomes in therapeutic recreation?* A presentation at the 29th annual Midwest Symposium on Therapeutic Recreation, Lake Geneva, WI.

Negley, S. K. (1994). Recreation therapy as an outpatient intervention. *Therapeutic Recreation Journal, 28,* 35–40.

Olson, R. G. (1962). *An introduction to existentialism.* New York, NY: Dover Publications.

Richter, K. J. and Kaschalk, S. M. (1996). The future of therapeutic recreation: An existential outcome. In C. C. Sylvester (Ed.), *Philosophy of therapeutic recreation volume II* (pp. 86–91). Arlington, VA: NRPA.

Stumbo, N. J. and Peterson, C. A. (1998). The leisure ability model. *Therapeutic Recreation Journal, 32,* 82–96.

Thompson, S. C. and Janigian, A. S. (1988). Life scheme: A framework for understanding the search for meaning. *Journal of Social and Clinical Psychology, 7,* 260–280.

Widmer, M. A. and Ellis, G. D. (1998). The Aristotelian good life model: Integration of values into therapeutic recreation service delivery. *Therapeutic Recreation Journal, 32,* 290–302.

Yoshioka, N. (2001). *Le raison d'etre: Existentialism and therapeutic recreation philosophical position.* Unpublished master's thesis, University of Iowa, Iowa City.

Chapter 3

Theory, Research, and Development of TR's Body of Knowledge

Learning Objectives

1. Identify and define the two principles on which knowledge is built. Explain why both are important.

2. Summarize the basic principles of effectance motivation.

3. Define the various sources of feedback that may be used to assist clients in forming perceptions of control, and provide an example in TR for each.

4. Define the two types of causal attributions clients may make and give an example of each in a leisure activity.

5. Identify the three characteristics of learned helplessness. Suggest individual cases especially vulnerable for developing learned helplessness.

6. Suggest strategies the TR specialist may use to counteract learned helplessness among clients, and give specific examples.

7. Explain the following quote from Iso-Ahola (1980a), which is contrary to the way most TR specialists think about activity interventions (that the activity does matter):

   It is not the recreational activity in itself that is critical but the extent to which such activity induces a sense of control and responsibility over one's own behavior, environment, and entire life.

8. Explain how optimal incongruity theory relates to stress and boredom in leisure. Suggest interventions to deal with stress and boredom based on optimal incongruity .

9. Discuss the two different approaches to the competing responses hypothesis: one using exercise and motor activities, the other using client choice to identify intrinsically motivated activities.

10. Identify the weaknesses of the competing responses hypothesis.

A profession rests its reputation and credibility on its body of knowledge. A body of knowledge is not developed overnight, but rather is typically built through the collective scholarship of many over a long time. Knowledge is built on two pillars: (a) observation or empirical data and (b) theory or logic.

Observation refers to the collection of facts that confirm or refute a hypothesis or prediction. Empirical methods tend to dominate professions that rely on the hard sciences, where the confirmation of concrete interventions is necessary. Medicine is a good example of a profession that stakes a large proportion of its body of knowledge on empirical research.

But even empirically driven fields must include theory or risk losing connection with logic. *Theory* helps to make sense of the evidence gathered through observation. For instance, studies concerned with identifying risk factors for coronary artery disease have been instrumental in motivating changes in risk behavior. This has helped people to avoid heart attacks. Some of the risk factors identified include high cholesterol, sedentary lifestyle, smoking, and so on. But another risk factor identified was baldness. Indeed, baldness was predictive of increased risk for heart disease, but some questioned the logic of this finding.

What the skeptics found was that baldness was correlated with a second risk factor, ethnicity. Some ethnic groups are more likely to develop baldness than others, and at the same time are more at risk for heart disease. This correlation produces a spurious finding—in other words, a false reading. It underscores the importance of including the second pillar of knowledge: theory or logic. Failing to include theory sometimes results in findings that may be empirically sound but logically questionable.

Besides using empirical data to establish a body of knowledge, a profession relies on theory. The simplest definition of a theory is an explanation for some aspect of a body of knowledge. Theories allow researchers to make a prediction (hypothesis) about some relationship of interest (e.g., Do stretching exercises for older adults increase their flexibility?). Researchers often test the validity of a hypothesis. If the prediction represented by the hypothesis is confirmed, then more confidence can be placed in the validity of the theory.

Just as empirical data were useless without logic and theory, likewise, logic and theory are no good without empirical confirmation. For example, consider the logic in the following two syllogisms:

All men are mortal.   All unicorns are white.
Socrates is a man.   Fred is a unicorn.
Therefore, Socrates is mortal.   Therefore, Fred is white.

Both syllogisms are equivalent according to the rules of formal logic. In a vacuum that ignores reality, both syllogisms are the same, equally logical. However, common sense leads most of us to question the validity of the second syllogism, because unicorns have no existence in reality. Hence, logic or theory without empirical verification—without a reality check—is weak.

Theories and TR

While admitting the development of a body of knowledge relies on both empirical findings and theory, this chapter focuses on theory. Theories are important because they guide research by forming and testing hypotheses. Theories are especially important to TR because they not only guide research, but also provide a logic or rationale for TR practice. Thus, it is especially important for practitioners to understand the theoretical bases for TR.

Why is TR effective? Why should a hospital financially support a TR program for its clients? Why should children with disabilities be allowed to play in a youth baseball league? Although the practitioner and student may not think of their answers to these questions as theories, they offer one or more explanations for each of the queries. In other words, they offer theoretical explanations.

TR is not only a relatively new profession, but also one situated in a difficult political position—having to work with professions that typically have well-developed bodies of knowledge that rely heavily on empirically verified theories. By comparison, TR is on weak ground, not possessing many theories of its own. The result has been that TR specialists frequently have to answer questions related to the justification or rationale for service provision. The success of their responses depends on the extent of understanding of the theories on which TR intervention is built. In addition, practitioners need to understand why interventions are successful, and which interventions are successful with which problems, to be effective. Without theoretical understanding, the practitioner is working blindly. Each procedure becomes a blind experiment, using someone's best guess about what intervention might work with a particular client.

This chapter offers three major theoretical perspectives on TR. The first is based on competence/effectance motivation (including learned helplessness and flow). The second is founded on intrinsic motivation. The third, a new theoretical perspective on TR, is the competing responses hypothesis. The theories are summarized in **Table 3.1** (p. 58).

Competence, Effectance, and TR

Effectance Motivation Defined

Competence and effectance motivation are considered equivalent concepts for the purpose of this chapter. As a theory, *competence motivation* evolved from an increasing dissatisfaction among psychologists with so-called "drive theories" of motivation that dominated psychology into the 1950s.

Around 1960 several leading psychologists started to develop an alternative perspective on motivation referred to as *effectance motivation*. Instead of seeing humans as bound to innate drives, scholars such as White (1959) argued that humans were different from other animals, not bound exclusively to instinct-like behavior. Every action, especially sophisticated behavior such as learning, could not be attributed to built-in drives. Drive theories simply were not parsimonious and advanced enough to explain most human behavior.

Table 3.1   Theories Applied to TR

Theory	Basic Premises
Competence/ Effectance Motivation	Human nature is such that people want to feel a sense of "control" over their environment. They want to believe that they control their own fate rather than their future being controlled by random factors and chance events.
Learned Helplessness	After experiencing repeated failures, the person "learns" to become helpless and hopeless, demonstrating three symptoms: unwillingness to believe his or her behavior can make a difference, inability to perceive personal causation even when it occurs, and heightened emotions (anxiety and/or reactive depression).
Flow	When challenging activities make the actor use his or her skills and abilities to a near maximum extent, then a sense of "enjoyment" is more likely to occur, resulting in perceptions of control and support of self-confidence.
Optimal Arousal/ Incongruity	The best leisure environment is one that presents the actor with varied stimuli to maintain arousal level at a moderate level, leading to better mental health.
Competing Responses Hypothesis	Intrinsically motivating leisure activities block or interfere with pathological behaviors, based on the assumption that both the pathological behaviors and leisure activities are intrinsically motivating.

White (1959) and others provided an alternative: effectance motivation. The human need to have a sense of control over the environment (instead of being controlled *by* the environment) was cause enough for some of the more complex behaviors exhibited by man. For White, competence referred to the ability to effectively control one's environment. Effectance was the feeling or perception of control that resulted when interactions with the environment were successful.

For example, when a client with a spinal cord injury (SCI) first learns how to play wheelchair basketball, he develops a certain amount of skill or competence in that activity. Continued practice of wheelchair basketball will advance his skills even more. It will also increase the probability for success in the sport. Though "success" can mean different things to different people, the resulting effect on cognitive interpretation of one's performance of the activity is the same—effectance.

Two further points are important to recognize early on. First, the feeling of effectance is pleasant and positive, even sought after. Human nature, argued the authors of effectance motivation, is such that humans find it desirable to control their environment rather than to be controlled by their environment. Second, behaviors that lead to feelings of effectance are intrinsically motivated. They are self-sustaining and desirable in their own right. Competence and effectance, therefore, have motivational properties.

As time went on, other psychologists added details to effectance motivation and refined the concept. Much of the development of effectance motivation is attributable to its clinical application. For example, while working with clients with various phobias, Bandura (1977) found effectance motivation to be most useful. He added the idea of *expectancy* to effectance motivation. In anticipating a future act/behavior, the person forms efficacy and outcome expectations. The person essentially makes predictions about how well he or she will perform (i.e., efficacy expectation) the act (e.g., wheelchair basketball) and what the rewards will be (i.e., outcome expectation). "Through cognitive representation of future outcomes individuals can generate current motivators of behavior" (Bandura, 1977, p. 193).

The client then can set his or her own goals for performance (of a recreational activity in this case), set a standard for performance, and evaluate himself or herself based on a comparison between the expected level of performance and actual performance. By setting an expectation for performance, the clients also "create self-inducements to persist in their efforts until their performances match self-prescribed standards" (Bandura, 1977, p. 193). Hence, Bandura built the foundation for practical application of effectance motivation for goal-oriented behavior in general, and for leisure behavior for the purpose of this book. There was not only a self-generated motive to initiating an activity, but also a motive for persisting in an activity until performance matched expectations.

Effectance and TR

When our client with an SCI makes a judgment about how well he performed in wheelchair basketball, Bandura states there are four sources of information available to use in evaluation: performance feedback, vicarious feedback, verbal persuasion, and physiological/visceral sensations (see **Table 3.2**). Each has direct application in TR practice.

Performance feedback is just what it suggests it is—the actual performance of wheelchair basketball and various subskills needed to be successful. Hence, the results of each game or practice are compared to the standard of performance the client holds for himself, and he reaches a judgment of how close he came to meeting his performance expectation.

Vicarious feedback about performance might be more relevant earlier in wheelchair basketball, when the client is still wondering if he has the capability to participate or not. Here, the TR specialist might introduce the activity by having the client watch a wheelchair basketball game. Optimally, the feedback that the person receives is gleaned from watching "people like me" play the sport successfully. The more the client identifies with the wheelchair basketball participants, the more likely he will conclude it is possible for him to participate with some degree of success too.

Table 3.2   Feedback Sources for Effectance

Source	Definition
Performance Feedback	Feedback information that results from practice of the activity; thought to be the most effective way of enhancing perceptions of competence and control.
Vicarious Feedback	Observe a peer or role model ("someone who is like me") perform a skill successfully; results in a perception of associated control ("if he can do I can do it").
Verbal Persuasion	Perceptions of control are formed on the basis of affirmations from a trusted confidant (e.g., TR specialist, friend, family member) who states that I can successfully perform the activity.
Physiological/ Visceral Sensations	Internal feelings associated with "nervousness" and anxiety; the TR specialist typically tries to counterbalance these feelings within the client through reassurance.

Third, the TR specialist could use *verbal persuasion* to convince the client that wheelchair basketball is something he could participate in if he is interested—that it is within his ability to do so if he wishes. The credibility and persuasiveness of the TR specialist will depend on several factors: (a) whether the TR specialist is considered a trusted (credible) source of information, (b) whether the arguments used "make sense" to the client, and (c) whether the goals set and standards for performance are within reach. Regarding the third point, the TR specialist should play a role in helping the person to set a realistic standard for success, one that will not lead to discouragement early in the activity, when "failure" is more likely. (See Chapter 8 on building a therapeutic relationship for more information.)

Finally, the TR specialist can alert the client to some *physiological/ visceral sensations* he or she might experience and guide him in his interpretations of those feelings. For example, when almost anyone tries a new activity for the first time or two he or she is apt to be nervous. The TR specialist is there to remind the client that feeling nervous because of uncertainty is normal.

Bandura's refinement of effectance motivation remains consistent with White's original version insofar as it is still rewarding for the actor to set goals and try to attain those goals generally in life, and specifically in leisure behavior. Bandura's interpretation of effectance motivation also is consistent with the emphasis of another researcher, Martin Seligman.

Learned Helplessness and TR in Theory

In the late 1960s and early 1970s, Seligman and his associates were occupied with a concept they named *learned helplessness*. Seligman integrated attribution theory to apply effectance motivation to the treatment of psychiatric patients, especially those with depression. Attribution theory maintains people not only want explanations for their behavior and that of others, but also actively seek to attribute cause of the behavior to something or someone (Iso-Ahola, 1980b).

There are two types of attributions. *Dispositional attributions* are made when a client attributes cause of a behavior (e.g., a successful free throw in wheelchair basketball) to his own skill. *Environmental attributions* occur when a client attributes cause of some action (e.g., a successful free throw in wheelchair basketball) to an external variable (e.g., luck). An analysis of these two patterns of attributions should lead the TR specialist to predict that the client apt to make dispositional attributions for success at a leisure activity is more likely to be more healthy psychologically. A second client, not as well off psychologically, may be prone to make environmental attributions, even in the face of evidence to the contrary—that luck led to the successful completion of the leisure activity. This is the sort of person that Seligman found to be at risk for developing learned helplessness.

Learned helplessness results when the person is repeatedly exposed to situations (usually negative) that he or she cannot control with resulting environmental attributions. A series of personal failures in work and relationships, even when the person makes his or her best effort, can lead to feelings of helplessness and lack of control. In the worst cases, feeling helpless in one sphere of life is generalized to all aspects of life. A person has "learned" that his or her efforts make no difference in life—he or she comes to believe life is controlled more by forces outside his or her influence than by one's own actions.

Seligman maintained that the more severe cases of learned helplessness can be recognized when three characteristics are evident: decreased motivation to respond, inability to perceive success, and heightened emotionality (Iso-Ahola, 1980a, 1980b). The result is often referred to as reactive depression (Iso-Ahola & Mobily, 1982). The TR specialist should be clear that this is not the same as psychotic depression. First of all, anyone with any disability can suffer from reactive depression—the person who sustains an SCI caused by a random accident, a cancer patient who does not understand the cause of the affliction, or the person who did nothing to deserve being born with a developmental disability (Iso-Ahola, 1980b). All of these clients have one thing in common: each experienced a significant change because of an environmentally determined etiology that they were unable to control.

Second, reactive depression is not the same as the depression exhibited by chronic mental health patients. When a client is reluctant to try a new or even old preinjury leisure activity, the TR specialist may suspect reactive depression and learned helplessness. The symptom may be evident even if the client does participate in a leisure activity, such as the earlier example of wheelchair basketball. Here the TR specialist may have to make heroic efforts just to get the client to watch the activity, much less participate. We recognize this first characteristic of helplessness as apathy in everyday life. In the case of learned helplessness, the apathy has generalized to every aspect of life—work, school, relationships, and leisure.

Reluctance to make an effort must be accompanied by an inability to perceive success. Again, in the earlier example of the successful free throw in wheelchair basketball, the person suffering from learned helplessness is unable to attribute the made shot to his own ability and effort. Even when evidence to the contrary is presented to the person (e.g., the TR specialist provides persuasive verbal feedback: "Your free throw shooting has really improved. You have been practicing a lot.") and his environmental attribution comes into question, the client persists in attributing outcomes to external forces rather than his own skill.

The final characteristic of learned helplessness is heightened emotionality. It manifests as elevated anxiety at first, but later evolves into reactive depression. Usually, the TR practitioner does not see the client in the earlier stages of learned helplessness where anxiety is the emotion exhibited. Certainly most people have frustrating experiences. Often frustration results when actions do not produce the desired effect—that is, the result seems to be out of our hands. At first we may be anxious, later resignation sets in, and we eventually give up trying. This is the same sequence of feelings experienced by the client on the way to developing learned helplessness, except it is magnified a thousandfold. Emotional deterioration spirals downward into reactive depression and generalizes to all aspects of life. The person becomes behaviorally and emotionally paralyzed.

Learned Helplessness and TR Intervention

The general strategy for the TR specialist when it comes to addressing learned helplessness is to use leisure activities and interpersonal techniques to reverse the psychological state of the client (Iso-Ahola, 1980a, 1980b). The variety of methods to accomplish this task is limited only by the imagination and creativity of the TR practitioner. Some of those strategies are presented in this section.

More than any other scholar, Iso-Ahola is responsible for importing theories of effectance motivation, learned helplessness, and perceived control into TR practice. Even though he accomplished this task more than 20 years ago, the principles still apply. He still identifies learned helplessness and perceived control as "core constructs" for TR (Iso-Ahola, as cited in Mobily, 2000).

If clients can be convinced their actions and behaviors make a difference in leisure activities, there is a chance the perceived control that results may generalize to other aspects of the client's lifestyle. To continue the example of the person with an SCI participating in wheelchair basketball, the client convinced his efforts are effective in producing successful results (e.g., a successful free throw, a completed pass, ability to dribble) comes to believe he can control his environment. Of course, perceptions of control and effectance are incompatible with reactive depression and learned helplessness. "It is in this process of increasing the client's perceived control and avoiding a feeling of helplessness that recreation activities are used as a treatment modality" (Iso-Ahola, 1980b, p. 323).

The question then is: How are perceptions of control and effectance encouraged in the person experiencing helplessness or the person at risk for helplessness? Specifically, what is TR's role in producing these favorable perceptions?

Some interventions suggested by Lee's analysis of transitions from preinjury to postinjury leisure were discussed in Chapter 2. If the client accomplishes continuity by participating in a leisure activity that approximates preinjury participation (Lee, Dattilo, Kleiber & Caldwell, 1996), then reaffirmation of competence and perceptions of control are likely. In a sense, continuing participation in a familiar activity restores competence and control. The resulting perceptions are incompatible with helplessness. "Consequently, the person continues to engage in the same leisure activity and tries to overcome problems in such a way that attribution of behavior to personal competence is creditable" (Iso-Ahola, 1980b, p. 334). Every practiced free throw serves as evidence that skills are improved and more likely the cause of successful participation than random events and environmental variables.

Another strategy to address helplessness is to adopt a new leisure activity. This recommendation from Iso-Ahola is consistent with another of Lee's (Lee et al., 1996) styles of transition from preinjury to postinjury: accommodating for continuity. "The person may turn to new leisure activities and acquire new skills which are more congruent with personal talents, and which more readily allow dispositional attributions" (Iso-Ahola, 1980b, p. 334). Practically speaking, the strategy may be implemented when the client finds it impossible to participate in preinjury leisure activities in a personally satisfying manner. For instance, if basketball (wheelchair or otherwise) is no longer accessible or desired because of the person's impairment, then seeking competence and control through a new postinjury activity may be in order. In this case, learning skills and acquiring abilities necessary for successful participation serve to support favorable perceptions. As with the first example, practice can be used to encourage perceptions of competence and control.

The net result of both of the strategies suggested here is perceived control in leisure. Whether learning a new activity or relearning an old favorite, the probability for perceptions of control in leisure is very high. Hence, Iso-Ahola (1980b) reasoned psychological health is improved as a result. Although there is no guarantee perceptions of control will generalize from leisure to other spheres of life (e.g., work, relationships), Iso-Ahola maintained there is good reason to believe self-concept may be maintained or restored through leisure competence.

Iso-Ahola's efforts were directed toward persons with mental illness and older adults. The former group attracted attention because it represents a situation where one would often find persons experiencing reactive depression. Older adults, too, are at great risk of acquiring learned helplessness because the prevalence of chronic conditions (e.g., arthritis, diabetes mellitus, high blood pressure) increases with age, putting the person in an impaired or limited state through no particular fault of his or her own. Furthermore, as people age their control over the environment is constrained. Many events associated with aging cannot be controlled. Retirement, which may jeopardize financial control, and the loss of a spouse or partner, friends, and acquaintances, which limits social contact, create an optimal medium for the formation of learned helplessness through repeated "failures." Social expectations and biases limit control of lifestyle (e.g., grandmothers are not supposed to lift weights). The issue of learned helplessness among older adults is magnified by the sheer number of elderly in North American society, a trend likely to continue for the foreseeable future.

Early work by Langer and Rodin (1976) pioneered the application of recreation as a preventive and "curative" measure against helplessness among older adults. Langer and Rodin encouraged control in one group of older residents of a nursing home, while discouraging control in a second group of older adults in the same nursing home. After a short time they found that the "responsibility induced" group, who had control over some small aspects of their environment, thrived and were rated psychologically healthier than the group deprived of control over a small part of their environment.

The key to Langer and Rodin's (1976) work for TR practice was that one of the aspects of the environment they were allowed to control was their recreational activities. As Iso-Ahola (1980a, 1980b) pointed out, the importance of control over even small aspects of life means more when one has lost control over many of the other traditionally self-determined aspects of living (e.g., vocation, residence, relationships). These findings confirmed Haun's (1966) earlier intuitive observation that it is vital to retain control over one's "tillable acreage" no matter how small. Plainly, when you have no control, securing even a little control is significant.

"It is not the recreational activity in itself that is critical but the extent to which such activity induces a sense of control and responsibility over one's own behavior, environment, and entire life" (Iso-Ahola, 1980a, p. 38). Perceptions of control regulate the benefits resulting from an activity. This means two clients could be involved in the same activity but not receive the same benefit because of the differences in "attitude" associated with the activity.

Badminton could be a meaningless part of a daily routine in a nursing home, or it could be an empowering activity because the client was allowed to choose the activity and performed it with an acceptable degree of competence. Hence, competence and choice (perceived freedom) seem to be the keys to empowering clients through recreation, and thus addressing the paralyzing effects of learned helplessness. The net result of competence and choice is perceived control, and prevention or cure of helplessness.

Shary and Iso-Ahola (1989) replicated the findings of Langer and Rodin (1976) by emphasizing choice and responsibility in leisure activities for one group of older residents in a nursing home. A comparison group in the same care center was not allowed choice in their leisure activities. The group with more freedom and control over their leisure reported more opportunity to choose, more control, and more responsibility than the comparison group. In addition, the responsibility induced group was rated higher on self-esteem and perceived competence. The results confirmed the earlier findings of Langer and Rodin (1976), with special emphasis on the role of leisure activities in fostering perceptions of choice, control, and competence.

Iso-Ahola also researched learned helplessness and reactive depression among persons with mental illness. In one study (Iso-Ahola & Mobily, 1982) he compared the recreation involvement of persons with clinical (endogenous) depression compared to those affected with reactive depression. Iso-Ahola reasoned that persons diagnosed with cancer were at great risk for developing reactive depression because of the loss of control the illness precipitated in their lives—cancer put future possibilities in question (Lee, Brock, Dattilo & Kleiber, 1993). The hypothesis—cancer patients would participate significantly less in recreational activities than patients admitted for clinical depression—was confirmed. Cancer patients participated 10 times less frequently than patients with mental health difficulties.

Iso-Ahola (Iso-Ahola & Mobily, 1982) reasoned that less frequent participation on the part of clients with cancer was consistent with one of the hallmark symptoms of helplessness—a decrease in the motivation to initiate a response. The person with cancer who accepts this lack of control also accepts his or her helplessness, thus reducing participation in recreation and increasing evidence of reactive depression.

The obvious weakness of Iso-Ahola and Mobily's 1982 study was that the lower participation on the part of cancer patients could very well have been because they were experiencing genuine physical symptoms (e.g., pain, nausea, malaise) that limited energy and physical capacity to participate. Cancer itself could cause symptoms that limited the ability to participate, and/or treatment (e.g., chemotherapy) may have imposed its own set of limitations.

To address this limitation, Wassman and Iso-Ahola (1985) investigated the relationship between recreation participation and depression in psychiatric clients. The researchers followed the clients for 30 days, noting their recreation participation and levels of depression (rated by staff nurses) over the same time period. They found a significant negative relationship between recreation participation and levels of depression—high rates of recreation participation were associated with lower ratings of depression.

Taken together, the theoretical and empirical work of Iso-Ahola began a new era in the way TR professionals thought about what they did, why they did it, and how they did it. For the first time, cognitive processing was implicated in a systematic fashion to explain why TR "worked." This groundbreaking work not only was significant in its own right, but also motivated others to explore new and more sophisticated ways of thinking about and explaining TR.

Flow and Effectance Motivation

One of the researchers motivated by Iso-Ahola's work was John Dattilo. Dattilo and Kleiber (1993) and later Dattilo, Kleiber, and Williams (1998) developed a practice model for TR (see Chapter 9) using a concept closely related to effectance motivation as a basis—the concept of flow.

Flow is an idea developed by Csikszentmihalyi (1975) to examine the nature of "peak experiences." Csikszentmihalyi's interest also included nonrecreational activities (e.g., surgery), although many of the activities he investigated are often considered recreational (e.g., rock climbing, chess). Typically, Csikszentmihalyi investigated an activity by having the participant keep a journal during the activity experience itself, thus chronicling the moment-to-moment feelings and perceptions of the participant in the midst of active engagement in the activity. His results pointed to a predictable set of feelings and perceptions, which he labeled flow. These predictable feelings and perceptions included being deeply absorbed in the activity, a loss of a sense of time, a merging of action and awareness, and a focus or concentration of effort on the task at hand.

Flow was conceived of as an intense experience, an extraordinary experience—one that challenged the actor's skills and abilities to the maximum. The probability of experiencing flow (i.e., a peak experience) is most likely when the person's skills and abilities are stretched and challenged by the activity. Hence, our wheelchair basketball player would have to force himself to take on ambitious challenges to experience flow. He might try out for a very good team, he may set a goal of making a competitive team, or he may seek out tough opponents. The task is to not overwhelm oneself with an impossible challenge, but to set a reachable goal.

When challenge is matched closely with the actor's skills and abilities, flow is most likely. Dattilo and his associates labeled the phenomenon of flow "enjoyment." They further argued this very special kind of enjoyment is the primary purpose of TR.

Flow and TR Practice: Enjoyment/Self-Determination Model

Dattilo and Kleiber (1993) originally developed the enjoyment/self-determination model based on the concept of flow. They argued that enjoyable leisure experiences amounted to flow experiences. Enjoyment meant the actor invested a substantial amount of attention in the activity—concentrated, exerted, considerable effort—and was in control of the activity. The last point of control means the patient has a choice. Dattilo added if the person could meet the challenge presented by the activity with skill and ability, perceptions of competence resulted. Together, the perceived choice (freedom) and perceived competence associated with the flow concept in general, and Dattilo's practice model specifically, are consistent with effectance motivation and Iso-Ahola's application of learned helplessness to TR practice.

Dattilo's practice model also revealed practical techniques that may be employed by the TR professional to engender perceptions of competence and freedom in his or her clients. The TR professional can therefore manipulate the environment to be more "responsive" (Dattilo & Kleiber, 1993, p. 62) to the patient, serving as a source of feedback about competence for the patient. For example, the practitioner can help the patient to set challenging yet attainable activity participation and performance goals. The client is more likely to aspire to reach a goal that requires intense effort, but is within reach. (Further discussion of techniques that may be used to enhance perceptions of competence and control can be found in the discussion of the TR process in Chapter 8.)

Like Iso-Ahola earlier, Dattilo viewed the client's perceptions of the activity as more important than the activity itself. The results of the perceptions of control should be familiar to the reader by now. "As enjoyment comes under one's own power, it offers an orientation for making the most of one's circumstances, and enhancing the quality of life" (Dattilo & Kleiber, 1993, p. 60). Therefore, like Iso-Ahola before, Dattilo and Kleiber submitted the resulting perceptions of control and effectance were associated with more favorable states of mental health.

Dattilo and his colleagues (Dattilo, Kleiber & Williams, 1998) further refined the enjoyment/self-determination model of TR practice. They added functional outcomes to their model. That is, as a result of the enjoyable experience, functional improvements may also result. They further stated both enjoyment and the promise of functional improvement serve as a "precipitating experience" (p. 260), an experience that feeds back to the actor and motivates continued participation. Simply, participation in an enjoyable experience (according to Dattilo's definition of "enjoyment") is sufficient to motivate continued participation. Recreation participation within TR, then, is self-reinforcing. Assuming the TR specialist can configure the environment in a way that is "responsive," the environment will underscore the patient's accomplishments, make those accomplishments more likely in the first place, and serve as a source for lifetime activities in the long run.

Optimal Incongruity and TR

Optimal Incongruity Defined

Optimal incongruity finds its origin in the neurophysiology of the brain. An arrangement of neurons (nerve cells) throughout a portion of the brain called the brainstem is responsible for the arousal of the individual. This diverse arrangement of neurons is known as the Reticular Arousal System (RAS). The RAS receives input from many sensory sources. Its major role is to maintain an appropriate arousal or alertness level within the individual. The so-called "optimal" level is thought to be moderate in intensity. Hence, as White (1959) speculated, humans are in possession of a "neurogenic" motive—built into the very character of the human nervous system is a need for optimal stimulation.

Too much arousal or alertness and the individual attends to everything in the environment and is unable to separate important environmental information from unimportant environmental information (often referred to as "noise"). Too little arousal and the person does not attend to any or most information in the environment, missing environmental cues crucial to successful adaptation to environmental demands. Hence, a moderate level of alertness that best serves the individual is optimal. Excessive information is not attended to, nor is important information missed, when the person is in a state of optimal arousal.

Iso-Ahola (1980b) applied the idea of optimal arousal to leisure behavior. He hypothesized that a play environment presents an individual with a series of stimuli that could be optimal, excessive, or insufficient. For example, Iso-Ahola maintained that traditional playgrounds are too predictable and therefore understimulating. Instead he submitted that playgrounds should be designed to encourage exploration and manipulation to optimally arouse the child with an interesting stimulus array.

Three assumptions support the application of optimal arousal to leisure behavior. First, the state of being optimally aroused is pleasant if not pleasurable. Second, the human organism is capable of learning behaviors that maintain an optimal level of arousal. Third, the normal state of the organism is activity and not quiescence. The final assumption contrasts markedly with some of the early definitions of play, insofar as definitions such as surplus energy and the like assume that the normal condition of the human organism is one of quiescence.

Because the human species is capable of learning behaviors that lead to the manipulation of the environment in a stimulating manner, humans are sometimes said to be *sensoristaic* (Ellis, 1973). This means that people will make the environment more stimulating if it falls short of a level necessary for optimal arousal. The term *sensoristasis* is adapted from the physiological term homeostasis. *Homeostasis* means the body works to maintain a balanced environment among physiologic systems (e.g., cardiovascular, respiratory). Similarly, the individual works actively to keep the amount of sensory stimulation at a proper (optimal) level.

Leisure activities are thought to afford the individual one of the best means of manipulating the environment in new and interesting ways to produce optimal arousal. Some authorities (Iso-Ahola, 1980b) believe that an incongruent play environment is best because it leads to an ideal level of stimulation. Several strategies are available to the individual to accomplish this end. For example, if someone is a good golfer, the individual may alter this very familiar activity by playing at different golf courses, playing with different partners, playing at different times of the day, or playing during different seasons. Clearly, through active manipulation of the play environment, the individual has attained an ideal level of stimulation by rearranging a very usual and familiar situation (e.g., golf).

The idea of optimal incongruity, therefore, has ample application to the configuring of all sorts of leisure environments, activities, playground designs, and so on. Iso-Ahola (1980b) asserted one main task of a recreation professional is to create optimal arousal in patrons to maximize enjoyment.

Optimal Incongruity and Well-Being

Likewise, Iso-Ahola (1980b) applied optimal incongruity to health and well-being, especially mental health. He argued optimal arousal is prerequisite to sound mental health. A person is better off when a balance is struck between stimulating elements in the environment and predictable elements. In cases of too much stimulation, chaos results; with too little stimulation, monotony and boredom result.

The consequences of failing to maintain an optimally incongruent pattern of leisure behavior is one of two conditions may manifest. First, if the individual is unsuccessful at manipulating the environment and making enough changes to keep familiar activities stimulating, boredom (underarousal) may result (Weissinger, Caldwell & Bandalos, 1992). Alternatively, if the environment is changed too often or too quickly, then chaos results and the person is overstimulated (overarousal). Stress is the result when too much stimulation is present in the environment.

Neither condition is desirable from the point of view of optimal arousal, and neither state is in the interest of the person's mental health. Iso-Ahola (1980b) argued leisure is one of the best ways to maintain an optimal level of arousal. Because people are generally able to change their activities during free time in almost any manner, leisure affords the person an excellent means for adjusting the amount of stimulation in his environment.

Optimal Incongruity and TR

The results of overstimulation or understimulation allow for a connection between optimal incongruity and TR. Overstimulation results in stress. Understimulation results in boredom. Neither is a desirable condition, and persons with disabilities are more at risk for developing both.

Stress has been implicated in several disease processes, most notably the development of heart disease. The high-stress, driven personality is associated with a greater risk of a heart attack. Other studies have linked stress to a variety of chronic conditions as well. Some forms of cancer and high blood pressure have been linked to prolonged exposure to high stress (i.e., overstimulating) conditions. Stress also increases a person's susceptibility to a variety of illnesses in general. For example, Neiman (1994) found high levels of stress were associated with an increased incidence of upper respiratory infections (e.g., the common cold). Fortunately, exercise at mild to moderate levels attenuates the negative effects of excess stress.

Of course, exercise and physical activities are popular activities used as interventions by TR professionals. Exercise as an intervention technique is therefore especially important to those working with persons (e.g., cardiac rehabilitation patients) with a negative risk profile for the development of stress-related conditions.

Leisure activities may have at least two other beneficial effects on stress. Through diverting the person's attention away from the stress producing elements in the environment, leisure activities decrease the amount of stimulation in the environment to bring the client closer to an optimal level of arousal. Use of the word "diversion" may cause many a TR specialist to cringe. But clearly, the diversionary aspect of leisure activity does have its benefits, especially for the individual who has difficulty ignoring an overstimulating/ stress-filled environment. Effectively, leisure activities interrupt the person's attention to negative stimuli (e.g., trouble at work) by substituting a less aggravating stimulus array.

Leisure activities may also be used to evoke a relaxation response. Guided imagery, massage, and progressive relaxation techniques number among the interventions used by TR specialists. Unwittingly perhaps, TR service may have stumbled on a way to reduce the chaos in the environment. True, the environment of interest is restricted to the client's free time space. But if the relaxation technique is effective, then the person is less apt to bring the "baggage" of work-related stress into leisure activities (by worrying about the stressful transactions at work).

Both the diversionary effects of leisure and the relaxation response associated with some leisure activities are considered palliative measures. *Palliative measures* treat the symptoms of a problem but not the actual cause of the stress itself. Thus, properly arranged and manipulated leisure environments can provide the client with the means to manage but not cure the problem of an overstimulating/stress-filled environment. As such, the interventions suggested here may be thought of as more preventive than curative.

Boredom represents the opposite end of the environmental array: the understimulating environment. Because of the nature of disabling conditions and the constraints associated with impairments, the potential for understimulation is probably greater than for stress (overstimulation). Numerous authors (Caldwell, Adolph & Gilbert, 1989; Caldwell & Weissinger, 1994; Coyle & Kinney, 1990) observed that persons with physical impairments live in the shadow of boredom. Persons with disabilities commonly describe their leisure as sedentary, isolated, homebound, and passive. Certainly these words describe a low stimulus environment, and one that has great potential to produce boredom.

The trouble with boredom among persons with disabilities is that it is associated with conditions that may exacerbate an illness (Coyle & Kinney, 1990). For example, substance abuse is higher among persons with physical impairments. Smoking, alcohol consumption, and more serious drug abuse put the person at risk for development of secondary impairments. The client is less likely to attend to his or her hygiene and self-care, risking development of skin lesions, urinary tract infections, and heart disease. (See Blake's 1991 case study of a person with an SCI and his development of secondary impairments.)

Boredom Interventions

Caldwell, Weissinger, and others actively researched boredom during free time among persons with disabilities. Caldwell et al. (1989) followed 155 persons with SCIs after discharge from inpatient rehabilitation and found those most active in leisure during hospitalization were most likely to report boredom and dissatisfaction after discharge. Similar findings were referred to as "relapse" phenomenon among recently discharged clients with SCIs (Caldwell, Dattilo, Kleiber & Lee, 1994/95).

Just as stress/overstimulation can be addressed through leisure-based interventions, so can boredom. In simplest terms, harking back to Iso-Ahola's advice, TR practitioners should endeavor to make constituents' free-time environments more stimulating. However, because persons with disabilities typically have fewer resources for the meaningful use of free time in the first place, they not only experience greater risk for developing boredom, but also experience more leisure constraints to hurdle. Common leisure constraints reported by persons with disabilities include inaccessible facilities, financial limitations, and fear of crime (Coyle & Kinney, 1990).

Leisure education is an especially promising intervention available to enrich the leisure of clients who find their free time boring. Obviously, teaching the client new leisure activities will provide new options for stimulating use of free time. Leisure awareness exercises can also be integrated into the leisure education curriculum to convince the patient of the importance of leisure in life (see Peterson & Stumbo, 2000, for leisure awareness exercises). Building on preinjury leisure can also supplement the acquisition of new leisure skills through leisure education. Adaptations in rules, temporal and spatial configuration, and pace can make previous activities accessible once again.

Still, if activities are pursued repeatedly, inevitably those activities may be seen as boring by participants. Iso-Ahola (1980b) suggested several methods for augmenting the amount of stimulation inherent in frequently repeated activities. Subtle variations in participation patterns can be planned to increase the client's arousal level.

Spatial, temporal, and social differences can be built into a person's regular pattern of participation. For instance, the wheelchair basketball player may change his practice schedule, change his opponents, change the level of competition, or play with a different group of friends each time. Moreover, the client should be instructed in how to make modifications in leisure participation patterns. In this manner he is empowered with the means to adjust his leisure on his own. Self-regulation of leisure through activity modification seems essential given the finding that persons with disabilities frequently report that boredom sets in after discharge from inpatient rehabilitation (Caldwell et al., 1989).

Another benefit of leisure education is that it likely leads to the expansion of the client's leisure repertoire (Mobily, Lemke & Gisin, 1991). Although Mobily et al.'s discussion of leisure repertoire was in association with the constraints on leisure experienced by older adults, it is applicable to all persons with disabilities. *Leisure repertoire* refers to all leisure activities available to an individual. It is essentially the person's leisure library—activities the person can perform competently and comfortably. As the client acquires more leisure skills through leisure education, he or she likewise acquires more activities and thereby combats boredom. In other words, the client has more options and is less susceptible to boredom.

Hence, leisure education is an especially effective modality for inoculating the client against bouts with understimulation and boredom. It is effective because it gives the person something better to do in preference to stimulating but abusive alternatives (e.g., cigarettes, alcohol).

Competing Responses Hypothesis

Giving clients "something better to do" is also the theme of the next rationale for TR's effectiveness. But the reasoning behind the *competing responses hypothesis* is somewhat different than for optimal incongruity.

Stereotypic behaviors are frequently found in persons with autism (Levinson & Reid, 1993) or schizophrenia (Wong et al., 1987). The behaviors tend to be perseverative motor responses (e.g., self-abuse) thought to be motivated by the person's need for more than the usual amount of stimulation (Levinson & Reid, 1993). This explanation for stereotypic behaviors is consistent with White's (1959) assumption that the normal condition for the human nervous system is neural activation and not quiescence. White maintained the human species exhibits a *neurogenic motive*, an incentive built into the nervous system to find an optimal amount of stimulation. The argument for autism suggests the person has a higher than normal threshold for what is considered optimal. It follows that substituting a socially acceptable alternative might replace the need for self-stimulation (e.g., exercise, arts and crafts).

Similarly, noted stress theorist and researcher Hans Selye (1975) argued to be without stress is to be dead. Life, he maintained, is fraught with a certain degree of stress and intensity. The key to healthful living is not to avoid stress altogether but to avoid excess stress or negative forms of stress ("distress"). Like White's neurogenic explanation, the stress theory rationale for stereotypic behaviors of persons with schizophrenia or self-stimulating behaviors of persons with autism is that the person is seeking to create a more stressful environment through these actions. Because self-stimulation often stigmatizes the client with a mental health disorder, or leads to self-abuse in the case of the client with autism, it needs to be channeled toward less damaging alternatives.

In a sense, the strategy behind using activities such as exercise and other leisure activities to treat people who manifest stereotypic behaviors is one of intrinsic motivation. The reasoning is as follows: If stereotypic behaviors have intrinsic appeal to the client—a "self-maintaining" characteristic (Wong et al., 1987, p. 81)—then it stands to reason if another intrinsically appealing activity could be substituted the stereotypic behavior might subside. The leisure activity that holds intrinsic appeal for the client with schizophrenia, then, is the competing response. Presentation of the competing leisure activity forces the client to decide which activity he or she wants to perform—the stereotypic behaviors or the leisure activity. Similarly, the child with autism is faced with the same choice—the self-stimulating behavior or the leisure activity. This is the competing responses hypothesis.

The idea is to have the client choose the leisure alternative in preference to the stereotypic behavior. When TR specialists observe a desirable effect by distracting a client's attention away from a stereotypic pattern of behavior, the leisure activity acted as a successful competing stimulus. A further assumption necessary to the competing responses hypothesis is that humans have limited processing capacity; they can only attend to a limited number of stimuli at one time. Hence, the client cannot exhibit the leisure activity and the stereotypic behavior simultaneously. Ideally, the TR specialist discovers the leisure activity or activities that are effective in competing for the client's attention—forcing a choice between leisure and a less desirable behavior.

The diversionary aspect of leisure takes on added significance under this scenario—the diversion is from one (undesirable) behavior to an alternative (desirable) activity. The literature reveals two means of effecting the competing responses hypothesis.

The first has received more attention. Researchers involved children with autism in reasonably vigorous exercise programs of various types and observe the effects on subsequent self-stimulating behaviors. The idea is to redirect or rechannel the self-stimulating behaviors into more constructive alternatives (Fine, Feldis & Lehrer, 1982).

Two studies reported success in accomplishing a diversionary effect among children with autism. Levison and Reid (1993) found that (vigorous) exercise activities replaced self-stimulating behaviors. Immediately after exercise, the display of stereotypic behaviors by subjects declined significantly.

Reid, Factor, Freeman, and Sherman (1988) completed a related study. Calisthenics, muscle toning, and stretching decreased inappropriate behaviors and increased on-task time among subjects with autism. Again, immediately following the administration of an exercise regime the subjects displayed fewer stereotypic behaviors. The authors concluded exercise was a viable substitute for stereotypic behavior because it offered the same inducements (e.g., motor activity and self-stimulation).

These studies and others like them show that physical activity can serve to rechannel the need for motor activity (some of it self-abusive) during exercise trials and immediately following the exercise intervention. However, the long-term effects of exercise on stereotypic behaviors have been disappointing on two counts. First, the subsiding of stereotypic behaviors is short-lived; the long-term effects are negligible. Second, removal of the exercise program is associated with a return of self-stimulating behaviors.

Researchers (Levison & Reid, 1993; Reid, Factor, Freeman & Sherman, 1988) pointed out that what may be occurring is simply the result of fatigue from the exercise. Once rested, the subjects returned to their stereotypic behavior pattern. Researchers have not been completely successful in explaining the delayed return of autistic behaviors.

Hence, one must question whether the latent return of stereotypic behaviors means the exercise did not compete at all. Wong and his associates (1987) employed an alternative method of addressing this problem. Two clients with schizophrenia were asked to select recreation activities and instructed to interact with the recreation materials for 20 minutes. Both clients had a previous record of frequent stereotypic behavior (vocalizations). Without any other direction, both subjects reduced their stereotypic behaviors by more than one half *during* the leisure activity. The authors (Wong et al., 1987) concluded:

> replacement of inappropriate behavior was achieved by introducing a competing as opposed to physically incompatible alternative responses. Subjects were able to engage in stereotypic vocalizations during recreation sessions, and did so, but for shorter average duration per session. Recreational behavior was activated with fewer prompts and was independently sustained, probably by reinforcement intrinsic to the activity. (p. 81)

Clearly, Wong et al. (1987) conceived of the competing response differently than researchers studying autistic behaviors and exercise. Unlike the studies using exercise as an intervention, the study of stereotypic behaviors among clients with schizophrenia allowed for client choice without using a physically incompatible activity (i.e., subjects cannot exercise and display self-stimulating behaviors at the same time). Therefore, the type of "competition" provided by the leisure/exercise activity was different in studies of autism versus schizophrenia.

This means competing responses can be of two varieties. First, getting the client involved in an activity that requires physical effort can provide direct motor interference. The incompatibility of carrying on two motor functions at once blocks the practice of self-stimulating behaviors by redirecting the client's (physical) effort. The second type of competing response is afforded by allowing the client to choose a leisure activity that presumably holds some intrinsic value. The competition provided is different than in the case of exercise. Here, the client is self-directed and the competition is not a matter of physical incompatibility. Instead, the competition is of the person's own design—of his or her own choice.

In sum, both approaches to capitalizing on competing responses hold promise as TR interventions. The challenge to exercise-induced competition is to find a way to sustain the beneficial effects over the long term. The challenge to competition afforded by intrinsically valuable activities is to extend the hypothesis to different disability groups and to study the long-term effects of the competing responses hypothesis.

Summary

This chapter reviewed three theoretical frameworks for explaining the effectiveness of recreation as "therapy" (in the broadest sense of the word). The first framework of effectance is the most developed and supported by theoretical and empirical literature. Effectance is expressed in at least two other ways: learned helplessness and flow. The second framework for understanding TR is intrinsic motivation expressed as optimal incongruity. This approach also has a broad application in the sense that the activity does not have to be bound by the label of "therapy" to be offered to persons with disability. So long as the activity is enjoyable and stimulating, the client should reap benefits in terms of improved mental health and outlook. The last framework is intentionally identified as a hypothesis because the evidence and theoretical reasoning is not yet well-developed. But the competing responses hypothesis does hold promise for discovering another explanation for the effectiveness of TR.

References

Bandura, A. (1977). Self-efficacy: Toward a unifying theory of behavioral change. *Psychological Review, 84*, 191–215.

Blake, J. G. (1991). Therapeutic recreation assessment and intervention with a patient with quadriplegia. *Therapeutic Recreation Journal, 25*, 71–75.

Caldwell, L. L., Adolph, S., and Gilbert, A. (1989). Caution! Leisure counselors at work: Long term effects of leisure counseling. *Therapeutic Recreation Journal, 23*, 41–49.

Caldwell, L. L., Dattilo, J., Kleiber, D. A., and Lee, Y. (1994/95). Perceptions of therapeutic recreation among people with spinal cord injury. *Annual in Therapeutic Recreation, 5*, 13–25.

Caldwell, L. L. and Weissinger, E. (1994). Factors influencing free time boredom in a sample of persons with spinal cord injuries. *Therapeutic Recreation Journal 28*, 18–24.

Coyle, C. P. and Kinney, W. B. (1990). Leisure characteristics of adults with physical disabilities. *Therapeutic Recreation Journal, 24*, 64–73.

Csikszentmihalyi, M. (1975). *Beyond boredom and anxiety: The experience of play in work and games*. San Francisco, CA: Jossey-Bass.

Dattilo, J. and Kleiber, D. A. (1993). Psychological perspectives for therapeutic recreation research: The psychology of enjoyment. In M. J. Malkin and C. Z. Howe (Eds.), *Research in therapeutic recreation: Concepts and methods* (pp. 57–76). State College, PA: Venture Publishing, Inc.

Dattilo, J., Kleiber, D. A., and Williams, R. (1998). Self-determination and enjoyment enhancement: A psychologically based service delivery model for therapeutic recreation. *Therapeutic Recreation Journal, 32*, 258–271.

Ellis, M. J. (1973). *Why people play*. Englewood Cliffs, NJ: Prentice Hall.

Fine, A. H., Feldis, D., and Lehrer, B. E. (1982). Therapeutic recreation and programming for autistic children. *Therapeutic Recreation Journal, 16*, 6–11.

Haun, P. (1966). *Recreation: A medical viewpoint*. New York, NY: Teachers College Press.

Iso-Ahola, S. E. (1980a). Perceived control and responsibility as mediators of the effect of therapeutic recreation on the institutionalized aged. *Therapeutic Recreation Journal, 14*, 36–43.

Iso-Ahola, S. E. (1980b). *The social psychology of leisure and recreation*. Dubuque, IA: Brown.

Iso-Ahola, S. E. and Mobily, K. E. (1982). Depression and recreation involvement. *Therapeutic Recreation Journal, 16*, 48–53.

Langer, E. J. and Rodin, J. (1976). The effects of choice and enhanced personal responsibility for the aged: A field experiment on an institutional setting. *Journal of Personality and Social Psychology, 34*, 191–198.

Lee, Y., Brock, S., Dattilo, J., and Kleiber, D. (1993). Leisure and adjustment to spinal cord injury: Conceptual and methodological questions. *Therapeutic Recreation Journal, 27*, 200–211.

Lee , Y., Dattilo, J., Kleiber, D., and Caldwell, L. (1996). Exploring the meaning of continuity of recreation activity in the early stage of adjustment for people with spinal cord injury. *Leisure Sciences, 18*, 209–225.

Levison, L. J. and Reid, G. (1993). The effects of exercise intensity on the stereotypic behaviors of individuals with autism. *Adapted Physical Activity Quarterly, 10*, 255–268.

Mobily, K. E. (2000). An interview with professor Seppo Iso-Ahola. *Therapeutic Recreation Journal, 34*, 300–305.

Mobily, K. E., Lemke, J. H., and Gisin, G. J. (1991). The idea of leisure repertoire. *Journal of Applied Gerontology, 10*, 208–223.

Neiman, D. C. (1994). Exercise, upper respiratory tract infection, and the immune response. *Medicine and Science in Sports, 26*, 128–139.

Peterson, C. A. and Stumbo, N. J. (2000). *Therapeutic recreation program design: Principles and procedures.* Boston, MA: Allyn & Bacon.

Reid, P. D., Factor, D. C., Freeman, N. L., and Sherman, J. (1988). The effects of physical exercise on three autistic and developmentally disordered adolescents. *Therapeutic Recreation Journal, 22*, 47–56.

Selye, H. (1975). *Stress without distress.* New York, NY: Mentor, Plume, and Meridian Books.

Shary, J. M. and Iso-Ahola. (1989). Effects of control-relevant intervention on nursing hone residents' perceived competence and self-esteem. *Therapeutic Recreation Journal, 23*, 7–16.

Wassman, K. B. and Iso-Ahola, S. E. (1985). The relationship between recreation participation and depression in psychiatric patients. *Therapeutic Recreation Journal, 18*, 63–70.

Weissinger, E., Caldwell, L. L., and Bandalos, D. L. (1992). Relationship between intrinsic motivation and boredom in leisure. *Leisure Sciences, 14*, 315–323.

White, R. W. (1959). Motivation reconsidered: The concept of competence. *Psychological Review, 66*, 297–333.

Wong, S. E., Terranova, M. D., Bowen, L., Zarate, R., Massel, H. K., and Liberman, R. P. (1987). Providing independent recreational activities to reduce stereotypic vocalizations in chronic schizophrenics. *Journal of Applied Behavior Analysis, 20*, 77–81.

Section 2

Nature of Disability

Chapter 4

Health, Well-Being, and the Role of TR

Learning Objectives

1. Justify the use of health promotion by therapeutic recreation (TR). Why should TR be involved in health promotion when so many other allied health professions already implement health promotion programs?

2. Compare and contrast the traditional definition of health as the absence of disease with the more contemporary definition of health associated with health promotion and prevention programs.

3. Discuss the role enjoyment plays in health promotion offered under the auspices of TR. Why is it important to have fun when you are exercising?

4. Explain the ways TR directly benefits health.

5. Summarize the physiologic pathway by which stress affects health.

6. Explain the two ways recreational activities can help people to cope with stress.

7. Identify the TR practice models that incorporate health promotion as a function of TR service delivery. Explain how each model includes health promotion as part of a continuum of TR services.

8. Define relapse as it relates to TR and health promotion. Describe a case example of relapse following discharge from an inpatient rehabilitation facility.

9. Explain how the role of a TR specialist would change if a health promotion approach was adopted at a rehabilitation facility.

10. Suggest activities and services that could be offered by a community TR program within a community recreation department. Discuss how much you think you could charge for each activity and service.

Three models of practice in TR include health promotion and wellness as service components: (1) the Health Protection/Health Promotion Model, (2) the TR Service Delivery/Outcomes Model, and (3) the Optimizing Lifelong Health Model. Noteworthy scholars in the field have advocated for health promotion within the context of TR practice.

> Doesn't the word therapeutic have a heavy connotation to health promotion? So, therapeutic recreation is all about physical and mental health. Prevention, maintenance, and promotion of health is at the heart of the profession—be it clinical or community settings. (Iso-Ahola, cited in Mobily, 2000, p. 304)

"It is likely that major areas more specifically addressing health and wellness will be added [to the Leisureability Model], as healthcare moves toward a more preventive and self-care mode" (Stumbo & Peterson, 1998, p. 95). Austin (1998) even maintains that health is an inherent aspect of the human experience: "all human beings have an inherent drive for health and wellness" (p. 112). Likewise, when defining TR, professional organizations have directly incorporated or implied health promotion and wellness (see Chapter 1, p. 6). TR interventions support the goal of assisting the individual to maximize independence in leisure, optimal health, and the highest possible quality of life (CTRA, 1999).

With the watershed changes in healthcare that marked the 1980s came a new set of initiatives. Healthcare professions were now rewarded for preventing illness and impairment, for decreasing a person's risk profile for acquiring an illness or a chronic condition, and for slowing the progression of deterioration once the client became impaired. Everyone and almost every healthcare profession responded with one or more variants of health promotion. TR is late in entering the arena of health promotion and wellness.

This leads one to query whether TR belongs in the health promotion area at all. What is the justification for including health promotion as a service component in one or more models of practice? On what basis can the profession justify health promotion and wellness as part of a definition of TR? A rationale for including health promotion in practice, in models of practice, and in definitions of TR requires more than simply advocating for health promotion. The danger of casually recommending health promotion as an aspect of TR service is that it will appear as yet another instance of being faddish and self-serving, as the profession has been prone to adopt whatever "hot topic" or intervention is in fashion at the time (e.g., protocols). Hence, the first step in this discussion of health promotion and wellness in TR service is to provide a rationale/justification for including it in the first place, and this will require a clearer contemporary definition of health.

Health

Early definitions of health centered on the absence of illness. This was understandable because of the incidence of infectious diseases that claimed many victims and disabled many more (e.g., poliomyelitis). With the advent of better medications and antibiotics, many of the diseases that caused mortality and morbidity in western cultures have all but disappeared. The new "disease" of western nations is the chronic condition, the diseases of lifestyle and aging: heart disease, diabetes, high blood pressure. This change in the nature of illness caused many to reconsider the simplistic definition of health as the absence of disease. This older definition of health emphasized negation rather than affirmation—health was assumed if certain symptoms were absent. The new version of health is positive/affirmative—not only the absence of illness, but also the presence of certain desirable attributes that serve to prevent, delay or minimize the effects of chronic conditions.

Several facts about the "new" illnesses of western culture also urge a holistic view of health. First, most chronic conditions develop over an extended period of time and result (in part) from sustained lifestyle abuse (e.g., lack of exercise, cigarette smoking, excessive drinking). Second, once manifested, chronic conditions cannot be cured, only managed. Third, because the window available to correct variables that contribute to the development of chronic conditions is usually lengthy, prevention through altered lifestyle is feasible and is now emphasized. This is why health promotion and preventive approaches make sense only within the context of a holistic perspective on health.

Austin (1997) maintained there is a difference between not being ill and being well. This perspective on health, reflected in the service models of several authors, assumes a *holistic* view of health. Holistic health is generally seen as a perspective that fits better with a health promotion/preventive approach to healthcare. By holistic the author usually means that mind and body are not considered separately, but as a unified whole. The old definition of health considered health of the body in isolation from the mind. What holistic views of health assume is that the health of the body affects the health of the mind and vice versa. And in the long run, it is one's mental approach to health and the cognitive choices one makes that have a profound affect of health, both physical and mental (e.g., choosing to smoke or not). A holistic approach to health also includes how we react psychologically to our environment, and how that reaction affects our mental and physical health. Hence, holistic interpretations of health usually include several dimensions of health—physical, mental, emotional, and so on. These more comprehensive/holistic definitions of health are well-represented in the TR literature.

For example, Van Andel (1998) maintained health includes sound physiological, mental, spiritual, emotional, and social functioning. Carter, Van Andel, and Robb (1995) agreed, stating an interrelationship between mind, body, and spirit is requisite to health. Likewise, Coyle (1998) argued health refers to holistic health and represents an approach to living that includes personal responsibility, empowerment, and informed choices that help to maintain or to advance toward higher levels of wellness.

Iso-Ahola (in Mobily, 2000) articulated a mechanism for implementing Coyle's approach to health promotion in TR. He asserted that leisure education is an optimal method for developing knowledge and skills in clients that translate into positive health behaviors, such as a regular program of exercise, proper nutrition, and cessation of substance abuse. Knowledge and skills taught during leisure education therefore empower the client to self-regulate (see also Austin, 1998; Wilhite, Keller & Caldwell, 1999) and to lead a healthier life.

While Iso-Ahola and others who included health promotion in practice models aptly demonstrated that TR can contribute to well-being and wellness, few tackled the problem of conceptualizing how to discuss health among people already impaired or disabled. Further interpretation of the notion of holistic health for TR service is necessary and has been provided by Lee, Dattilo, Kleiber, and Caldwell (1996) in their articulation of Kagawa-Singer's model of health.

Alternative methods of interpreting health must be available to persons with chronic conditions. Otherwise, they are doomed to live out their lives under the specter of being considered "sick" and impaired. The label of sickness taints the manner in which the person is treated and affects how they see themselves and the quality of life available to them. Hence, Kagawa-Singer's alternative view of health would seem to be a productive one for persons already impaired.

"They [persons with impairments] must create socially valued positions for themselves by reestablishing the fact that they are still the same individuals even though they are inside bodies which no longer meet society's requirement of 'health'" (Kagawa-Singer, 1993, p. 296). Lee et al. (1996) underscored Kagawa-Singer's thesis, suggesting that the person could still perform important social roles in spite of physical constraint.

To reconceptualize health more holistically, Kagawa-Singer developed a two-dimensional model based on an axis of physical function and an axis of social function. She maintained if the person with an illness can retain social abilities, then they may still be considered "healthy" within the limitations of the impairment. Although Kagawa-Singer focused on clients with cancer, the idea has much broader application. Hence, the client with cancer, the person with a spinal cord injury, and the older adult with chronic arthritis can be healthy because they all may "maintain a sense of integrity as productive, able, and valued individuals within their social spheres, despite their physical condition" (Kagawa-Singer, 1993, p. 295). Some in the TR profession have echoed Kagawa-Singer's sentiments, notably Lee et al. (1996), Van Andel (1998), and Wilhite and Keller (2000).

Furthermore, if Kagawa-Singer's thesis is correct, then part of "rehabilitation" involves coming to terms with the meaning the illness has for the person's lifestyle. Or, to paraphrase Kagawa-Singer (1993), clients do not deny the reality of their impairment, but rather try to make sense of their altered social reality. A serious illness or the prospect of the remainder of life with a chronic condition will no doubt give anyone pause to reframe his or her present and foreseeable future. Part of the new rehabilitation will have to involve a reconstruction of reality. (See Chapter 2 for an in-depth discussion of this topic.) The point for TR, of course, is that only a holistic view of health is compatible with the social reconstruction necessary to deal with the chronic condition in modern society. The alternative is that without a holistic view of health, persons with disabilities are condemned to live a considerable portion of their lives labeled as "sick" in strictly biomedical terms.

Rationale for Health Promotion in TR

Three lines of reasoning support TR's involvement in health promotion, prevention, and wellness programs: conceptual, moral, and practical.

Conceptual

We have already noted the definitions of TR include well-being and health as part of the conceptualization of TR service. Likewise, some recent practice models include health promotion as a service component for TR (Austin, 1998; Van Andel, 1998; Wilhite et al., 1999).

TR customarily works with those at risk for development of secondary conditions and those with negative health habits that put them at risk for complications that may contribute to further disability (e.g., falls, hip fractures, smoking, substance abuse, sedentary lifestyle, boredom, heart disease). TR may intervene with persons who have disabilities to prevent further impairment and exacerbation of their handicap due to secondary impairments (e.g., heart disease among persons with spinal cord injuries). Thus, a role for therapeutic intervention based on prevention is feasible.

TR may be able to provide the skills and knowledge needed for health promoting behaviors (e.g., nutrition, exercise, stress management). Leisure education should be a featured part of health promotion services offered by TR. An educational approach to health promotion is consistent with similar efforts made by other health professionals (e.g., nursing, physical therapy) because of the limited time any professional has to bring about therapeutic change on an inpatient unit. The new script for rehabilitation, with few exceptions, is to give the client a "taste" of the therapeutic intervention (e.g., exercise prescription) while in the hospital, and then to teach the client to continue the rehabilitation program on his own, after discharge. Therefore, many clients are discharged without having completed their rehabilitation program, with the assumption they have been taught the skills necessary to complete their rehabilitation on their own. (Whether this is a valid assumption is debatable; more on this later.) The point for now is much inpatient rehabilitation (and health promotion) amounts to client education.

Reliance on client education assumes consumers will comply with health promoting behaviors once discharged. Taking this point one step further, one might predict compliance would improve if behaviors were enjoyable (e.g., exercise can be fun). Some literature does exist in the area of exercise compliance that indicates people are more likely to continue to adhere to an exercise program perceived as enjoyable (e.g., Dishman, 1988). Naturally, the challenge for the TR profession is to devise ways to make health-promoting behaviors enjoyable. But this is not a far-fetched notion. There is no reason to believe exercise should not be enjoyable. The most current recommendation for *Healthy People* (U.S. Department of Health and Human Services, 2000) takes a lifestyle exercise approach; that is, exercise should be incorporated into the daily routine (e.g., 30 minutes of daily activity in a variety of activities, such as walking, gardening, biking, strength training), does not have to be strenuous (mild to moderate intensity), and does not have to be continuous (e.g., a 10-minute walk, 15 minutes of light weightlifting, and 5 minutes of pedaling an exercise bike yields 30 minutes for the day). The hope is that compliance on the part of the general public will improve. Likewise, a similar approach by TR with persons with disabilities might have more success because of the "enjoyment" factor.

Although it did not include health promotion as a service component, one TR practice model (Dattilo, Kleiber & Williams, 1998) maintained that the basis for intervention is to engender enjoyment. Applied to health promotion, this means that enjoyable TR programs will be more successful because persons with disabilities will want to participate. Efficacy of programs should get better as well when compliance improves because most health promoting behaviors rely on long-term lifestyle change to be effective (e.g., exercise must be completed on a regular basis to bring about any benefit and to promote health).

Moral

TR has a long tradition of supporting and promoting "wholesome" recreation. Health promotion is certainly captured within the context of this founding ideal of the recreation profession (see *History of TR* in Carter et al., 1995). From this moral imperative, health promotion is seen as a natural part of the usual and customary tradition of recreation service that has been offered for the past century or so. Simply put, healthy recreation is the sort of use of free time encouraged by the profession since its inception.

Furthermore, if recreation activities can promote physical and mental health, then the profession is obligated to make such services available for the good of society (see *Code of Ethics*, NTRS, 1994). TR's duty to society, to fulfill its "calling," requires services that might potentially benefit persons with disabilities are not withheld (Sylvester, 1992). Hence, the TR profession has an obligation to fulfill its calling, which includes a tradition of offering healthy recreational choices.

As suggested earlier in this chapter, some question exists regarding the wisdom of discharging clients before they have completed their rehabilitation programs. The motivation is healthcare cost containment, and the justification is clients are capable of taking responsibility for aspects of their own rehabilitation (e.g., completing an exercise prescription). With healthcare reform (e.g., shorter hospital stays), the increasing prevalence of chronic conditions, and the aging of society, many of the clients discharged today from clinical facilities are not "cured," not completely rehabilitated, or not well. Those left to their own devices to continue self-regulated rehabilitation and those with chronic conditions, who will never be completely well, are in need of ongoing health-promoting/rehabilitative services. This need frequently continues throughout the remainder of the person's life (Beaudoin & Keller, 1994; Rath & Page, 1996). TR, especially community-based TR, is well-positioned to offer health promotion programs to these individuals. And the moral imperative is TR *should* offer health promotion services to these individuals in need.

Practical

TR often works within healthcare settings; therefore, focusing on health-related outcomes makes sense. Instead of backing away or apologizing for health-related outcomes, more frequently contemporary practice models are proactive in including health benefits as a legitimate TR outcomes (e.g., ATRA, 1993; Austin 1998; Coyle, Kinney & Shank 1991).

Although other professions (e.g., nursing) may be involved in health promotion, TR can provide many of the very same services more efficiently (and TR is less expensive). TR programs tend to be delivered to groups rather than individuals, driving down per capita costs and increasing efficiency.

TR practitioners employed by public recreation agencies are strategically positioned to deliver community-based health promotion to clients after discharge because community recreation agencies have much of the needed infrastructure for health promotion (e.g., pools, gymnasiums, exercise facilities, parks) already in position.

How Does TR Promote Health?

Van Andel (1998) suggested three ways in which TR can promote health among persons with disabilities. First, recreation may be used as a "tool" by which health is pursued—leisure is an activity/place where health-promoting behaviors are typically practiced. For instance, early studies of exercise behavior focused on work-related physical activity and attempted to predict the incidence of heart disease at some future time. Epidemiologic studies of physical activity have more recently turned to physical activity during free time, recognizing that almost all manual tasks of the past have been mechanized to the extent that work-related physical activity is no longer common. Exercise and physical activity during free time have become far better predictors of heart disease and other chronic conditions.

Second, Van Andel suggested health promotion during leisure could be beneficial because of the attitude the participant assumes—a more leisurely way of life. He argued a leisure lifestyle approach to life induced an orientation to life favorable to good health. This notion is certainly consistent with research pertaining to the toll stress and stress-related illness takes on society.

Third, the concept of leisure includes some inherent qualities germane to health. This point was implied earlier when pointing out that the heritage of the TR profession was skewed toward wholesome recreation. Some research has pointed toward this relationship: an active leisure lifestyle is correlated with better health, especially psychological health, and well-being (Caldwell & Weissinger, 1994; Coleman & Iso-Ahola, 1993; Ragheb, 1993).

In the following sections, the potential contributions of TR in the area of health promotion are explored in more depth.

Direct Effects

Substantial literature in medicine, epidemiology, and exercise science supports the direct benefits of exercise and physical activity. Cardiovascular health may be improved and/or maintained through a program of regular aerobic activity. However, the recommendation for the intensity of aerobic exercise needed to reap these benefits has been altered. No longer is the recommendation for all or most people one of regular vigorous exercise. Instead, moderate to mild levels of exercise are now recommended for most people, including those with disabilities and chronic conditions (U.S. Department of Health and Human Services, 2000).

The scope of exercise recommended by experts has been broadened to include not only aerobic exercise, but also exercise designed to enhance muscle strength. A decade or more of research on strength training for older adults and those at risk for falls underscored another priority for exercise besides the traditional cardiovascular fitness—functional fitness. *Functional fitness* refers to the physical fitness necessary to carry on independent activities of daily living. Most activities required for independent living have to do with the abilities needed to take care of their immediate environment—cooking, reaching, cleaning, light lifting, and walking. Another important research finding is that the major means to reducing the risk of falls and improving balance among older adults is through improvement of lower extremity strength. With the aging of society, this feature of exercise delivered through health promotion programs available in the community by TR specialists has considerable upside potential. Older adults fear one thing above all others: losing independence. The two means they have to avoid dependency are avoiding falls and retaining functional fitness necessary to take care of themselves independently.

Another area of behavior that promises to promote health through leisure is nutrition/cooking. The family cookout, traditional holiday foods, and sharing food as a part of many social gatherings urge consideration of food preparation/cooking as a promising intervention point for health promotion through recreational activity. Intuition suggests when cooking is done for enjoyment participants are more apt to take the time necessary to prepare healthier meals using fresh foods. Little research has been completed in the area of nutrition/cooking as a recreational activity, and whether it is effective in improving health. However, Coroleo (1988, 1994) has been an advocate for cooking/nutrition programs delivered within a context of recreation programs for person with HIV/AIDS with the intent of improving the health of consumers.

Direct benefits accrue from exercise, and much exercise occurs during free time, but this does not necessarily mean TR should be delivering exercise/health promotion programs. However, because most recent recommendations are skewed in the direction of mild to moderate exercise, and most community-based exercise facilities operated by municipal recreation departments have TR programs, TR service is qualified and well-positioned to deliver health promotion programs to persons with disabilities, especially those residing in the community.

Indirect Effects

Three potential indirect benefits of health promotion programs are offered within the context of TR services. The first relates to decreasing the risk exposure of the person with the disability to some of the concomitants of his or her primary impairment (Parker & Carmack, 1998; Wilhite et al., 1999). These benefits include the rather obvious reduction in the risk of secondary impairments—skin lesions, diabetes, heart disease. Also related to the risk of developing comorbid conditions is the reduction of risk exposure by decreasing the incidence of negative lifestyle behaviors, such as sedentary lifestyle, smoking, alcohol abuse, and drug abuse. The net result of practicing positive lifestyle patterns and behaviors should be a decrease in recidivism rates resulting from either complications of physical impairments or exacerbations of mental illness.

The second area in which health promotion through TR services promises to benefit clients pertains to stress and stress-related illnesses. This area has been the focus of considerable research and theoretical development lately. Stress is both a new and an old etiology for illnesses, particularly various forms of heart disease, made more notorious as a part of the so-called Type A personality. The competitive, driven, obsessive executive typifies this personality variant.

But the more stress is researched, the more scientists are finding it is not only the prototypical Type A personality who has all the problems associated with stress. Another approach to stress research made famous by Holmes and Rahe (1967) is known as the "life events" method. Researchers ask subjects how many "life events" (e.g., marriage, divorce, minor traffic violation, incurring significant debt) they experienced in the past year. The person who experienced more life events is usually more stressed, and theoretically more susceptible to certain diseases of lifestyle, such as heart disease.

The ideological kernel that gives impetus to the life events approach to chronicling stress is the inspiration of noted stress researcher Hans Selye (1974). His pioneering work in stress research altered how scientists think about stress today. Stress is not simply nervous tension. Selye (1974) maintained stress is the "nonspecific response to any demand" (p. 27). More simply, it is how the body/person responds anytime adaptation is required. The life events approach to stress research is consistent with Selye's hypothesis—life events can be negative or positive. Negative and positive life events share one thing in common: they both require adaptation and adjustment on the part of the individual, and that adjustment is *not* specific to the event—it is a generalized adaptive response. Adaptation/stress responses take energy, and according to the life events approach, the more energy expended in adaptation, the more fatigued the individual is, and the more susceptible he or she is to illness and disease.

Selye was quick to point out, however, that we are always stressed somewhat—stress cannot be completely eliminated. A person who is not stressed at all is dead. The key is to find as acceptable level of stress, provoked primarily through positive life adaptations (e.g., exercise, positive social interactions).

More recently researchers have taken the initiative in investigating how stress (physiologically) causes its damage, and how positive life events result in favorable stress (called *eustress* by Selye). Russoniello (1994) articulated an explanation of how stress contributes to disease as a basis for his Medicine Model of TR. Russoniello correctly implicated structures in both the nervous system and endocrine (hormone) systems as parts of a pathway that causes pathology. The physiologic mechanism is called the hypothalamic pituitary adrenal cortical axis (HPAC; LaPerriere et al., 1994). It is a holistic concept that seeks to explain how physiological stress is translated into physical disease. It works like this:

1. The person perceives an event (e.g., an argument with the boss) as a "threat."

2. The perception of threat causes anxiety and psychological stress.

3. The hypothalamus in the brain sends biochemical messages to the pituitary gland.

4. The pituitary gland secretes hormones that affect other glands (in this case, the adrenal gland).

5. The adrenal gland secretes its hormones when stimulated by specific pituitary hormones.

6. Adrenal hormones suppress host immunity through several mechanisms (e.g., suppressing the activity and potency of white blood cells important in resisting infections).

At the same time, part of the nervous system (the sympathetic division of the autonomic nervous system) causes the body to marshal resources for an emergency ("fight or flight") response directly, and through a sympathetic/

adrenal medulla (SAM) connection indirectly (LaPerriere et al., 1994). In the case of genuine physical threat, this response is useful in mobilizing resources to respond to the threat. Unfortunately for the human species, however, this fight or flight response is not very useful in combating psychological threats (unless one gets into a fight with the boss). Therefore, chronic exposure to psychologically induced stress responses wears down the body's reserves and depresses capacity for resisting infections, viruses, and even some forms of cancer.

Based on the biochemistry of stress, common sense suggests two general approaches to controlling stress and minimizing HPAC and SAM activation. The first approach is to nip the perception of threat in the bud by altering perceptions of potentially stressful life events. This strategy is best articulated within the leisure studies literature by Coleman and Iso-Ahola (1993), and relies on control through psychological techniques. The second approach described by Russoniello (1994) hypothesizes that bonafide physiological changes in the body intended to counteract the detrimental biochemistry of the stress response (HPAC and SAM activation) are manifested during certain types of recreation participation.

Consistent with a life events approach to measuring stress, Coleman and Iso-Ahola (1993) defined stress as the accumulation of an inordinate number of negative life experiences that overcome the person's ability to cope. They further suggested the psychological manifestations of being excessively stressed induce physical and mental illness. Finally, they suggested leisure participation can assist the person in coping with stress in two ways: through social support and/or through augmented capacity to cope.

Coleman and Iso-Ahola (1993) speculated that "leisure impacts health by providing buffering mechanisms that come into play when life presents significant problems" (p. 113). They cited the stress research literature, which supports two methods of coping: cognitive reappraisal and palliation. *Reappraisal* means the person is able to successfully reevaluate a potentially threatening life event (e.g., an argument with the boss) and this diminishes the detrimental stress response, psychologically (e.g., less depression and anxiety) and physiologically (e.g., decreased HPAC and SAM activation).

In the case of reappraisal, Coleman and Iso-Ahola (1993) argued that the social nature of many leisure activities may help to build a social support network available in times of crisis/stress that the person can turn to for assistance. Each companion may help the person (impartially) to reappraise the stressful event and to defuse potential psychological and/or physical damage.

Leisure at its best also means the actor comes to perceive himself or herself as free or self-determined. Coleman and Iso-Ahola (1993) further argued a person who perceives himself or herself as self-determined is "hardier" or more resilient, better able to cope successfully and to reappraise a potentially stressful event as nonthreatening. Hence, it is through psychological mediation, a social effect and an autonomy effect, that leisure participation holds the promise of helping the person cope with his stress.

The other mechanism by which leisure participation may help a person cope falls under the category of palliation. *Palliative* means that the activity is successful in addressing the symptoms of stress. For instance, participating in leisure may decrease the person's anxiety. Palliative mechanisms for coping with the symptoms of stress are not well-understood, although they likely work by blocking HPAC and SAM activation. The diversionary aspect of leisure participation may be the mechanism by which relief from stress symptoms (e.g., anxiety) is realized. This is not to trivialize leisure participation— when the actor becomes wholly absorbed in an activity (Dattilo et al., 1998, p. 261), then his or her attention is directed toward the dynamics of leisure participation and he is less apt to worry about a stressful confrontation at work or home. However, the diversionary hypothesis of leisure participation as a coping device awaits testing through empirical research. Clearly, in the minds of Coleman and Iso-Ahola, as well as most stress researchers, stress cannot be avoided, but it can be managed.

Coleman and Iso-Ahola (1993) speculated that hormonal and immune systems may provide an explanation for the leisure/stress reduction relationship. Russoniello (1994) took this notion one step further by describing a TR practice model based on the relationship between mind and body. He maintained that leisure activities of various intensities promote hormonal/biochemical changes that counteract the stress response and depressive symptoms. Unlike the cognitive reappraisal/perceptual mechanisms for change in Coleman and Iso-Ahola's (1993) views, Russoniello hypothesized that some properties of recreational activities (e.g., exercise, laughter, music, thrill) can translate into favorable changes in some hormones. In addition, Russoniello (1994) went so far as to state that "*prescribed* [italics added] recreational therapy can significantly increase HGH [Human Growth Hormone] and these changes could be correlated with changes in reported mood states" (p. 248).

Mobily (1996) conducted a careful analysis of the research Russoniello used to support this theory and found it flawed in at least two respects:

1. The data were collected and analyzed using poor scientific methodology. Research subjects were recovering alcoholics and drug/hormonal interactions confounded the findings. Proper statistical analysis was not performed on the data.

2. It was theoretically unsound. For instance, Russoniello equated exercise to leisure. Conceptually, not all exercise is considered recreational (e.g., mowing the lawn).

Nevertheless, although flawed, Russoniello's thesis should not be dismissed. The idea that leisure activities, particularly physically active ones, can blunt the detrimental effects of stress has some validity. In what follows, the TR/stress relationship is reconstructed along theoretical lines, suggesting TR may have something to do to offer in preventing or attenuating stress.

La Perriere et al. (1994) outlined a causal model that implicated stress in suppressing the individual's resistance, making him or her more susceptible to a variety of disorders. Likewise, the same authors articulated a second pathway, one that showed how exercise counteracts stress-induced physiological changes. Exercise channels SAM activation constructively because sympathetic stimulation is part of a normal exercise response. Secondly, exercise seems to blunt HPAC activation, thus decreasing the secretion of hormones from the adrenal cortex, which in turn depress the immune system. Thirdly, some research suggests that exercise may stimulate the secretion of endogenous opiads (natural analgesics), such as endorphins.

Although this collection of exercise-induced responses is promising and scientifically sound, the question remains: Does exercise qualify as leisure or recreation? The answer is sometimes, perhaps usually. Recreational-level exercise of a mild to moderate intensity is more likely to be enjoyable. An additional benefit is long-term compliance with a program of exercise is better when the exercise is enjoyable. And it is long-term, chronic exercise that accrues benefit, not occasional or sporadic exercise. Mild to moderate intensity exercise is appropriate to offer as an aspect of TR programming.

In sum, reasonable theoretical support and some empirical support exist for the ability of some leisure activities to help clients to cope with stress. Psychological benefit may be realized through social support and cognitive reappraisal of threat. Physiologic benefit may be realized through nervous/hormonal mechanisms as well as secretion of endogenous opiads.

Health Promotion in TR Practice

Is health promotion as a service component in TR something of a fad, or a long-term reality (Mobily, 1999)? Others have expressed concern over integrating health promotion in TR because of a lack of research support (Ross, 1998) or a lack of clarity (Freysinger, 1999). Although the TR literature on health promotion is full of promise, more work still needs to be done on exactly how TR serves as a means to better health (Ross, 1998). Health promotion has arrived and represents a more or less central feature in at least three TR practice models.

Health Promotion in TR Practice Models

Three TR models include health promotion. Two state health is an outcome toward which TR should strive, and a third suggests health is an outcome and a service component.

1. The purpose of therapeutic recreation is to assist the person to recover following threats to health (health protection) and to achieve as high a level of health as possible (health promotion). (Austin, 1998, p. 110)

2. The purpose of this paper is to initiate a dialogue about the incorporation of health enhancement concepts into TR practice and to propose a nonlinear model of TR that is grounded in a life course perspective which merges health enhancement and self-care approaches. (Wilhite et al. 1999, p. 99)

3. The essential components for the delivery of health and human services are activities and strategies that contribute to (a) diagnosis or assessment of client needs, (b) treatment or rehabilitation, (c) client education, and (d) health promotion/prevention activities. (Van Andel, 1998, p. 181)

The three models that include health promotion share similarities. First, each places health promotion at a higher level than therapy or education, which is closer in some models to attaining a higher state of being. For Austin (1998) this higher state of being is self-actualization, for Van Andel (1998) it is leisure. What all three models suggest is health promotion activities are conceptually close to attaining a state of leisure and to manifesting the best leisure's attributes—perceived freedom and self-regulation.

Second, with freedom and choice comes responsibility. This aspect of health promotion in TR practice suggests the TR specialist will perform roles different from the traditional professional in the field. Hence, models that include health promotion typically stress concepts such as the client taking more responsibility (TR specialist acts more as a facilitator, less directive) and empowerment (TR specialist helps the client to acquire the skills and abilities needed to take responsibility for his or her own health).

Austin's Health Protection/Health Promotion (HP/HP) model linear and offers a continuum of services ranging from prescriptive activities (therapy) to leisure, with the latter service being most consistent with attaining high-level wellness. Austin (1998) equates high-level wellness with self-actualization. Another important assumption of the HP/HP model is health is thought to be an inherent human drive.

Van Andel (1998) employs two illustrations to articulate two models of practice intended to function together. The first is the Service Delivery model, which specifies a continuum of services in a manner similar to that of Austin (1998). The services specified by Van Andel differ somewhat from those of Austin, with the scope of services ranging from assessment to prevention/health promotion services. Notably, health promotion activities bring the nature of service closest to the attributes that customarily characterize the state of leisure. Van Andel's second model is called the Outcome Model. Here Van Andel details the results that should occur as a result of TR services. The three outcomes are functional capacity, quality of life, and wellness/health status.

The models described by Austin and Van Andel provide an interesting contrast as far as health promotion in TR is articulated. For Austin (1998) optimal health is an outcome to be achieved by way of self-determined activities (e.g., leisure). For Van Andel (1998) health is both an outcome (optimal wellness) and a service component (health promotion).

The final TR practice model that is explicit about including health promotion concepts is the Optimizing Lifelong Health (OLH) model authored by Wilhite et al. (1999). Wilhite et al. describe a nonlinear model in which a premium is placed on client/therapist interaction and cooperation (interdependence), a sharing of responsibility seen in the health promotion features offered by the Austin and Van Andel models as well.

The OLH model is based on the premise that the client will have to adapt and accommodate to maintain or advance health throughout life. The TR specialist is very nondirective and responsibility for leisure activities is conceived of most often as shared by client and therapist. This characterization of leisure within the OLH model is consistent with the way in which health promotion is incorporated into the HP/HP and Service Delivery/Outcome models. That is, all three models that include health promotion assume the client will take considerable responsibility for his or her own leisure lifestyle. Accordingly, the OLH model does not specify a directive therapist role, but rather educator and facilitator roles only for the TR specialist.

Besides some skepticism about the inclusion of health promotion in TR and the concern over health promotion being a passing fad, some have identified other faults in health promotion as it is currently conceived of in TR. In particular, Austin's assumption that "all human beings have an inherent drive for health and wellness" has come under question. His assumption may be questioned along two lines of reasoning. The first pertains to the use of the word "drive." Drives were discounted as a theoretical grounds for the explanation of motives some time ago (e.g., White, 1959), because to hypothesize a drive for all but the most basic of motives is simply not parsimonious and inconsistent with the manner in which the central nervous system is thought to work. Second, and more importantly, people simply do not always inherently know what is good for them with respect to health. Healthy behaviors do not always have intuitive appeal because of some associated discomforts (e.g., muscle soreness and fatigue when beginning an exercise program). It is probably valid, however, to assert that people in general do wish to stay healthy even though they may not always recognize what health is. All the while it would be prudent to admit that health as a concept is likely to change in the future as it has in the past (e.g., without the conceptualization of health in a holistic sense advocating for health promotion in TR would be groundless).

Further conceptual development should help to solve the dilemma the Outcome Model finds itself in as well. Three outcomes are specified: functional ability, health/wellness, and quality of life. The problem is the manner in which these outcomes are portrayed suggests they are interdependent. Correlation between health, function, and quality of life has a commonsense appeal, and certainly it is true most of the time that people who function well and who are relatively healthy report a good quality of life. But it is not necessarily true that healthy, well-functioning people are inevitably leading a high quality of life. Certainly depression is rampant in western society; some have said it is the "common cold" of mental illness. Hence, a person could function very well, and be physically very healthy, but not report a high quality of life because of depression, or a sense of meaninglessness, or a perception of hopelessness and despair. Conversely, a person with a disability could be functioning as well as possible within the limitation of his or her impairment, be only marginally healthy, and still report a high quality of life.

The OLH model (Wilhite et al., 1999) is likely the most contemporary when it comes to the development of the health concept. It assumes maintaining health throughout life requires constant adaptation and adjustment. This notion of health is consistent with the previous discussion of the stress concept, also based on adjustment and adaptation. The OLH model's conceptualization of health as a developmental process makes it more inclusive, because there is room for different perspectives on the definition of health within an adaptive framework—health for an older adult or for a person with a spinal cord injury is different than health for an asymptomatic 21-year-old. The thread that connects the health of these three individuals is that all of them are faced with an ongoing task of adjustment and adaptation necessary to maintain or to improve health.

None of these criticisms of health promotion means it is incorrect to include health promotion in TR. But it does indicate a need for further theoretical work and certainly more research on the topic. Ross (1998) advises, "therapeutic recreation students and professionals will need more knowledge and higher level skills related to health and wellness" (p. 127).

Clearly, capricious use of the phrase "health promotion" is to be avoided. For example, Ross (1998) pointed out one obvious precaution—not all leisure activities contribute to health. This notion is similar to the problem found in Russoniello's conceptualization of exercise and leisure, wherein he assumed that exercise and leisure were nearly identical. Plainly, Ross is correct—not all leisure contributes to health.

With these conditions in mind, community-based TR is ideally positioned to serve persons who fit into one or more of these categories of those needing continuity during transition from inpatient rehabilitation to community.

Need for Health Promotion in TR Practice

Besides stress, stress symptoms, and stress-related illnesses, can the TR profession take any other initiatives with respect to health promotion among persons with disabilities and chronic conditions? At least two other problem areas have been identified in the literature that may call for health promotion services delivered by TR specialists.

Caldwell and associates (Caldwell, Adolph & Gilbert, 1989; Caldwell, Dattilo, Kleiber & Lee, 1994/95) hypothesized that persons with disabilities are at risk for relapse once discharged from inpatient rehabilitation programs. For example, TR was seen as a very positive force in the rehabilitation experience of clients with spinal cord injuries, except for one criticism (Caldwell et al., 1994/95). Clients reported that some aspects of TR service "may have created a false sense of security with oneself in the 'real world' and one's ability to cope in it" (Caldwell et al., 1994/95, p. 24).

Caldwell et al. (1989) maintained TR likely raises expectations of clients during the rehabilitation process, first by enhancing self-efficacy. Leisure skills and abilities acquired while in rehabilitation skewed clients' expectations for effective and satisfying leisure participation after discharge. Inevitably, many clients reported their actual experience after discharge did not live up to the gratifying experiences they had while inpatients. Armed with a repertoire of leisure skills and abilities, clients anticipated continuation of the satisfying participation they tasted while recuperating.

Second, after discharge, former clients are apt to report disappointment with the attitudes and accessibility of leisure facilities and resources in the community. Leisure skills and abilities are of little use if the person cannot get into the facility or if negative attitudes constrain participation. The user-friendly attitudes of staff and the community of other clients with similar problems made the inpatient experience more receptive to the actor's participation in leisure, and likely enhanced the satisfaction of the participant. Of course, few if any of these characteristics were present after discharge, and many clients reported disappointment, frustration, and relapse.

Third, Caldwell et al. (1989) found leisure skills and attitudes learned by their clients did not persist after discharge. Perhaps the lack of opportunity to use the skills learned or the capitulation that results from repeated bouts of frustration caused former clients to let their leisure skills slip into disuse. The hard-earned competence in adapted leisure activities was surrendered out of frustration. Data pertaining to the recreation participation patterns of persons with disabilities are consistent with relapse and frustration—boredom, sedentary, homebound, and isolated are words used to characterize the leisure participation patterns of persons with disabilities residing in the community (Caldwell et al., 1989; Coyle & Kinney, 1990).

The relapse hypothesis points to several preventive initiatives that can be taken under the rubric of health promotion. First, more work needs to be directed toward strengthening the inner resources of the client transitioning out of inpatient services into the community. Earlier work on discharge planning may bolster the client's mental toughness and "hardiness" to help him or her persist in leisure participation after discharge despite the frustrations. As Caldwell et al. (1989) stated, TR "should not only raise expectations about abilities and opportunities, but also should educate as to what might thwart an individual's postdischarge efforts to positively engage in leisure opportunities" (p. 48).

The second preventive approach on the part of the TR profession concerns community TR. Once discharged, the client should be put in contact with the community TR specialist to receive support that mimics the conducive environment for participation found in the clinical setting. Similar to the types of services advocated by the OLH model, in this situation the community TR specialist would serve primarily as an educator and facilitator, creating an environment conducive to the successful experience of the patient once discharged. Binkley (1999) alerted the profession that the introduction of health promotion as a service component has skewed TR specialists more in the direction of an educational role, and away from a classic therapist role.

Avoiding relapse/boredom may also be considered as preventive because of the negative health habits and outcomes associated with it. Caldwell and Weissinger (1994) reminded us an excess of free time without productive (leisure) alternatives can produce negative health habits, such as cigarette smoking, poor eating habits, or binge drinking, that contribute to obesity, alcohol abuse, and a sedentary lifestyle. These risky health behaviors, in turn, likely contribute to the exacerbation of the client's primary condition and development of secondary/comorbid conditions (e.g., accelerated heart disease in a person with a spinal cord injury).

Lee, Mittelstaedt, and Askins (1999) suggested boredom may also lead to the development of secondary psychological conditions, such as depression, suicidal ideations, and other stress-related symptoms (e.g., anxiety).

(Remember the use of leisure activities to cope with stress directly and indirectly, as suggested previously.) Hence, community-based TR programs emphasizing health promotion may also find stress reduction and coping activities useful in working with patients following discharge. The net result of health promotion intended to prevent relapse and boredom may be measured by decreased recidivism rates, lower incidence of secondary conditions, and fewer inpatient days if the client does have to return to the hospital (Coyle, 1998).

A Case Study in Health Promotion in TR

Sable, Craig, and Lee (2000) reported the results of a health promotion intervention delivered in a community TR situation to a client who had sustained a spinal cord injury. Their report may serve as a template for TR service in the not too distant future. The incentives in healthcare have shifted away from cure toward prevention. Even among persons with disabilities, a dollar spent on prevention will save many dollars later as a result of preventing the onset of comorbid conditions or the delay on onset of the same secondary complications. Sable et al.'s (2000) report suggested a larger presence in patient education and may predict the future of TR.

The subject in the Sable et al. (2000) study sustained a spinal cord injury and was diagnosed as paraplegic. The authors suggested health promotion education was needed because the subject was at risk for the development of several secondary conditions—decubiti (skin lesions), respiratory and urinary tract infections, chronic pain, depression, anxiety, and alcohol or substance abuse.

The health promotion intervention was delivered in a community TR setting, focusing on the junction between discharge of the patient from a supportive, rehabilitation situation into a home environment. Life adjustment subsequent to discharge was of central interest. The authors maintained there is a "critical window" of opportunity for conveying information to the client necessary for the prevention of secondary conditions. This critical window is hypothesized to be immediately after discharge from direct, inpatient treatment, because that is the time at which the client is most impressionable—that is, still concerned enough to take a conscientious interest in the seriousness of his primary impairment.

The TR services illustrated in the Sable et al. (2000) study included wellness education, fitness programming, recreational skill development, accessibility, and advocacy training. These services are typically seen in a health promotion/prevention program. Assessment of a number of variables was also central to the program, and included preinjury leisure, home and community, nutrition, exercise and stress management, social support, recreational interests, and goals.

As a result of the assessment, individual strengths and weaknesses were identified. The young, male participant had assets in the area of social network/support, but many liabilities in the areas of nutrition (too much fast food), lack of concern about his weight (although it had not been a problem to date), and a competitive attitude (in sport). The reader should note the health promotion interventions described in Sable et al. (2000) anticipated potential problem areas—it was proactive, not reactive. This represents the new thinking required of the TR profession if health promotion and preventive programs are to become a genuine aspect of TR services.

The participant was constantly assessed and reassessed throughout the health promotion experience. Competency testing for various health behaviors and wellness awareness were sprinkled throughout the experience to monitor the client's actions and emerging awareness of his own responsibility for his future health and how current behaviors and choices would have a significant impact on future health.

The effectiveness of the health promotion intervention was evaluated after the subject completed the program. Results indicated no significant medical problems developed during the intervention. More importantly, he complied with an exercise prescription, and demonstrated knowledge of sound nutrition, secondary conditions, fitness, and stress management. The subject also improved functional skills, muscular strength, and endurance, and reported more leisure choices comprising a broader repertoire of leisure skills and abilities.

In sum, the evaluation suggested the health promotion intervention helped to keep the subject free from medical complications and assisted in community transition during the year following discharge from inpatient rehabilitation. The authors (Sable et al., 2000) concluded:

> with the decreased in length of stay in rehabilitation settings, many people with spinal cord injuries are discharged with an exposure to skills rather than mastery of the skills they need to make a successful transition to home and community. (p. 361)

This study illustrated the unique opportunity available to community TR programs. Most of the lessons in prevention pertain to lifestyle decisions— the person must take responsibility *after* discharge from rehabilitation. In addition, community TR departments have available many resources (e.g., parks, pools, facilities) that may be used to promote health. Third, health promotion programs for persons with disabilities can be offered at low cost, in group settings in the community. Programs may be offered at a cost low enough that consumers may be willing to pay for the services out-of-pocket, creating a positive cash flow service that may pay for itself and other less profitable programs.

In conclusion, TR is ideally positioned in the community to offer health promotion programs to the many persons with chronic conditions who need ongoing attention and support to prevent or to retard the onset of costly (in monetary and quality-of-life terms) secondary impairments and comorbid conditions.

Summary

With the advent of healthcare reform and managed care, most allied health fields have become increasingly aware of health promotion and disease prevention as a companion to curative, clinical approaches to care. TR is no exception to this trend. Several models of TR practice directly or indirectly address the health-promoting aspects of leisure behavior. Some theoretical evidence supports a mind–body linkage that may be exploited to promote health by TR practitioners. Finally, from a practical point of view, community-based TR is ideally positioned to deliver health-promoting services to persons with chronic conditions who reside in the community.

References

American Therapeutic Recreation Association. (1993). *Standards for the practice of therapeutic recreation.* Hattiesburg, MS: Author.

Austin, D. R. (1997). *Therapeutic recreation: Process and techniques.* Champaign, IL: Sagamore Publishing.

Austin, D. R. (1998). The health protection/health promotion model. *Therapeutic Recreation Journal, 32,* 109–117.

Beaudoin, N. M. and Keller, M. J. (1994). Aquatic solutions: A continuum of services for individuals with physical disabilities in the community. *Therapeutic Recreation Journal, 28,* 193–202.

Binkley, A. (1999). OLH-TR model critique: A practitioner view. *Therapeutic Recreation Journal, 33,* 116–121.

Caldwell, L. L., Adolph, S., and Gilbert, A. (1989). Caution! Leisure counselors at work: Long term effects of leisure counseling. *Therapeutic Recreation Journal, 23,* 41–49.

Caldwell, L. L., Dattilo, J., Kleiber, D. A., and Lee, Y. (1994/95). Perceptions of therapeutic recreation among people with spinal cord injury. *Therapeutic Recreation Journal, 5,* 13–26.

Caldwell, L. L. and Weissinger, E. (1994). Factors influencing free time boredom in a sample of persons with spinal cord injuries. *Therapeutic Recreation Journal, 28,* 18–24.

Canadian Therapeutic Recreation Association. (1999). About CTRA. Retrieved from http://www.canadian-tr.org/about_ctra.htm

Carter, M. J., Van Andel, G. E., and Robb, G. M. (1995). *Therapeutic recreation: A practical approach* (2nd ed.). Prospect Heights, IL: Waveland Press.

Coleman, D. and Iso-Ahola, S. E. (1993). Leisure and health: The role of social support and self-determination. *Journal of Leisure Research, 25,* 111–128.

Coroleo, C. C. (1988). AIDS: Meeting the need through therapeutic recreation. *Therapeutic Recreation Journal, 22,* 71–78.

Coroleo, C. C. (1994). Loneliness and anxiety as two of the psychosocial factors associated with HIV illness and their implications for recreation programming. *Leisureability, 21,* 30–36.

Coyle, C. P. (1998). Integrating service delivery and outcomes: A practice model for the future? *Therapeutic Recreation Journal, 32,* 194–201.

Coyle, C. P. and Kinney, W. B. (1990). Leisure characteristics of adults with physical disabilities. *Therapeutic Recreation Journal, 24,* 64–73.

Coyle, C. P., Kinney, W. B., and Shank, J. W. (1991). *Benefits of therapeutic recreation: A consensus view.* Ravensdale, WA: Idyll Arbor.

Dattilo, J., Keliber, D., and Williams, R. (1998). Self-determination and enjoyment enhancement: A psychologically based service delivery model for therapeutic recreation. *Therapeutic Recreation Journal, 32*, 258–271.

Dishman, R. K. (1988). Determinants of physical activity and exercise for persons 65 years of age or older. *American Academy of Physical Education Papers, 22*, 140–162.

Freysinger, V. J. (1999). A critique of the "optimizing lifelong health through therapeutic recreation" (OLH-TR) model. *Therapeutic Recreation Journal, 33*, 109–115.

Holmes, T. H. and Rahe, R. H. (1967). The social readjustment rating scale. *Journal of Psychomatic Research, 11*, 213–218.

Kagawa-Singer, M. (1993). Redefining health: Living with cancer. *Social Sciences in Medicine, 37*, 295–304.

LaPerriere, A., Ironson, G., Antoni, M. H., Schneiderman, N., Klinos, N., and Fletcher, M. A. (1994). Exercise and psychoneuroimmunology. *Medicine and Science in Sports and Exercise, 26*, 182–190.

Lee, Y., Dattilo, J., Kleiber, D. A., and Caldwell, L. L. (1996). Exploring the meaning of continuity in the early stages of adjustment for people with spinal cord injuries. *Leisure Sciences, 18*, 209–225.

Lee, Y., Mittelstaedt, R., and Askins, J. (1999). Predicting free time boredom of people with spinal cord injuries. *Therapeutic Recreation Journal, 33*, 122–134.

Mobily, K. E. (1996). Therapeutic recreation philosophy re-visited: A question of what recreation is good for. In C. Sylvester (Ed.), *Philosophy of TR II* (pp. 57–70). Arlington, VA: NRPA.

Mobily, K. E. (1999). New horizons in models of practice in therapeutic recreation, *Therapeutic Recreation Journal, 33*, 174–192.

Mobily, K. E. (2000). An interview with Professor Seppo Iso-Ahola. *Therapeutic Recreation Journal, 34*, 300–305.

NTRS. (1994). *NTRS Code of ethics and interpretive guidelines*. Arlington, VA: NRPA.

Parker, V. B. and Carmack, R. W. (1998). A critique of Van Andel's service delivery and TR outcome models. *Therapeutic Recreation Journal, 32*, 202–206.

Ragheb, M. G. (1993). Leisure and perceived wellness. *Leisure Sciences, 15*, 13–24.

Rath, K. V. and Page, G. (1996). *Understanding financing and reimbursement issues*. Arlington, VA: NRPA.

Ross, J. E. (1998). Critique of Austin's health protection/health promotion model. *Therapeutic Recreation Journal, 32*, 124–129.

Russoniello, C. V. (1994). Recreational therapy: A medicine model. In D. Compton and S. E. Iso-Ahola (Eds.), *Leisure and mental health* (pp. 247–258). Park City, UT: Family Development Resources.

Sable, J., Craig, P., and Lee, D. (2000). Promoting health and wellness: A research-based case report. *Therapeutic Recreation Journal, 34,* 348–361.

Selye, H. (1974). *Stress without distress.* New York, NY: HarperCollins.

Stumbo, N. J. and Peterson, C. A. (1998). The leisure ability model. *Therapeutic Recreation Journal, 32,* 82–95.

Sylvester, C. (1992). Therapeutic recreation and the right to leisure. *Therapeutic Recreation Journal, 26,* 9–20.

U.S. Department of Health and Human Services. (2000). *Healthy people 2010* (2nd ed.). Washington, DC: U.S. Government Printing Office.

Van Andel, G. E. (1998). TR service delivery and outcome models. *Therapeutic Recreation Journal, 32,* 180–193.

White, R. W. (1959). Motivation reconsidered: The concept of competence. *Psychological Review, 66,* 297–333.

Wilhite, B. C. and Keller, M. J. (2000). *Therapeutic recreation: Cases and exercises* (2nd ed.). State College, PA: Venture Publishing, Inc.

Wilhite, B., Keller, M. J., and Caldwell, L. L. (1999). Optimizing lifelong health and well-being: A health enhancing model of therapeutic recreation. *Therapeutic Recreation Journal, 33,* 98–107.

Chapter 5

Services for People With Disabilities

Learning Objectives

1. Investigate factors that influence the formation of attitudes toward people with disabilities.

2. Create an awareness of personal experiences and their impact on attitude formation.

3. Discuss how the media influence our attitudes toward people with disabilities.

4. Explain and apply the principle of normalization.

5. Develop an awareness of issues related to supporting people with disabilities in communities.

6. Understand the importance of valued social roles for people with disabilities.

7. Identify person-first terminology and appropriate use of sensitive language.

Every person working in therapeutic recreation or leisure services should be aware of issues related to delivering quality services to people with disabilities. Regardless of chosen employment, profession, or recreational pursuit, people with disabilities will be included or involved. Approximately 12.4% of the Canadian population (Statistics Canada, 2001) and 15% of the population in the United States (Kraus, Stoddard & Gilmartin, 1996) have disabilities that limit activity participation. Yet despite the statistics, people with disabilities are still largely misunderstood and misrepresented.

This chapter addresses issues related to service delivery, including terminology and language that support therapeutic recreation for people with disabilities. It focuses on developing and understanding attitudes and values toward people with disabilities by exploring how attitudes are formed, types of attitudes, and where values come from. The chapter covers terminology, with an emphasis on "person first" language and media treatment of people with disabilities, and suggests some guidelines for positive portrayal of people with disabilities. The end of the chapter introduces the concepts of normalization and social role valorization.

To introduce the topic of attitudes toward people with disabilities, read the following passage and respond to the questions that follow.

> A *middle-aged* woman got into her *expensive* car to go to her *high-paying* job in a *big* city on a *cold* day.

1. Do you understand this passage?

2. Give a number value to each italicized word in the passage. For example, what age do *you* think represents middle age? How much does an expensive car cost? How much does a person in a high-paying job make? How many people do you believe live in a big city? What temperature constitutes a cold day?

3. Review your findings with other classmates. If possible post your findings on the blackboard or on a flipchart so class numbers can be compared.

When asked if students understood the passage, the answer is universally yes, with little hesitation. Students rarely report concern or confusion over the passage. However, when numerical meanings for each item in the passage are compared there are frequently different understandings on specific parts of the passage. The results of this activity usually indicate a great variance in the numbers people attach to a passage that everyone understood. For example, the perception of "middle-aged" often shows a vast difference, from 30–65. So even though the understanding of the passage is universal, the meanings and values associated with the passage are very different.

1. Why such differences in the numbers?

2. Where do these values come from?

3. Why would there be so many differences, especially given that everyone understood the same passage?

This passage attaches a number to specific values; however it is difficult to quantify values since value systems are shaped by many factors.

From Where Do Our Values Come?

- Our communities—where we live, with whom we interact, our experiences in and out of schools, religious institutions, community agencies, and access to different services in the community all shape the way we look at the world.

- Our families—where our families come from, our parents, our family size, family relationships, siblings, and extended families all influence the development of our value and meaning.

- Our close friends, support networks, and our enemies all influence our experiences and our values.

- Our work provides us with examples and context for how we relate to specific tasks and specific clientele.

- Our leisure choices provide exposure, opportunity, and access to specific social networks, skill development, and interests. Our leisure preferences also influence our exposure to different cultures and environments.

Many factors influence our perceptions and beliefs. The previous example shows there can be great variation of understanding of the same passage. Our understanding of people with disabilities and our personal attitudes will be very different for each individual, depending on different life influences. In the provision of quality therapeutic recreation services for people with disabilities, it is important to understand that everyone approaches issues and events from a different value and belief system. As TR specialists, we must recognize personal values and attitudes because they impact the leisure service provision for people with disabilities.

How Are Attitudes Formed?

Fishbein and Ajzen's (1975) Theory of Planned Behavior/Reasoned Action describes the relationship between antecedents, beliefs, attitudes, intentions, and behaviors. All of these factors in attitude development influence each other, and TR specialists must understand how they shape behavior toward people with disabilities. It is important to address all aspects of attitude development in TR, as many individuals in society hold negative attitudes and beliefs toward people with disabilities.

- *Antecedents* are conditions that form the foundation for beliefs to develop. The sources that shape values (e.g., community, family, friends, work, and leisure choices) can influence our attitudes. We could also include gender, age, socioeconomic status, religion, race, or ethnic background.

- *Beliefs* involve what people perceive or believe to be true. Beliefs form during a process of acquiring information and forming an opinion.

- *Attitudes* are learned predispositions to respond in a consistently favorable or unfavorable manner with respect to a given "object." Once opinions (learned predispositions) are developed, attitudes reflect positively or negatively based on past experience.

- *Intentions* are motivations that influences behavior toward other people.

- *Behaviors* are any observable and measurable acts by an individual.

Terminology

When discussing attitudes toward people with disabilities, it is important to understand relevant terminology. Many terms are used interchangeably, but actually have very different meanings. It is important to understand the consequences for people with disabilities related to the language we use in forming positive and negative attitudes. Our day-to-day language may convey negative attitudes toward people with disabilities. To clarify meanings, the following terms are described and differences between terms are highlighted. Clarity of terms helps to develop positive attitudes (Dattilo, 2002).

- *Stigma* is an undesired "differentness" that separates the person from society (Goffman, 1963). A disabling condition or illness may have such negative perceptions that the person is devalued by a single attribute. For example, a person with a sexually transmitted disease may be given a stigmatized labeled and ultimately this can lead to negative self-perceptions.

- *Stereotype* is a standardized mental picture held in common by members of a group and represents an oversimplified opinion, attitude, or judgment (Dattilo, 2002). Society develops stereotypes, which lead to a narrow view and imply that all individuals in the grouping are similar. Stereotypes promote categories, and in doing so also promote misconceptions rather than highlighting individual capabilities. An example of a stereotype is that all Asians are good at math.

- *Prejudice* involves the development of a judgment while disregarding a person's rights, resulting in the individual being injured or damaged in some way (Dattilo, 2002). It comes from the prefix *pre*, and *judic*, the root word for judge. Being stigmatized and stereotyped by the development of prejudicial attitudes can result in discrimination, segregation, self-fulfilling prophecy, labeling, or spread phenomenon.

- *Discrimination* occurs when people make judgments or decisions based on a person's affiliation with a specific group rather than on an individual basis. In recreation it involves making decisions about disability and leisure interests, rather than on individual needs.

- *Segregation* results because stigmatization, stereotypes, and prejudices place people with disabilities in the different or deviant category. As a result of being perceived as different, people with disabilities are segregated or isolated in society. An act of segregation further alienates people with disabilities. Hutchison and McGill (1992) reported that segregation is based on beliefs that people given similar labels have the same needs and can be best served in a congregate environment. Segregation and congregation lead to further stigmatization and ostracization of the person by accentuating differences (McGill, 1996, pp. 18–19) If people with disabilities are segregated they are open to further stereotypes and generalizations.

- *Self-fulfilling prophecy* is the result of misconceptions that lead to lowered expectations of people with disabilities. As a result people with disabilities create lowered expectations for themselves.

- *Labeling* encourages self-fulfilling prophecy. A person's behavior becomes consistent with the label. Labels are like stigmas.

- *Spread phenomenon* refers to ascribing more limitations to a person with one disability. For example, one may assume persons with significant physical impairments also have mental retardation. Tripp and Sherril (1991) identified spread phenomenon as an association of additional imperfection on the actual disabling condition—for example, yelling at someone with vision limitation (making an assumption that the person also has a hearing impairment) or speaking slowly to someone with a physical disability (making the assumption that the person also has a cognitive impairment).

Sensitive Terminology

Often the terms we use convey attitudes or misunderstandings about disadvantaged populations (e.g., people with disabilities, minorities, people from economically or socially disadvantaged backgrounds). To understand sensitive terminology, we begin with a word association activity.

What do you think of when you hear the word *disability*?

1. Take one minute and list as many words as you can think of that you associate with disability.

2. Exchange lists with a fellow student and indicate whether each word has a positive (+), negative (–), or neutral connotation (0).

3. Return the list to the original person and add up how many positive, negative and neutral terms you have listed.

4. Discuss your findings with fellow classmates.

Often people associate many more negative words with disability than positive terms. When discussed, it is usually determined that students with more positive word association with the word *disability* have experienced positive situations with people with disabilities. Those who listed more negative associations usually include a majority of people who have little or no exposure to people with disabilities or who have had negative experiences. Students generally report very few neutral terms associated with the word disability, and report significantly more negative terms associated than positive ones.

There is often confusion over the terms disability, impairment, and handicap. These three terms are often used synonymously. However, there are important distinctions.

- *Impairment* is a loss or abnormality of psychological, physiological, or anatomical structure or function that may result from disease, accident, birth disorder, or environmental agents.

- *Disability* is a restriction or lack of ability to perform an activity in the manner or range considered normal for a human being.

- *Handicap* is a disadvantage for a given individual that limits or prevents the fulfillment of a role that is normal (depending on age, gender, social, and cultural factors) for that individual. The term "handicap" originated from a game in which forfeits were drawn from a cap. It is also linked with the practice of beggars who held "cap in hand" to solicit charity. This historical image creates a negative image for people with disabilities (Dattilo, 2002).

For this reason it is important to know more about disability and handicap. Often the words handicap and disability are used interchangeably when they have two distinct meanings. A *disability* is a functional challenge caused by an impairment, whereas a *handicap* is a function of the relationship between an individual and their environment. Here are two examples to distinguish the difference between each of the terms.

Dominic is a 10-year-old boy with a developmental disability who has a mother who does everything for him.

Impairment	Deficit in intellectual functioning.
Disability	Slow in learning developmental skills.
Handicap	Does not play with other children the same age, mother speaks and does things all the time for the child.

Malti is a college-age woman recently diagnosed with multiple sclerosis.

Impairment	Weakness in lower limbs as a result of MS.
Disability	Mobility limitations. Malti uses a wheelchair to cover long distances.
Handicap	Difficulty in attending classes on her university campus because of accessibility of buildings and walkways, winter weather, and poor snow removal.

Person-First Terminology

Hutchison and McGill (1992) suggested language tends to shape beliefs about a person. Our vocabulary and choice of words can orient an entire perception of people with disabilities. Negative terms not only bias a person's understanding, but also trivialize genuine community support for people with disabilities. Many examples exist of inappropriate terminology focused on grouping people with different disabilities together in one descriptor. For example, consider categorizations such as disabled persons, the mentally retarded, the disabled, the handicapped, handicapped people, or even the elderly. This categorizing of people assumes everyone in this group is the same. Other terminology highlight negative characteristics of disabilities, such as retard, dummy, feebleminded, retarded, crippled, invalid, lunatic, psycho, dumb, and mute. Other inappropriate terms highlight the specialized equipment used such as wheelchair user, crutch user, and cane user.

One goal of TR is to foster an individual, not categorical, approach to understanding people with disabilities. The language used contributes to the development of positive or negative associations with disabilities. By adopting person-first terminology, one emphasizes individual abilities rather than disabilities with the use of words and phrases. To avoid devaluing people with disabilities or members of marginalized populations, it is important to consider people individually and to not make generalizations about their group affiliation. If it is relevant to use a label, place the person first to avoid stereotypes and generalizations about a person who happens to have a disability. In placing the person first it is important to use a label only as a noun to describe the condition (e.g., a person with a visual impairment) rather than generalizing (e.g., "blind," or "the blind," or "the blind guy"). In person-first terminology it is also important to avoid group referencing by disability, illness, or diagnosis. Be clear in terminology references to disability. The use of acronyms might be unclear and demonstrate a generalization of abilities. By emphasizing the person first, abilities and uniqueness are highlighted. Using people first terminology emphasizes the person before the disability. The Canadian Active Living Alliance (1995) suggests examples of more appropriate sensitive terminology (**Table 5.1**).

Therapeutic recreation must ensure the uniqueness of individuals in services and programs. This involves use of empowering terminology that focuses on abilities. In referring to populations participating in TR services, words such as program participant, client, or resident would be preferred to patient or case, which imply dependency or illness. Positive emphasis could be placed on the selection of wording when referring to clients.

Role of the Media in Shaping Attitudes and Values

Have you ever considered how people with disabilities are portrayed by the media? Media are an integral part of society both in shaping and reflecting values of society (Gilbert, MacCauley & Smale, 1997). The media influence and reinforce our attitudes and values with messages in television programs, commercials, magazines, news coverage, printed advertisements, and films. Media often contribute to negative self-images of people with disabilities, which can have cognitive, emotional, and motivational impacts.

Table 5.1 Sensitive Terminology

Instead of ...	Use
disabled the disabled the handicapped	person with a disability
feebleminded retard mentally retarded mentally challenged	person with a developmental disability
deaf and dumb deaf mute hearing impaired	person who is deaf, hard of hearing
special child	child
crippled by... afflicted with... suffering from... victim of...	person who has... person with...
lame	person who is mobility impaired
confined to... bound by... dependent on.. (a wheelchair)	person who uses a wheelchair
physically challenged	person with a physical disability
mental patient mentally ill mental insane	person with a mental illness, person with schizophrenia
learning disabled learning difficulty	person with a learning disability
visually impaired (as a collective noun)	persons who are visually impaired persons who are blind
spastic (as a noun)	person with cerebral palsy

Adapted from Canadian Active Living Alliance (1995)

History of Media Treatment of People With Disabilities

An abundance of examples show how people with disabilities have been portrayed negatively by the media. Many historical examples show how people with disabilities were used as tools for amusement. Historical patterns of portrayal also show people with disabilities as "horror movie monsters" and "psychos." These images serve to further develop negative attitudes toward people with disabilities (Bedini, 1991).

In the 1800s people with disabilities were seen as forms of entertainment, such as those short in stature being used as comedians or pets (Bedini, 1991). This practice became so popular that some parents stunted the growth of their children to sell them for a profit. The mid-1880s included circus and freak shows in the United States. These shows were advertised as "mysterious, amazing, and frightening." People in these shows were portrayed as part human, part animal (Fiedler, 1978). These forms of entertainment continued to perpetuate misinformation related to people with disabilities.

With better access to information through education related to disability there is less "out of the ordinary" portrayal. Have things changed since the 1880s? Society is more educated and more aware of persons with disabilities than in the mid-1880s, yet there is still a great deal of exploitation of people with disabilities in magazines, comics, phrases, terminology, movies, and literature (Bedini, 1991). Examples of the 1880s freak shows continue to exist on the front pages of tabloid newspapers found at the grocery store checkout. Some examples since the year 2000 include front page photos of Siamese twins with full details of their physical features, a front page article featuring a boy as an alien because of physical features, and a little girl described as part frog because she had no hair.

Cartoons

Modern examples of how people with disabilities were used as a source of entertainment can be found in cartoons. Consider popular North American cartoons from the 1940s. Characters were often given disabilities to appear funnier—for example, Porky pig stutters, Sylvester the cat has a lisp, and Goofy has cognitive limitations. These characters develop and promote stigmas (Bedini, 1991). Recent cartoons for preschoolers have demonstrated more positive portrayals of characters with disabilities. Cartoons such as Franklin (Benjamin) the Turtle, Caillou, Sesame Street, Clifford the Big Red Dog, and Dragon Tales include people with disabilities as main characters in the stories—showing characters with disabilities as regular members of society with similar activities and involvement to other characters without disabilities. Some specific examples of positive cartoon portrayals include the following:

- *Franklin (Benjamin) the Turtle* shows friends with disabilities as part of the gang—disability is not an issue. The program demonstrates regular integration of characters with and without disabilities in play and in the classroom. Characters with disabilities are not seen as special guests or having special talents.

- *Dragon Tails* often includes characters with disabilities as regular friends in the story rather than focusing on the disability. The cartoon also shows how certain tasks can be individually modified without difficulty to ensure everyone can be involved.

- *Arthur* shows lots of different children with different abilities playing together.

Even with improvements in the portrayal of cartoon characters in preschool stories, characters with disabilities are still not featured as main characters and are largely underrepresented. In addition, there are very few feature length cartoons with characters with disabilities represented in a positive way.

News

Biklen (1987) identified images of people with disabilities in the newspapers range from very positive (e.g., superheroes) to very negative (e.g., burdens, menaces, or dependents) but rarely as ordinary citizens.

In a study of disability portrayal in the *Canadian Globe and Mail*, Gilbert et al., 1997) examined language and characteristics concerning people with disabilities for patterns of preferred terminology usage over an 11-year period (1980–1990). The results of their investigation indicated minimal positive change in the language and characteristics of articles concerning people with disabilities. Their findings revealed frequent contradictory terminology, with 72.9% of news articles including both positive and negative language related to people with disabilities. Gilbert et al. (1997) concluded the public is receiving mixed messages. These mixed messages remained unchanged despite the international year of people with disabilities (1981) and the UN declaration that the decade (1980s) was devoted to persons with disabilities.

An earlier study by Fletcher, Marino, and Everett (1988) also reports on negative images of people with disabilities in the news. According to their study of 12 daily newspapers, the most negative images suggested people with disabilities depend on charity (22%) or are victims as a result of their disabilities (11.2%). Their study also revealed people in wheelchairs were shown significantly more often than people with other disabilities, implying a hierarchy of disabilities covered by the media. The study also reported 8.9% portraying people with disabilities as capable in a positive way and 6.4% with depictions as ordinary citizens.

Television

One of the learning activities at the end of the chapter invites you to carefully examine how often people with disabilities are portrayed as main characters in prime time television. In an *Introduction to TR* course (2003), 161 students studying in Canada reported their findings following watching television one evening during prime time (7:00–10:00 p.m.) during the month of January. Their findings were summarized as follows:

- Very few people with disabilities were represented in prime time television programs.

- No people with disabilities were included in any commercials during prime time television.

- Few programs (with the notable exceptions of *ER, CSI,* and *Becker*) included people with disabilities.

- The most common portrayal of people with disabilities was as victims of violent crimes.

- No people with disabilities were found on prime time French television except on news stories related to disability or illness.

- The only shows that featured someone with a disability beyond the shows mentioned earlier were shows or documentaries about specific conditions or disabilities.

In summary, the students reported being consistently surprised by the lack of representation of people with disabilities in prime time television. From the media portrayal and representation one might conclude that people with disabilities do not drink beer, drive cars, or use shampoo or toothpaste. People with disabilities are not seen as consumers and are underrepresented by prime time television coverage.

Role of Therapeutic Recreation in Changing Attitudes Toward People With Disabilities

Many examples show how the media portrayal of people with disabilities could support the development of negative attitudes. The role of a TR specialist is to create positive leisure experiences for people with disabilities. One main barrier in the inclusion of people with disabilities is negative attitudes held by others about their limitations. It is important that TR specialists serve as advocates and positive representatives for people with disabilities. When reporting stories and news to the media a TR specialist can take on the role of educator and influence positive portrayal and language associated with people with disabilities. News reporters can be given summaries that stress the importance of sensitive terminology. TR specialists should be aware of the messages they send when using terminology associated with persons with disabilities, and clients.

The primary focus of TR specialists is to provide leisure opportunities to maintain or improve functional abilities. To do this people with disabilities need to be supported in their communities and programming environments. TR services can play a significant role in changing attitudes. To begin, TR services offer opportunities for people without disabilities to interact in a positive meaningful way in programs with people with disabilities. This direct contact can lead to positive formation of values, beliefs, and attitudes toward the abilities of people with disabilities (Hoenk & Mobily, 1987).

Leisure services or recreational activities provide an ideal context where people can have positive experiences with people with disabilities. TR specialists can have a significant role in creating positive perceptions of people with disabilities. By designing services inclusive of people with disabilities, recreational activities can offer opportunities for structured interaction between people with and without disabilities. TR services with specific designs help to facilitate equal status among participants and allow for effective communication and openness between people of all abilities. A TR specialist can also play a role in facilitating age-appropriate and skill-appropriate programs and service offerings.

The Canadian Active Living Alliance (1995) offers specific guidelines for positive media portrayal of people with disabilities, including

- a person with a disability is a person first.

- describe the person, not the disability.

- refer to a person's disability only when relevant.

- avoid stories or images designed to evoke pity or guilt.

- portray the human, not the superhuman.

- treat persons with disabilities with dignity.

- recognize that disabilities occur along a spectrum and not all people with the same disability have the same limitations.

- use words with dignity.

According to the Canadian Active Living Alliance (1995) a positive portrayal of people with disabilities in the media focuses on three components: individuality, integration, and imagination.

- *Individuality* refers to the uniqueness of the person, highlighting capabilities and portraying people with disabilities in all levels of authority. In highlighting the individual, both work and leisure accomplishments should be presented.

- *Integration* refers to emphasizing people with disabilities in shared activities, not just alone or with others with disabilities.

- *Imagination* refers to being creative when portraying people with disabilities, beyond familiar, dependent images. Whenever possible, demonstrate that people with disabilities are active and involved in the community, rather than using passive, solo depictions.

Normalization/Social Role Valorization

This final section examines two important concepts in therapeutic recreation: normalization and social role valorization. As discussed earlier, our culture devalues people with disabilities by minimizing media representation, promoting negative attitudes and values, and using nonsupportive terminology. As a result, often people with disabilities are not given the same access to valuable social roles that many people take for granted (McGill, 1996). These negatively valued roles are commonly perpetuated to the extent that members of society rarely question them. According to Wolfensberger (1983), society unconsciously places people with disabilities into negatively valued roles such as dependent person, object of charity, holy innocent, eternal child, and object of pity and ridicule. Often, because of unquestioned assumptions, values, and beliefs, people with disabilities are seen as *deviant*. A person is said to be deviant if they are perceived to be significantly different in some aspect considered important and if the difference is negatively valued. We develop our self-perceptions and image based on our interactions with others. For people seen as deviant and devalued, access to many social roles are more difficult or denied.

Normalization

In the late 1960s and early 1970s, the term *normalization* was influenced by the writings of Wolfensberger. There was an increased awareness of the rights of people with disabilities to live "normal," valued lives. Normalization is defined as

> the use of culturally normative means (familiar, valued techniques, tools and methods) in order to enable persons' life conditions (income, housing, health services) which are at least as good as the average citizens, and to enhance or support their own behavior (skills, competencies), status, and reputation. (Wolfensberger, 1983)

The framework of normalization serves to reinforce the recognition that normalization could be more fully realized in the mainstream community settings and to advocate for the development of supports that facilitate normalization in community recreation settings (Pedlar & Gilbert, 1997). Normalization advocates for supporting people with disabilities in normal everyday settings and environments rather than in segregated environments.

Principles of Normalization

In discussing the need for everyone to have access to regular, "normal" patterns of everyday life Wolfensberger identified five principles of normalization: integration, avoidance of deviancy juxtaposition, dignity of risk, behavioral expectations, and advocacy.

Integration. Bengt Nirje (a Scandinavian pioneer of normalization) wrote extensively on the need to recognize normalization in everyday life including education, employment, shelter, and leisure. According to Nirje, normalization was synonymous with *integration*. His concept of integration included the following (Nirje, cited in Pedlar and Gilbert, 1997):

- *Physical integration* refers to the location of homes, schools, work places, and recreation facilities accessible to all individuals.

- *Functional integration* means the opportunity exists to function in ordinary segments of the environment (e.g., eating out at restaurants, use of transportation, use of rest rooms).

- *Social integration* provides interpersonal, social relationships at all levels, from neighborhoods to the community at large.

- *Personal integration* refers to relationships with significant others (e.g., parents, siblings, friends, partner) that allow for an opportunity to experience normal steps in the lifecycle.

- *Societal integration* relates to those expressive elements of functioning as a citizen, including the extension of legal rights and opportunity for growth and self-determination.

- *Organizational integration* means accessible generic services that avoid the necessity of segregating support services.

Hutchison and McGill (1992) maintained the notion of integration must be considered beyond a continuum approach, and they challenged people to consider a new integration philosophy. According to the authors, integration means

- a process of people who are valued—support to establish relationships with ordinary members of the community.

- support to participate in typical, everyday education, recreation, work, and family settings with ordinary peers in the community.

- having a range of valued social roles in the community similar to other citizens.

- participating and interacting with ordinary citizens, not just being physically present in the community.

- eliminating segregated settings and reallocating segregated resources to create integrated opportunities and safeguarding resources in the process to ensure they are not lost.

- new areas of involvement and changing roles for recreationists and advocates, including planning, community building, coordinating individual and system supports, educating, and connecting.

- building competencies in the community so that it becomes inclusive and accepting of diversity.

The integration process is complex. There are no simple solutions. For integration to occur there needs to be opportunity and support within communities.

Avoidance of Deviance Juxtaposition. A second principle of normalization is the *avoidance of deviance juxtaposition*. To ensure a "normal" environment, every effort should be made not to group people together because of their disabilities. People should be organized by program and services according to interests, not limitations. When people with different disabilities are grouped together it could create a further lowered social role value and perpetuate myths and stereotypes. There are many examples of community programs where a "special" or separate set of programs and services are offered to people with disabilities. These programs are offered with the idea that they are specially designed to service the needs of people with disabilities, yet by being segregated they are not highly supported or valued in the community.

Dignity of Risk. The third principle of normalization is *dignity of risk*. All people regardless of their abilities or limitations must be given the right to take risks and potentially to make mistakes. With regard to risk, persons with disabilities should be no exception. Risks provide challenges and allow for normalcy of life.

Behavior Expectations. The fourth principle of normalization is *behavior expectations*. We should expect the same behavior of everyone. Standards or expectations should not be altered because someone has a disability. If behavior difficulties are a function of a person's limitations, and a reward system is used to promote positive behaviors, rewards should be realistic and should work toward natural reinforcement (e.g.,verbal praise instead of a piece of candy). Program offerings and role models should be age appropriate. Not all people with disabilities have behavior difficulties, but sometimes lowered or altered societal expectations of people with disabilities leads to devalued social roles.

Advocacy. The fifth principle of normalization is *advocacy*. To create opportunities for people with disabilities, there must be advocacy and education of the general public on principles of normalization. As discussed in the integration section, it is important to recognize the need for normalization and to go beyond supporting people with disabilities. Advocacy includes creating programs and services, using appropriate terminology, creating valued opportunities for social role development, creating opportunities for people with disabilities to advocate for themselves, and promoting policy and legislation to ensure the rights of people with disabilities are enhanced.

Consider the following questions when applying normalization principles to recreation situations:

- Does this program or service teach participants skills that can be applied in real life situations?

- Are participants learning skills that make them less dependent on others?

- Does this program serve as an avenue to opportunities that will help participants to grow, to develop, and to enhance inclusion?

- Do the activities participants engage in enhance their acceptance and value among peers?

- Do participants really like the activity?

- Does the community value the activity?

At the end of this chapter (in the learning activities) two scenarios test your understanding of the principles of normalization.

Social Role Valorization

Many people strongly believe and support the principles of normalization. However, disagreement exists over the term, because it is difficult in a complex diverse society to determine what is considered *normal*. It implies it is possible those who follow principles of normalization do so because they work with clients seen as "not normal." As a result the term *social role valorization* is gaining popularity. It means ascribing value to people in their roles. People who have been devalued by society have the need and right to experience the same everyday opportunities as other citizens including holding valued social roles (Wolfensberger & Thomas, 1983). The goal of social role valorization is "the creation, support, and defense of valued social roles and life conditions for people who are at risk of social devaluation" (Wolfensberger & Thomas, 1983, p. 236). Through our social roles we become intertwined with others. To support valued roles, TR specialists need to enhance the social image or perceived value of clients in the eyes of others, as well as enhance that person's competencies (Hutchison & McGill, 1992). Social role valorization places emphasis on two elements: enhancing personal competence and enhancing social image of people with disabilities.

Enhancing Personal Competence

Enhancing one's personal competence includes creating accessible comfortable environments in close proximity to other services in the community. Personal competence is developed through the promotion of appropriate social and sexual identity.

Enhancing Social Image

Leisure services provide an ideal context for supporting valued social roles, because they provide a powerful context for identity creation and expression. The leisure context provides a means of developing social identification, memberships, and community affiliations in groups and organizations outside of family. It is in recreation and leisure where friendships are developed, expressed, and enhanced.

Roles can be either positive or negative. The goal of a TR specialist is to enhance the opportunities for positive roles. Roles we play can impact our personal worth, status, associations, values, and beliefs. In our free time much of what is done is defined by roles. Following are examples of leisure influences and personal roles:

- What does what you do in your free time say about you?

- What kinds of beliefs and values are associated with what you do?

- What social roles do you have? How many were developed through work? through family?

- What social networks have you developed as a result of your leisure interests?

- How has your background influenced your leisure interests?

- What personal qualities do you attribute to experiences in leisure?

McGill (1996) identified that the typical roles given to devalued citizens do not emphasize the abilities of individuals. Rather than being seen as a valued family member or someone in a valued intimate relationship, people who are devalued are viewed as dependents. The roles for devalued citizens need to be expanded to include positive roles such as volunteer, neighbor, community club member, board member, etc.

Everyone is identified by social roles in our work and in our leisure. We are known as figure skaters, shoppers, travelers, belly dancers, tennis players, skiers, wine tasters, campers, and quilt makers (Hutchison & McGill, 1992). Often people with disabilities are not given the same access to social roles. People with disabilities are more frequently recognized as people who take part in activities but are not recognized in these roles. Often people with disabilities are seen as needing these activities rather than pursuing them for enjoyment.

According to McGill (1996), "The process of marginalization or devaluation has meant that persons with disabilities have been taught to view leisure primarily as a 'treat,' as a programmed diversion forming part of the monotony of being a client in human service." (pp. 7–8). Therapeutic recreation can offer people with disabilities an opportunity to gain access to valued social roles in leisure. Unfortunately people with disabilities have been denied opportunities by recreational program offerings, which only offer a sampling of activities rather than an opportunity to gain skills and recognition in leisure pursuits.

Learning Activities

Media and People With Disabilities

The following learning activities will help you to gain awareness of the role of media in the promotion of positive attitudes of people with disabilities.

Television

For this activity select one evening and watch prime time television from 7:00–10:00 p.m. While watching, record the numbers of times you see a person with a disability appear during the programming. When a character with a disability appears, indicate whether it is a main character and what the story is about. During the advertisements, watch to see how often people with disabilities are included. What products are they promoting? Bring your information back to your class and report your findings.

Advertisements

Select a recent issue of a popular magazine and examine all advertisements. Identify all people with disabilities found in the advertisements and the types of products they are promoting. In addition include the type of disability.

Movies

Rent *My Left Foot* from local commercial video store or from your public library. For the discussion answer the following questions:

- What are your overall impressions of the film?
- What influences your attitudes toward Christy Brown?
- Do you feel it was a realistic portrayal of a person with a disability?
- How were the guidelines set out by the Canadian Active Living Alliance followed in the film?

Print

Read Leandra Bedini's (1991) "Modern Day 'Freaks'? The exploitation of people with disabilities."

Normalization/Social Role Valorization

To understand the principles of normalization, examine one of the following scenarios in a small group. For each scenario, identify issues relate to the principles of normalization and social role valorization.

Scenario A

Each year a campus sorority selects a charity and puts on a fundraising event to raise money and awareness for the local nonprofit organization. This year the sorority chose to raise money for summer programming for a network of group homes called Seashore Support System, which supports adults with cognitive disabilities to live independently in the community. The sorority decided to do a spring fashion show as this year's event. The fashion show titled, "Make a Dream Come True," would feature fashion from local area merchants and would include a special section featuring models from the group homes. The sorority would take care of all the details related to planning the event. The adults in the Seashore Support Systems Group home would work on organizing the special section in their group homes with Seashore employees. What principles of normalization and social role valorization apply in this scenario? If you were the therapeutic recreation specialist how would you modify the situation to follow principles discussed in the chapter?

Scenario B

"Le Soleil" is a community day center for older adults with dementia and other physical disabilities. The role of the center is to provide recreation, lunch, and an opportunity to socialize with other adults. The center also provides respite for family caregivers. The center is staffed by a social worker, a dietician/cook, an activities director, and university student volunteers.

You have decided you would be interested in volunteering some time to gain experience with this population in a community TR setting. To be a volunteer, you take part in a volunteer orientation on the services and programs. During the orientation you learn about the *Five Alive Sensory Program* offered each morning to the entire group. The five alive program consists of different sensory activities, such as holding teddy bears, playing with musical toys (designed for toddlers), playing with Play-Doh, finger painting, and choosing different types of foods by color. You decide not to volunteer at "Le Soleil" because you believe the organization does not follow principles of normalization and social role valorization. Give some examples of principles from this chapter that were not followed. How would you change the program to offer services that promote valued social roles?

Summary

This chapter provides an overview of services for people with disabilities. The chapter highlights the importance of our attitudes, beliefs, and values in terms of developing quality recreational services for people who are disadvantaged. The chapter also identifies the influence of the media and stresses the importance of access to social roles for everyone. Sensitive language, valued roles, media portrayal, and understanding the roots of our own values and attitudes all influence the opportunities for inclusion in services for people with disabilities.

References

Bedini, L. (1991). Modern day "freaks"? The exploitation of people with disabilities. *Therapeutic Recreation Journal, 25*(4) 61–69.

Biklen, D. (1987). Framed: Print journalism's treatment of disabling issues. In A. Gartner and T. Joe (Eds.), *Images of the disabled, disabling images* (pp. 79–95). New York, NY: Praeger.

Canadian Active Living Alliance. (1995). Federal government initiative published through the Ministry of Sport, Fitness, and Recreation.

Dattilo, J. (2002). *Inclusive leisure services: Responding to the rights of people with disabilities* (2nd ed.). State College, PA: Venture Publishing, Inc.

Fishbein, M. and Ajzen I. (1975). *Belief, attitude, intention and behavior: An introduction to theory and research.* Reading, MA: Addison Wesley.

Fiedler, L. (1978). *Freaks: Myths and images of the secret self.* New York, NY: Simon and Schuster.

Fletcher, F., Marino, D., and Everett, R. (1988). *News coverage of disabilities and disabled persons in the Canadian media.* Unpublished report prepared for the House of Commons Committee on the Status of Disabled Persons.

Gilbert, A., MacCauley M., and Smale, B. (1997). Newspaper portrayal of persons with disabilities over a decade. *Therapeutic Recreation Journal,* 108–120.

Goffman, I. (1963). *Stigma: Notes of the management of the spoiled identity.* Englewood Cliffs, NJ: Prentice Hall.

Hoenk, A. H. and Mobily, K. (1987). Mainstreaming the play environment: Effects of previous exposure and salience of disability. *Therapeutic Recreation Journal, 21*(4), 23–31.

Hutchinson, P. and McGill, J. (1992). *Leisure, integration, and community.* Concord, Ontario, Canada: Leisurability Publications.

Kraus, L., Stoddard, S., and Gilmartin, D. (1996) *An info use report.* Washington, DC: U.S. National Institute on Disability and Rehabilitation Research.

McGill, J. (1996). *Developing leisure identities: A project of Brampton Caledon Community Living and the Ontario Ministry of Citizenship, Culture, and Recreation* (p. 14). Brampton, Ontario, Canada: Brampton Caledon Community Living.

Pedlar, A. and Gilbert, A. (1997). Normalization for individuals with disabilities: The Canadian model. In D. Compton (Ed.), *Issues in Therapeutic Recreation* (pp. 489–506). Champaign, IL: Sagamore Publishing.

Statistics Canada (2001) Participation and Activity Limitation Survey. Retrieved from http://www.statcan.ca

Tripp, A. and Sherril, C. (1991). Attitude theories of relevance to adapted physical education. *Adapted Physical Activity Quarterly, 8*, 12–27.

Wolfensberger, W. (1983). Social role valorization: A proposed new term for the principle of normalization. *Mental Retardation, 21*(6), 235–239.

Wolfensberger, W. and Thomas, S. (1983). *PASSING (Program analysis of service system, implementation of normalization goals): Normalization criteria and ratings manual* (2nd ed.). Toronto, Ontario, Canada: National Institute on Mental Retardation.

Chapter 6

The TR Profession

Learning Objectives

1. To understand how TR meets the criterion set out for a profession by Sessoms.

2. To articulate arguments for the public good and the benefits of TR services.

3. To compare and contrast services and philosophical orientations of ATRA, CTRA, and NTRS.

4. To understand the professional and educational preparation of TR specialists in Canada and the United States.

5. To highlight the importance of continuing education in the TR profession.

6. To develop an awareness of the criteria for professional competence.

7. To develop an understanding of the differences in the credentialing of TR specialists in Canada and the United States.

What Is a Profession?

According to the United States Department of Labor's Bureau of Labor Statistics (2004), in 2000 there were approximately 29,000 recreational therapists. "Employment of recreational therapists is expected to grow faster than the average for all occupations through the year 2006 because the anticipated expansion in long-term care, physical and psychiatric rehabilitation, and services for people with disabilities." (U.S. Department of Labor, Bureau of Labor Statistics, 2004). Despite this predicted growth, therapeutic recreation is considered a relatively new profession. Becoming a profession is a long, complex process.

According to Reynolds and O'Morrow (1985), a *profession* refers to the provision of services that require "specialized knowledge and skills." Professions are necessary in complex societies to sustain and support health, education, and human services. Professions can improve quality of life for clients through ethically enlightened efforts (Sylvester, 1998).

Many occupations have sought to gain professional status. All aspects of healthcare have evolved into professional designations. While many occupations are considered professions, few have attained the attributes of the professions of law and medicine (Carter, 1998). In TR, professionalization is seen as a way to ensure practitioner competence, to maintain service quality and uniformity, and to gain status for recognition (Carter, 1998). Many authors have highlighted criteria for a profession. Opinions vary on whether therapeutic recreation meets the criteria set out for professions.

This chapter provides an overview of the therapeutic recreation profession. It explores criteria in determining professions, professional preparation, the role of professional associations, continuing education for professionals, professional competence and standards, and some differences between Canadian and American therapeutic recreation.

Sessoms (1991) identified four requirements for an occupation to be designated as a profession:

1. recognition by the public of its importance to the welfare of the public (a social mandate).

2. formulation of professional organizations that assume responsibility for the control and destiny of the profession.

3. body of knowledge and programs of formal professional preparation to impart that knowledge to those who wish to practice.

4. acceptance by both those who practice and those who receive the service that the practitioner needs specialized knowledge and training to perform service correctly.

Public Welfare

For a profession to be recognized there needs to be recognition by the public that the services provided are important to the welfare of clients. While definitions of TR often conflict or contain different emphases, general agreement exists that the role of TR is to enhance and to maintain health and skills and well-being, which ultimately contributes to an enhanced quality of life.

The benefits of TR services are well-documented in the literature. Anecdotal evidence supports the notion that TR contributes to numerous benefits.

The National Therapeutic Recreation Society (NTRS) identifies numerous benefits of TR, such as

- improving or maintaining physical abilities.

- increasing self-confidence.

- promoting greater independence.

- strengthening interpersonal skills.

- managing stress.

- learning new leisure skills.

Therapeutic recreation is recognized as an important part of the service spectrum in most healthcare agencies. Clinical (hospital) environments recognize the value of TR by ensuring all settings include recreation as a part of the treatment process. In most healthcare settings, TR specialists are considered a part of the multidisciplinary team. In the community, TR is recognized for the services provided, which are inclusive and offer increased participation opportunities to people who have disabilities.

Sylvester (1992) maintained TR cannot and should not justify its social calling based on the same functional outcomes as other allied health professions (e.g., physical therapy/physio therapy). In attempting to quantify all outcomes of service provision, TR runs the risk of becoming the poor stepchild of physical therapy or occupational therapy, especially if it seeks its social mission in the same functional outcomes of traditional therapies: Why does society need another discipline that improves functional outcomes when it already has physical therapy and occupational therapy? Others expressed similar concerns, suggesting TR will lose its identity if it follows the same path as physical therapy and occupational therapy.

Instead, Sylvester (1992) maintained TR can serve the public good only if it makes clear its unique contribution to enhancing quality of life. Leisure is a modality quite distinct from exercise (used by physical therapy) or activities of daily living (used by occupational therapy) insofar as it usually requires enjoyment, some measure of participant self-determination, and intrinsic motivation. Leisure is a basic human right, not a privilege. Regardless of the person's condition, impairment, or disability, he or she has a right to leisure.

Those maintaining the right to leisure advances the public's welfare, for example, cite cases where those most constrained have an abundance of free time. There are many people with severe and multiple disabilities that have few opportunities for employment. This leaves most persons with physical disabilities with a large amount of free time. Likewise, people convicted of crimes are arguably the most constrained people in society, and even they are granted one hour of recreation a day by law. Both of these phenomena underscore the distinct possibility that leisure is viewed as a right, not a luxury. Hence, TR promotes the public welfare by acting on society's will to guarantee the right to leisure of all its citizens, even those most constrained by condition or impairment.

Professional Organizations

The second criterion of a profession is the formulation of professional organizations that assume responsibility for the control and destiny of the profession. What are professional TR associations? What role do they play? According to Keller (1989)

> Professional associations are organized by volunteers working in the field with the primary purpose of organizing resources of members for effective service to others, advancing the quality and standards of the profession and its members, and advancing the welfare of its members. (p. 35)

In addition to national professional associations, there are also regional, state, and provincial professional organizations. Most TR practitioners belong to both a regional and a national professional organization. In Canada, participation and involvement in regional and provincial TR associations is often much greater than national membership.

There are several benefits to belonging to professional TR organizations. The main benefits to students are the opportunities to network, to attend conferences, and to become exposed to the latest trends in the field at a reduced cost. Professional organizations offer students special programs and opportunities to gain experience as a volunteer at conferences or on committees, and may offer scholarships or designated awards for outstanding student contributions to the field.

Professional associations require some form of belonging often in the form of membership registration. In North America three national organizations (introduced in Chapter 1) have played a significant role in the development of the TR profession.

American Therapeutic Recreation Association (ATRA)

The American Therapeutic Recreation Association (ATRA) is the largest national membership organization representing the needs and interests of recreational therapists. ATRA offers many services to members, including continuing education, *TR Annual*, a treatment network, educational program information, conferences and workshops, a career network, professional standards of practice and code of ethics, and a variety of groups on specific topics.

The vision of ATRA includes

- providing an open organization that encourages critical thinking among members.

- a professional commitment to continuously assess the healthcare environment.

- an opportunity to exchange information with members and to act swiftly and decisively in areas that have current and potential impact on the profession.

- upholding a strict code of ethical directives that include such concepts as equality, honesty, fairness, and justice for all members of the association and for the members of the profession.

The ATRA website (http://www.atra-tr.org) offers a comprehensive online service that includes links to services provided by the organization. The website also offers discounts for members.

Canadian Therapeutic Recreation Association

The mission of the Canadian Therapeutic Recreation Association (CTRA) is to advocate for the TR Profession and members by

- promoting and facilitating communication between and among members in TR.

- developing and implementing a plan that will lead to national certification of TR practitioners.

- promoting and advancing public awareness and understanding of TR.

- developing and promoting the adoption and implementation of professional standards for the delivery of TR services.

- supporting excellence and advancements in education and research in TR.

The CTRA website (http://www.canadian-tr.org/about_ctra.htm) offers support to practitioners, educators, and students working in the field of TR. The organization publishes the *Tribune* quarterly, which contains regional updates, conferences and workshop opportunities, articles on TR issues, information on innovative TR initiatives, and suggestions for resources and the promotion of TR. CTRA sponsors a national conference every year in conjunction with a provincial or regional professional association with specific themes.

National Therapeutic Recreation Society (NTRS)

The National Therapeutic Recreation Society is a membership organization for those interested in the provision of TR services for people with disabilities in clinical facilities and in the community. NTRS is a branch of the National Parks and Recreation Association.

NTRS members include practitioners, administrators, educators, volunteers, students, and consumers. The goals of NTRS are

- to unite professional and paraprofessional therapeutic recreation personnel.
- to encourage professional development of all TR personnel.
- to advocate for the leisure rights of individuals with disabilities.
- to advocate for the professional interests of TR personnel.
- to encourage and conduct research to improve the quality of TR services.
- to promote relationships between therapeutic recreation personnel and those professions and agencies concerned with the health and well-being of people with disabilities.

NTRS offers technical assistance services to agencies, institutions, and individuals on professional issues and trends in the field of TR. NTRS publishes books and brochures on the provision of TR services and sponsors national and regional conferences on program development, management, professional issues, and trends. *Therapeutic Recreation Journal* and the NTRS Report are provided quarterly to NTRS members. For more information visit the NTRS website at http://www.activeparks.org/branches/NTRS.

Professional Preparation

The third criterion for an occupation to be considered a profession is professional preparation. This section of the chapter discusses the professional preparation and educational background of TR specialists in the United States and Canada. Chapter 12 will address curricula preparing TR specialists in other parts of the world. The role of continuing education, conferences, and workshops is highlighted as an important element of keeping current with trends and issues in TR.

The role of theory in professional education can be traced to Plato's *Republic*. The notion of educational preparation being a part of any defined profession is common. Millerson (1964) found "being based on theoretical knowledge" was among the most frequently cited characteristic of a profession. On assessing the TR profession, Reynolds and O'Morrow (1985) confirmed that publicly sanctioned authority to practice and mechanisms to protect the public, professionals are characterized by "both a general and specialized body of knowledge that can be used to benefit the consumer" (p. 11). Professional preparation serves as a foundation for rational for practice and serves as a basis for developing a rationale for why TR services are offered. Figure 6.1 illustrates how professional preparation requires three interrelated parts:

1. *Theory* is an explicative system of ideas that provides the basis for professional knowledge and activity. Theory is knowledge that guides the development of principles of practice.

2. *Practice* is the field of action where theory is structured and applied to achieve concrete goals.

3. *Techniques* involve specific skills used to make or to do something related to practice. It concerns is how to apply skill to achieve practical purposes.

All three components must be included as part of professional preparation (Sylvester, 1998).

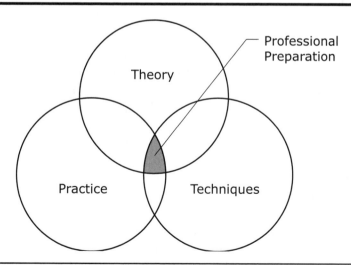

Figure 6.1   Professional preparation

United States

In the United States a baccalaureate degree is an entry-level requirement for the therapeutic recreation profession. Formal educational began as preparation for those working in hospital recreation. Over the past 60 years, professional preparation programs evolved, yet professional preparation continues to vary significantly in the United States. TR curricula varies significantly: some universities offer university degrees in TR, some offer recreation programs with TR options, and some offer coursework in TR.

Both ATRA and NTRS developed standards of practice for TR professionals, which is reflected in most TR curricula. But programs vary considerably from as few as 3 to as many as 13 courses in therapeutic recreation at the undergraduate level (Navar, 2001). Austin (1989) questioned assumptions concerning TR curricula in terms of professional preparation. He reported in the early 1980s lengthy discussions were held by TR educators to resolve curricular issues with no resolution because of variances of opinions and approaches in TR.

Resources, faculty availability, number of students, availability of options, and internship/practicum agencies all have an impact on the development of TR professional preparation programs in the United States. It can be confusing to find therapeutic recreation professional preparation programs because they fall into subsections of departments and under different degree titles. Because of the varied nature of TR curricula, the designation of degrees often refers more to the home department and history rather than the curriculum. The mission of a university (e.g., research, land grant, teaching, or religious foundations), the home in the university (e.g., Arts and Sciences; Health, Physical Education, Recreation, and Dance; Kinesiology; Social Sciences) and the department (e.g., Leisure Studies, TR, Applied Human Sciences) have different influences on the development of the curriculum and the credibility of TR in the curriculum. Usually degree titles have more to do with the home of the TR program rather than specific curriculum requirements.

In their study of TR curricula, Stumbo and Carter (1999) discovered TR curriculums vary significantly. There have been several attempts at standardization through accreditation by the National Recreation and Parks Association (NRPA) and the American Association of Leisure and Recreation (AALR) Council on Accreditation (COA). While these standards do not address the structure in which a curriculum is maintained or the number of classes in programs, they do specify content to be taught (O'Morrow, 1997). In 2000 the NRPA and AALR upgraded these standards.

In 1997 the National Council for Therapeutic Recreation Certification (NCTRC) completed a National Job Analysis that identified eight different knowledge areas for the professional preparation of TR graduates:

1. background (lifespan development, behavior change, leisure theories).

2. diagnostic groupings (understanding special populations, symptoms, incidence, and treatment).

3. assessment (types, process, interpretation).

4. planning (impact of impairment, nature of leisure activities).

5. implementation (program delivery techniques).

6. documentation (progress notes, charting).

7. program evaluation (organizing and managing services, supervision, budgets, and standards).

8. professional advancement (advocacy, professional associations).

Canada

The preparation of TR specialists in Canada differs from preparation in the United States. To begin with, there are fewer educational institutions preparing professionals in the field. Universities and community colleges across Canada share an interest in postsecondary education and training in TR, even though the form and function of program delivery and course content may vary considerably. College programs provide training for entry-level and technical positions, while university programs focus on skills for practitioners to attain increasing levels of responsibility and management (Searle & Brayley, 1993). Due to the broad emphasis of the university undergraduate curriculum, TR is often not seen as a profession within the discipline, but rather as subset of leisure studies programs with specific coursework in TR. As a result there is greater variance between TR programs in Canada.

Currently there is only one TR undergraduate degree program (Concordia University), several TR undergraduate specializations (Brock University, University of Waterloo, University of Manitoba, Dalhousie University), one post degree diploma (Georgian College) and a few universities offering graduate programs with coursework in TR. Some provinces (many in western Canada) have limited access to university TR course offerings and other provinces (Ontario and Quebec) include both college and university preparation opportunities.

In the fall of 2002, fewer than 10 full-time faculty/educators worked in therapeutic recreation in Canada. University and college programs in Canada do not follow standardized curricula, and no national program of accreditation exists. Each university and college curriculum offers unique programs and course offerings. Many university curricula place an emphasis on community therapeutic recreation and the role of recreation in integration and creating inclusive, supportive communities. Support coursework relates to the study of leisure, understanding diversity, and developing general skills in social sciences, such as research and evaluation, and interpersonal and group leadership skills (Dieser & Ostiguy, 2004).

Few formal studies examined the educational preparation of TR specialists in Canada. Hutchison (1983) examined curriculum issues that affected people with disabilities in the community. The results of her study indicated entry-level practitioners were underprepared to deal with issues in communities. A gap was identified between education and practice. There was little connection between theory and practical application of coursework. Hutchison confirmed a need for more focus on practical every day problems and issues that arise in the TR field. In addition, the Hutchison investigation highlighted that concepts taught were based on models from the United States, and only 21% of Canadian university recreation and leisure studies programs had a strong concentration in the area of TR. Since the study in 1983, there have been many changes to TR curriculums in Canada. Most programs at universities have designed coursework that provides a broad understanding of leisure (theory) and professional preparation opportunities (practice).

Continuing Education

Educational training and professional preparation does not end with a degree or completion of an undergraduate program. Continuing education in the form of conferences, workshops, and seminars provides ongoing access to new knowledge and techniques and promotes the understanding of issues in the profession. Continuing education is essential to maintain a current body of knowledge.

Graduates of TR programs typically have been exposed to only a few professors in coursework. It is important to attend workshops and conferences to obtain different TR perspectives. TR programs at universities and colleges are often limited by resources, historical influences, faculty expertise, and size of program, which means that courses in all areas of TR cannot always be covered. Conferences provide important opportunities to build on current TR curricula.

Conferences and workshops also provide opportunities to keep up with current TR issues and trends. Langsner (1994) identified many benefits associated with participation in continuing education:

- staying abreast of new developments in the field, professional knowledge, and skills.

- becoming more competent in current work.

- matching knowledge and skills with demands of work situations.

- learning from the interaction of other professionals.

- exchanging ideas with professional colleagues.

- sharpening perspectives of professional role or practice.

- maintaining personal identity with a profession.

- assessing the directions in which a profession is going.

- obtaining leadership capabilities for the profession.

- enhancing the image of the profession.

- reflecting on the value of the profession's responsibilities.

Conferences and workshops are easy to locate if the student or practitioner is a member of a professional association. ATRA, CTRA, and NTRS all include continuing education/conference and workshop information on their websites and in print materials sent to members. Provincial and state professionals and TR regional groups also offer workshops and conferences to members.

According to Austin, Dattilo, and McCormick (2002) a common misperception associated with attending professional conferences is only professionals working in the field attend it. As students, attending conferences and workshops provides an excellent entry into the field of TR. It also serves as an orientation to issues and the breadth of TR service delivery, as well as an important opportunity to network with practitioners. Of course the practical reason for pursuing continuing education is that it is required for continued professional certification through the National Council for Therapeutic Recreation Certification. Completion of between 30 and 50 hours of continuing education every five years is required to maintain professional certification.

Profession Competence

The final criteria for a profession outlined by Sessoms (1991) is the acceptance by both those who practice and those who receive the service that the practitioner needs specialized knowledge and training to perform service correctly. The phrase "your organization is only as good as your people" has never been more true. As service providers, we know that competent and well-trained staff members are the cornerstone of our organizations' ability to provide quality services. The purpose of this part of the chapter is to develop an awareness of issues related to developing professional competence and to understand initiatives to ensure competence within the TR profession.

With ongoing budget and resource constraints in healthcare, TR service providers are faced with a continuous demand for standards of effectiveness and efficiency with at best modest budget increases. In this climate of "doing more with less and doing it better," it is clear why employers increasingly focus on methods to ensure professional competence and performance.

An important rationale for professionalism is based on the belief that competence can be ensured in the workplace by adherence to measures such as job standards. While the issue of professional competence is a crucial concern in all human service disciplines, there is little unanimity as to what it means in terms of job requirements. According to Stumbo and Carter (1999) the profession generally agrees on what constitutes the boundaries of the field in terms of practice, yet there is less agreement on curriculum and design.

Competence is a multifaceted, complex, and value-laden term. According to MacNeil, Teague, and Cipriano (1989) competence is based on three inter-related elements: knowledge, skill, and performance. Competence should not be determined by static knowledge or skills that may quickly become obsolete. Hence, continuing education is absolutely essential to keeping current and maintaining competence.

It is clear from this description that efforts to ensure competence must be flexible and individualized to respond to differences in practitioners' backgrounds, their degrees of ability, and myriad job functions (Stumbo, 1989). The measurement of professional competence is hindered by the difficulty in defining the concept of competence. It is difficult to distinguish differences between knowledge, skills, and performance because they interrelate.

Defining and delineating the practice is essential to many activities germane to an emerging profession, including standards of practice, certification, and accreditation (Connolly & Riley, 1995/1996, p. 26.). The competencies identified by certification and accreditation standards were derived from the profession's body of knowledge and a job analysis assumed to define the scope of practice.

Credentialing

Credentialing is an umbrella term used for any type of program that defines and recognizes professional competence. There are several different approaches to assuring professional competence: licensure, registration, certification, and accreditation. This chapter introduces four common methods used by different professions. Each has a unique mission and has advantages and disadvantages.

Licensure is the most restrictive form of credentialing because it requires a government agency to enact legislation defining professional practice. Licensure identifies the scope of professional practice and sets out criteria that a professional (with a license) can do. To obtain a license, a profession must convince the government agency the public may be harmed in the absence of a specific law or regulation.

The most common form of licensure in North America is a driver's license. To obtain a vehicle operator's (driver's) license one must demonstrate a set of minimum skills and knowledge identified by a government agency. Usually a license is time-bound, has demographic requirements, residence requirements, and a renewal process to become a member in good standing. While licensure ensures a minimal skill set, it does not address incompetent practice and does not promote current aspects of the field. Licensure usually requires a one-time demonstration of skill, with some record of performance and a cash transaction. Licensure in TR is uncommon. At the time of printing, licensure is a measure of professional competence only in Utah and North Carolina (Riley, 2004).

Registration is another term often associated with professional credentialing. Registration generally means all individuals who wish to engage in a given occupation need to register with a designated agency. Registration processes vary considerably. Some registrations involve the listing of one's name and paying a fee, other professional registrations require proof of educational background and specific demonstrated practice information. Because of the variance of registration processes it is difficult to determine how much registration will demonstrate TR competence. In Canada, registration in professional orders associations is common and often a requirement for employment. Professional orders verify the backgrounds of those registered and ensure they have minimal qualifications and related experience.

Certification is a voluntary national process whereby a nongovernmental agency or association grants recognition of competence to an individual who has met predetermined qualifications (Carter, 1998). Usually qualifications include graduation from an approved educational program, acceptable performance on a qualifying exam, and completion of some type of work experience. Certification requirements do not prohibit uncertified individuals from practice (not a government law), but they do prevent the use of professional titles or form delineations, such as the use of the title Certified Therapeutic Recreation Specialist (CTRS). Certification is usually a voluntary process not required to practice in the profession. Certification in TR in the United States and Canada will be highlighted in the next sections (Riley, 2004).

Accreditation is a process by which an institution, agency, organization, or program is reviewed to determine whether it meets specific standards or competencies (Zabiskie, 1998). Accreditation of educational programs may be used as a mechanism for upgrading and maintaining quality of personnel entering a given profession. It is a mechanism for ensuring educational programs have met certain requirements for faculty, resources, and curriculum.

According to Zabiskie (1998) the process of accreditation involves the following areas: determination of eligibility for evaluation, initiation process, self-appraisal of quality, formal hearing before accrediting commission, and ongoing evaluation. There are two types of accreditation: institutional and program specialization. *Institutional accreditation* for higher education facilities is implemented by regional associations that focus on the adequacy of the entire university and its personnel in terms of providing quality education (Reynolds and O'Morrow, 1985). *Specialized program accreditation* is usually conducted by a professional association and focuses on a narrower aspect of the university, such as a professional preparation program. In Canada, there is no formal program of accreditation. Colleges, departments, and programs typically have designed curricula to be consistent with the mission of the entire university. Only one Canadian university has sought accreditation for the leisure studies program. The Council on Accreditation (COA) administers accreditation of professional preparation programs in the United States through a cooperative agreement between NRPA and AALR.

United States

Much of what is known about professional competencies in therapeutic recreation has been developed within the United States. The first credentialing program for TR specialists began in 1956, when the Council for the Advancement of Hospital Recreation (CAHR) created the national Voluntary Registration Plan for hospital recreation personnel (Carter, 1981). CAHR established standards, decided on mechanism for implementing those standards, and formed the board of registration. Standards for professional registration included both education and experience, although educational requirements were sometimes waived for persons considered pioneers in the field (Carter, 1981). Registration was a two-part process: voluntarily listing one's name and a review of the candidate's education and experience. In 1967 the NTRS registration board continued the voluntary registration program for the TR personnel.

As the profession continued to develop and progress, expectations were also raised. It became clear that a higher level of competence was necessary. Initially the National Council for Therapeutic Recreation Certification (NCTRC) was managed by volunteers. In 1985, three part-time staff were added to manage the certification process. In 1986, the first full-time executive director was hired. By 1998, NCTRC staff had grown to 12 full-time and 3 part-time staff (Carter, 1981).

In 1982 the NCTRC established the test development and research committee. The committee established links with testing companies and conducted a variety of studies of entry-level practitioners in the field and undergraduate curricula in the United States. These activities led to the development of a test to ensure minimum competence of TR specialists. The certification test was based on a job analysis to identify content areas for examination. The test was first used as a part of the certification process in 1990. In addition, the NCTRC established a comprehensive list of requirements to become eligible for certification. The number of credentialed professionals has also grown since 1959, from the original 68 hospital recreation personnel to the current 17,000 certified TR practitioners. Approximately 2,000 new candidates apply each year (Carter, 1981).

There are two paths to professional certification of TR specialists in the United States: the academic path and the equivalency path. The *academic path* is for individuals who have completed a baccalaureate or higher in TR, or completed a major in recreation or leisure with a TR option. The *equivalency path* is for individuals with a related degree in another area of study. The NCTRC identifies specific requirements for certification, including coursework in TR, coursework in general recreation, supportive coursework and experience in TR practice. The NCTRC website (http://www.nctrc.org) lists the current requirements necessary to be eligible for certification. For 2003 applicants, the academic path requirements included a baccalaureate degree from an accredited college or university with a major in TR *or* a major in recreation or leisure with an option in TR, an official transcript to verify degree, and coursework including the following:

1. 18 semester hours of TR and general content coursework with no less than 9 semester hours of specific TR content (each course must be a minimum of 3 hours) ***and***

2. Supportive courses to include a total of 18 semester hours with a minimum of 3 semester hours in anatomy and physiology, human growth and development, and abnormal psychology. The remainder of coursework must be fulfilled in the content area of human services as defined by the NCTRC *and*

3. A minimum 480-hour, 12-week consecutive field placement in TR, which follows the TR process defined by NCTRC under the supervision of a TR specialist certified by NCTRC.

A full booklet of certification requirements can be downloaded from the NCTRC website (http://www.nctrc.org).

Canada

There are significant differences between Canada and the United States in terms of professional credentialing and determinants of TR competence. While understanding the experience of the United States is helpful, it is based on a much different model of government and quasi-governmental (e.g., corrections, hospitals nursing home) support. Canadian TR has a larger role in community service delivery. The diversity of Canadian TR makes the task of identifying universal standards difficult (Robertson, 1989). Over a decade ago, Hare and Frisby (1989) were critical of the lack of commonly accepted Canadian standards. While this is still true, some progress has been made.

CTRA was founded in 1993 (incorporated in 1996) in large measure to respond to the increasing interest in professionalization and accountability. Certification was identified as an important method to ensure professional competence through measures such as job standards, performance indicators, and outcome measures. Within Canada there has been significant support for making certification of TR professionals a reality. Thomas and Ostiguy (1998) reported on several provincial initiatives to certify individuals practicing in the TR field. Efforts to designing a system of credentialing are underway in Canada. Therapeutic Recreation Ontario (TRO) developed a working framework for a proposed plan of certification. CTRA set up a national task force to look at issues involved in certification. The CTRA annual conference (May 2004) focused on issues and challenges related to professional certification and standards.

Few studies have examined the TR profession in Canada. There is a general lack of knowledge of educational competencies and professional preparation of those working in the TR field. Nogradi, Weile, and Iles (1991) identified the learning needs for Ontario recreation (including TR) practitioners. Necessary skills in order of importance included human resource management, planning, public relations, education, collaboration, self-management, and computer technology. In a similar study in 1992, the Saskatchewan Recreation Society (SRS) identified educational competencies for TR professionals. The 24 competency areas—such as etiology of disease and illness, human anatomy, and medical charting—largely reflected the needs of practitioners in clinical settings. In 1994, Nogradi assessed the impact of a competency-based certification program sponsored by the Parks and Recreation Federation of Ontario. Based on 323 questionnaires and 41 focus groups Nogradi concluded there was widespread support for a competency based certification program. The key elements to such a plan, according to respondents, including continued learning, standards for acceptable performance and ethical practice, clear purpose and mandate for the profession, specific competencies for practice, and objective assessments of these competencies (Nogradi, 1994).

Some Canadian educational institutions and practitioners advocated that the TR professionals in Canada should pursue certification via the U.S. NCTRC process. Carter (1998) highlighted how certification increased professionalism in the United States, suggesting a model Canadians may want to follow. Contrary to the U.S. approach, Dieser (2000) maintained, "...jumping on the American certification bandwagon is a short sighted solution to increase the professionalization of TR in Canada and does not reflect the complex nature of certification in Canada" (p. 6). Further, Dieser argued, "Canadian TR professionals need to develop a therapeutic recreation philosophy and a model of practice that reflects a Canadian multicultural perspective, rather than simply adopting the Leisureability Model which embraces individualistic values that are prevalent in the United States" (p. 7).

Dieser and Ostiguy (2004) suggested a Canadian certification process should

> separate itself from the United States National Council on TR Certification (NCTRC) melting pot amalgamation ideology in which competencies must be a uniformed united one homogeneous body and develop a framework of certification based on the Multicultural Act of Canada and the Canadian political ideology of creating a mosaic of cultures. (pp. 22–23)

Many significant differences between Canada and the United States make the adoption of a universal (international) certification for TR a challenge and undesirable (Dieser & Ostiguy, 2004). To begin, Canada has a different political structure, with a liberal federal government with a mandate to support education, family, healthcare, and social programs. In Canada, universal healthcare coverage supports clinical and nonclinical initiatives in the community, especially in disease prevention and health promotion. Canadian TR practitioners work in many settings that would be considered nontraditional in the United States, such as school boards, municipalities, federal and provincial parks, and transitional environments (e.g., shelters for victims of violence and centers supporting immigrants). Each province is supported federally, but maintains autonomy over decisions related to priorities and administrative structure. This means that in each province TR may play a slightly different role and may be aligned with different professional unions, associations, and organizations (Dieser & Ostiguy, 2004).

Delamere and Ostiguy (2004) highlighted the challenges and feasibility of implementing the current NCTRC program in Canada. The few education programs make it difficult to ensure TR specialists across Canada have access to required coursework. The national association is small with limited representation from specific parts of the country. Costs for practitioners to be certified are much higher than required professional fees for organizations.

Canada is a bilingual country and offers services and programs in two official languages. This means that TR specialists may come from different educational backgrounds and may have studied in English, French, or both. To bridge the differences in language, educational preparation, and provincial policy, and to advance the profession of therapeutic recreation in Canada, Dieser (2002) argued the CTRA should separate itself from the NCTRC and design a certification process keeping with the multicultural policy in Canada—a policy that recognizes and promotes understanding and appreciating multiculturalism and reflects the cultural and racial diversity of Canada.

Several leaders voiced similar positions on multiculturalism. Watt (1995) suggested that social policies in human and social services in Canada would be most effective if they reflected a Canadian perspective premised on multiculturalism. Hutchison and McGill (1998) and Lord, Hutchison, and VanDerbeck (1991) argued in support of recreation and leisure services being based on multicultural and interdisciplinary models.

Dieser (2002) proposed a system of certification that supports the mosaic approach, including three requirements: core courses, support courses, and multicultural courses. With this proposal for a framework for Canadian certification, all university programs in Canada offering TR programs, specializations, or degrees would develop three uniform courses in TR, develop diverse support coursework in multiculturalism that reflects the strength of departments and university and require diverse coursework in multiculturalism that draws on the expertise of other disciplines. The only standardized (melting pot) component would be the three core courses in TR. Different universities would develop different multicultural coursework and support courses. University curricula could therefore build on the strengths and interest areas of the faculty. The benefits of this approach are that it

- reflects the mosaic philosophy and Multicultural Act of Canada.

- develops creative and innovative thinking in terms of TR.

- draws from a number of disciplines to support the profession and body of knowledge.

- has greater flexibility to respond to clients from diverse backgrounds.

- supports diversity in thinking.

- addresses the reality of the increasing challenge of finding qualified faculty to teach TR courses.

In the proposal by Dieser (2002), CTRA and universities would develop a formal partnership in creating the three core classes, thus maintaining accountability to consumers and employees by underscoring how TR specialists should have a solid set of skills and knowledge to be an effective practitioner.

The Canadian Therapeutic Recreation Association task force on certification is working to establish professional standards, review job descriptions and roles, and examine a variety of proposed models for credentialing. Information and updates on the certification process can be found on the CTRA website (http://www. canadian-tr.org/about_ctra.htm).

Summary

This chapter outlined the professional development of therapeutic recreation in the United States and Canada. In so doing similarities and differences between the two nations were featured. Because of different political systems, social support, health networks, and cultural mix, therapeutic recreation is exposed to varied external forces in each country. As a result the profession looks somewhat different in each country today, and likely will continue to be different in the future. This presents both a challenge and an opportunity to professional organizations representing therapeutic recreation. An appreciation and respect for the varied development of the profession in the global community will likely bring practitioners together to share research, knowledge, and skills that will enrich the lives of their clients. Conversely, parochial attitudes about what therapeutic recreation should be—a "one size fits all" approach—will likely promote the continued unraveling of therapeutic recreation across national borders.

References

Austin, D. (1989). Therapeutic recreation education: A call for reform. In D. Compton (Ed.), *Issues in therapeutic recreation: A profession in transition* (pp. 145–156). Champaign, IL: Sagamore Publishing.

Austin, D., Dattilo, J., and McCormick, B. (2002). *Conceptual foundations for therapeutic recreation.* State College, PA: Venture Publishing, Inc.

Carter, M. (1981). Registration of therapeutic recreators: Standards from 1956 to the present. *Therapeutic Recreation Journal, 15*(2), 17–22.

Carter, M. (1998). Increased professionalism: An experience from the United States. *Journal of Leisureability, 25*(2), 20–25.

Connolly, P. and Riley, B. (1995/1996). Entry level job skills: Reinvestigation of the national job analysis of the practice of therapeutic recreation. *Annual in Therapeutic Recreation, 6,* 26–37.

Dieser, R. (2000). Professionalization and certification: The need for critical thinking and discussion. *Tribune, 1,* 6–7

Dieser, R. (2002). *Accreditation, certification, registration—What should we do? Outlining a Canadian vision for TR professionalism.* Paper presented at the Canadian TR Association annual conference, Calgary, Alberta, Canada.

Dieser, R. and Ostiguy, L. (2004). A proposed framework for TR certification in Canada. *Expanding Horizons in Therapeutic Recreation, XXI,* 21–26.

Delamere, F. and Ostiguy, L. (2004). Where do we go from here? TR in Canada. Presentation at the Canadian TR Association Annual Conference, Montreal, Quebec, Canada.

Hare, L. and Frisby, W. (1989). The job competencies and educational needs of therapeutic recreationist in Ontario. *Journal of Applied Recreation Research, 15*(1), 15–24.

Hutchison, P. (1983). *Curriculum guidelines for Canadian colleges and universities: Leisure and disabled persons.* Ottawa, Ontario, Canada: Canadian Parks and Recreation Association.

Hutchison, P. and McGill, J. (1998). *Leisure integration and community* (2nd ed.). Toronto, Ontario, Canada: Leisureability Publications.

Keller, J. (1989). Professional leadership: Honor or responsibility. In D. Compton, *Issues in therapeutic recreation: A profession in transition.* Champaign, IL: Sagamore Publishing.

Langsner, S. (1994). Deterrents to participating in continuing professional education: A survey of NTRS. *Therapeutic Recreation Journal, 28*(3), 147–162.

Lord, J., Hutchison, P., and VanDerbeck, F. (1991). Narrowing the options: The power of professionals in daily life and leisure. In T. L. Goodale and

P. A. Witt (Eds.), *Recreation and leisure: Issues in an era of change* (3rd ed.; pp. 275–305). State College, PA: Venture Publishing, Inc.

MacNeil, R., Teague, M., and Cipriano, R. (1989). The discontinuity of continuing education. In D. Compton (Ed.), *Issues in therapeutic recreation: A profession in transition* (pp. 157–182) Champaign, IL: Sagamore Publishing.

Millerson, G. (1964). *The qualifying associations: A study of professionalization.* In D. Compton (Ed.), *Issues in therapeutic recreation: A profession in transition* (pp. 1–15). Champaign, IL: Sagamore Publishing.

Navar, N. (2001). Keynote: Thoughts on therapeutic recreation education. In N. Stumbo (Ed.), *Professional issues in therapeutic recreation: On competence and outcomes.* Champaign, IL: Sagamore Publishing.

Nogradi, G. S. (1994). The importance and impact of certification for parks and recreation practitioners in Ontario. *Journal of Applied Recreation Research, 19*(1), 23–40.

Nogradi, G., Weile, K., and Iles, L. (1991). Partners in training: Working toward a desired future for training and development. *Journal of Applied Recreation Research, 16*(2), 93–115.

O'Morrow, G. (1997). Does accreditation of therapeutic recreation programs make a difference? Pro and con. In D. Compton (Ed.), *Issues in therapeutic recreation: Toward a new millennium* (2nd ed.; pp. 237–254). Champaign, IL: Sagamore Publishing.

Reynolds R. P. and O'Morrow G. S. (1985). *Problems, issues and concepts in TR.* Englewood Cliffs, NJ: Prentice Hall.

Riley, R. (2004). The value of a national certification program. Presentation at the Canadian Therapeutic Recreation Association conference, Montreal, Quebec, Canada.

Robertson, T. (1989). Standards versus practice: Is there a gap? In D. Compton (Ed.), *Issues in therapeutic recreation: A profession in transition.* Champaign, IL: Sagamore Publishing.

Sabine, G. H. (1961). *A history of political theory* (3rd ed.). New York, NY: Holt, Rhinehart and Winston. In D. Compton (Ed.), *Issues in therapeutic recreation: A profession in transition* (pp. 1–15). Champaign, IL: Sagamore Publishing.

Searle, M. S. and Brayley, R. E. (1993). *Leisure services in Canada: An introduction.* State College, PA: Venture Publishing, Inc.

Sessoms H. D. (1991) The professionalization of parks and recreation: A necessity. In T. L. Goodale and P. A. Witt (Eds.), *Recreation and leisure: Issues in an era of change* (3rd ed.; pp. 247–261) State College, PA: Venture Publishing, Inc.

Stumbo, N. J. (1989). Credentialing in therapeutic recreation: Issues in ensuring minimal competence. In D. Compton (Ed.), *Issues in therapeutic recreation: A profession in transition* (pp. 67–86). Champaign, IL: Sagamore Publishing.

Stumbo N. J. and Carter M. J. (1999). National therapeutic recreation curriculum study part A: Accreditation, curriculum and internship characteristics. *Therapeutic Recreation Journal, 33*(1) 46–60.

Sylvester, C. (1992). Therapeutic recreation and the right to leisure. *Therapeutic Recreation Journal, 16*(2), 9–20.

Sylvester, C. (1998). Careers, callings and the professionalization of TR. *Journal of Leisureability, 25*(2), 3–13.

Thomas, M. and Ostiguy, L. (1998). Therapeutic recreation: Profession at a crossroads. *Journal of Leisureability, 25*(1), 26–36.

U.S. Department of Labor, Bureau of Labor Statistics. (2004). Recreational therapists. Retrieved February 17, 2004, from http://www.bls.gov/oco/ocos082.htm

Watt, S. (1995). Canadian realities. In J. C. Turner and F. J. Turner (Eds.), *Canadian social welfare* (pp. 120–129). Scarborough, Ontario, Canada: Allyn & Bacon Canada.

Zabiskie, R. (1998). Accreditation: Are we there yet? Perspectives of a doctoral student. In B. A. Hawkins (Ed.), *Historical perspectives on the development of NRPA/AALR council on accreditation* (pp. 103–116). Ashburn, VA: National Recreation & Parks Association.

Section 3

Practice of TR

Chapter 7

Recreation Therapy Versus Recreation Services

Learning Objectives

1. Summarize the means/ends controversy.

2. Explain how the scientific method (used by the medical professions) is reflected in therapeutic recreation practice.

3. Explain how healthcare reform has supported a means approach to therapeutic recreation.

4. *Can* therapeutic recreation prove its effectiveness and/or *should* therapeutic recreation prove its effectiveness (with respect to functional outcomes and the medical model)?

5. Identify the professional organizations that have participated in the means/ends debate. Summarize the position of each.

6. Compare and contrast the three different versions of the means approach articulated by Goodzeit, Shank and Kinney, and Russoniello.

7. Explain recreation as an end using a social psychological (optimal incongruity) approach.

8. Define White's neurogenic motive for human behavior. Explain how it pertains to therapeutic recreation.

9. Summarize Sylvester's criticisms of the means approach to therapeutic recreation.

10. Defend either the means or the ends approach to therapeutic recreation, supplying arguments consistent with the strength of the approach you have selected.

> This history of therapeutic recreation has at least one consistent theme: the uneasy fit between recreation as a contribution to the normalization and life quality of persons with disabilities and recreation as a means to improve an individual's psychological and physical functioning. (Shank & Kinney, 1987, p. 65)

This quote captures the essence of the disagreement about the primary purpose of therapeutic recreation among practitioners and educators. This historical problem dates back to the formation of the first organizations that represented therapeutic recreation professionals. This chapter describes and discusses the problem: the conflict between recreation (and leisure) as a worthy outcome of the therapeutic recreation process in and of itself versus the use of recreation (and leisure) as a means to improve some other health-related concern (e.g., depressive symptoms, physical strength) or as means to develop specific skills.

What Is the Problem?

Representatives for each position (recreation therapy and recreation services) can be found in the literature, although few are straightforward about their thinking. Three representatives for each of the possible positions on therapeutic recreation serve to underscore the salient features of each approach: means, ends, and combined.

Means Approach (Recreation Therapy)

The means approach can be expressed directly as "therapy means treatment" (Goodzeit, 1967). Goodzeit emphasized therapy is required to ameliorate disease and symptoms associated with such conditions, and enjoyment is a trivial byproduct of the therapeutic process.

Ends Approach (Recreation Services)

The ends approach is repeated throughout Haun's (1966) *Recreation: A Medical Viewpoint*. It emphasizes recreation/enjoyment is a basic human need. Simply because a person is impaired does not mean the individual can be walled off from customary human needs and rights. From this perspective therapeutic recreation is offered as a necessary service because it is an end in itself—a normal human need not suspended just because the person is ill.

Combined Approach (Recreation Therapy and Recreation Services)

The combined approach maintains recreation may be used as both a "tool" for therapeutic change and simultaneously as an enjoyable outcome "for its own sake." Hunnicutt (1980) articulated the combined position well in stating, "therapeutic recreation is unique because it rests on recreation's subjective quality (the individual's own state of mind, his fun) at the same time it provides tangible evidence that real medical and health goals are served through recreation" (p. 132). While this chapter focuses on the extremes of the means/ends continuum, the reader would do well to appreciate the middle ground described by Hunnicutt, which more accurately represents how therapeutic recreation is actually delivered in real world settings.

The means/ends problem will not likely be solved, because it comes down to values. Therapeutic recreation is usually defined in value-laden terms (Widmer & Ellis, 1998). Whenever issues amount to deciding on what is "right," the inevitable result will be that at least one other alternative will be "wrong." And no final truth, no lasting proof, no scientific gold standard exists to make the decision for the student or practitioner. This chapter provides the reader with a comprehensive review of the means and the ends approaches, the strengths and weaknesses of each position, and the implications of each position for practice. In the end, however, because the means/ends controversy is a moral and ethical question, only the reader can make a decision about which approach (or compromise) is appropriate or correct.

Why Is It a Problem?

Following a comprehensive assessment of the literature on the means/ends debate in therapeutic recreation, Yoshioka (2001) concluded in the United States, the medical model was the template for how allied healthcare professions implemented services. In a similar vein, Rusalem (1973) remarked earlier that thinking in treatment terms underlies much of what therapeutic recreation had become in the 1970s. These same observations are true today. Therapeutic recreation, indeed most of allied healthcare services in clinical environments (e.g., physical/physio therapy, occupational therapy), conforms to a medical model of thinking about rehabilitation—cure and remediation of illness and symptoms.

First of all, as a clarification for the reader, the medical model implies the same approach to therapeutic recreation thus far described as the means approach. Since the Hippocratic oath, medicine has pledged to take control over the recuperation of the client from impairment, doing everything humanly possible to help the person to recover. To advance medicine's capacity to "cure" clients, a particular method of doing the business of medicine was adopted—the scientific method. While the scientific method is not unique to medicine, medicine has been the premier field to use the scientific method in its routine practice, and the influence is both unmistakable and widespread.

The scientific method is easy to recognize if restated in terms of the therapeutic recreation process: assessment, planning, implementation, and evaluation. Like doctors, therapeutic recreation professionals assess the client to determine problem areas and to find a baseline for comparison. One cannot know whether improvement has occurred unless one knows where the client begins. Next, based on the assessment, the practitioner uses logic and research evidence to select an intervention with the best prospects for reversing the illness, the condition, or its symptoms. The intervention is implemented for a predetermined period of time and the client's response to the intervention is monitored through ongoing evaluation. If clinically significant improvement is observed, the treatment may be continued, augmented, attenuated, or stopped depending on what the practitioner deems in the best interest of the patient.

Hence, the medical model provides a template for other allied health professions to imitate when designing an approach to illness and rehabilitation. Its influence has been widespread, and most readers will have little difficulty recognizing the assessment, planning, implementation, and evaluation (APIE) process that has become the prototype for therapeutic recreation program design.

The medical model is also intuitively appealing because of its compelling logic. It represents a systematic way of thinking that helps the practitioner to avoid casual, haphazard, and thoughtless intervention. It mimics the manner in which most research is conducted. Finally, because of its heritage as a way of showing cause–effect in research, it has great appeal when allied health professions are mandated to show how they are effective in bringing about functional improvement in clients served. Therapeutic recreation has been and will continue to be influenced by this way of thinking. The medical model provides a concrete approach to demonstrating outcomes of therapeutic recreation.

Given the environment in healthcare over the last 20 years or so, it is understandable that therapeutic recreation practitioners, especially clinicians, gravitated to the medical model/means approach to implementing services. In 1987 Shank and Kinney summarized the pressures under which clinically based therapeutic recreation specialists operated, and their observations are especially true today. They maintained that healthcare reform had changed rehabilitation into a business. No longer can practitioners in any profession simply do as much as they could for the client, with some assurance that most expenses would be compensated (retrospective payment system).

By the mid-1980s in the United States, a prospective payment system was all but put in place. This new brand of healthcare scrutinized every potential treatment and intervention prior to its application, evaluating variables such as prospects for success, research support, and value (i.e., how likely is the treatment to work and how much better off will the patient be for having received the treatment). Based on this before-treatment cost–benefit analysis, decisions were made about what kinds of treatments were effective (in functional terms), and which patients were good candidates for which treatments. What was implemented was a system of healthcare gatekeeping that continues today.

The prospective payment system was necessitated by skyrocketing healthcare costs and irresponsible practices on the part of the healthcare professions (especially prescribing interventions not medically necessary). Although clients were told the reason for reform was quality assurance, lurking just below the surface was the real issue of cost containment: It had become too expensive to do everything possible (medically) for every client.

Given this environment, it should be of little surprise that therapeutic recreation ascribed to the same medical model template for planning and implementing services. Likewise, casual review of the professional literature from the mid-1980s to the present aptly demonstrates that the therapeutic recreation field has been calling for efficacy studies for almost 20 years. Efficacy research is designed to show the effectiveness of any number of therapeutic recreation interventions in bringing about significant functional improvements (e.g., less depression, better self-esteem, increased endurance, less perceived pain) in clients.

Hence, adoption of the medical model, the emblem of the means approach to therapeutic recreation, seems to have been a natural response to the pressures and problems of working in a clinical environment and trying to "fit in" with that culture—of trying to be accepted as legitimate members of that culture. Two questions emanate from the use of the medical model by therapeutic recreation.

1. Can therapeutic recreation live up to the expectations for rigorous research to substantiate the effectiveness of recreation in causing clinically important changes to occur?

2. Should therapeutic recreation pursue the means approach, patterning itself after the medical model template like the balance of allied health professions?

The first question is answered briefly here and in more detail later in the chapter (see Recreation as a Means, p. 167). In short, considerable effort has gone into therapeutic recreation research over the last 20 years, with mixed results. The studies most reliable at demonstrating the effectiveness of therapeutic recreation interventions have been small sample studies of five people or less. While these findings are laudable, they do not amass the kinds of data sufficient to persuade the community of healthcare professions and insurers that rely on large sample (e.g., hundreds or thousands of subjects), highly controlled, clinical trials (e.g., as in testing a new drug). The few studies in therapeutic recreation that have employed larger samples tend to show positive correlations between recreation and some functional improvements, but these studies do not show the kind of cause–effect evidence needed to prove the effectiveness of therapeutic recreation as a means of clinical change.

The lack of sufficient empirical evidence to support the effectiveness of therapeutic recreation in bringing about functional gains in clients disturbs the clinical practitioner, but the emphasis on locating the value of therapeutic recreation in instrumental outcomes equally disturbs practitioners in less clinically oriented settings, especially where reimbursement for services does not depend on demonstrating functional improvements. Another group of therapeutic recreation practitioners is more interested in responses to the second question posed: Should therapeutic recreation be focused primarily on bringing about functional improvement through the use of recreation as a treatment modality? Is something important lost when the means/medical model approach is taken with patients?

Rusalem (1973) was among the first to suggest another method of understanding the value of therapeutic recreation might be superior to following the medical model. Rusalem imported an ecological model for understanding therapeutic recreation from education. The ecological model was later supported by Howe-Murphy and Charboneau (1987). An ecological approach (one of several "ends" approaches to therapeutic recreation) stresses changing the *environment* in preference to changing the client as in most intervention biased models. Rusalem argued in many cases the pathology did not lie with the individual, but instead with an insensitive society that failed to make the adaptations and accommodations necessary to lead a quality life. Rusalem recommended changing the surroundings ought to be the value imperative of the therapeutic recreation specialist through the provision of enjoyable recreational experiences that could be taken on their own terms. Free of concern over manipulating recreational activities, the practitioner could concentrate on what recreation is best suited for—an enjoyable experience and worth experiencing for its own sake.

Moreover, Rusalem (1973) pointed out the means/medical model approach failed many times, citing cases of relapse and high recidivism rates among clients with cognitive and emotional impairments. Tangible outcomes are also difficult to evaluate with clients with terminal illness or progressive conditions. In sum, Rusalem suggested the medical model was not even working for medicine and another method was indicated. In Rusalem's opinion, therapeutic recreation, as well as most other allied health professions and special education, would be better served and more effective if they adopted an ecological approach that emphasized changing environments and attitudes to be more receptive to the needs and interests of persons with disabilities. Under an ecological paradigm, it made sense that therapeutic recreation would be more interested in configuring environments to enhance the recreational opportunities and enjoyment of the clients served.

However, to understand Rusalem, one must appreciate the historical context in which he wrote. Sweeping social reform and social reform legislation loomed on the horizon. The dawn of accessibility and advocacy was at hand. This time of the 1970s was a time of social concern and social reform. The federal government in particular mandated sweeping changes in the way persons with disabilities could live, generally advancing the quality of life for these individuals dramatically. Equal access to public education and public facilities became the law, and aggressive deinstitutionalization allowed more persons with mild to moderate impairments to live in the "mainstream" community and to hope for a better quality of life. Recreation service provision was seen as a part of this initiative. People with disabilities deserved the same "right to leisure" as part of a larger government assurance of the right to life, liberty and the pursuit of happiness (Sylvester, 1992). The NTRS even adopted a philosophical position statement in 1982 that declared that all persons had a "right to leisure" regardless of ability. Likewise, the Leisure Ability Model (Peterson & Gunn, 1984; Stumbo & Peterson, 1998) of therapeutic recreation became the dominant model of practice, also based on the ultimate aim of cultivating an appropriate/satisfying leisure lifestyle.

A Brief History of the Problem

Although many students of therapeutic recreation may have read recent versions of what has come to be known as the means/ends controversy, the problem is not a new one. Disagreement about the primary intent of recreation with and for persons with disabilities, impairments, and chronic conditions is at least as old as the assembly of therapeutic recreation specialists into professional organizations. In the United States, the Hospital Recreation Section (HRS) of the American Recreation Society (ARS) first formed in 1948. It comprised mostly hospital recreation workers with a long tradition of providing recreation programs for veterans in military hospitals both during and between wars.

Shortly after organization of the HRS, other organizations affiliated with therapeutic recreation were formed. One in particular brought the means/ends controversy into greater relief: the National Association of Recreational Therapists (NART). NART was formed in 1953 in response to the absence or the lack of emphasis by ARS on clinical outcomes and the role of recreation in bringing about functional improvement in clients.

Carter, Van Andel, and Robb (1995) summarized the distinction between therapeutic recreation services (ARS position) and recreational therapy (NART position). *Therapeutic recreation services* provide meaningful leisure experiences that promote the enjoyment of the clients during their time as inpatients, whereas *recreational therapy* focuses on the use of recreational activities to bring about functional improvement and remediation of an illness or its symptoms. Clearly, the latter approach emphasizes recreation as therapy and treatment; the former approach sees leisure as part of quality healthcare and quality of life within a civilized society.

But the controversy may have started well before the formation of professional organizations such as ARS and NART. Recreation workers in veterans and military hospitals were the heirs to a tradition of therapeutic recreation services provided for wounded soldiers by Red Cross workers during the First World War. However, by the late 1930s a new version of therapeutic recreation was on the horizon, cultivated primarily by the play therapy approach of the Meninger Clinic. Based on Freudian psychoanalysis, the play therapy approach assumed the client (usually a child) had some internal conflict to be resolved, and play was one modality for working through that turmoil. Further, "selected recreational activities were carefully matched with the particular needs of the individual and used to alleviate or reduce the primary symptoms of illnesses" (Carter et al., 1995, p. 41). Clearly, the practitioners at the Meninger Clinic had in mind that therapeutic recreation (play therapy) could be adapted to specific treatment goals.

The merger of NART and HRS (1966) into the National Therapeutic Recreation Society (NTRS) branch of the National Recreation and Parks Association (NRPA) appeared to put the conflict between means and ends to rest. But the truce was only temporary. Dissatisfied with the support given to NTRS regarding clinical concerns and governance issues by its NRPA parent organization, Peterson (1984) and others formed an organization completely devoted to therapeutic recreation issues and concerns in 1984—the American Therapeutic Recreation Association (ATRA). Although ATRA did not start out as an organization that represented a particular approach (means or ends) to therapeutic recreation, it soon became the representative of clinical concerns with a focus on the means argument and medical model. Its 1990 definition of therapeutic recreation (see Chapter 1) clearly underscores its bias toward functional outcomes and an instrumental approach to therapeutic recreation (recreational therapy) practice. ATRA resurrected the NART-preferred "recreational therapy" to refer to treatment services. Understandably, clinical practitioners began to gravitate to ATRA, and community-based practitioners found NTRS more in line with their (leisure outcome) orientation toward therapeutic recreation.

Hence, although ATRA did not begin as an organization that represented clinical interventions (and functional outcomes emphasis), it soon came to be understood as the preferred organization for clinical practitioners in therapeutic recreation. And although NTRS did not begin as an organization that represented primarily community-based therapeutic recreation, it evolved into that role. The net effect of this dual representation of the profession was to deepen the rift between the two camps and to polarize the field further.

In Canada, the Canadian Therapeutic Recreation Association (CTRA) formed in 1993 (incorporated in 1996) to address TR professional issues and the goal to unit TR practitioners across the country. (For more information on TR in Canada, see Chapter 6.) The CTRA has not focused specifically on the means/end debate. Since CTRA members come from all types of the facilities and settings where TR is practiced, no distinction is made between clinical and community TR. The orientation of the CTRA is to provide support for TR practitioners across the country following a combined approach supporting TR specialists working in both clinical and community environments. The association provides suggested standards of professional practice similar to U.S. organizations with criteria related to assessment, program development, program delivery, documentation, evaluation, research, and professional development (Canadian Therapeutic Recreation Association, 1996, p. 3).

Recreation as a Means

Goodzeit (1967) was certainly among the first since the inception of the NRPA/NTRS to advocate for an instrumental/means approach to therapeutic recreation. The intervention is designed to lead to the remediation of disability, disease, and/or symptoms associated with the person's primary condition. Goodzeit made the distinction between specific planned recreation interventions and recreation offered as a diversion. Exposure to nondirective recreational activities cannot be confused with the systematic and purposeful interventions reserved for therapy. In short, the activity cannot be the primary intent of the recreative experience—fun, enjoyment, and participation for its own sake cannot qualify as therapeutic recreation. According to Goodzeit, fun is secondary—remediation of disease or symptom is the focus and emphasis.

Goodzeit (1967) further maintained recreational pursuits were the means through which children with disabilities (his primary area of focus) developed activity skills (presumably he is referring to motor activity here) leading to developmental progress and amelioration of symptoms. And it was because the recreation was directed at advancing the development of the child and addressing the symptoms that *therapeutic* was a deserved adjective in therapeutic recreation. Someone who merely observes a recreational activity cannot benefit, it was the active involvement that qualified as therapeutic recreation's active ingredient—the "stuff" that made it work.

According to Goodzeit (1967), it was acceptable for an activity to be enjoyable because the "fun" was an inducement to draw the child into active involvement. But fun could not be the ultimate reason for participation, at least in the mind of the recreational therapist. Enjoyment was a lubricant to ease the child's involvement in the activity.

Furthermore, therapy could take place only in a rehabilitative setting. Goodzeit used this assumption as a justification for segregation of therapeutic recreation efforts. When children with disabilities are integrated and included in regular (presumably community-based) programs "...we remove them from the therapeutic and rehabilitative milieu" (p. 31). Treatment for Goodzeit not only meant therapy, it also occurred only in "protected settings." This latter point is very consistent with a medical model—a Hippocratic-like approach to therapeutic recreation—and very paternalistic.

The arguments in favor of therapeutic recreation as a means to rehabilitation became more sophisticated in the decades following Goodzeit's rather uncompromising point of view. Shank and Kinney (1987) argued supporting a leisure lifestyle was an impractical goal for therapeutic recreation. But, perhaps as a result of the burgeoning healthcare reform movement of the mid-1980s, they also recognized the setting did not determine whether recreation was being used as a therapeutic device or an outcome.

Unlike Goodzeit, they did not insist on segregation of the client as a criterion for therapy. Likely, a decade or more of mainstreaming and inclusion as well as the increasing emphasis on outpatient and community-based health care led to this conclusion. Although the setting did not qualify the activity as therapy, Shank and Kinney (1987) argued two criteria did.

1. The agency mandate/mission should point to the overall purpose of activity/business carried on by the agency. Under this condition recreation would be used as therapy if the agency's mission were one of rehabilitation or improvement of functional skills.

2. A therapy context is characterized by a special relationship that develops between the client and the therapist, and that relationship serves as a catalyst for change (in the client).

Similar to the Leisure Ability Model of practice, Shank and Kinney (1987) maintained the person must regain competencies necessary for satisfying leisure before talk of a satisfying leisure lifestyle is even a prospect. They use the term *preleisure* to represent that class of competencies that were necessary precursors to satisfying leisure participation. These competencies laid the necessary foundation for subsequent leisure.

Like most medical model approaches, the preleisure concept of Shank and Kinney (1987) stressed a paternalistic attitude toward the client. But they maintained this was especially necessary in the case of persons with cognitive and neurological impairments, whose judgment may be impaired. This means client consultation, or the "informed consent" seen as part of some more recent models of practice, is invalid. According to Shank and Kinney choice is not a right for all clients. Sometimes clients make bad or incorrect choices, especially during their free time. Examples include smoking, alcohol, and other substance abuse; eating disorders; and criminal or delinquent behavior.

Shank and Kinney (1987) placed conditions on choice by clients, perhaps believing this was what separated therapy and autonomous leisure participation. They maintained the person had to be cognitively sound and able to act on his or her choice—to be empowered to take action based on that choice.

Besides using preleisure to acquire competencies, Shank and Kinney (1987) also believed therapeutic recreation could serve an important role in the area of illness-induced stress, the stress associated with the fact that the person is sick or impaired. Specifically, they suggested therapeutic recreation could help the patient to cope with stress and feelings of helplessness and hopelessness. Hence, they concluded therapeutic recreation served a dual role as therapy

1. by helping the person adapt by coping with stress.

2. by using recreational activities to build functional skills needed later to lead a satisfying leisure lifestyle.

Russoniello (1994) crafted a more clinical version of the instrumental approach to therapeutic recreation shortly after the appearance of the Shank and Kinney work. He claimed therapeutic recreation could bring about physical changes that lead to functional improvement of the client. He based his medicine model of therapeutic recreation on the use of variables inherent to recreation activities to bring about changes. These inherent characteristics of recreation were exercise, laughter, and a thrill response. All three characteristics of recreation activity were thought to act in the same manner—by stimulating the endocrine (hormone) and nervous systems to change in ways that resulted in less physiologic stress. In addition, he argued recreation participation caused the release of hormones thought to be beneficial for the individual, especially with respect to depression.

Scientists have known for many years there is a genuine connection between body and mind—how we "feel" affects our physical and emotional health. This is accomplished through a connection between the endocrine system and nervous system in at least two places. The most important connection is between part of the brain known as the hypothalamus and a vital endocrine gland, the pituitary gland. The other connection is between the nervous system and another endocrine gland, the adrenal gland. Hormones secreted by both glands can have beneficial or detrimental affects on physical and emotional health depending on timing and amount of secretion. Hence, Russoniello's foundation in the science of mind–body relationships is sound.

Based on these assumptions and facts, Russoniello (1994) designed a version of the medical model of therapeutic recreation that would, on most accounts, qualify as the most aggressive yet. Based on knowledge about how the endocrine and nervous systems responded to exercise, he maintained therapeutic recreation could actually prescribe dosages of recreational activities to address specific problems. This amounted to prescriptive therapeutic recreation practice, very closely approximating the practice of medicine, and the exercise prescription approach of traditional physical therapy practice.

Russoniello (1994) also presented research data he asserted lent support to his medicine model approach to therapeutic recreation. Certain hormonal concentrations changed with each of three types of recreational activity, and these changes were associated with positive changes in mood states, especially depression.

Based on his findings, Russoniello (1994) advocated for the prescription of specific recreational activities for specific problems and conditions. "The key signs, symptoms, and the disease or illness itself, henceforth, become the clinical indicator from which the therapist prescribes treatment and evaluates effectiveness" (p. 255). Based on Russoniello's hypothesis, the challenge for therapeutic recreation researchers and practitioners alike is to identify specific treatment approaches for specific problems—which symptoms and impairments respond to which activities. The recreation activity, then, becomes the medicine—the active ingredient of therapeutic recreation.

Research Support

Each position on therapeutic recreation places a specific demand on the kinds of research and scholarship support required. For the means/instrumental position, the burden is on therapeutic recreation to demonstrate its efficacy with respect to functional and symptom-driven outcomes. The most pressing research need for an instrumental approach to therapeutic recreation "...continues to be the demonstration of the degree to which and the conditions under which therapeutic recreation services make a significant difference in clients' physical and mental well-being and their functioning" (Iso-Ahola, cited in Mobily, 2000, p. 304). Hence, the means approach relies heavily on efficacy studies.

Two types of sources may be used to illustrate the partial fulfillment of this research challenge. The first is an impressive compendium of studies published in the early 1990s, *Benefits of Therapeutic Recreation: A Consensus View* (Coyle, Kinney, Riley & Shank, 1991). The work grew out of a conference that gathered experts in subspecialties in therapeutic recreation at Temple University. Delegates were given the task of assembling evidence in the form of comprehensive literature reviews to support various aspects of therapeutic recreation effectiveness with various disability groups (e.g., physical medicine, gerontology). Authors in each area were successful at gathering impressive lists of citations and wrote summaries based on those works.

The second encouraging source of efficacy studies in therapeutic recreation is *Therapeutic Recreation Journal* for the last two decades. Within the articles published by the journal there has been a decided change in the theme. The shift has been more in the direction of intervention/efficacy studies. The results have been encouraging—most of the studies have found significant improvement in one or more functional or symptom-driven outcomes after exposure to some type of therapeutic recreation intervention.

The problems with both of these sources of evidence are apparent. As far as the benefits of therapeutic recreation literature review is concerned, most of the evidence supporting the use of recreation as a therapeutic modality is correlational. This means the findings of studies pertaining to the efficacy of therapeutic recreation, while encouraging, do not meet all of the standards for "proof" in the scientific community. A typical finding might be demonstrating that a group of clients is less depressed after participating in recreation over the course of time than before they participated in recreation. While this is certainly a heartening result and points toward a causal relationship between therapeutic recreation and depressive symptoms, it cannot handle criticism from skeptics.

Taken at face value, this finding may be questioned if a control group (i.e., a comparable group of clients who did not receive therapeutic recreation services) was not used so that the changes in depressive symptoms of the treatment group (i.e., the group receiving therapeutic recreation services) could be compared to a group not receiving recreation. If a control group was used but clients were not randomly assigned to treatment and control groups, then there is reason to question whether the groups were comparable to begin with. The real danger lies in the risk that those in the treatment group were in some way biased (i.e., more likely to become involved in the first place) toward responding favorably to recreation participation than those in the control group. Another challenge of control group studies is the reality of excluding clients from TR services offered in an agency. The challenge for therapeutic recreation in research and practice is many of the traditional methods of science used to establish causal relationships are not easily exported to practical settings (Coyle, Kinney & Shank, 1993). This leaves the findings of therapeutic recreation research on the efficacy of services encouraging but not scientifically convincing.

The second category of studies published in *Therapeutic Recreation Journal* may be questioned because of small sample sizes and qualitative data. While the small sizes of single subject research alone are not a problem, small sample studies do limit the extent to which findings can be generalized to other clients with similar problems or impairments. Further, although qualitative studies offer information and provide a rich source of detail about a specific intervention, the client–therapist relationship, and the client's response to the intervention, the small sample size and inability to test a hypothesis statistically limit the impact of these findings.

In summation, the kind of research needed to provide convincing evidence therapeutic recreation is effective in bringing about functional change or improvement in symptoms related to impairment remains an urgent need if the means argument is to be supported and promoted. Therefore, although the results of research on the efficacy of therapeutic recreation are heartening, limitations in data quality have hampered the advancement of therapeutic recreation as a treatment modality on par with other health professions focused on therapy (e.g., physical/physio therapy). The next section dedicated to satisfying leisure as the preferred result of therapeutic recreation intervention calls into question the need for research pertaining to functional outcomes.

Recreation as an End

The plainest expression of the "ends" or intrinsic position in therapeutic recreation is associated with the Leisure Ability Model. (See Chapter 9 for details on this model.)

> Leisure, including recreation and play, is an inherent aspect of the human experience....Some human beings have disabilities, illnesses or social conditions which limit their full participation in the normative social structure of society. These individuals with limitations have the same human rights to, and needs for, leisure involvement. (Peterson & Gunn, 1984, p. 321)

A more recent version of the Leisure Ability Model restates this same sentiment: "the first assumption is that every human being needs, wants, and deserves leisure" (Peterson & Stumbo, 2000, p. 8). Clearly the authors of the Leisure Ability Model have consistently based therapeutic recreation service on the assumption that leisure is a basic human need and deserved by all people, regardless of ability. Other authors have supported the intrinsic value of leisure as the primary outcome and purpose of therapeutic recreation.

Sylvester (1987) and others (Hemingway, 1987; Lee, 1987) maintained leisure is an innate human need. The study of leisure behavior in general over the last 30 years serves as a foundation for the intrinsic approach to therapeutic recreation.

The body of leisure theory and research demonstrated two clear patterns. First, people are more likely to report experiencing leisure when they believe (perceive) they are free. Second, when people are free (self-determined) they believe (perceive) they are in control of their (leisure) behavior. The net effect of these two relationships is that people are psychologically healthier when participating in self-determined leisure activity (Iso-Ahola, 1980).

The groundbreaking work of Ellis (1973) and Iso-Ahola (1980) sets the stage for a social psychological approach to therapeutic recreation, which largely supports the intrinsic approach to therapeutic recreation. Ellis developed a position on the research that accompanied the reconstruction of motivational psychology in the late 1950s and early 1960s. An *optimal incongruity* view of leisure behavior suggested people (primarily children in Ellis's research) play because the play environment presents (stimulates) them with challenge and uncertainty. The actor then behaves in a manner that reduces uncertainty, mastering the environment along the way.

The other half of Ellis's (1973) hypothesis referred to behavior once the actor has mastered the environment—that is, achieved competence. In theory, the actor becomes bored with the play environment once he or she has eliminated all of the uncertainty and challenge. The play environment then becomes too predictable, and to maintain leisure motivation the actor must find a new challenge, a new place, or a new game to play. While this may explain much of play in young children, it fails to explain much of adult leisure, because adults tend to return to the same (mastered) leisure activities again and again.

The answer to this problem lies in recognizing adult leisure is much more complex and people only *seem* to behave in a repetitious, boring manner. For example, shooting the same 18 holes of golf on the same course for many years remains stimulating because golf is a very difficult game to master. The same course may seem identical to the novice, but on closer examination of the activity, the social company may change (e.g., playing with friends vs. playing in a competitive league) or the context may change (e.g., pin placement, altered traps). In this way a person can seek competence and optimal incongruity at the same time—he or she has achieved a certain degree of competence in becoming a better golfer, but the course remains challenging because certain variables are altered to exert subtle but unmistakable challenges that continue to stimulate participation.

Iso-Ahola's (1980) version of the intrinsic position is grounded more in clinically driven research, mostly found in the psychological and social psychological literature, but later replicated to a limited extent in the therapeutic recreation literature (e.g., Shary & Iso-Ahola, 1989). Iso-Ahola constructed a rationale for therapeutic recreation based on the fact that patients in healthcare settings can be given choices in their leisure activities, and they can come to perceive themselves as competent and capable participants in their world. In this sense, they can reclaim some of the control they lost when they became sick.

An extension of this point was applied to a related concept—learned helplessness. People who repeatedly lose control over their personal environment may come to perceive themselves as helpless. Those most vulnerable are affected by some traumatic event that changes their life, especially if the person was not responsible for the traumatic event. Many illnesses and injuries play out this way; they are often unpredictable and the victim frequently concludes that the injury means he or she is no longer in control of his or her destiny.

Iso-Ahola (1980) maintained leisure was a method for reclaiming at least a portion of control. When therapeutic recreation provides leisure opportunities that translate into a choice for the actor, the actor perceives he or she is free. When therapeutic recreation provides instruction through leisure education or reeducation, the actor is empowered; he or she is taught or retaught how to perform competently in an array of activities. This two-fold benefit of leisure participation is especially effective in countering learned helplessness, because therapeutic recreation provides instances of exactly the opposite experience: control and empowerment. Further, Iso-Ahola contended when people believe they have a choice (in leisure) and when they come to perceive themselves as competent (in leisure), the net result is intrinsic motivation—the ends approach to therapeutic recreation.

Earlier Haun (1966) expressed the intrinsic position of therapeutic recreation more directly, arguing that fun is a basic human need and a primary biologic activity. His arguments in support of the intrinsic position began as more philosophical in character than either Ellis or Iso-Ahola. Haun believed recreation was essential, but recreation was not therapeutic in the traditional sense of the word *therapeutic*. He insisted therapeutic recreation would head down a blind alley if it pursued the traditional therapy approach to justifying itself (the means approach), because he was convinced therapeutic recreation could not establish its effectiveness based on a medical model approach. "If we hold that it [recreation] is therapeutic, then recreation must be judged on its effectiveness in arresting and relieving illness" (Haun, 1966, p. 57).

Instead Haun (1966) preferred that therapeutic recreation base its justification on its role in developing the *therapeutic milieu*. He thought of therapeutic recreation as "...an important means of increasing the effectiveness of therapy. While not curative in itself, it helps create the milieu for successful treatment" (Haun, 1966, p. 55). This may be seen as a sort of enzymatic effect of recreation (Mobily, 1996); it potentiates the rehabilitation process. The presence of therapeutic recreation services then serves to catalyze the effectiveness of physical therapy, occupational therapy, and so on.

In rejecting mind–body dualism (e.g., the notion that what people think has little to do with how they feel physically), Haun (1966) maintained therapeutic recreation can be justified in part because it is biologically built into the human species. White's (1959) seminal work on competence motivation further supported Haun's observation of recreation's biological link. White contended humans are unlike most other animals—they actively seek stimulation and possess a "neurogenic motive" (a need to be stimuated). While most other species are content with predictability and their nervous systems find quiescence the normal state, the human nervous system is designed for activity and activation. White claimed the *normal* state for the human nervous system, unlike our animal cousins, is activation; the human nervous system needs and wants stimulation. The human will actively work in ways to make the environment stimulating if it is not. And this behavior, White insisted, we recognize as play (leisure and recreation).

When Haun said recreation is a primary biological activity and when Ellis stated people play to make the environment optimally stimulating, they intuitively referred to White's neurogenic motive for human behavior. White (1959) used many examples of play to illustrate his hypothesis about the human need for stimulation.

The End as a Moral Matter

Regardless of the hypotheses forwarded by various scientists, the debate over whether therapeutic recreation is best suited as a mechanism to promote a "cure" or an end in itself is a philosophical one—a matter of ethics and morals. The following underscores some of the moral issues that bear on the quality of the leisure experience as an outcome for therapeutic recreation.

Earlier we cited Haun (1966) as an enthusiastic supporter of therapeutic recreation in clinical settings, but not as therapy. Rather, he insisted recreation's value for patients related to the fact it was not traditional therapy in the way physical therapy is therapy. Haun contended therapeutic recreation's value was "extra clinical," implying its value as a necessary part of the human experience.

Like Haun (1966), Widmer and Ellis (1998) and Sylvester (1992) argued that the primary purpose of therapeutic recreation is to help clients achieve well-being through leisure. But well-being here is used to imply more than physical health or rehabilitation. For these authors, well-being implies persons served by therapeutic recreation will advance their freedom and responsibility and increase their prospects for happiness and a good life.

In this case "happiness" is used in its traditional, philosophical sense; it means much more than mere pleasure. A good life (happiness) includes finding meaning and purpose to living. It assumes people make choices, act on those choices, and take responsibility for those choices. Happiness, in this case, comes close to the meaning implied by life satisfaction.

Sylvester (1992) asserted the pursuit of well-being through leisure was the better purpose of therapeutic recreation on moral and ethical grounds. He further based his assertion on two weaknesses in the instrumental (means) approach to therapeutic recreation.

1. Efficacy studies in therapeutic recreation were neither abundant nor of the quality necessary to make strong cause–effect assertions about recreation's effectiveness as a therapeutic modality.

2. Even if therapeutic recreation was able to produce convincing and conclusive evidence of recreation's effectiveness as a therapeutic device, there would remain a question of duplication. Specifically, if therapeutic recreation was configured in such a way as to produce functional outcomes, then the activities would look more like tasks and chores than leisure. If the activities were no longer recognizable as leisure (enjoyment), the effective services would amount to a duplicate of occupational therapy.

Instead, Sylvester (1996) suggested therapeutic recreation would be advised to stake its future on something more closely related to the true nature of recreational and leisure activities—seeking to promote well-being through participation in enjoyable activities. He maintained (as did Richter & Kashalk, 1996) that leisure helps clients to find a purpose to life—"having something worth getting up for...requires a substantive goal or end, like a friend to visit....Without meaningful activities in one's life, standing and walking eventually lose their attraction..." (Sylvester, 1996, p. 101). In other words, functional outcomes only have "function" when harnessed to another meaningful activity. The point of relearning how to walk after a traumatic injury is not to be a proficient walker, but to be able to walk with a purpose.

From Sylvester's point of view, this makes leisure (and therapeutic recreation) as an end a higher purpose than recreation as a means.

Another argument along the same lines as Sylvester's is found in Mobily (1996). He argued leisure offered through therapeutic recreation services represented the client's opportunity to have a glimpse at normalcy in an otherwise routine, scheduled, and predetermined day. Certainly, schedules and prescribed rehabilitation are necessary for efficient achievement of treatment goals. The respite offered within therapeutic recreation is a symbolic expression of normal, an "oasis of happiness" (Fink, 1974) in an otherwise regimented day of rehabilitation.

Advantages of Each Position

Advantages of the Means Approach

The intuitive reaction is to associate the means approach to therapeutic recreation with clinical settings, and the ends approach to therapeutic recreation with community-based settings. However convenient this may be, it would be shortsighted and unduly simplistic to reduce this discussion to such a black and white solution.

Nevertheless, the means approach to therapeutic recreation does fit well with clinical culture, an environment commonly driven by one's capacity to demonstrate functional outcomes and to secure compensation for services rendered. And the practical reality for many therapeutic recreation specialists is that they must attempt to blend with the clinical culture of inpatient services. While a practitioner may harbor an affinity for implementing therapeutic recreation using leisure activities to promote a satisfying leisure lifestyle, the priority of inpatient services is functional outcomes. With the costs of inpatient care today, hospitals cannot afford to spend time and resources on "nice but not necessary" interventions. With shorter stays and a decrease in funds available, the means approach is practical, functional, and necessary.

Some in-roads with respect to insurer reimbursement for therapeutic recreation services have been made, especially in the areas of leisure education, transition planning, and assessment (Rath & Page, 1996). With some inventiveness, therapeutic recreation practitioners may find a silver lining to the dark cloud of healthcare reform and cost containment. Another reality is therapeutic recreation specialists can perform some of the tasks commonly assigned to physical/physio therapy and occupational therapy more efficiently. Therapeutic recreation can, for example, plan and implement a program of mild to moderate, low risk exercise for persons with arthritis-related syndromes. Furthermore, costs will be lower because therapeutic recreation specialists do not cost as much as physical therapists, and therapeutic recreation services are commonly delivered on a group rather than individualized basis. This approach has two advantages: (1) it frees the physical/physio therapist to work with more serious and demanding cases, and (2) it allows the therapeutic recreation specialist to deliver services efficiently (i.e., group activities are cheaper per capita).

In addition, with the rise in chronic conditions that comes with an aging population, the demographics suggest an ongoing need for "therapy" in outpatient settings. For instance, a person with arthritis needs a lifetime of supportive services, including regular exercise, symptom management education, and social support. The problem is that these "therapies" are not cost-efficient when offered by rehabilitation professionals (e.g., occupational therapy) in traditional rehabilitation settings (e.g., hospitals). The window created between pent-up demand for continuous, preventive therapy (e.g., health promotion) and the inability of conventional medicine to deliver the needed services in an efficient manner represents *the single biggest opportunity for therapeutic recreation in the last 50 years.* Therapeutic recreation is capable of delivering many of the needed services, in an outpatient (community-based) setting, for a fraction of the cost of traditional, inpatient rehabilitation.

The preceding example illustrates why it is not always prudent to associate the means or instrumental approach to therapeutic recreation with only clinical settings. Clearly therapy using recreation as a modality for bringing about functional improvements in clients is feasible and even practical in community-based settings as well.

Finally, recent research in therapeutic recreation provided a reason for optimism with respect to the means approach to therapeutic recreation. Over the last decade or so, small scale intervention studies have proven to be reliably favorable with respect to the effectiveness of a variety of modalities. In particular, leisure education, aquatic therapy, strength training, and health promotion initiatives demonstrated remarkable effectiveness with a variety of impairments and chronic conditions. Although small sample and qualitative studies are not a substitute for clinical trials and quantitative research, these studies do mark an improvement over the correlational results characteristic of studies of the 1980s and early 1990s. Even small sample studies can demonstrate efficacy through functional relationships between the intervention and the outcome. Through replication, therapeutic recreation will build a body of research knowledge that eventually will demonstrate the effectiveness of therapeutic recreation interventions.

In Canada, healthcare is provided through a socialized (subsidized) system. Even though health services are publicly supported through tax dollars, there is an increasing need to be accountable in the provision of services. To manage increasing costs of healthcare, there is a movement to greater emphasis on measuring and evaluating outcomes of therapeutic recreation. The means approach provides greater opportunity to fund TR because of direct links to functional improvements, which ultimately have greater cost benefits.

On moral grounds, one of the advantages of the means approach to therapeutic recreation is the link to a Hippocratic tradition of care. This tradition of care has persisted even though it is difficult to provide all the care one would like in an era of healthcare cost containment. However, the tradition of altruistic care should not be jettisoned. Instead, the profession should come to terms with the realities of ever expanding healthcare costs. This may mean the healthcare professional endeavor to provide as much of the best quality of care feasible, with the recognition that the client may have to share some of the financial burden himself or herself, out-of-pocket. Hence, the client may choose to pursue some therapy programs and not others.

For the practice of therapeutic recreation, the combination of maximum service provision at a minimum of price means services using the means approach may be provided in a community-based setting. Services would compliment inpatient services, but the patient would be free to choose which services he or she wished to consume. The patient would likely share the expense with an insurer—out-of-pocket, but at a reduced rate. For example, mild to moderate intensity exercise programs, offered on a group basis, may be provided by therapeutic recreation professionals for outpatients, instead of by physical/physio therapists on an inpatient basis.

Although some (Lahey, 1987) rightly argued the medical model (means approach) may give rise to paternalism, it is hard to argue that its intent is not altruistic. Others (Widmer & Ellis, 1998) pointed out some clients may not be able to choose and to act on their choices. With the aging population and the increased incidence of chronic conditions, the probability that more clients will be affected by dementia and other neurological impairments is high. This suggests that the number of clients unable to make informed and rational choices for themselves will increase, and they will look to healthcare professionals, including therapeutic recreation specialists, to guide them. Hence, one could argue the means approach and the directive approach it fosters is a matter of necessity.

Lastly, the advantage of the perspective of the medical model is it fosters a scientific, systematic approach to research and practice in therapeutic recreation. A scientific approach to therapeutic recreation is one of the advantages associated with the means approach. We ought not to forget the legacy of systematic thinking about practice inherited from the medical model, even if the practitioner adopts an ends approach to therapeutic recreation. It has been the difference between the purposeful intervention associated with therapeutic recreation and a diversional approach to service provision.

Advantages of the Ends Approach

Intuitively, most believe the ends approach correlates well with community-based therapeutic recreation. This is because community recreation in general responds to all consumers by providing recreational services and programs consistent with the needs and wishes expressed by constituents. On the surface of things, ideas such as the right to leisure, perceived freedom, and self-determination through leisure are the therapeutic recreation equivalent to basic community recreation services. The only difference between services to persons with disabilities and general able-bodied consumers in the community from this point of view is that consumers with disabilities may need accommodations to receive services in as normal an environment as possible.

But this interpretation would not do justice to the ends approach to therapeutic recreation. The ends approach avoids the need for convoluted arguments and rationales designed to justify therapeutic recreation's place in clinical settings or in rehabilitation, whereas the means approach has to reconcile (sometimes through tortuous and questionable arguments) the fact that recreation should be "fun" with the claim that therapeutic recreation services can improve functional outcomes. Those espousing the ends approach to therapeutic recreation have the luxury of resting their services on something close to the very nature of recreation and leisure activities—enjoyment. The community recreation specialist providing services to persons with disabilities is free to market his or her "product" based on a claim that therapeutic recreation can support, with little argument required. Providing leisure to persons with disabilities because they are citizens in a community just like able-bodied persons is a right to leisure claim. It needs little in the way of extensive rationale because it is self-evident that leisure and recreation are part of the aggregation of rights the citizen in the community inherits.

Citizens in a democratic society have the right to life, liberty, and the pursuit of happiness. Persons with disabilities are no less citizens of that same community. Therefore, they have the same rights as other members of the community. They have the right to leisure.

Leisure under the ends approach takes on a moral meaning not only because it belongs to a collection or rights the person has, but also because it may be the most exquisite expression of freedom available to the person with a disability. Few other opportunities are as freeing as leisure. The freeing aspect of leisure relates to its position "in but not of the world" (Huizinga, 1950). People play and pursue leisure in the real world, but they do so in a "playground"—a place marked off from the real world but residing in the real world. Special rules apply within the playground, different from those of the ordinary world. It is this aspect of leisure (and play) that maximizes freedom—the person freely chooses to be in the playground.

If freedom means being able to choose and carry out purposes (Muller, 1978), then one would be most free in circumstances in which an activity held consequences only for the actor. This is because the results of the act do not affect anyone else, and in a free society citizens are free to act as they wish so long as they do no harm to themselves or others. Hence, because leisure's consequence is enjoyment, pursuit of leisure presents very little risk for harm.

Second, leisure represents a collection of activities the actor can carry out with some degree of competence. Furthermore, leisure activities maximize the probability for a perception of competence on the part of the actor because "success" is often subjective and individually defined. Everyone, regardless of ability, can achieve a sense of competence, if he or she balances ability against an activity-based challenge (reflected in the concept of "flow"; Csikzentmihalyi, 1975).

In sum, if freedom means the ability to choose and to carry out purposes as Muller (1978) suggested, then leisure is the most eloquent expression of freedom. This is especially the case for persons with disabilities, who may not have the capacity or opportunity to choose and carry out purposes in other spheres of life (e.g., work).

The right to leisure and the pursuit of leisure may lead to other expressions of freedom. Over the last 50 years or so, the recreation movement in general and the field of therapeutic recreation in particular have been linked to normalization (and to related initiatives, such as inclusion). Normalization is the right of a person with a disability to live as normal a life as possible. Part of living as normally as possible is to live openly and publicly, integrated with able-bodied citizens whenever and wherever feasible. The research and programming literature in therapeutic recreation has developed into a substantial knowledge base to underscore the fact that the leisure experience of the person with a disability is enriched when it takes place in an integrated setting. Certainly, an integrated leisure activity is not something to enter into haphazardly—considerable education, planning, and design of program and community are prerequisites to success. Nevertheless, research in therapeutic recreation supports the fact that the effort is worth it because it often results in advancing the quality of the person's leisure experience.

Therefore, the case for an ends approach to therapeutic recreation is based on its fit with community-based therapeutic recreation efforts. But focusing on the quality of the leisure experience reveals other advantages. The ends approach may be more appropriate in certain clinical environments that focus less on functional improvement and more on designing TR services and programs to improve or to maintain quality of life (e.g., nursing homes). Therapeutic recreation is on solid moral ground, because the purpose of participation is enjoyment. Freedom is often realized through leisure when emphasis is placed on enjoyment as well. And leisure activities provided through therapeutic recreation services make available opportunities to advance the lifestyle of the person with a disability toward normalcy.

Disadvantages of Each Position

The short answer to the matter of disadvantages is differences among professionals pertaining to the best path for therapeutic recreation to follow have polarized the TR field in the United States into two camps. The means approach is more aligned with ATRA and clinical therapeutic recreation, whereas the ends approach is more commonly associated with NTRS and community-based therapeutic recreation. These perceptions, like most, are only partially true and exaggerated. But real or not, they nevertheless contribute to the polarization of the field. Part of the explanation for why therapeutic recreation has less impact on healthcare legislation and the health insurance industry is that we have taken a growing but small field and divided it into two cultures of care.

For those espousing the ends approach to therapeutic recreation, any functional improvement is characterized as a "side effect" (e.g., Haun, 1966; Lee, 1987)—a benefit not central to the true nature of recreation and leisure activities (e.g., enjoyment). Understandably, this attitude does not sit well with clinical therapeutic recreation specialists who must answer to treatment teams, medical directors, and financial officers concerned about necessary service and outcomes that make a difference in the patient's ability to function independently in the real world.

Conversely, the professional espousing the means approach maintains that while enjoyment is fine as an inducement for participation, it is not the element that makes recreation a therapy. Central to the interests of the clinical practitioner are functional outcomes. If enjoyment is the purpose of recreation for persons with disabilities, then the practice is not measurably different than recreation for a person without a disability.

Summary

In truth, it is almost impossible for the practitioner to identify many agencies using an exclusively means approach or an exclusively ends approach. Most settings articulate some version of a combined approach to therapeutic recreation, and show concern both about clients achieving functional improvement and about clients enjoying their participation. The practitioner must attempt to interpret and to understand the prevailing culture of care in the agency, then decide whether one's own philosophy of therapeutic recreation fits with the agency's culture. But what happens most often is the practitioner will find an eclectic approach, combining both means and ends.

Perhaps this is the final answer to the controversy that will not likely ever be settled. Using recreation as both a means and an end may be forever linked, impossible to separate (Hunnicutt, 1980; Mobily, Weissinger & Hunnicutt, 1987). The instrumental value of therapeutic recreation is jeopardized if the activity is not enjoyable, and if the TR specialist is too directive and prescriptive. Some of the best research (e.g., Iso-Ahola, 1980; Shary & Iso-Ahola, 1989) in therapeutic recreation that substantiates the efficacy of services relies on the perceptions of freedom and control on the part of the client. In other words, the moment therapeutic recreation professionals attempt to deliver their services in a prescriptive manner is the same moment those services fail to have a functional impact. However, if TR services focus only on the ends and fail to demonstrate the direct impacts of TR interventions, then it will not be supported within healthcare. Functional outcomes and enjoyment join in therapeutic recreation.

References

Canadian Therapeutic Recreation Association. (1996). *CTRA member manual.* Quebec, Canada: Author.

Carter, M. J., Van Andel, G. E., and Robb, G. E. (1995). *Therapeutic recreation: A practical approach* (2nd ed.). Prospect Heights, IL: Waveland Press.

Coyle, C. P., Kinney, W. B., Riley, B., and Shank, J. W. (1991*). Benefits of therapeutic recreation: A consensus view.* Ravensdale, WA: Idyll Arbor.

Coyle, C. P., Kinney, W. B., and Shank, J. W. (1993). Trials and tribulations in field-based research in therapeutic recreation. In M. J. Malkin and C. Z. Howe (Eds.), *Research in therapeutic recreation* (pp. 207–232). State College, PA: Venture Publishing, Inc.

Csikzentmihalyi, M. (1975). *Beyond boredom and anxiety: The experience of play in work and games.* San Francisco, CA: Jossey-Bass.

Ellis, M. (1973). *Why people play.* Englewood Cliffs, NJ: Prentice Hall.

Fink, E. (1974). The ontology of play. *Philosophy Today, 18,* 147–161.

Goodzeit, J. M. (1967). Therapeutic recreation vs. recreation for the handicapped. *Therapeutic Recreation Journal, 1*(2), 6–9, 30–31.

Haun, P. (1966). *Recreation: A medical viewpoint.* New York, NY: Teachers College Press.

Hemingway, J. (1987). Building a philosophical defense of therapeutic recreation: A case of distributive justice. In C. Sylvester, J. L. Hemingway, R. Howe-Murphy, K. Mobily, and P. Shank (Eds.), *Philosophy of therapeutic recreation: Ideas and issues* (pp. 1–16). Alexandria, VA: National Recreation and Park Association.

Howe-Murphy, R. and Charboneau, B. G. (1987) *Therapeutic recreation intervention: An ecological perspective.* Englewood Cliffs, NJ: Prentice Hall.

Huizinga, J. (1950). *Homo ludens.* Boston, MA: Beacon Press.

Hunnicutt, B. K. (1980). To cope in autonomy: Therapeutic recreation and the limits to professionalization and intervention. In G. Hitzhusen, J. Elliott, D. J. Szymanski, and M. G. Thompson (Eds.), *Expanding horizons in therapeutic recreation VII* (pp. 121–134). Columbia, MO: University of Missouri.

Iso-Ahola, S. E. (1980). Perceived control and responsibility as mediators of the effects of therapeutic recreation on the institutionalized aged. *Therapeutic Recreation Journal, 14,* 36–43.

Lahey, M. P. (1987). The ethics of intervention in therapeutic recreation. In C. Sylvester, J. L. Hemingway, R. Howe-Murphy, K. Mobily, and P. Shank (Eds.), *Philosophy of therapeutic recreation: Ideas and issues I* (pp. 17–26). Alexandria, VA: National Recreation and Park Association.

Lee, L. L. (1987). A panic attack in therapeutic recreation over being considered therapeutic. *Therapeutic Recreation Journal, 21*, 71–78.

Mobily, K. E. (1996). Therapeutic recreation philosophy re-visited: A question of what leisure is good for. In C. Sylvester (Ed.), *Philosophy of therapeutic recreation: Ideas and issues volume II* (pp. 57–70). Arlington, VA: National Recreation and Park Association.

Mobily, K. E. (2000). An interview with professor Seppo Iso-Ahola. *Therapeutic Recreation Journal, 34*, 300–305.

Mobily, K. E., Weissinger, E., and Hunnicutt, B. K. (1987). The means/ends controversy: A framework for understanding the value potential of TR. *Therapeutic Recreation Journal, 21*(3), 7–13.

Muller, H. J. (1978). Freedom is natural, acquired, and circumstantial. In J. A. Gould (Ed.), *Classic philosophical questions* (3rd ed.; pp. 490–501). Columbus, OH: Merrill.

Peterson, C. (1984). A matter of priorities and loyalties. *Therapeutic Recreation Journal, 18*(3), 11–16.

Peterson, C. A. and Gunn, S. L. (1984). *Therapeutic recreation program design* (2nd ed.). Englewood Cliffs, NJ: Prentice Hall.

Peterson, C. A. and Stumbo, N. J. (2000). *Therapeutic recreation program design* (3rd ed.). Boston, MA: Allyn & Bacon.

Rath, K. V. and Page, G. (1996). *Understanding financing and reimbursement issues.* Arlington, VA: National Recreation and Park Association.

Richter, K. J. and Kaschalk, S. M. (1996). The future of therapeutic recreation: An existential outcome. In C. Sylvester (Ed.), *Philosophy of therapeutic recreation: Ideas and issues volume II* (pp. 86–91). Arlington, VA: National Recreation and Park Association.

Rusalem, H. (1973). An alternative to the therapeutic model of therapeutic recreation. *Therapeutic Recreation Journal, 7*, 8–15.

Russoniello, C. V. (1994). Recreational therapy: A medicine model. In D. Compton and S. E. Iso-Ahola (Eds.), *Leisure and mental health* (pp. 247–258). Park City, UT: Family Development Resources.

Shank, J. and Kinney, T. (1987). On the neglect of clinical practice. In C. Sylvester, J. L. Hemingway, R. Howe-Murphy, K. Mobily, and P. Shank (Eds.), *Philosophy of therapeutic recreation: Ideas and issues I* (pp. 65–75). Alexandria, VA: National Recreation and Park Association.

Shary, J. M. and Iso-Ahola, S. E. (1989). Effects of a control relevant intervention on nursing home residents' competence and self-esteem. *Therapeutic Recreation Journal, 23*, 7–15.

Stumbo, N. J. and Peterson, C. A. (1998). The Leisure Ability Model. *Therapeutic Recreation Journal, 32*, 82–96.

Sylvester, C. (1987). Therapeutic recreation and the end of leisure. In C. Sylvester, J. L. Hemingway, R. Howe-Murphy, K. Mobily, and P. Shank (Eds.), *Philosophy of therapeutic recreation: Ideas and issues I* (pp. 76–89). Alexandria, VA: National Recreation and Park Association.

Sylvester, C. (1992). Therapeutic recreation and the right to leisure. *Therapeutic Recreation Journal, 26*, 9–20.

Sylvester, C. (1996). Instrumental rationality and therapeutic recreation: Revisiting the issue of means and ends. In C. Sylvester (Ed.), *Philosophy of therapeutic recreation: Ideas and issues volume II* (pp. 92–105). Arlington, VA: National Recreation and Park Association.

White, R. W. (1959). Motivation reconsidered: The concept of competence. *Psychological Review, 66*, 297–333.

Widmer, M. A. and Ellis, G. D. (1998). The Aristotelian Good Life Model: Integration of values into therapeutic recreation service delivery. *Therapeutic Recreation Journal, 32*, 290–302.

Yoshioka, N. (2001). *Le raison detre: Existentialism and therapeutic recreation philosophical position.* Unpublished master's thesis, University of Iowa, Iowa City.

Chapter 8

The TR Process

Learning Objectives

1. Define the eight components of the therapeutic recreation (TR) process.

2. Define the three fundamental principles of a therapeutic relationship based on a Rogerian approach to the client.

3. Explain how being a teacher (in leisure education) can help to establish a therapeutic relationship with a client. Consider front-loading, debriefing, feedback, and metaphor.

4. Define self-disclosure. Explain why a TR specialist needs to use this technique cautiously.

5. Define the three basic techniques of data collection used during assessment.

6. Define validity, reliability, and practicality. Explain why they are desirable characteristics of a measurement instrument.

7. Identify the three parts to a behavioral/performance objective. Write a sample behavioral/performance objective for the following three areas of behavior: physical, mental, and emotional.

8. Explain the differences between standardized programs and protocols that may be used during the implementation part of the TR process. Provide one example of each.

9. Define and distinguish between evaluation and monitoring. Explain when each would be of value to the practitioner.

10. Define documentation. Give three examples of items that may be documented in a patient's chart (written or electronic).

11. Define the roles of professionals on a treatment team with whom a TR specialist may work.

12. Discuss the role of TR in transition planning. Pay particular attention to the usefulness of leisure education in transition planning.

The TR process includes the following features: establishment of a therapeutic relationship, individualized assessment, goal setting and the design of an individual treatment/program plan, implementing TR services with selected interventions, evaluating progress toward the plan, developing a discharge/transition plan, coordination of services, and documenting the outcome of services. (Luken & Rios, 1998, p. 3)

Clearly, the therapeutic recreation (TR) process is not unique to the clinical environment. Built from years of job analysis research that polls certified therapeutic recreation specialists (CTRS), the TR process represents a succinct description of the tasks and duties that a "typical" TR specialist engages in during the day. The TR practitioner can work in clinical settings, community settings, or any variation of these settings. The important point is the TR process is shared among all TR professionals, regardless of where the service delivery occurs.

The TR process delineates the characteristic tasks of the TR specialist, though most would admit that the delivery of TR services involves more. The TR process statement seeks to identify the common ground shared by all TR workers, the duties that unite the profession, and the basis on which a common dialogue can rest (e.g., assessment implies the same meaning to the clinical CTRS and the community CTRS). Said simply, the TR process can occur anywhere and is feasible in any setting.

The definition of the TR process that began this chapter implies two other facts about the profession. First, it clarifies that the TR process is more than the familiar acronym APIE (assessment, planning, implementation, evaluation). This chapter seeks to demonstrate that the therapeutic relationship between the client and the therapist is perhaps the most important aspect of practice. Without an effective therapeutic relationship, implementing the remaining parts of the TR process will be difficult if not impossible.

Second, as pointed out elsewhere in this textbook, the practice of TR is systematic, calculated, and purposeful. The description of the TR process supplied by Luken and Rios (1998) underscores the careful planning and implementation that occur when the consumer or client is served by a TR specialist. The plan, once implemented, is monitored and adjusted, if warranted. The plan includes coordinating TR service with those complimentary services provided by allied professions also working with the client. Finally, provisions are made by way of a transition plan for the client once he or she is through receiving direct services.

Collectively, the TR process is a minimal job description for the field and a set of agreed on tasks shared by all members of the profession. It is the tie that binds TR specialists together—whether working in a transition program for adults with developmental disabilities, a clinical rehabilitation unit for persons with brain injuries, or a community-based program for older adults. Regardless of position or setting, the TR process joins the profession together.

The Therapeutic Relationship

A TR practitioner once said to be an effective TR specialist "you have to be a good and mature person." Of all of the tasks a practitioner has before him or her, establishing a good (effective) and mature relationship (not a friendship) with the client is the most essential. All else depends on the kind of relationship the therapist and the client have with one another. Therefore, we begin the presentation of the TR process with the keystone to the entire process: the therapeutic relationship.

TR specialists must consider themselves to be instruments of change. The most important therapeutic device the practitioner has is himself or herself. No assessment, plan, or protocol can be as effective as the personality the therapist imparts to interactions with the client. And although helping relationships bear a striking resemblance to friendships, they are not the same. "Professional helping relationships have much in common with social relationships. Nonetheless, there are distinctions between helping as a professional and helping as a friend" (Austin, 1997, p. 201). The practitioner has a professional obligation to be self-aware—that is, to be alert to his or her own interests and motives for the relationship with a client.

A Rogerian Heritage

The TR specialist must keep the needs and interests of the client foremost in his or her mind, suppressing his or her own needs for affiliation until with peers and friends. Austin (1997) described characteristics of the therapeutic relationship that have a long history in humanistic and Rogerian psychology.

In the 1950s and 1960s Carl Rogers' approach to psychotherapy was a dominant force in psychology, education, and counseling. Although his contributions (Rogers, 1961) have been modified and configured to fit many different professions, his basic tenets for a productive helping relationship have weathered time and remain largely unaltered.

Like most practitioners with existential leanings, Rogers believed the capacity for productive change resided within the individual. The therapist was present only to stimulate, to evoke, and to facilitate the patient's progress toward productive therapeutic change. The client would discover his or her inner strength and capacity for change as a result of this relationship with the therapist. The result would be a change in attitude toward oneself (e.g., more favorable self-esteem) that would translate into positive behavioral changes.

Through various means and publications Rogers laid out his framework for therapeutic relationships founded on three fundamental principles: being genuine, being accepting, and expressing a desire to understand. Although the words used to describe this relationship vary from source to source, the final account always comes down to these three attributes.

Being Genuine

First, the therapist must be aware of his or her own feelings and be willing to express them, tempered with tact and without malice. Rogers (1961) thought "being real" would induce the client to behave in the same way, to say what was really on his or her mind. In other words, the therapist helps the client to seek his or her reality by expressing his or her (the therapist's) reality.

Being Accepting

Second, the therapist should be accepting of the person as someone with worth and value. Furthermore, this acceptance should be unconditional. This is not to say that the therapist endorses antisocial behaviors or nonproductive actions, strategies, or attitudes. But it means the client deserves respect as a person with the right to search for his or her own meaning and life.

Expressing a Desire to Understand

Third, the therapist should reflect a sincere attitude to understand—a sensitive empathy. "Traveling" with the client metaphorically, accompanying the client, trying to imagine how the client really feels—this is what Rogers (1961) meant by being understanding. This attitude frees the person to look inside and to change (positively) his or her attitude toward oneself. Rogers (1961, p. 34) maintained:

> the relationship which I have found helpful is characterized by a sort of *transparency* on my part, in which my *real* feelings are evident; by an *acceptance* of this other person as a separate person with value

in his own right; and by a deep empathetic *understanding* which enables me to see his private world through his eyes [italics added].

The TR literature is frequented by essentially the same description of the
therapeutic relationship that we seek to establish with our clients. It is also
worth noting that the therapeutic relationship described by Rogers, and later
Austin (1997) and others, exhibits an important congruence with leisure theory.

Much of our understanding of leisure behavior is based on the notions of
perceived freedom and self-determination. Further, many practice models of
TR include choice, freedom, and responsibility on the part of the client and
the therapist. It seems fitting that the fundamentals of Rogerian psychology
fit well with leisure theory and models of practice, because Rogers believed
the motivation for change is ultimately the person's choice and responsibility.

Methods of Helping

Although it goes without saying that the primary means of establishing a
sound therapeutic relationship with a patient is through conversation and
verbal interactions, several other methods can initiate this relationship. These
include journaling (Murray, 1997) and several teaching techniques (Hutchinson & Dattilo, 2001).

The manner in which Murray (1997) described journaling leaves ample
room for the client to share experiences through written, artistic, or other
means. Journaling may be immediately less threatening for the client because
the narrative or picture is addressed to an inanimate object to start (the piece
of paper in the journal). Depending on the amount of control the client has
over who sees the journal, he or she can release aspects of his or her personal
and subjective experience gradually, discovering whether the reader can be
trusted with the client's shared experience. Journaling, therefore, qualifies as
another means of sharing one's subjective reality.

On reading the journal, the TR specialist should reflect the behaviors
characteristic of any humanistic/Rogerian transaction (e.g., being genuine,
accepting, and understanding). As with Rogerian techniques used in conversation, so too in reflecting on a client's journal the TR specialist can help the
patient to make sense of living.

Murray (1997) is careful to use the phrase "supportive witnessing" to
describe the therapist's role in reading and responding to the journal. This
nonjudgmental attitude is consistent with the characteristics of the humanistic
approach to a helping relationship. By supportive witnessing Murray means
the TR practitioner "...must make room to let self-discovery occur without
exerting too much control..." (p. 73).

Likewise, through teaching (via leisure education), the TR specialist may seize the opportunity to build trust and to establish a therapeutic relationship with the client. Hutchinson and Dattilo (2001) described four strategies the therapist (as teacher) may use to enhance the learning experience of the patient: frontloading, debriefing, feedback, and metaphors Hutchinson and Dattilo do not mention a therapeutic relationship directly, but by facilitating client learning, trust is built between the therapist and client. Further, they describe the purpose of the teacher–student relationship as one in which the therapist is "...escorting people through the [learning] process..." (p. 43).

Frontloading is a technique wherein the instructor highlights the material/skills to be learned before the actual learning activity. In other circles, this technique is sometimes called providing an advance organizer. In either case, the information provided primes the client and helps to focus his or her attention on the lesson. Therefore, with the advanced information the client can anticipate the events of learning. In addition to anticipating, the information provided may review previous material, review the aims of the activity, allow for reflection on motivation, and identify detrimental behaviors that stand in the way of learning.

The second technique mentioned by Hutchinson and Dattilo (2001) is *debriefing*. As the word suggests, debriefing refers to the reflective questioning and other types of discussion and communication that may occur after the learning activity is complete. Debriefing stimulates immediate mental rehearsal of the lesson or skill, focusing the client's attention on what was right and what was wrong about the learning activity. This is particularly useful if the client displays behaviors that obstruct the learning (e.g., impulsive behavior on the part of a patient with a brain injury).

While frontloading refers to the teaching in advance of the lesson and debriefing refers to communication after the activity, the third technique, *feedback,* refers to teaching moments that occur during the activity. According to Hutchinson and Dattilo (2001), feedback is the provision of supportive comments during the activity. But feedback is more than providing encouragement. Well-chosen feedback contains two attributes: encouragement (positive reinforcement via verbal comment, gestures, or body language) and informational value. The latter aspect of feedback adds measurably to learning. If a client is shooting free-throws and misses, the therapist should provide feedback that will encourage him or her to continue trying, but the effective feedback will also clue the patient into what he or she is doing incorrectly. For instance, "I can see you are really trying hard. Do you think the ball is rebounding far from the basket because you are shooting it too hard?" The latter part of the verbal feedback clues the learner in to the means to correct his or her performance without directly telling him or her what to do and exactly what is wrong. This way the client is guided in correction of his or her performance—steered to the solution without being given the answer outright.

The final technique for facilitating learning (and building a therapeutic relationship) mentioned by Hutchinson and Dattilo (2001) is the use of *metaphors*. A metaphor, of course, is a phrase paired with another word or phrase that it usually does not accompany. The intent is to create an image in the client's mind's eye by evoking an analogy to a situation the client does understand. For example, "You should shoot free throws by imagining you are placing a book on a tall shelf in front of you." If the metaphor works, then the client will picture his or her hand reaching up high above his or her head and raise up on his or her toes to execute a proper free throw.

Collectively, if the facilitation/teaching techniques suggested by Hutchinson and Dattilo are effective in moving the client's learning forward, one would imagine an emerging therapeutic relationship would develop gradually over time. This teacher–student relationship bears a marked similarity to the therapeutic/helping relationship we have described. Hence, direct conversation is not the only way to establish a therapeutic relationship with a client—journaling and teaching techniques afford ample opportunity for building such a relationship as well.

Challenges in Establishing a Therapeutic Relationship

Several problems face the motivated TR specialist who takes the initiative to establish a therapeutic relationship with a client. These pitfalls include relying excessively on self-disclosure, obstructing the development of friendships with peers, and not being aware of patient preferences. The more serious and more common of the problems is the use of self-disclosure.

Self-disclosure is the practice of sharing information about oneself with the client that will advance the relationship and build trust. While there is nothing wrong in principle with self-disclosure, it must be used with caution. Widmer (1995) reviewed the practice of self-disclosure in TR and found several potential dangers. He warned, "...self-disclosure exposes the therapist to considerable emotional and professional risk" (p. 266). New practitioners, especially, are vulnerable to internal and external pressure to be successful and effective, and establishing a therapeutic relationship is critical to one's effectiveness as a therapist. This pressure may lead the therapist to disclose personal information to gain client approval or acceptance. One risk is that the client may come to perceive the TR practitioner as someone other than a professional—gaining a "friend" but losing confidence in the therapist as a professional. Another risk in self-disclosure is giving clients information about personal beliefs or values. A client may not reveal information or give honest responses if they believe the TR specialist may disapprove or not support the behavior.

It is difficult to know where to draw the line in terms of self-disclosure because it can be an effective technique in helping relationships. Effective self-disclosure narrows the distance and differences between the client and therapist. But used to excess or abused, self-disclosure can deteriorate into "selling" personal information in preference to more advised interventions with the prospects for long-term and permanent client improvement. And if the TR specialist is ultimately effective in bringing about patient improvement, then the best-case scenario is that the relationship between the therapist and client will end. If the therapist has invested an ill-advised amount of emotional energy in the relationship by way of self-disclosure, then he or she may be vulnerable as a result of the eventual separation (see Negley, 1994).

In other words, if we as TR specialists do our jobs well, our clients will no longer need us. Termination is the inevitable result of an effective TR process in general and an effective therapeutic relationship specifically. Hence, while self-disclosure is a useful technique, it should be used judiciously and with considerable caution.

Being a friend instead of a helping professional is fraught with dangers as well. Confidentiality is among the most common problems for the novice practitioner. Hemingway (1993), for example, reported on a case of a young man with a substance abuse problem and noted that the client often shared considerable personal information with the TR specialist before anyone else. Owing to the relaxed atmosphere of the recreation environment and the helping relationship established with the therapist, the client felt enough at ease to share with a trusted professional. Hence, the TR specialist bears a heavy responsibility for confidentiality. Little wonder that confidentiality is a prominent part of the ethical standards for all professional organizations that represent TR (e.g., NTRS, ATRA, CTRA).

Being a friend instead of a professional helper can present other difficulties that impede the progress of the client. For example, Green and Schleien (1991) pointed out building friendships with staff members is easy because the staff typically display accepting and tolerant attitudes toward persons with disabilities. The ease with which friendships form between client and staff means the client does not feel as much of a need to venture out and form friendships with peers, which is not as easy a process and takes much more work. Therefore, friendships with accepting staff members become the default, undermining the motivation to form genuine and lasting friendships with peers.

The final problem the novice practitioner should be aware of is *client preference*, of which he or she may or may not be conscious. Barber and Magafas (1992) surveyed 76 undergraduate TR majors and inquired into their client preferences. Not surprisingly, the students most preferred younger clients with physical disabilities. Those least preferred were chronically ill, older adults. The problems associated with client preference are numerous, not the least of which is that it can interfere with establishing a therapeutic relationship. Client preference as a problem is further magnified because of the aging of Canadian and U.S. societies and the fact that chronic conditions are far more common that acute problems. Naturally, it is rewarding to work with someone near one's own age who shares many of the same life experiences as the therapist and is cognitively lucid. Preferences are natural and unavoidable. We all set goals for ourselves, imagining ourselves working in a particular environment with a specific type of impairment we are most comfortable with. In reality, few practitioners have the latitude for picking a "best world" and have to settle for the best opportunity available at the time. An awareness of one's preferences and how those preferences might affect interactions with clients is the best way to avoid problems that may develop as a result of not getting to work with the type of clients most preferred.

Assessment

Because most professionals think of assessment as a process that ends with hard data, the relationship between assessment and a therapeutic relationship is not immediately obvious. However, Pedlar, Hornibrook, and Haasen (2001) investigated the assessment process at one agency in Canada and found the link between a therapeutic relationship and assessment vital to the success of the assessment effort. The general purpose of their study was to understand the initial encounter between the therapist and client at one agency. Of course, the initial encounter between therapist and client usually pertains to assessment.

Practitioners at the agency investigated were dissatisfied with the nature of interactions with clients and the quality of assessment information they collected. Upon intensive study of the assessment process and interactions between the clients and therapists during assessment, Pedlar et al. (2001) discovered the therapists were more inclined to be "telling, advising, managing, and controlling" instead of "listening, exploring, and clarifying."

Further analysis of the interactions between practitioners and their patients revealed several emerging relationships quickly established during the initial (assessment) interaction. These tended to run counter to the principles of a sound therapeutic relationship between client and staff member. Assessments at the agency investigated were aimed at the nature of the client's leisure experience. But many times the researchers found staff members were invalidating (ignoring, redirecting) the client's description of their own leisure in an effort to expedite acquisition of the information they wanted to elicit by means of the facility's standardized assessment instruments (questionnaires). In the rush to move patients through the healthcare system, many allied health professionals lost sight of their initial reason for being in healthcare. The system, though culpable, should not deter professionals from rediscovering their sensitivity to patients, during assessment and any other part of the rehabilitative experience.

Pedlar et al. (2001) also discovered the assessment instruments used were often irrelevant and confusing to specific clients. Again, in an effort to automate rehabilitation, many fields (not just TR) have engineered shortcuts to increase productivity. One of these is standardized instrumentation and a "one size fits all" approach. Clients are moved along a conveyor belt and assessed, treated, and evaluated in a uniform manner with the hope that a standardized assessment here and a standardized protocol there will suit everyone, moving rapidly toward discharge in three to seven days. As Pedlar et al. observed, the experience is not only dehumanizing and dissatisfying (from a humanistic point of view), but also largely unsuccessful. Recidivism rates and premature discharge of patients tell us as much.

As a result of their study, Pedlar et al. (2001) developed a new approach to assessment and pilot-tested it at the same agency. The new assessment approach, the Personal Leisure Profile, integrated many principles of Rogerian psychology and the humanistic approach described earlier. In contrast to the earlier approach to assessment used at the agency, the Personal Leisure Profile focused on the therapist's attitudes and characteristics during the assessment interview with the patient. The authors suggested several basic principles that should be true of the initial encounter with the patient.

1. Be present or "go with" the patients by listening, accepting, and empathizing instead of trying to channel the conversation in the direction of gaining assessment data as quickly as possible. This means that you should display the characteristics conducive to a helping relationship—listening, paying attention, acting interested, empathizing, and accepting. These characteristics will also induce perceptions of freedom and control on the part of the patient, which we know through research are very helpful.

2. Use simple and understandable language with the client instead of technical terminology. The client must understand if he or she is to make a decision about how the treatment program should proceed.

3. Make certain the patient knows why you are there. Many patients have no understanding of TR, and there is a good chance they may not have ever heard of TR. Take time to explain yourself and your purpose.

4. Contribute personal experiences through self-disclosure (but be cautious given the points raised earlier in this chapter).

5. Eliminate assessment tools/instruments during the first interaction and focus on present leisure interests. Although this seems contrary to the purpose of assessment, taking some time to establish a good relationship with the client and to show your genuine concern will make assessment go much more smoothly on your subsequent visit. We all like to feel that we (as people) are more important than some piece of paper—make sure to send this message early.

In sum, Pedlar et al. remind us not to lose sight of the reason why we are doing the assessment in the first place—the client.

Defining Assessment

Client assessment is the systematic process of gathering and analyzing selected information about an individual client and using the results for placement into a program(s) that is designed to reduce or eliminate the individual's problems or deficits with his or her leisure and that enhances the individual's ability to independently function in leisure pursuits. (Peterson & Stumbo, 2000, p. 200)

[Assessment] is concerned with data collection and analysis in order to determine the status of the client. Once baseline assessment information is available, the therapeutic recreation specialist can help identify and define the client's problems and strengths. (Austin, 1997, p. 153)

...assessment can be defined as a systematic process for gathering select information about an individual for the purpose of making decisions regarding that individual's program or treatment plan. (Peterson & Gunn, 1984, p. 268)

All of these definitions of assessment share common characteristics. All emphasize the collection of information and data. All stress the information is gathered for a purpose—identifying problems, strengths, and needs. Definitions of assessment suggest it is the beginning of a process that leads to the placement of the client in one or more programs or activities designed to help the client make progress toward productive change.

Furthermore, all of these definitions of assessment avoid the problem identified by Fain (1973): assessing patients to place them into existing (standardized, prepackaged) programs. Readers were alerted to this same problem earlier, insofar as standardization for efficiency and productivity in modern healthcare have desensitized the rehabilitation process. Specifically pertaining to assessment and placement into programs, the practitioner must not allow the assessment process to be reduced to a matter of determining which of several existing programs the client will be funneled into. This practice leads to pigeonholing clients into "canned" programs that may not meet their needs, all for the sake of efficiency. The primary purpose of assessment is *not* to place clients into programs (especially preexisting programs). Its purpose is to identify strengths and weaknesses, problems for the treatment team to work on with the client. However, assessment information does ultimately affect the kind of intervention program recommended to the client.

Assessment Methods

Most practitioners would agree the usual source for assessment information is the client; hence, the importance of building a sound relationship with the client. But other sources for information important to the client's case are commonly used, either to supplement and verify what the client says, or as an alternative source of information when the client is unable to represent himself or herself. These sources include other staff, family members, neighbors, friends, and preexisting data (e.g., from earlier admissions, incidents, or events related to the client's present condition). Secondary sources would be consulted if the client were confused (e.g., dementia), brain-injured, or had a cognitive deficit (e.g., mental retardation) that affected his or her ability to think logically. Alternatively, secondary sources could be used if the client were prone to being dishonest about his or her case (e.g., some psychiatric disorders). Three basic techniques for data collection are typically available to the practitioner.

1. *Direct observation* refers to the collection of information about the client through watching and/or listening and then recording the measure of interest, usually some category of behavior (e.g., good manners).

2. The practitioner may administer a standardized *questionnaire* or one of his or her own invention. (Use of questionnaires is limited by cognitive and psychological considerations.)

3. The TR specialist may *interview* the client and either complete a standardized questionnaire based on the client's responses or

record the conversation and review it for emerging themes later (as in Pedlar et al., 2001).

What to Measure

What to assess is almost as varied as the different types of clients one could see in clinical or community-based settings. Certainly leisure behavior and leisure-related indices are commonly assessed in many settings. *Assessment Tools for Recreation Therapy: Red Book #1* (Burlingame & Blaschko, 1990) is a source students should consult for several standardized leisure related-instruments. Other leisure-related areas that may be assessed include leisure preferences, past leisure behavior, leisure attitude, perceived freedom in leisure, leisure constraints and barriers, leisure satisfaction, and leisure ethic.

Functional skills and abilities are very popular areas of assessment, depending on the breadth and extent of areas with which the TR specialist is to work in a given facility. *Functional skills* are loosely defined as those skills and abilities needed to conduct oneself in a relatively independent manner. Occupational therapy and physical therapy commonly work on activities of daily living (ADLs) or independent activities of daily living (IADLs). These represent basic skills such as getting dressed, bathing, cooking, or shopping. Sometimes TR is involved with ADLs or IADLs as well. But many other functional measures and indices are relevant to TR, depending on the situation.

For instance, the TR specialist may be working with older adults in a community setting and focusing on reducing the risk of falls and improving functional fitness so clients can continue to live independently. In this case using the Functional Fitness Assessment for Adults Over 60 Years (Osness et al., 1996) would help the TR practitioner to obtain measures of arm strength, endurance, flexibility, hand–eye coordination, and dynamic balance. With older adults in a preventive setting, the practitioner may also choose to assess chronic pain (Tait, Chibnall & Krause, 1990), static balance (Berg, Wood-Dauphinee, Williams & Gayton, 1989; Duncan, Weiner, Chandler & Studenski, 1990), and lower extremity strength (Csuka & McCarty, 1985). The area of leisure may be combined with functional skills, resulting in the need to measure functional skills that pertain to leisure. Peterson and others developed the Functional Assessment of Characteristics for Therapeutic Recreation (FACTR) scale for use in such circumstances (consult the *Red Book* for the FACTR).

Other areas the TR specialist may assess include perceptions of health, developmental level, some impairments, and problems. It should be clear that a comprehensive list of areas to assess cannot be represented in one text. Those mentioned here do seem to be typical and of frequent interest to the field of TR. However, the TR practitioner must be prepared for the distinct possibility that he or she may have to develop his or her own assessment. It is with that possibility in mind that a discussion of the characteristics of good assessment devices follows.

Criteria for Good Assessment

Dunn (1989) and Austin (1997) enumerated a list of criteria for sound assessment. Although it is not feasible to review all of these criteria here, several of the more important criteria for good assessment are discussed.

Validity

As obvious as it may seem, the first criterion means that the measurement device is measuring what the practitioner intends to measure. *Validity* refers to the accuracy of the measurement device—is it hitting the proper target? Some issues of validity are plain: if one wants to measure leisure preferences, then the practitioner would administer a questionnaire that contained a list of activities and solicit the patient's preferences, or the practitioner could simply ask the client about his or her favorite leisure activities. Either way, the measure has a certain amount of common sense and directly measures what you intend to measure. This sort of validity is called *face validity* because the questionnaire appears to measure what it claims to measure.

The problem with validity, however, is that many variables the TR specialist wants to measure are not straightforward. Take a test for arm strength, for example. One test on the Functional Fitness Assessment Battery for Older Adults claims to be a test of muscle strength. The subject is to assume a seated position and curl an eight-pound weight (four-pound weight for women) as many times as possible in 30 seconds. At what point does the test change over from a test of muscle strength to one of muscle endurance? In fact, the classic definition of muscle strength is the maximum exertion that can be expended at one time. This means that the subject's muscle strength would be better assessed using a maximum, one repetition bench press. For obvious safety reasons, it would not be desirable for older adults to push themselves to a maximal exertion. So we settle for an approximation of muscle strength using a task that is better called muscle endurance (submaximal, repeated contractions over an extended period of time). Validity is indeed a trickier matter than meets the eye.

Content validity is similar to face validity, but the practitioner relies on "experts" to help with development of the measurement device. The method begins with a complete review of the relevant literature on measuring a particular variable. Once the measure is developed, a panel of experts in the area then screens it. They comment on the content of the measure and modify it accordingly. This process continues until the experts agree the instrument measures what the user claims it measures—until it reflects the content it purports to measure.

Another way to demonstrate validity is known as *criterion-referenced* or *predictive validity*. For example, the practitioner may be interested in measuring leisure attitude. Once leisure attitude of a patient is assessed (e.g., using Crandall and Slivken's [1980] Leisure Attitude Scale) one might reason that if a person's leisure attitude improved (e.g., through leisure education), then one should be able to predict leisure behavior. The reasoning is that a positive leisure attitude would translate on average into more leisure activity. Hence, the patient's leisure behavior should be predicted by leisure attitude. The predictive power of the Leisure Attitude Scale reflects its validity. That is, if leisure attitude has been measured accurately, and attitude is a learned predisposition to behave in a way consistent with positive (or negative) feelings toward the object of the attitude (leisure), then an attitude measure should be able to predict behavior relative to the same area (leisure).

Other means of showing validity exist (e.g., *construct validity*), but tend to be used mostly by the research community. The good news for the reader with respect to validity is most measures used for some time have already established measures of validity. It is the practitioner's task not only to be aware of validity and its importance, but also to be discriminative when selecting a measurement device. The practitioner should scrutinize the literature pertaining to the measurement instrument and determine whether validity has been demonstrated, and if so, by what means. Not all measures are created equal. It is the practitioner's job to find the best measure available, or to develop his or her own measure.

Reliability

The companion of validity is reliability. *Reliability* refers to the consistency with which a measure performs. If validity means being accurate, then it is even more desirable to be consistently accurate. Only two main types of reliability exist, although there are several methods for measuring each. As with validity, if the author of a measure has done his or her homework, reliability should be reported along with validity. It is the responsible professional's task to learn if a questionnaire, performance measure, or observation scale is reliable *and* valid.

The first type of reliability, *stability*, tells the user how consistent the measure is over time. Therefore, if a TR specialist administers a leisure satisfaction index today and then again tomorrow, the patient's score on the index should be about the same. Assuming that 24 hours is too short a time to effectively change a person's satisfaction with their leisure, then similar or identical scores indicate that the measure is reliable—stable over time. This type of reliability is sometimes also called *test–retest reliability* because it depends on two measures using the same instrument at different times. The time interval between measures is usually 24–48 hours.

The second type of reliability is *internal consistency*. Internal consistency refers to how consistent each of the items on a questionnaire is with the other items on the questionnaire. The reasoning behind internal consistency is that if each item on a questionnaire measures the same concept, then the patient's response to each item should be about the same. This means, for example, each measure of a 10-item social skills function assessment should correlate with the total score (which is a global measure of social skill) and each of the remaining nine items that also measure the same social skills function. Hence, if someone is rated high on "eye contact during conversation" they should also be rated high on "not interrupting during conversation," assuming the assessment device is consistent and reliable. Optimally the author of a measure will report both types of reliability.

Practicality

A measurement device may be both reliable and valid, but still unsuitable for use in practice. Many measurement instruments are developed by researchers in very controlled settings. Although control is desirable for establishing reliability, validity, and other psychometric properties of measures, it may mean that the measure does not perform well in field trials (i.e., realistic settings).

Hence, one must also ask if the measure is practical: Does it lend itself to use in the field? If a questionnaire is too long, clients will become bored and refuse to continue or give any response just to finish. If the measure requires sophisticated technology or complicated equipment, then most practitioners may find the measure impractical. In addition, with increasing reliance on technology, expense may become an issue. Can the setting afford to purchase the device? Price may be an issue if a questionnaire must be purchased because of its copyright, or if equipment needed to complete testing must be purchased. Practical considerations figure into the decision to use one measure in preference to another, even after reliability and validity matters have reduced choices.

Planning

Assessment information collected from the patient and other sources serves as the basis for planning. Data are gathered not only by the TR specialists, but also by the entire treatment team or support network. Assessment data form a foundation for the four steps of planning (Austin, 1997), including setting priorities, drafting goals and objectives, formulating strategies, and monitoring client progress.

Setting Priorities

The process of setting priorities is usually a consensus effort by all members of the treatment or rehabilitation team. In different settings that team may include different members. In clinical settings the team could include TR, physical therapy, occupational therapy, speech pathology, social work, and a physician. In a community setting working cooperatively with the school system the team may include TR, special education, school counseling, teachers, parents, and other school officials. In a residential care center, such as a nursing home, the team may include TR, social work, a transition specialist, a caseworker, other family members, and a representative from the local community recreation department. Hence, the use of the word "team" here broadly references all those working to improve the status of the client, regardless of setting.

Once the team is gathered, the process setting priorities begins. Austin (1997) suggested categorizing priorities into three groups: tasks the patient can perform independently, tasks that require professional assistance, and most critical needs. A short list of priorities is then developed from the latter two categories.

Next, the priorities are ranked from most important to least important. The experienced team will know all needs cannot be met, and they must focus on the most crucial ones. This part of planning may be made somewhat easier if the team leader (e.g., head of physical medicine and rehabilitation in a clinical setting) has a clear picture of the optimal future placement for the client. For example, different needs will be prioritized if an older adult patient is a candidate for independent living than if the patient is likely to be discharged to a nursing home or assisted living center. In the former case IADLs would be the priority since those are the skills he or she will need to live on his or her own in an apartment or home. Leisure skills necessary in this case would be identifying preferred activities and whether they were accessible in the community. In the latter case, the focus might be directed toward ADLs and remaining independent with respect to self-care as long as possible. Leisure skill development for the nursing home patient would focus more on activities available within the residential center, and what the professional staff made available through regular recreation programs.

Drafting Goals and Objectives

Once priority needs have been selected, then goals and objectives may be developed. Usually there are global goals and objectives that all members of the team work on. In addition, each team member will have goals and objectives specific to his or her discipline. For instance, for the patient destined for discharge to an independent living situation, all members of the team would work on IADLs. The TR specialist might also work on functional skills for leisure (e.g., if the patient had a stroke, then TR might work on alternative communication skills necessary for participating in a favorite leisure activity).

Whether the goals and objectives are the responsibility of all team members or only the TR practitioner, the model for writing goals and objectives remains the same. *Goals* are broad statements of intent not directly measurable. In contrast, *objectives* are very specific and directly or indirectly measurable. Good objectives have three basic components: the behavior, the criterion (for success), and important conditions.

Mager (1997) is considered by many to be the authority on preparing objectives. But most authors list the same three components. The *performance* or *behavior* is rather obvious and refers to what the patient is expected to do. The sound objective will employ action words to make a performance/behavior come to life and easier to recognize.

- *Memorize* directions to the recreation center closest to home.

- *Distinguish* between recreation activities that do and do not pose the potential for substance abuse.

- *Walk* one mile three days per week to improve endurance.

- *Manipulate* playing cards and sort them into suits in a cardholder.

- *Appreciate* the importance of leisure as part of a well-balanced life.

- *Adhere* to a regular exercise program after discharge.

All of these performance/behavior statements express an action to be taken by the patient. Some are overt behaviors and therefore directly measurable, while others are covert behaviors and must be inferred from behaviors and/or measured indirectly. In the previous example, two objectives are written for each of the three fundamental domains of behavior. The cognitive domain (mental activity) is the focus of the first two behavior statements—*memorize* and *distinguish*. The psychomotor domain (physical activity) is of interest in the next two statements—*walk* and *manipulate*. Lastly, the affective domain (feelings and emotions) is expressed in the final two objectives—*appreciate* and *adhere*. The key is always to make certain the main intent is expressed in the objective and that an action word is used.

The second important component of a performance/behavioral objective is the criterion. A complete objective should tell the reader how success is to be recognized; it indicates how well the behavior must be performed. Performance criteria usually refer to accuracy, quality, or speed. Criteria (in italics) have been added to the previous examples using two of the performance/behavior statements with which we started (referring to accuracy, quality and speed respectively).

- Memorize directions to the recreation center closest to home *with 100% accuracy.*

- Walk one mile three days per week to improve endurance *at a speed of three miles per hour.*

The final component to a complete performance/behavioral objective is to specify *conditions*. Conditions important to the performance should be specified if they clarify the circumstances under which the behavior must take place. Although some authors contend that conditions may be omitted, for all practical purposes complete objectives include important conditions. This is especially true when working with persons with disabilities. Building on the aforementioned examples, important conditions (in italics) have been added.

- *After a leisure education session on identifying community resources,* Sarah (a patient recovering from substance abuse) will memorize directions to the recreation center closest to home with 100% accuracy.

- *Following instruction and practice,* Phil (patient recovering from a stroke) will walk one mile three days per week to improve endurance at a speed of three miles per hour.

In both cases the conditions add important information about the circumstances under which the target behavior must be performed. In Sarah's case, the TR specialist does not expect her to know and appreciate the importance of remembering the directions to her local recreation until after a session of leisure education. In Phil's case, without instruction and practice, it would not be realistic to expect a person recovering from a stroke to be able to walk well (depending on the extent of the impairment). Hence, the conditional statements add to the clarity of each objective.

Formulating Strategies

Once team goals and TR-specific goals and objectives have been completed, strategies for achieving those goals and objectives are determined. This amounts to selecting activities, programs, or protocols best suited to satisfying goals and objectives for the client. The means for determining which activities, programs, or protocols to use varies. Some standardized activities and programs exist. Standardized protocols likewise have their own following. But most commonly the TR specialist will individualize the activity or the program to the patient's unique needs expressed through goals and objectives.

Before selecting an activity/program strategy the practitioner may wish to complete an activity analysis. This task is most frequently completed if the activity or program is designed to meet unique patient needs or problems. Considerable consensus in the literature suggests the need for activity analysis, but uniformity in the definition of activity analysis is not always found.

> Activity analysis involves identifying each cognitive, social, physical, and psychological behavior present in a specific leisure experience. (Carter, Van Andel & Robb, 1995, pp. 127–128)

> Activity analysis can be defined as a process that involves the systematic application of selected sets of constructs and variables to break down a given activity to determine the behavioral requirements inherent for successful participation and that may contribute to the achievement of client outcomes. (Peterson & Stumbo, 2000, p. 142)

> Activity analysis is the procedure for breaking down and examining an activity to find inherent characteristics that contribute to program objectives. (Peterson & Gunn, 1984, p. 180)

Two themes run through the various definitions of activity analysis: breaking down an activity into smaller parts and identifying behaviors necessary for participation in various domains. Breaking down the activity into subunits will help the practitioner to determine whether the client can participate in all aspects of the activity or whether the patient will only be able to participate in a portion of the activity (with or without adaptations). Identifying the behavioral requirements of the activity will help the TR worker to focus on one domain as the most vital to successful participation.

For example, even though a game of cards requires cognitive (game rules and strategies), emotional (keeping a positive mood regardless of the outcome, controlling emotions), social (carrying on a friendly conversation, taking turns), and physical (manipulating the cards in one's hand or a cardholder, playing cards in the middle of the table) skills, cognitive skills are the most important. If the participant does not understand the game or rules, then it will not matter if he or she can manipulate the cards, control emotions, or carry on a conversation. Hence, in the case of a card game, cognitive skills are most important.

Peterson and Gunn (1984) further reminded readers that an activity analysis should be undertaken independent of the client the activity intends to serve. The reason for analyzing an activity independent of the client (and his or her impairment) is because the analysis should yield behaviors necessary for successful participation without adaptation. Only when the practitioner knows the usual behaviors required for participation can he or she determine whether adaptations need to be made in the activity.

Following completion of activity analysis, the treatment plan (also called program plan, intervention plan, educational plan, or care plan, depending on the setting) can be assembled. The treatment plan may include the original assessment(s); client needs/problems to be addressed; client strengths, goals, and objectives; activities, programs, and protocols selected for implementation; and a plan for monitoring and evaluation (Austin, 1997, p. 182).

Monitoring Client Progress

The final part of the planning process really continues during implementation of the treatment plan. It consists of devising an evaluation/monitoring plan. The purpose of an evaluation/monitoring plan is to guide the practitioner to evidence of the relative success of the plan and its implementation. Perhaps the monitoring aspect of the plan is most important. Monitoring, in this case refers to ongoing, constant oversight of the implementation of the plan and the patient's response to it. Is the patient responding favorably? Is the client making progress toward treatment goals and objectives? Are there adaptations and adjustments that can be made early in the implementation phase if the client is not responding as expected or not making progress on goals and objectives? If the practitioner waits until the completion of the implementation phase and the treatment is not effective, then a considerable amount of time and effort has been wasted. This can be avoided if the TR specialist views evaluation and monitoring as an ongoing process and not just something to be left until after the implementation phase is finished.

Implementation refers to the actual provision of the treatment/program plan (Austin, 1997, p. 192). Clearly, the effectiveness of implementation depends greatly on interpersonal skills, communication, and leadership abilities, as we have discussed elsewhere in this text. We will not repeat that discussion here. However, one should consider two other topics during implementation: scheduling conflicts and the activity program resources available.

Scheduling

Scheduling, in theory, should not be a problem with a team approach to treatment because all members of the team have a shared vision of where the client is headed with respect to treatment goals and all disciplines are equal members of the team. In reality, not all professions are treated equally, and TR is not always considered an equal partner in the process. As a result scheduling conflicts may occur, either initially or later during implementation. More than one TR specialist can relate stories of patients being removed from the middle of activities and programs because this or that therapy was more "important." Obviously, this action does not inspire a cooperative and trusting attitude on the part of "team" members. Effective teams are built on mutual respect among disciplines and recognition of the contribution of each discipline to the total rehabilitation effort.

Scheduling conflicts undermine mutual respect of team members. When clients are habitually removed from TR programs by other disciplines, it sends a disturbing message that TR is not an equal member of the team. Without mutual respect, practitioners will become discouraged and this will effect recruitment and retention of staff. Continuity and organization of the TR program will erode with high turnover as a result because no one will want to remain at an agency where mutual respect and appreciation are not evident.

Although scheduling conflicts are less prevalent today, they still occur frequently enough to be a concern for the TR profession. This concern is supported by the fact that National Therapeutic Recreation Society includes scheduling as part of its Standards of Practice document: "A master schedule for the client is established in cooperation and coordination with other services" (National Therapeutic Recreation Society, 1995, p. 7).

Standardized Programs

Usually, the TR specialist will deliver a series of programs and activities that represent a combination of individualized activities designed especially to meet a specific patient's needs along with standardized programs that meet a variety of needs. Standardized programs are typically delivered in the same manner with each repetition and delivered on a group basis. In this section we identify and define some common standardized programs employed by TR practitioners. It is important to realize that standardized programs, though often used by TR, are not exclusively used by TR (other allied health professions use the same techniques as well). In addition, some of the standardized programs listed here require additional certification and training.

Aquatic therapy uses a water environment to improve physical or psychological functioning. Pain management, range of motion, flexibility, and strength are typical physical function indicators that may be improved. Psychological benefits include building trust, self-esteem, and confidence. Training is available through the Arthritis Foundation and the Aquatic Therapy and Rehabilitation Institute.

Strength training is especially useful in working with older adults at risk for falls or losing functional independence. Considerable research over the last 15 years demonstrated improvements in strength among older adults can be very beneficial to maintaining a high quality, independent lifestyle. Familiarity with principles of exercise is needed, but no formal training program in TR exists as of this writing.

Leisure education involves the use of teaching principles to improve the patient in one of four leisure-related areas. The four main topics addressed in leisure education are leisure awareness, social interaction skills, leisure resources, and leisure activity skills (Peterson & Stumbo, 2000). Currently, there is not a training program for leisure education distinct from professional preparation in TR.

Remotivation is the use of a series of group encounters for persons with dementia (senility) designed to improve memory and active involvement in the everyday world. Additional training and certification is required to practice remotivation.

Reality orientation (RO) is similar in intent to remotivation, but not delivered in a group situation. Reality orientation refers to any action taken by any staff with the purpose of orienting the patient (usually an older adult) to the present context and time. RO boards are displayed in prominent locations in the facility to remind patients of where they are, and the year. Activity calendars are often used with the intent of serving this purpose as well. Reality orientation is an affirmative attitude on the part of the facility to remind the patient of where he or she is, and it is practiced by the entire staff accordingly.

Sensory stimulation involves just what one might intuitively guess it would—stimulating the senses with various modalities and having the client identify scents, objects, pictures, and sounds using the basic senses. This exercise capitalizes on the intact senses if one or more senses is failing.

Coping/stress management refers to a general intent of a variety of programs and activities designed to relieve stress or to prepare the patient to cope with stress following discharge. Techniques in this category range from exercise programs and relaxation techniques to mental imagery and mental rehearsal of positive affirmations. Assessment of stress and coping styles may also be part of this program. The approach is often used by TR in psychiatric facilities and with recovering cardiac patients who need to decrease stress in their lives.

Protocols are categories of programs related to standardized interventions. A protocol is a standardized (programmatic) response to a specific problem (Knight & Johnson, 1991)—a feature that distinguishes them from standardized programs and activities. Protocols are frequently used in nursing for responsibilities repeated many times as part of the nursing process that must be performed in the same manner every time (e.g., distribution of narcotic drugs to patients). The use of protocols in TR has not been as frequent, although some protocols have been developed for indecisiveness (Knight & Johnson), impaired mobility (Knight & Johnson), dementia (Connolly & Keough-Hoss, 1991; Land, Marmer, Mayfield, Gerski & Murphy, 1989), spinal cord and head injuries (Land, et al.), stroke (Land, et al.), substance abuse (Land, et al.), and frailty in older adults (Mobily & MacNeil, 2002).

Evaluation (Monitoring)

As pointed out earlier, evaluation should include periodic reassessment of the client to determine if he or she is progressing toward treatment goals and objectives in the predicted manner. The periodic review of client progress is often referred to as monitoring or formative evaluation. The final evaluation of the client following completion of the intervention program is sometimes called a summative evaluation. In terms of the day-to-day operation of TR, monitoring is more important.

Monitoring and evaluation employ the same measurement techniques as assessment, including questionnaires, interviews, observation, and physical and skill performance measures. Monitoring allows the TR specialist to determine how the client is responding to treatment and whether he or she is making expected progress. Monitoring provides the means for adjusting the intervention program plan if the patient is not responding well or if the client is not making progress. It stands to reason it is far better to discover early that a program is not working or the patient is not responding as expected. With the shorter stays in hospitals and rehabilitation centers typical nowadays, adjustments must be made quickly because of the narrow window of opportunity the therapist has to work with the client.

Although monitoring and evaluation differ in timing, the mechanics are identical. In either case, monitoring or evaluation refers to an assessment of the client following the initial assessment (used to determine problems, needs, and concerns to be addressed) with the intent of determining whether he or she has made progress. Three different techniques for executing monitoring and evaluation include pretest and posttest, parallel forms, and treatment goals and objectives.

Pretest and Posttest

The first technique, known in research circles as *pretesting and posttesting,* is to simply use the same measurement device employed during the initial assessment. This straightforward technique is particularly good for physical and functional measures. For example, if the TR specialist is conducting a program designed to reduce the risks of falls among at-risk older adults and measures leg strength using the "timed stands" test (recording the time it takes the client to stand up and sit down 10 times; Csuka, & McCarty, 1985), then using that very same test subsequently makes considerable sense. This is because research has shown leg strength (or lack thereof) is one of the best predictors of falls among older adults.

Physical performance measures involve very little bias and only minimal instrument learning effect, both of which produce measurement error. The problem with some paper and pencil or interview measures of cognitive function is they are subject to many sources of bias. The patient may want the therapist to like him or her and behave in ways that cultivate that relationship (e.g., responding in ways he or she knows the therapist expects). Patients often know what their treatment goals and objectives are, and they may want to impress the therapist with their progress and effort (known as the "social desirability" effect). For example, a psychiatric patient may respond to a leisure attitude measure favorably because he or she values the therapist's friendship and fears a negative attitude might jeopardize that friendship, not because his or her leisure attitude is really better. This sort of bias produces measurement error.

Instrument learning refers to the tendency of individuals to figure out what a device is trying measure following a first exposure (during assessment) to the instrument. Subsequent use of the same device is therefore skewed by the client's knowledge of the purpose of the measure. For instance, if the patient figures out that the purpose of the measure is to determine the risk of abusing alcohol again, then that knowledge may well influence how he or she answers the questions on the survey (i.e., the client may answer questions in way that conform to a lower perceived risk of abusing alcohol after discharge). It is not always bad that the client knows the intent of the measurement device, but there is a great risk of the client's response being biased by any number of factors (e.g., "If I improve my attitude, then they will discharge me earlier."; "If I demonstrate the social skills they want, then I can get back together with my wife/husband."). The problem with these outcomes is, of course, they do not measure genuine improvement, only a temporary condition motivated by some other factor (e.g., early discharge).

If the TR specialist wishes to use a pretest/posttest technique because it is the simplest and most direct method of monitoring or evaluation, then some alternative strategies may be employed. One technique for protecting against bias and instrument learning is called the *split-half method.* Imagine that the practitioner has a 20-item leisure attitude questionnaire. In theory, each item on the questionnaire measures 1/20th of the subject's leisure attitude. With the spilt-half technique, the client responds to 10 of the items at the initial assessment and the remaining 10 items subsequently for monitoring or evaluation purposes. Theoretically, either half of the questionnaire should measure a variable identical to the remaining half. There are differing ways to divide the 20-item questionnaire in half. Some will take the first 10 items and use the second 10 for monitoring or evaluation; other prefer to randomly select 10 items for use at assessment and leave the remaining 10 available for monitoring or evaluation. Lastly, 10 items could be selected at random every time the measure is used. Although some items would be repeated (just by chance alone), the totally random method would assure a completely unbiased set of 10 items would be used at each assessment, monitoring, or evaluation interval. The key to being able to use a split-half technique is the quality of the original 20-item questionnaire. If each item on the questionnaire is not as "good" an indicator as every other item, then the halves selected will not be equally valid.

Parallel Forms

A second approach to the completion of monitoring and evaluation, *parallel forms*, is similar to the pretest/posttest method, but two different measures are used. This is another way to avoid instrument learning and other sources of bias. Usually, the outcome variable of interest is a commonly measured problem, such as depression. The therapist then has to find two good (parallel) measures of the outcome of interest. Alternatively, the therapist may design two forms of the same device, if he or she is using an instrument he or she developed. This is the same thinking that underlies the split-half method. Therefore, parallel forms can be thought of as a hybrid of the split-half technique, and is in this respect similar to the theory behind the split-half technique. However, finding two good measures of the same outcome variable presents a serious challenge for the practitioner. This is especially true with respect to leisure-related outcomes, because for many variables only one measurement has been developed.

Treatment Goals and Objectives

The final approach to monitoring and evaluation relies on the use of *treatment goals and objectives.* Instead of using the same measurement device to determine client progress, the therapist monitors client progress by comparing client behavior or performance to stated treatment goals and objectives. Approximating stated goals and objectives constitutes progress and suggests the intervention program brought about the desired change(s) in the patient. Failure to make progress toward treatment goals and objectives suggests a change in the intervention might be warranted.

The use of goals and objectives as monitoring and evaluation indicators frees the practitioner from the problems associated with using the same measure in evaluation as was used in assessment (e.g., bias, instrument learning). It also avoids the problem of having to find another device to measure the same outcome (a parallel form) or dividing the original measurement device into two equivalent halves (split-half technique).

However, the use of goals and objectives as indicators of client progress for monitoring and evaluation creates a different set of challenges. First, the performance or criterion may be set at too "easy" a level. Behaviors tend to be identified based on what is reasonable for the client to achieve, with the therapist often taking a mastery approach.

For instance, one goal/objective for a psychiatric patient anticipating discharge is to be able to ride the bus to the recreation center. Normally, the therapist would set the criterion for this behavior at a 100% level because of the risk of failing to perform this task correctly just once means the patient may be lost. As a result the client may react adversely and lose any progress made with respect to confidence to live outside the institution on his or her own. In other words, the behavior (taking the correct bus and getting off at the right stop) must be mastered (i.e., correct) all of the time. And chances are that the patient would be able to master the behavior while working with the therapist at a clinical agency. Although the behavior in this example may not be "easy" for every patient, the objective does reflect the concern associated with a mastery approach cultivated by goals and objectives.

Would it not be more desirable for the client to be able to think on his or her feet and to be prepared for the inevitable "glitches" associated with public transportation (e.g., buses do not always run on time, buses break down, stops may be missed on occasion)? Obviously, the answer is affirmative. But to prepare the patient to face these challenges would likely result in several different objectives and take a longer time than is typical of inpatient treatment. Hence, while the patient may achieve treatment goals/objectives, it does not always mean he or she is as ready as we would like for discharge into an unforgiving world.

Another less serious problem associated with using goals and objectives as markers of patient progress also relates to the tendency to write objectives using too "easy" of behaviors and at a mastery level. Objectives do not give the patient credit for doing better than expected, or performing at a level that might make him or her eligible for a more desirable community placement (e.g., assisted living rather than a nursing home). Hence, the risk is the client may not find himself or herself in an optimum lifestyle situation, thus hurting the person's quality of life.

However, careful design of goals and objectives can compensate for the lack of an opportunity to demonstrate performance above the expected level. The technique that integrates goals and objectives into a scheme that allows the patient to exceed expected levels of performance is called Goal Attainment Scaling (GAS). Katsinas (1986) and Touchstone (1984) successfully applied GAS to TR situations using very practical examples. The examples aptly demonstrate there is room for the client to exceed expected/satisfactory performance levels and to go beyond mastering minimally acceptable objectives. The reader should consult the aforementioned citations for more information about GAS.

Documentation

Documentation refers to the written (or electronic) record of the client's experience in the agency. It may include assessments, goals and objectives, progress notes, intervention plans, monitoring and evaluation data, discharge plans, and a variety of other written documents that describe the client's stay at the agency. Some documentation is similar from agency to agency (e.g., practically all agencies complete progress notes or their equivalent) while others are unique to one type of agency (e.g., psychiatric assessments of patients at mental health facilities).

The written record serves many purposes, outlined by Peterson and Stumbo (2000) and Austin (1997). Most importantly, documentation serves as a means of communication among members of the allied treatment team. It may not be convenient to meet on a daily basis, but professionals can report to one another through a common source—the chart, the client's written record. Regular review of patient charts can avoid duplication of services, confusion, and scheduling conflicts. And since all members of the treatment team are supposed to be working toward a common set of goals and objectives, the regular consultation of the patient's chart can provide up-to-date information about how close the patient is to discharge relative to the progress he or she has made.

Documentation also provides one means for determining the quality of services. Many agencies conduct a periodic review of the quality of services rendered. A source of information about the quality of patient care is found in the charting/documentation that occurred. One standard may require that an agency assess patients within 48 hours of admission. A random sample of charts could be selected and checked to determine whether the assessments were completed in a timely (within 48 hours) manner. If so, then that standard is met. When an external agency reviews a healthcare facility or program, the process is known as *accreditation*. For example, in the United States the Joint Council on the Accreditation of Health Care Organizations is one such organization and in Canada standards are set by each province.)

Documentation may serve the purpose of accountability even if the organization is not reviewed by another agency for accreditation purposes. Some healthcare and human service organization conduct their own internal reviews as a means of self-regulation. Some even employ personnel whose sole purpose is to maintain or to improve the quality of services (i.e., quality assurance). Whether a healthcare organization is accredited by an outside entity or whether it assumes responsibility for its own quality assurance internally, documentation proves to be a critical data source for either process.

Types of Documentation

Many documents may become part of the client's record, from initial assessments to final discharge plans. Most of these aspects of documentation have already been described. This section focuses on the progress note (charting) part of documentation. Progress notes are the day-to-day written reports entered by the healthcare staff and members of the allied treatment team.

The first type of documentation is called *source-oriented* documentation. Here each therapist working with a client "tells their story" about if/how the client is progressing according to the intervention plan. Recommendations may be added about whether to continue treatment as planned or to alter the intervention plan because the patient is not progressing as expected. Sometimes concerns expressed through documentation in the client's chart may lead to a staff or team meeting, at which time the client and the intervention plan are reviewed.

A second more standardized version of documentation is known as *problem-oriented* charting or documentation. With this type of documentation, the therapist has more responsibility for gathering and analyzing information/data. Problem-oriented medical records (POMR) require initial assessment data, a problem list, a treatment plan, progress notes, and a discharge plan/summary (Peterson & Stumbo, 2000). Clearly, POMR expects more of the therapist than the typical progress note in terms of documentation.

Similarly, *SOAP notes* ask the therapist for more than a narrative comment on how the patient is doing. SOAP stands for

- *S*ubjective information (what the client reports about the problems).

- *O*bjective information (what the therapist observes and quantifies, or data gathered through the use of formal assessment).

- *A*nalysis (the reasoning used by the therapist as he or she interprets the subjective and objective data and justifies a course of action).

- *P*lan (the course of action, the activities and programs that will be used to address the problem).

Sometimes an "E" is added to the SOAP approach to documentation so that *e*valuation (and monitoring) is included in the documentation process (the result is SOAPE).

In sum, documentation often amounts to creating a record of many of the steps in the TR process. Although documentation styles and patterns vary from one organization to the next, in the end much of the same information is found in the client's chart. The TR professional is expected to document in a manner consistent with other professionals on the allied treatment team. In this regard, a clear and concise writing style pays off. Although this is not the place to embark on a discussion of professional writing, the future professional is reminded that practice is necessary for the development of a sound professional writing style.

Coordinating Services

Coordination of services is essential to avoid conflict and confrontation between disciplines. If professionals working on the treatment team have a mutual respect for one another, and see each other as credible, then scheduling conflicts should be minimal. If team members appreciate the role and contribution made by other members of the team, then mutual respect should grow and foster the cooperation necessary for an effective team approach. However, if the opposite is true, if team members do not respect one another as professionals, if some members of the team see others infringing on their therapeutic territory, then conflict is unavoidable.

Some of the more common members of the treatment team are defined in **Table 8.1**. Of those, physical/physio therapy (PT) and occupational therapy (OT) are the two professions where the most potential for conflict with TR exists. Conflicts with PT are usually minimal because there is little overlap in modalities, with the exception of the use of exercise. Even with the use of exercise, PTs are typically using exercise in a corrective manner to treat a mobility impairment, deficit functional skill, or cardiac disability, whereas TR may use exercise in a preventive manner primarily in community-based settings (e.g., an exercise program for people with arthritis) or in a clinical setting to maintain function (e.g., range of motion and toning in a nursing home). Corrective intervention is usually not the intent when TR uses exercise. Furthermore, with the significant increase in chronic conditions and the aging of society, more demand for preventive and maintenance programs from community-dwelling older adults means demand has outpaced the capacity of both PT and TR to provide community-based exercise programs. Simply put, there is plenty of exercise demand in the community for both professions.

The most common conflict that interferes with a coordinated team effort is between TR and OT. One study by Smith, Perry, Neumayer, Potter, and Smeal (1992) shed light on the source of the problem. The disagreement centers on the use of play, leisure, and recreation as a modality.

Smith et al. (1992) surveyed 147 TR specialists and 153 OT practitioners and asked them questions pertaining to the barriers to interdisciplinary cooperation. They speculated that several barriers interfered with effective team work, including lack of trust in professional judgment, status differences,

Table 8.1	Professions and Definitions
Physical/ Physio Therapy (PT)	PTs assess and evaluate clients impairments and provide treatment for pain and mobility impairments.
Social Work (SW)	SWs focus on family systems and social change to enhance responsiveness of human service between society and the individual and family.
Speech Pathology (SP)	SPs provide remedial services to individuals with speech, language, and hearing problems in clinical, community, and school settings.
Occupational Therapy (OT)	OTs help people who have an illness, injury, developmental or psychological impairment build skills important for independent functioning.
Clinical Psychology (CP)	CPs work with persons with psychopathologies related to aggression, personality disorders, anxiety disorders, affective impairments, and cognitive disabilities.
Nursing (RN)	RNs are involved with the primary medical care of patients in hospitals and other healthcare organizations. More recently nursing has expanded into community service in schools, homes (visiting nurses), and nurse practitioner roles.

lack of understanding, ethical concerns, professional language differences, role ambiguity, role conflict (overlap), and role overload.

The results indicated that TR and OT practitioners disagreed about a number of favorable attributes that characterized the other profession (e.g., status, training, understanding the capabilities of the other profession, and ethical behavior). These misperceptions translated into a lack of trust in professional judgment. Sixty-seven percent of TR practitioners reported that OTs cooperated with them, whereas 90% of OT believed that TR cooperated with them.

Encroachment was also an issue for both professions. Both disciplines thought of play, leisure, and recreation as their modality. Eighty percent of TR specialist believed that OT encroached into their professional area, and 70% of OT thought that TR practitioners encroached into their area of professional practice.

Sadly, Smith et al.'s (1992) findings did not indicate an environment conducive to cooperation is always present, at least in clinical settings and between TR and OT practitioners. The authors urged both professions to place the client's interests before professional and personal interests. For a treatment team to work, there is a need for more understanding and appreciation for the contributions made by other allied health team members to the real reason the team was put together in the first place—the client.

Discharge and Transition Planning

Discharge and transition planning begins the first day a client is seen in a healthcare setting and continues throughout the rehabilitation or recovery period. In fact, it begins with assessment. "Assessment acts as an excellent tool in ascertaining each patient's individual community reintegration/adjustment needs" (Rath & Page, 1996, p. 25). Discharge planning should be on the mind of every member of the rehabilitation team, because the eventual goal of all rehabilitation efforts is the return of the client to as normal a living circumstance as possible under the best quality of life conditions possible. In some cases the focus on discharge planning is discussed in staff or team meetings, in other more standardized rehabilitation scenarios discharge planning appears as an important aspect of care (e.g., clinical pathways; see Rath & Page, 1996).

TR's role in discharge planning usually relies heavily on leisure education (Luken, 1993; Rath & Page, 1996). For example, in reporting the results of a transition program, Luken maintained leisure education was used based on the assumption that one important problem for persons with mental illness was the misuse of free time. Difficulty managing free time then led to other problems related to independent living in the community.

The reliance on leisure education during discharge and transition planning should come as no surprise. Recalling the major topical areas frequently included in leisure education content reveals the natural fit between leisure education and preparation for independent living in the community. First, being aware of the important role of leisure in one's life leads to the recognition that free time holds both the promise for facilitating adjustment to community living (e.g., a way of making friends and building a support system) and the threat associated with its misuse (e.g., substance abuse is associated with some forms of leisure). Second, leisure skills needed to use free time meaningfully are commonly taught during leisure education. Third, social skills are likewise common topics during leisure education and may be impossible to separate from the learning of leisure skills (e.g., being a good sport is part of learning a sport skill). Finally, leisure resources must be identified along with the logistics of accessing those resources (e.g., transportation, expense, building accessibility). All of the skills learned in leisure and social skill development are of little use if the person cannot negotiate his or her environment and locate the resources necessary for participation once discharged.

The reliance on leisure education is clear in one report of a clinically based TR program at an adult and child psychiatric facility. Rath and Page (1996) described their intervention program and explained how it was supported by leisure education. Their particular approach was very similar to the leisure education content areas enumerated previously. It included leisure skill development (e.g., frustration management), social skill development (e.g., sharing), and community skill development (e.g., ability to plan).

Discharge planning may occur within the context of regular patient rehabilitation during staff or team meetings. But with the reduced length of stays in inpatient settings, more creative approaches to discharge and transition planning begin to emerge. Two creative endeavors are Reintegration Through Recreation (RTR) and use of a Therapeutic Recreation Community Liaison (TRCL).

RTR is a program developed to assist persons with serious mental illness make the transition back to independent functioning in the community. RTR begins in the client's own community, using recreation as a medium for exercising personal choice and practicing independent activities of daily living. It emphasizes choice and personal responsibility for those choices. RTR relies heavily on leisure education in "...identifying personal interests, needs and resources, specific activity skill development, exploring community resources, practicing the use of leisure skills in the community setting of choice, and using problem-solving and decision-making skills" (Luken, 1993, p. 54).

Baker-Roth, McLaughlin, Weitzenkamp, and Womeldorff (1995) reported another unique approach. The TRCL is a TR specialist who works one-to-one with a patient to facilitate his or her transition back into the community. The case study reported by Baker-Roth et al. details the transition of a female who had sustained a brain injury and chronicles her challenges and the barriers she encountered in successfully reintegrating back into the community. Along with her brain injury, the 30-year-old female had a history of alcohol and substance abuse to address. The TRCL provided emotional support, assisted with the identification of funding sources, and identified transportation to support the client's efforts to function independently in her leisure in the community. Together the client and therapist built a complex of support resources to ease the transition back into the community, with the client gradually assuming more responsibility and control for her leisure. The authors concluded that without the TRCL transition program the patient likely would have returned to her previous pattern of substance abuse during free time in reaction to stress and boredom.

Summary

The present chapter described the TR process. The process includes more than conventional assessment, planning, implementation, and evaluation. Building a therapeutic relationship with the patient was emphasized—without a sound helping relationship none of the other techniques and strategies would be productive. Problems associated with implementation and working on an interdisciplinary treatment team were pointed out to alert the student of potential conflicts. Ultimately, the entire TR process has the same goal of all allied health disciplines: discharge to as normal a living situation as possible. In the best of worlds that lifestyle includes independent leisure functioning where the client is self-determined and takes responsibility for choices made.

References

Austin, D. R. (1997). *Therapeutic recreation: Processes and techniques* (3rd ed.). Champaign, IL: Sagamore Publishing.

Baker-Roth, S., McLaughlin, E., Weitzenkamp, D., and Womeldorff, L. (1995). The impact of a therapeutic recreation community liaison on successful re-integration of individuals with traumatic brain injury. *Therapeutic Recreation Journal, 29,* 316–323.

Barber, E. H. and Magafas, A. (1992). Therapeutic recreation majors' work preference. *Therapeutic Recreation Journal, 26*(4), 43–54.

Berg, K., Wood-Dauphinee, S., Williams, J. I., and Gayton, D. (1989). Measuring balance in the elderly: Preliminary development of an instrument. *Physiotherapy Canada, 41,* 304–311.

Burlingame, J. and Blaschko, T. M. (1990). *Assessment tools for recreational therapy: Red book #1.* Ravensdale, WA: Idyll Arbor.

Carter, M. J., Van Andel, G. E., and Robb, G. M. (1995). *Therapeutic recreation: A practical approach* (2nd ed.). Prospect Heights, IL: Waveland Press.

Connolly, P. and Keough-Hoss, M. A. (1991). The development and use of intervention protocols in therapeutic recreation: Documenting field-based practices. In B. Riley (Ed.), *Quality management: Applications for therapeutic recreation* (pp. 118–136). State College, PA: Venture Publishing, Inc.

Crandall, R. and Slivken, K. (1980). Leisure attitudes and their measurement. In S. E. Iso-Ahola (Ed.), *Social psychological perspectives on leisure and recreation* (pp. 261–284). Springfield, IL: Charles C. Thomas.

Csuka, M. and McCarty, D. J. (1985). Simple method for measurement of lower extremity muscle strength. *The American Journal of Medicine, 78,* 77–81.

Duncan, P. W., Weiner, D. K., Chandler, J., and Studenski, S. (1990). Functional reach: A clinical measure of balance. *Journal of Gerontology, 45,* 192–197.

Dunn, J. (1989). Guidelines for using published assessment procedures. *Therapeutic Recreation Journal, 23*(3), 59–69.

Fain, G. (1973). Leisure counseling: Translating needs into action. *Therapeutic Recreation Journal, 7*(2), 4–9.

Green, F. P. and Schleien, S. J. (1991). Understanding friendship and recreation: A theoretical sampling. *Therapeutic Recreation Journal, 25*(4), 29–40.

Hemingway, V. G. (1993). Therapeutic recreation services for a chemically dependent client. *Therapeutic Recreation Journal, 27,* 126–130.

Hutchinson, S. L. and Dattilo, J. (2001). Processing possibilities for therapeutic recreation. *Therapeutic Recreation Journal, 35,* 43–56.

Katsinas, R. P. (1986). Goal attainment scaling as program evaluation for individualized leisure services. *Journal of Expanding Horizons in Therapeutic Recreation, 1,* 28–37.

Knight, L. and Johnson, D. (1991). Therapeutic recreation protocols: Client problem centered approach. In B. Riley (Ed.), *Quality management: Applications for therapeutic recreation* (pp. 137–147). State College, PA: Venture Publishing, Inc.

Land, C., Marmer, A., Mayfield, S., Gerski, M. A., and Murphy, C. (1989). *Protocols in therapeutic recreation.* Arlington, VA: NRPA.

Luken, K. (1993). Reintegration through recreation. *Parks and Recreation, 28*(4), 52–57.

Luken, K. and Rios, D. (1998, Fall). Clinical is NOT a place: The clinical process in TR. *NCTRC Newsletter.*

Mager, R. F. (1997). *Preparing instructional objectives* (3rd ed.). Atlanta, GA: Center for Effective Performance.

Mobily, K. E. and MacNeil, R. D. (2002). *Therapeutic recreation and the nature of disabilities.* State College, PA: Venture Publishing, Inc.

Murray, S. (1997). The benefits of journaling. *Parks and Recreation, 32*(5), 68–75.

National Therapeutic Recreation Society. (1995). *Standards of practice for therapeutic recreation services and annotated bibliography.* Arlington, VA: National Recreation and Parks Association.

Negley, S. (1994). Recreation therapy as an outpatient intervention. *Therapeutic Recreation Journal, 28*(1), 35–41.

Osness, W. H., Adrian, M., Clark, B., Hoeger, W., Raab, D., and Wiswell, R. (1996). *Functional fitness assessment for adults over 60 years* (2nd ed.). Dubuque, IA: Kendall-Hunt.

Pedlar, A., Hornibrook, T., and Haasen, B. (2001). Patient focused care: Theory and practice. *Therapeutic Recreation Journal, 35,* 15–30.

Peterson, C. A. and Gunn, S. L. (1984). *Therapeutic recreation program design* (2nd ed.). Englewood Cliffs, NJ: Prentice Hall.

Peterson, C. A. and Stumbo, N. J. (2000). *Therapeutic recreation program design* (3rd ed.). Boston, MA: Allyn & Bacon.

Rath, K. V. and Page, G. (1996). *Understanding financing and reimbursement issues.* Arlington, VA: National Recreation and Parks Association.

Rogers, C. R. (1961). *On becoming a person.* Boston, MA: Houghton Mifflin.

Smith, R. W., Perry, T. L., Neumayer, R. J., Potter, J. S., and Smeal, T. M. (1992). Interprofessional perceptions between therapeutic recreation and occupational therapy practitioners: Barriers to effective interdisciplinary team functioning. *Therapeutic Recreation Journal, 36*(4), 31–42.

Tait, R. C., Chibnall, J. T., and Krause, S. (1990). The pain disability index: Psychometric properties. *Pain, 40,* 171–182.

Touchstone, W. A. (1984). A personalized approach to goal planning and evaluation in clinical settings. *Therapeutic Recreation Journal, 18,* 25–31.

Chapter 9

Models of TR
Joining Theory to Practice

Learning Objectives

1. Explain the role of practice models in therapeutic recreation.

2. Identify the four different practice models in TR, explain the unique features of each model, and select appropriate approaches in different settings and with different clients.

3. Examine factors influencing diversity and scope of the TR field.

4. Identify multicultural considerations in the design of TR practice models.

Therapeutic recreation (TR) professionals are often asked to respond to the question, "What is therapeutic recreation?" It is common for TR students, faculty, and practitioners to initially explain the role of TR and the benefits of TR services. In the explanation of TR, various aspects of the field are usually addressed. Specific responses usually highlight the use of leisure as a tool to bring about positive changes, the benefits and advantages of services, the domains covered by TR services, and the uniqueness of TR from other therapies and other health professionals. To advance the understanding of the TR profession, it is critical TR service providers clearly represent the profession in an effective way.

This chapter introduces the role of TR practice models as a method to explain and to understand the diversity and scope of the field. Models offer a tool to explain the practice of TR to others. TR practice models provide a visual representation of TR service delivery and serve as valuable resources to facilitate communication and to support comprehensive program development. TR practice models help practitioners as well as those outside the field to understand how the TR field is organized and conceptualized. This chapter looks at four practice models with different philosophies and theoretical orientations as examples to demonstrate how models can be useful in the design and development of TR services. When selecting an appropriate practice model, a TR specialist must reflect on theory and philosophy to explain the rationale for service delivery.

Many different models, with different sets of assumptions and beliefs about the nature of development and growth, definition of health and illness, and the process and goals of therapy have emerged in TR (Selz, 2000). Models guiding TR interventions have evolved over time in response to research advances, social changes, and changes in healthcare. In the past 20 years, several models of practice have been proposed to guide TR practitioners.

It might simplify our explanations in TR if a single practice model were put forward. However, the field of TR is diverse in settings, in approaches, and in the clientele served. Clients vary with respect to level of ability and disability, age, and background. Currently the field of TR is represented by a range of professional associations, and services are offered by people with a broad range of backgrounds, including people with two-year college or associate degrees, people with undergraduate and graduate degrees, and people who hold degrees or diplomas in allied health and social service professions. Given the diversity of the TR field, one TR practice model is not feasible or desirable.

Practice models are needed to make the key elements of TR, including values, beliefs, customs, practices, norms, and language concrete (Freysinger, 1999). TR practice models allow for testing and research about theory and practices. From the examination and challenges to current models come improvements to services. Models are like metaphors, helping to organize abstract concepts into a picture, and making TR more real or concrete.

This chapter reviews four examples of TR practice models to demonstrate diversity and scope of services. It highlights the importance of studying TR practice models, and explains some criteria for selecting relevant TR service models. The chapter introduces the following four different TR practice models:

1. Leisure Ability Model (Peterson & Gunn, 1984; Peterson & Stumbo, 2000)

2. Self-Determination and Enjoyment Enhancement Model (Dattilo, Kleiber & Williams, 1998)

3. Optimal Lifelong Health Model (Wilhite, Keller & Caldwell, 1999)

4. Leisure Gyroscope for Enhancing Quality of Life in Long-Term Care (Côté, LaPan & Hallé, 1997)

For each of these models, there is a brief explanation and discussion on the practical applications of service delivery. The chapter closes with multicultural considerations when selecting TR practice models and learning activities to further develop an understanding and awareness of TR models and their relevance in TR service delivery.

Why Is the Study of TR Practice Models Important?

The study of models guides individual and professional practice. Models offer tools to compare, to evaluate, and to develop comprehensive services built on theory and shared philosophy of what services should be. TR models should be theoretically based and should direct practitioners in the process of client interventions (Austin, 1991). Practice models offer a blueprint of TR services, including the type of services provided, the client–therapist relationship, and the proposed outcomes (Voelkl, Carruthers & Hawkins, 1997). The identification of content and outcomes provides direction to TR specialists who design and implement programs. Models of practice help to explain TR service to clients, administrators, family members, client support services, the public, and third-party payers. Practice models also generate dialogue among professionals, which promotes the professional development of TR (Sylvester, Voelkl & Ellis, 2001).

Advantages of Studying TR Practice Models

1. Models help us to understand the foundation and beliefs that support TR practice.

2. Models provide a way to plan and to explain our approach to services to others. Specifically, they clarify our definition of TR and offer theory to guide our practice.

3. Models provide a visual diagram and help to make a useful action plan or design services.

4. Models provide a framework for visualizing services, including selecting, sequencing, and organizing interventions (Selz, 2000; Carter, Van Andel & Robb, 1995).

5. Models provide a clear picture, which can serve as a guide for our decision making and as a framework for making good choices (Austin, 1991).

6. Models allow the opportunity to compare approaches and to understand diversity of setting.

7. Models offer a range of interventions to consider when designing quality TR services.

8. Models are usually supported by clear concrete theory, which provides rationale for services.

9. Models explain the orientation of TR to all who deliver services to provide consistency and coherence in TR services.

Considerations for Selecting Relevant TR Service Models

Since many TR practice models exist, practitioners should have a framework for selecting models appropriate for TR service delivery. When selecting TR practice models, practitioners should address the following questions:

1. Does the model cover all essential components of TR service offered?

2. Is the model supported by theory relevant to your clientele, the mission of your agency, and your department goals for therapeutic recreation?

3. Is the model visual?

4. Does the model provide a blueprint that orients your clients and other professionals to TR services?

5. Does the model educate the uninformed on the role of TR in your agency?

6. Does the model support your agency and department definition of TR services?

7. Does the model address domains covered by TR services?

8. Does the model clearly identify the role of a TR specialist?

9. Does the model provide service direction based on conceptualization?

One Size Does Not Fit All: Multicultural Considerations and TR Models

Practice models are built on beliefs and a value system is inherent in the design of every model. Practice models reflect specific cultures by selecting variables, interrelationships, and importance of components in the models. It is essential to explore the cultural implications of models and how open or closed they are to diversity (Sylvester et al., 2001, p. 108).

In their multicultural critique of three therapeutic recreation models, Dieser and Peregoy (1999; cited in Sylvester et al., 2001, pp. 108–109) identified several culturally biased assumptions from the literature and identified these as problem areas in TR models:

- Definition of normal behavior is accepted as universal.

- Individuals (not communities) are the building blocks of society.

- Abstractions such as health and leisure are universally recognized as the same and have the same meaning in all cultures.

- Clients are helped more from formal therapy than by culturally appropriate supports.

- All people employ linear thinking to understand the worlds.

- Cultural history is not necessary for understanding contemporary issues.

- Most TR practice models emphasize western values of independence and individualism.

- Many TR practice models do not include cross-cultural assumptions.

TR Practice Models

Many models have been developed for TR practice. TR specialists should be aware of the different models and should review the relevance of their own practice and agency to solidify orientation and approach to TR services. Each existing model highlights specific components of service, philosophical arguments for service, strategies for TR service delivery, rational for TR in specific environments, health and wellness promotion strategies, and the role of the TR specialist.

The models in this chapter have been selected to demonstrate the different components of TR service and to show how orientation to service can vary significantly in the field. This chapter selects a few practice models currently being used in the TR field and discusses how they can be of use by TR practitioners.

Leisure Ability Model

The Leisure Ability Model (Peterson & Gunn, 1984; Peterson & Stumbo, 2000) was one of the first practice models to be introduced to the field (see **Figure**

9.1). The National Therapeutic Recreation Society in the United States adopted this model in 1982 as a philosophical basis for practice. The Canadian TR Association also supports the Leisure Ability Model as a philosophical foundation.

The Leisure Ability Model developed from the assumption that leisure is a basic human right and many people encounter barriers to enjoyable leisure experiences (Stumbo & Peterson, 1998). In the Leisure Ability Model, the purpose of TR is to "facilitate the development, maintenance and expression of an appropriate leisure lifestyle for individuals with physical, mental, emotional or social limitations." Leisure lifestyle is defined as the "day to day behavioral expression of one's leisure and related attitudes, awareness and activities revealed within the context and composite of the total life experience" (Peterson & Gunn 1984, p. 4).

An appropriate leisure lifestyle is comprised by a number of behaviors. Stumbo and Peterson (1998) identify some of these leisure lifestyle indicators as social skills, decision-making ability, knowledge of leisure resources, attitudes and behaviors, perception of choice, and independence (p. 91).

The theory that supports the Leisure Ability Model is based on concepts of learned helplessness, intrinsic motivation, locus of control, choice, and optimal experiences (Stumbo & Peterson, 1998). These concepts direct the design and focus of TR programs. In this model of TR practice, programs and services are designed to give opportunities for success and to promote leisure-related skills and knowledge. According to the model, intervention may occur in a wide range of settings and addresses individuals with "physical, mental, social, or emotional limitations" (Stumbo & Peterson, 1998, p. 4).

The Leisure Ability Model is conceptually divided into three major components along a continuum of client functioning and restrictiveness. The purpose of the service, the role of the TR specialist, and the degree of control on the part of the client is illustrated for each of the three components. The Leisure Ability Model promotes a client-centered, problem-oriented approach. Client needs are identified through an assessment process, and clients are referred to programs based on area of need.

Three essential components comprise the model: functional intervention, leisure education, and recreation participation. Each area reflects a different orientation and approach to TR services. The model also provides an optimal sequence of three phases and discusses the role of the TR specialist in each phase.

Components of the Leisure Ability Model

Functional Intervention. Functional intervention (formerly described by Peterson & Gunn, 1984) refers to activities specifically meant to improve functional abilities in the physical, social, cognitive, and affective domains. In this area of the model, there is an assumption that adequate functioning is a prerequisite for an independent leisure lifestyle. The activities selected in the

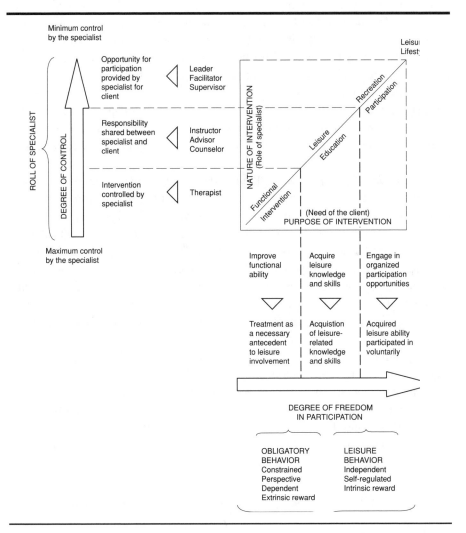

Figure 9.1   Leisure Ability Model (Fig. 2.2, p. 39 from *Therapeutic Recreation Program Design, 4th ed.* by Norma J. Stumbo and Carol Ann Peterson. Copyright ©2004 by Pearson Education, Inc. Reprinted by permission).

functional intervention component are not designed "for their recreation or leisure potential, but rather for their specific inherent contribution to behavioral change" (Peterson & Gunn, 1984, p. 18). This first phase has a prescriptive medical orientation and clients have little or no freedom to choose activities.

Leisure Education. Leisure education addresses "the development and acquisition of skills, attitudes, and knowledge related to leisure participation and leisure lifestyle development" (Peterson & Gunn, 1984, p. 22). In other words, at this phase the client is assumed to have the basic skills to participate in leisure. The four areas of leisure education include (a) leisure awareness, (b) social interaction, (c) leisure activity skills, and (d) leisure resources. Leisure awareness is explained further by including elements such as knowledge of leisure, self-awareness in relation to leisure, attitudes toward play and leisure, participating, and decision-making skills. Social interaction skills consists of communication, relationship building, and self-presentation skills. Leisure activity skills include both traditional and nontraditional leisure resources, such as personal resources, home resources, community resources, and government resources.

Recreation Participation. In the recreation participation phase, the client receives activity-based programs and services to "provide opportunity to engage in structured group recreation experiences for enjoyment or self-expression" (Peterson & Gunn, 1984, p. 7). Focused on involvement rather than specific functional outcomes, this area offers opportunity for choice and interaction. This component offers organized opportunity for fun and enjoyment, such as programs offered in community TR settings, diversional programs in long-term care or group homes, recreation offerings at integrated daycares, and community recreation offerings. In this phase, autonomy and self-determination are the orientation.

Sequence. The three phases are arranged in a sequence from greater therapist control to lesser therapist control and from client dependence to client independence. The ultimate outcome of the model is to develop an appropriate leisure lifestyle that can be utilized independently and freely. As a client moves along the continuum from functional improvement to recreation participation and begins to develop skills relevant to leisure, freedom increases and reliance on the TR specialist decreases.

Practical Advantages of the Leisure Ability Model

- The model is straightforward, basic, and easy to follow and logically identifies and explains the different components in the field.

- The model is well-known to TR practitioners and is currently used to support the philosophical orientation of the NTRS and CTRA.

- Graphics are clear and comprehensive and can be useful in communicating about TR to people outside the field.

- The model uses a systems approach for developing different service components (Peterson & Stumbo, 2000).

- Three components make it easy to focus on one client aspect at a time, making accountability for services easier.

- Programs can be designed with the model as a guide and can be adapted to suit client needs.

- The model can be useful in both group and individual TR services, and relevant to different settings and a range of client needs.

Self-Determination and Enjoyment Enhancement Model

The second practice model examined is the Self-Determination and Enjoyment Enhancement Model (Dattilo, Kleiber & Williams, 1998). This model highlights the purpose of TR as supporting participants in achieving goals of self-determination and enjoyment, and ultimately functional improvement (Dattilo, Kleiber & Williams, 1998, p. 259). If the purpose of TR is to treat physical, cognitive, and emotional conditions associated with illness, injury, or chronic disability, then TR specialists need to create environments conducive to enjoyment that will ultimately contribute to well-being. This model is based on the premise that self-determination and enjoyment lead to functional improvement and personal growth.

In TR it is important to develop "conditions that help concentration, effort and a sense of control, and competence while promoting freedom of choice and expression of preference" for clients to experience enjoyment from programs (Dattilo, Kleiber & Williams, 1998). To do this a TR specialist needs to understand theory related to self-determination and factors interfering with it to develop strategies. Enjoyment and associated functional improvements serve to reinforce experiences and to lead a person to greater challenges and higher levels of self-determination.

The Self-Determination and Enjoyment Enhancement Model offers specific service delivery strategies for each stage of the TR process. The main focus of the model is to create environments conducive to enjoyment and to teach participants to experience that enjoyment, contributing to participants' functional improvements.

As shown in **Figure 9.2** (p. 234), the Self-Determination and Enjoyment Enhancement Model is divided into two sections—functional improvement and

enjoyment—with aspects of TR service delivery designed to support participants in achieving the goals of self-determination, enjoyment, intrinsic motivation, perceptions of manageable change, and investment of attention. The
model adopts a circular approach. Each component of the model interacts
with other aspects of the model. All components are essential and the model
could not be effective if one component is isolated or left out.

The model is designed to be circular, in contrast with other linear or
hierarchical TR practice models. It is circular because it assumes that each
intervention impacts outcomes of other components. In this model, four
determinants influence enjoyment and functional improvement. The model
builds on the components and gives an overview of the range of services
outlined in the Leisure Ability Model. The model also proposes strategies for
enhancing participants' experience in the four areas.

The Self-Determination and Enjoyment Enhancement Model is not
aimed at defining program content. It outlines an approach to TR rather than
specific outcomes or content. The strategies employed by the TR specialist
depend on the abilities, awareness, and needs of the participant (Dattilo, Kleiber
& Williams, 1998).

Components of the Self-Determination and Enjoyment Enhancement Model

Self-Determination. According to Dattilo, Kleiber, and Williams (1998)
"Self-determination involves acting as a primary causal agent in one's life and

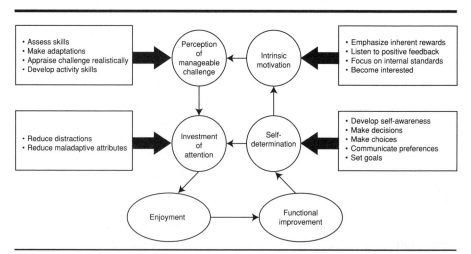

Figure 9.2   Self-Determination and Enjoyment Enhancement Model
(Fig. 2. A Psychologically-Based Therapeutic Recreation
Service Delivery Model to Enhance Self-Determination and
Enjoyment, *Therapeutic Recreation Journal, 32*(4), 263)

making choices and decisions free from external influence or interference." Self-determination involves autonomy and ability to choose options and the ability to adjust to situations when only one option is available.

When individuals are in control of their actions, they approach participation in activities with a sense of interest and commitment. The goal of many TR programs is to offer opportunities for enjoyment. By creating environments that offer many options and respond to client interests, a TR specialist can increase the likelihood of participants becoming self-determined (Dattilo, Kleiber & Williams, 1998).

Intrinsic Motivation. Self-determination is influenced by internal motivation. According to Dattilo, Kleiber, and Williams (1998) intrinsically motivated activities are energizing, exciting, challenging, and relaxing, and are often associated with recreation and leisure. People with intrinsic motivation generally seek challenges that match their competencies. They will avoid situations that are not challenging or too difficult. A person intrinsically motivated is more likely to learn, to adapt, and to develop competencies that contribute to well-being. This concept is extremely relevant to TR service delivery, because internal motivation is not linked to specific ability, so everyone can have it.

Persons with disabilities may be unaware of the possibilities for challenging experiences or discouraged from challenges or prevented by others from experiencing challenge. When success is achieved the challenge is perceived as manageable. Challenge can serve as a motivator.

Perceptions of Manageable Challenge. Therapeutic recreation must find a good match of challenge and skills through assessment. If an activity is too easy it causes boredom; if an activity is too hard it causes anxiety and frustration. Adaptations can increase or decrease the level of challenge, but to be successful one needs to examine instructional strategies. It is important to gain a realistic appraisal of the degree of challenge. One simple strategy is to introduce small, simple tasks then move on to the more difficult tasks. Carrying out a meaningful assessment of client skills, interests, and abilities will also assist in the development of challenging programs.

Investment of Attention. In TR services, many programs are offered to clients to attract attention; however, to maintain the person's attention the activity must remain challenging and keep with a person's expanding skills. If a person's skills decrease due to illness, perception of the challenge can be altered. Challenge must be constantly evaluated.

According to Csikszentmihalyi (1997), attention becomes ordered and fully invested when goals are clear, feedback is relevant, and challenge and skills are in balance. Investment of attention involves concentration, effort, and a sense of control. These factors must be understood and managed by TR specialists if attention and depth of involvement are to occur.

Enjoyment. According to Dattilo, Kleiber, and Williams (1998), enjoyment comes through the experience derived from *investing one's attention* in action patterns *intrinsically motivated.* Enjoyment is consistent with concentration, effort, control, and competence. Enjoyment is equated with fun, but also reflects a considerable amount of psychological involvement, including *perception of manageable challenge* and *self-determination.*

Functional Improvement. Functional improvement refers to developing and maintaining functional skills through enjoyment. When participants independently access creative environments conducive to enjoyment, functional improvements should result. When people participate in things they enjoy, it is possible to go beyond present abilities. Appropriately designed TR services allow clients the opportunity to reach farther, to communicate better, and to gain benefits of stress reduction. Dattilo, Kleiber, and Williams (1998) highlight the need to carry out research to document the link between enjoyment and functional improvement.

Practical Implications for TR Service Delivery

The Self-Determination and Enjoyment Enhancement Model offers TR professionals many practical implications and strategies. The interrelated items demonstrate the complexity of TR service offerings. This model has a number of valuable aspects for consideration. First, the model is tied to existing theory and well-researched constructs. Second, the model goes beyond a programming focus and highlights the importance of leisure awareness, choice making, decision making, and resource awareness. The model encourages the avoidance of oversimplified services and emphasizes the need for challenge.

This practice model highlights the importance of making choices and decisions as part of the leisure experience, which can ultimately lead to self-determination. If leisure is to foster independence, it is imperative that participants be encouraged to make decisions. Decisions about leisure involvement can be stimulated by having people identify resources, locate facilities, learn about requirements, and obtain answers. (Mahon 1994; Mahon & Bullock, 1992). Through this model clients can be encouraged to evaluate their decisions and to determine the effectiveness of their decisions. By allowing clients the opportunity to make timely, effective decisions, a greater interest may be developed, which subsequently promotes the investment of attention and enjoyment.

The Self-Determination and Enjoyment Enhancement Model is valuable because it has relevance in a variety of TR settings and with a diversity of disadvantaged populations. The model offers a number of specific strategies for TR specialists, including the following:

- Self-determination can be enhanced when people are encouraged and supported. Awareness of themselves in the leisure contexts, ability to make decisions, make choices, communicate preferences, and set goals can all be accomplished in TR service offerings.

- Intrinsic motivation is an important component of all programs in TR. Clients focused on internal standards emphasize inherent rewards, listen to feedback, and become aware of their interests more readily than those motivated by external rewards. To foster internal motivation, client choices can be reinforced and a focus on participation outcomes could be minimized. Helping participants to become aware of their interests through self-examination can also lead to intrinsic motivation.

- Since challenge relates directly to enjoyment, clients should have their skills accurately assessed. Then adaptations can be made to ensure realistic appraisals of challenge and development of activity skills. To promote self-determination, a TRS must have an awareness of the strengths, limitations, and unique learning needs of each client.

- Therapeutic recreation services should focus on sending messages that support and create environments of opportunity for both success and challenge, with some chance to take risks that might lead to failure.

- Goal setting is important. Clear goals provide direction and facilitate enjoyment as these goals are achieved.

- Environments that encourage self-determination assist clients in becoming personally aware of the benefits of leisure, promote relevant decision making and meaningful leisure choices, and consider the actions taken from those choices once they have been made.

- To develop self-determination, internal motivation, increased attention, and perceptions of manageable challenge it is imperative to include the client in the planning of TR services.

- Develop programs and services with enjoyment as a primary objective.

Optimizing Lifelong Health Model

Recreation services are recognized as having an influence in optimizing lifelong health and well-being through an emphasis on health enhancement and health promotion. Anecdotal reports suggest that involvement in recreation helps to prevent illness and further disability and promotes health of persons with physical, psychological, mental, or social disabilities (Wilhite, Keller & Caldwell, 1999). Given the links, TR services may be an ideal avenue to address health advancement needs.

The Optimizing Lifelong Health (OLH) model developed by Wilhite, Keller, and Caldwell (1999) is a nonlinear model supported by theory borrowed from developmental psychology (see **Figure 9.3**). The guiding principles addressed in the model include healthy leisure lifestyle, individualized resources and opportunities, and responsiveness to change. In this model, the role of the TR specialist is an educator and facilitator. The model allows for flexibility because it contends independence may not be realistic or desired. The OLH model takes a broad approach to service delivery that addresses both short-term and long-term outcomes. The OLH model is supported by three concepts: health advancement, reform in health and human service, and life course perspective.

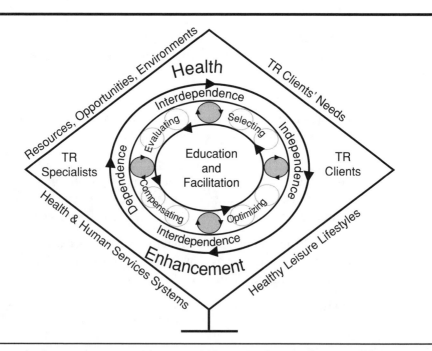

Figure 9.3   Optimizing Lifelong Health Model (Fig. 1. Optimizing Lifelong Health and Well-Being Through Therapeutic Recreation Model, *Therapeutic Recreation Journal, 33*(2), 102)

Health Advancement

Health advancement refers to a variety of behaviors individuals may use to prevent health risk, to maintain or to promote health, and to facilitate independence. These behaviors are often undertaken by individuals with assistance and support from others and can operate as formal services, such as specific programs offered by a TR specialist, or informal services, such as recreational activity with family or friends. Health advancement relies on many factors, including clients, support networks, environmental factors, and situational contexts. The role of the TR specialist is to prevent secondary consequences or to reduce further impairments (Wilhite, Keller & Caldwell, 1999).

Reform in Health and Human Service

Reforms are evident in North American systems that support health and human services. As changes are undertaken it becomes more challenging to provide comprehensive, integrative, systematic TR services with traditional service models. The role of TR services is changing due to changing clientele and shortened stays in long-term units, hospitals, and rehabilitation centers. The long-term impact of services may be increasingly difficult to assess, given that client contact is reduced and with so many clients making the transitions to community programs. The former emphasis of TR addressing immediate need and long-term need can be problematic. Since contact time with clients is unlikely to increase, the role of TR in certain settings, such as acute care, will need to adapt. Increasingly there is a need to enhance the role of TR services in the community. A primary goal of TR services could be to minimize the lifelong resources individuals require (Breske, cited in Wilhite, Keller & Caldwell, 1999). Costs need to be considered. A high level of client recidivism can be extremely costly. If illness prevention and health promotion are provided, transitions may be easier and less costly. In recent years healthcare has put a greater emphasis on client self-reliance, and there has been a greater increase in advocacy on the part of people with disabilities.

Life Course Perspective

People with disabilities, diseases, or illnesses continue to develop and to grow over the life course. This development is in relation to changing needs, resources, health status, and environments. During this process, clients constantly design procedures for coping, evaluating, or appraising outcomes (Baltes & Baltes, 1990; Leventhal, Levanthal & Shaefer, 1992). Goals, aims, interests, and resources change over the life course. People become aware of resources and their own skills within an environment, and conserve resources based on these changes. According to Kleiber (1985) leisure participation may influence health and well-being by facilitating coping behaviors in response to changes and transitions individuals experience over the life course. When people engage in healthy behaviors they actively participate in their own well-being.

The OLH model is grounded in developmental theory. Clients become active agents in securing and maintaining their own well-being over time, while maximizing their individual capabilities for growth and creative adaptations (Wilhite, Keller & Caldwell, 1999). The client-initiated strategies are critical and reflect self-determined decision making. The OLH model is supported by three basic principles adapted from the developmental theory proposed by Baltes and Baltes (1990):

1. Engagement in healthy leisure lifestyle reduces the probability of pathology or secondary consequences of disability over the life course.

2. Strengthening optimal health can be achieved by developing resources and opportunities, such as educational, motivational, or health-advancement activities.

3. Individuals must be prepared to alter choices or to find substitutes by changing personal and environmental characteristics across the life course. There is a need to be flexible and accommodating in response to internal and external changes. The role of the TR professional is to facilitate adjustments while allowing for maximum client choice, control, and preservation of self. In the OHL model, TR plays a central role in coping and adjusting to changing conditions and health factors (Wilhite, Keller & Caldwell, 1999).

As Figure 9.3 (p. 238) indicates, the OLH model components include four developmental features: selecting, optimizing, compensating, and evaluating. These four elements are the primary responsibility of clients supported by TR services. The TR specialist uses a systematic approach that includes assessment, program planning, implementation, and evaluation to support the individualized planning approach.

Components of the Optimizing Lifelong Health Model

Wilhite, Keller, and Caldwell (1999) identify four components to target in TR services:

1. ***Selecting***. The selecting component focuses on resources in functional domains that match environmental demands with the client

capacities, skills, and motivations. The selecting component supports efforts to achieve, to maintain, or to regain leisure lifestyles that optimize health. This component involves selecting target activities with clients to ensure maximum personal control and choice. The TR specialist can help clients to set limits and to increase choice according to changes in health status and environmental situations. The selection of appropriate activities involves goal setting and skill building to assist in achieving goals. The process of setting goals is an important tool for enhancing choice and decision making.

2. *Optimizing*. The optimizing component focuses on selection of activities that maximize general personal and environmental resources to make participation possible.

3. *Compensating*. The compensating component allows for the adoption of both new skills and lost skills. Compensating might mean substituting a new activity or adapting a familiar activity. There may be a need to learn skills to prevent further losses, secondary disabilities, or injuries. There may also be a need for new facilities and transportation.

4. *Evaluation*. As clients select, optimize, and compensate they are presented with many options. Learning skills related to evaluation can help clients to weigh the advantages and disadvantages of specific choices and decisions. This process of critical evaluation may lead to new activities that offer the same benefits with less costs and resources. Learning evaluation skills also fosters independence and less reliance on formal TR service intervention.

Role of the TR Specialist in the OLH Model

The OLH-TR model highlights an intervention approach that emphasizes education and facilitation in TR. According to the model, education focuses on awareness, knowledge, and understanding of various options for minimizing health risks and promoting health. Facilitation strategies include creating experiences for clients to apply learning, offering leisure opportunities, and advocating for clients. The role of a facilitator is to achieve a balance of "needs, resources, and goals for healthy (lifestyle) environments where needs can be met" (Wilhite, Keller & Caldwell, 1999). The model suggests a need for balance, ensuring all elements are addressed. The OHL-TR model suggests independent functioning with minimal support from TR and others is not always a reasonable goal depending on client capabilities. The model focuses on creating an environment to foster self-determination, yet health is not necessarily achieved when you move from dependence to independence.

Practical Applications of the OLH Model

This model offers many different applications for TR service providers. Some strengths of this model include the following:

- interrelatedness to all aspects of TR.

- interdependence between clients, others, and the environment.

- departure from traditional and curative models.

- flexibility to include diverse, social, personal, and cultural needs.

- emphasis on the value of an environment.

- opportunity to allow for changes as people change.

- support for personal responsibility and empowerment.

- the role of a TR professional as a facilitator and educator without focusing on a particular setting.

- consideration for clients who will not "get better."

Leisure Gyroscope for Enhancing Quality of Life in Long-Term Care Model

The Leisure Gyroscope for Enhancing Quality of Life in Long-Term Care Model, or Leisure Gyroscope Model (LGM) was developed by TR practitioners in Quebec, Canada, and for this chapter has been translated from French to English. In the translation several adaptations have been made where modifications and changes to terminology do not translate well into the English language. The original model—Modèle normatif d'Animation-loisirs en centre d'hébergement pour la création d'un milieu de vie animé (Côté, LaPan & Hallé, 1997)—is currently being used in several long-term care agencies in Quebec. The model has been included to demonstrate the diversity in practice models in the TR field.

Enhancing and maintaining quality of life is a main objective of the health system in Canada. Medical progress has enhanced the quality of life and for Canadians and increased their chances of living to an advanced age. The medical focus in healthcare, with all its advances in technology, has its limits. With more people living to an advanced age, there are less acute diseases and more people with chronic disabilities and illnesses. With the increase in the aging population, healthcare budgets are stretched. With greater demands on long-term care as population ages, the challenge becomes how to manage quality of care. The ideal situation is to give support for people in their homes, but for people with severe limitations as a result of illness or disability, long-term care becomes a reality. With an increase in the demand for long-term care, we must focus on identifying resources needed to support quality of life in institutions.

Many studies to addressed and identified indicators of quality of life in institutions. To break the cycle of devaluation one goes through when moving from a home environment to an institution, one needs to understand a client in the context of needs and environment in long-term care. In Quebec, the Department of Health and Social Services mandates every long-term care agency to create environments that enhance quality of life as a part of their mission. To address this mission, each long-term care agency is to create environments that enhance quality of life in a concrete way by offering appropriate therapeutic recreation services. In reality, a decrease in resources has made creating an enhanced quality of life in institutions a challenge. To create a positive long-term care environment that includes residents, family members, neighbors, volunteers, staff, and community, all members of the staff and residents must work together.

The LGM incorporates medical and therapeutic approaches. It promotes leisure as a significant tool to maintain natural human activity and normal (home-like) rhythm within the context of an institution.

To improve quality of life there is a need to create a substitute for the natural home environment in institutions. This is a challenge, because disability, illness, lack of support, barriers, shared living, patriarchal relationships with staff, architectural barriers, and lack of resources all contribute as influencing factors. According to the Quebec Federation of Leisure in Institutions the creation of a positive long-term care environment will not develop on its own (Côté, LaPan & Hallé, 1997).

In the LGM, TR serves as a catalyst to create a consistent, dynamic balance of quality of life in long-term care. According to the LGM, TR creates energy, hence the gyroscope indicates a circular design that rotates, balancing and supporting a number of elements. Variables of the model include significant others, disability, staff, volunteers, the community, and relationships with others. TR keeps equilibrium of these variables for enhanced quality of life. To keep a balance one needs to consider the weight of each element for each individual.

Foundations Supporting the Leisure Gyroscope Model

The LGM is supported by a number of statements serving as the foundation of the model, including the following:

- Organized and structured therapeutic recreation services have a positive influence on long-term care agencies.

- Individuals require different levels of support at different times.

- Increased quality and quantity of positive interactions and resources in TR will enrich quality of life of clients.

- There must be a specific plan of action with a philosophy of TR services that favors choices for clients.

- Agencies must support the client's right to live, laugh, and love.

- Free time should be viewed as a privileged opportunity, not enforced time.

- Agencies must give value to spontaneity, caring relationships, goodwill, and kindness.

- Daily routines that exist in client rooms and corridors must be transformed.

- There is a need to seek a balance between therapeutic interactions and spontaneity.

- There must be opportunities for clients to be democratic, with the ability to make informed decisions and to make significant changes in the social fabric of the agency.

- Interdisciplinary support should include all available social services.

- There is a need to open the long-term care agency to the community in a variety of meaningful ways.

- Leisure should be recognized as a vehicle for increased quality of life and a catalyst for positive change.

However, the developers of this model recognize these statements serving as a foundation do not happen easily. Simply providing TR services cannot be a guarantee of enhanced or increased quality of life. Anecdotally, there is recognition that leisure contributes to increased choice, improved well-being, and enhanced quality of life. This model highlights the importance of leisure to maintain and to enhance quality of life and allows for further development to support the role of TR and contributions to quality of life in long-term care. The model also serves to justify the need for TR services by addressing the formal link to the mission of promoting quality of life.

Key Components of the Leisure Gyroscope Model

The authors of the LGM (Côté, LaPan & Hallé, 1997) state that for recreation services to have an impact on quality of life six components must be in place: (a) administrative support for quality of life, (b) need for adapted services, (c) development of structured services, (d) resource development, (e) balance of program offerings, and (f) evaluation. In this model the role of a TR specialist would be to concretely address each component.

Administrative Support for Quality of Life. Decision makers and administration must consider quality of life a priority in long-term care. TR specialists can ensure this happens in several ways. To begin, there can be a review of agency missions and philosophical orientations, including TR services as a component linked directly to quality of life. TR specialists can arrange meetings with stakeholders and decision makers and highlight the importance of TR services for improving residents' quality of life. Educational sessions and workshops can be given on the TR profession to ensure the administration supports the hiring of qualified TR professionals with appropriate educational backgrounds and training. TR specialists can promote a culture of support through research and evaluation to demonstrate the outcomes of TR services and to secure adequate resource support from the administration. Finally TR departments can present a clear plan for the need for environmental resources, such as appropriate places for programs, and the need for different types of spaces, including workshops for skill building, outdoor programming, and adapted material.

Need for Adapted Services. If therapeutic recreation services are to impact quality of life, then programs have to be designed to address specific individual needs. To create effective, quality TR services, some strategies TR specialists can utilize include the following:

- carrying out a careful leisure assessment of each client to determine priorities in service delivery.

- analyzing assessment data regularly to design individual plans based on needs and to make program adaptations when necessary.

- modifying activities only when necessary, because an activity modified too much from its original form may not have the same benefits.

- developing monthly program standards that reflect community offerings.

Development of Structured Services. As mentioned earlier, TR programs need to be planned with the specific goal of enhancing quality of life. TR services need to be structured in a way that meets agency and client goals. Characteristics of structured services include the following:

- developing TR programs following consultation with clients (and, if appropriate, staff, family members, and volunteers).

- developing a plan of documentation that provides a written record of client interests, progress, and concerns.

- developing specific measurable program objectives with clearly stated outcomes.

- designing appropriate spaces and equipment for services.

- creating client program opportunities that build on skills before coming into the long-term care facility.

- offering opportunities to allow clients to understand the importance of TR services for quality of life through leisure education programs.

- encouraging client input on structured services through committees that include different clients and stakeholders in the institution.

- holding interdisciplinary meetings to discuss shared philosophy in approaching quality of life.

- developing client committees of active volunteers to assist in specific programs or service offerings.

- ensuring consultation with clients continues beyond the initial assessment.

- establishing a policy and procedures manual that includes a mission, focused department goals, and a detailed description of how services are defined (Côté, LaPan & Hallé, 1997).

Resource Development. Ongoing resource development is an important aspect of the delivery of quality TR services. This aspect can seem overwhelming for the TR specialist with a heavy caseload of clients, or with increasing demands for documentation of services. Strategies for TR specialists for resource development include the following:

- developing a strong network of volunteers, family, and community networks.

- securing supplemental income to support TR services from grants and community sponsors

- developing a long-term plan of ongoing support from the agency rather than relying on short-term funding solutions.

- developing partnerships (e.g., schools, municipalities, community organizations).

- designing programs that could enhance client autonomy and less reliance on the TR specialists for services.

Balance of Program Offerings. It is important to develop a wide variety of service offerings to maintain a positive social climate, to develop significant relationships within the long-term care facility, and to actualize individual clients through leisure. Some strategies for creating a balance of services include the following:

- ensuring TR services are developed based on interests of clients, not offered based on what has been done in the past or what equipment is available.

- scheduling both individual and group activities.

- offering opportunities for skill development in all domains.

- offering TR programs that allow for different levels of participation (e.g., spectator events, skill building, drop-in programs, and programs that involve full participation).

- designating active roles in programs for residents to realize potential.

- designing specific activities for people who prefer to be by themselves.

- ensuring TR services have a presence all the time in the long-term care agency, offering programs at different times each day, seven days a week.

- auditing monthly to determine the diversity of services in the physical, cognitive, social, affective, and spiritual domains.

- ensuring TR program offerings include different interactions, such as resident–resident, resident–family, and resident–community (Côté, LaPan & Hallé, 1997).

Evaluation. For services to be effective and to contribute to the quality of life in long-term care, regular, formal evaluation of program offerings must be carried out. In an evaluation, a TR specialist should look at the different elements of service and how they relate to the mission of the agency and to the orientation of the TR department. Specifically, an evaluation should include the following:

- reviewing each program to determine if appropriate for current clientele.

- reviewing assessment information to determine if specific needs are being meet.

- reviewing care plans to determine if goals and objectives are being met in a reasonable appropriate way.

- interviewing clients to address concerns about quality of life in the institution (Côté, LaPan & Hallé, 1997).

In addition, there needs to be a routine check on the orientation to services. TR specialists should review all components to address specific strategies, and should also consider the following:

- Do TR programs reinforce the routine, structured environment in long-term care?

- Do TR services complement what is currently being offered by a client's support network (e.g., family, friends, other staff)?

- Do the TR programs offer freedom of choice and the ability to make quality decisions?

- Do the TR service offerings allow for the maintenance of specific relationships?

- Is client quality of life and happiness at the root of all program designs?

- Are client preferences included in the service design?

Practical Applications of the Leisure Gyroscope Model

The LGM offers concrete strategies for TR specialists. The model highlights the interconnectedness of TR services with other aspects of long-term care. It demonstrates the impact of quality of TR services and how it can influence quality of life. The model provides an overview of key elements in developing TR services. It is easy to follow and highlights the role of systematically designed TR services in long-term care. The LGM is not formally tested. Links to the support of enhancing and maintaining quality of life need to be investigated further.

Summary

This chapter introduced practice models in therapeutic recreation. The chapter provided an overview of why practice models are important and also identifies how practice models can serve to explain, justify, and promote TR services. This chapter highlighted four practice models to demonstrate differences in approach, content, and foundation. Readers are encouraged to explore other practice models to understand fully the diversity of the scope of practice in TR. The learning activities for this chapter offer an opportunity to use practice models to support the answer to the question "What is therapeutic recreation?"

Learning Activities

1. Select a TR practice model and explain it in your own words.

2. Design a TR program plan based on one model presented in this chapter.

3. In small groups, select a TR practice model and address the strengths and challenges of the model. Discuss its relevance to TR service delivery.

4. Identify similarities and differences between each of the four models presented in this chapter.

5. Answer the question "What is therapeutic recreation?" using a model in this chapter to support your answer.

6. Identify examples of cultural considerations that might be relevant for the specific clientele with whom you plan to work.

7. The developers of each of the models presented in this chapter discuss the need to evaluate and to further test the models. How would you design an evaluation procedure that would test or evaluate the model you select in your agency?

8. Select one population and TR setting and choose an appropriate model. Develop arguments that support your choice.

9. Using criteria and examples of models presented in this chapter, design your own TR service delivery model. Justify each element of your model and explain the interrelationships of items. Share your model with others in class and offer critiques to fellow classmates on their models.

10. Visit two agencies and determine what practice models guide their TR services.

References

Austin, D. R. (1991). Introduction and overview. In D. R. Austin and M. E. Crawford (Eds.), *Therapeutic recreation: An introduction* (pp. 1–29). Englewood Cliffs, NJ: Prentice Hall.

Baltes P. B. and Baltes M. M. (1990). Selective optimization with compensation. In P. B. Baltes and M. M. Baltes (Eds.), *Successful aging: Perspectives from the behavioral sciences* (pp. 1–34). New York, NY: Cambridge University Press.

Carter, M. J., Van Andel, G. E., and Robb, G. M. (1995). *Therapeutic Recreation: A practical approach* (2nd ed.). Prospect Heights, IL: Waveland Press.

Côté, L., LaPan, B., and Hallé, A. (1997). *Modèle normatif d'Animation-loisirs en centre d'hébergement pour la création d'un milieu de vie animé* [Normative model for the leisure/animation in long-term care centers to enhance quality of life] (pp. 1–23). Quebec, Canada: Publication for the *Federation Quebecoise du Loisir en institution.*

Csikszentmihalyi, M. (1997). *Finding flow: The psychology of optimal engagement with everyday life.* New York, NY: Basic Books.

Dattilo, J., Kleiber, D., and Williams, R. (1998). Self-determination and enjoyment enhancement: A psychologically based service delivery model for therapeutic recreation. *Therapeutic Recreation Journal, 32*(4), 258–271.

Freysinger, V. (1999). A critique of the "optimizing lifelong health through therapeutic recreation" (OLH-TR) model. *Therapeutic Recreation Journal, 33*(2), 109–115.

Kleiber, D. A. (1985). Motivational reorientation in adulthood and the resource of leisure. *Advances in Motivation and Achievement, 4*, 217–250.

Leventhal, H., Leventhal, E., and Shaefer, P. (1992). Vigilant coping and health behavior. In M. Ory, R. Abeles, and P. Lipman (Eds.), *Health, behavior and aging* (pp. 109–140). Newbury Park, CA: Sage.

Mahon, M. (1994). The use of self-control techniques to facilitate self-determination skills during leisure in adolescents with mild and moderate mental retardation. *Therapeutic Recreation Journal, 28*(2), 58–72.

Mahon, M. and Bullock, C. (1992). Teaching adolescents with mild mental retardation to make decisions in leisure through the use of self control techniques. *Therapeutic Recreation Journal, 26*(1), 9–26.

Peterson, C. A. and Gunn, S. L. (1984). *Therapeutic recreation program design: Principles and procedures* (2nd ed.). Englewood Cliffs, NJ: Prentice Hall.

Peterson, C. A. and Stumbo, N. J. (2000). *Therapeutic recreation program design: Principles and procedures.* Boston, MA: Allyn & Bacon.

Selz, L. (2000). Introduction to therapeutic recreation: An evolving profession. In C. Bullock and M. Mahon (Eds.), *Introduction to recreation services for people with disabilities: A person-centered approach* (2nd ed.) (pp. 267–301). Champagne, IL: Sagamore Publishing.

Stumbo, N. J. and Peterson, C. A. (1998). The leisure ability model. *Therapeutic Recreation Journal, 32*(2), 82–96.

Sylvester, C., Voelkl, J. E., and Ellis, G. D. (2001). *Therapeutic recreation programming: Theory and practice.* State College, PA: Venture Publishing, Inc.

Voelkl, J. E., Carruthers, C., and Hawkins, B. (1997). Special series on therapeutic recreation practice models: Guest editors' introduction. *Therapeutic Recreation Journal, 31*, 210–212.

Wilhite B., Keller, M. J., and Caldwell, L. (1999). Optimizing lifelong health and well-being: A health enhancing model of therapeutic recreation. *Therapeutic Recreation Journal, 33*(2), 98–108.

Section 4

The Changing Healthcare Scene

Chapter 10

Disabilities
Chronic Conditions Versus Acute Conditions

Learning Objectives

1. Name the three variables associated with chronic conditions and give one example of each.

2. Describe lifestyle/quality of life of the "typical" person with a disability residing in the community.

3. Explain how the skeletal system is divided into axial and appendicular parts.

4. Provide an example of an impairment that affects the skeletal system versus one that affects the joint system.

5. Suggest three programs TR may use to address pain among patients with skeletal and joint impairments.

6. Explain why exercise programs for children and teens with Duchenne type muscular dystrophy are not as effective as exercise programs for frail older adults.

7. Compare and contrast injuries to the central nervous system (e.g., spinal cord) with injuries to the peripheral nervous system (e.g., a nerve to a muscle).

8. Explain how persons with spinal cord injuries make the transition from preinjury to postinjury lifestyle and the role leisure plays in this adjustment.

9. Explain why persons with visual or auditory impairments often need the assistance of a TR specialist to improve their low levels of physical fitness.

10. List the causes/risk factors for cardiovascular disorders. Next, divide the risk factors into two groups: those that cannot be altered and those that are modifiable. Suggest TR programs for the modifiable risk factors.

11. Explain why professionals should not assume a person with cancer is terminally ill.

Table 10.1 lists the leading causes of death in the United States for persons 65 years and older. In Canada, the leading causes of death of older adults are similar, with cancer attributed to 27.2% of deaths, heart disease 26.6%, stroke 7.4%, chronic lung disease 4.5%, pneumonia and influenza 3.7%, and diabetes 2.6% (Statistics Canada, 2001a). For the most part these and other leading causes of death are known as *chronic* conditions. In 1995 Statistics Canada identified that more that 80% of individuals over the age of 65 had some type of chronic illness. Because chronic conditions are associated with advanced age, and because of changes in healthcare policy over the last 20 years, the type of client seen in clinical practice has changed. Today clients are likely to be older, sicker, and more debilitated. Chronic conditions share several characteristics:

- They cannot be cured.

- They increase in incidence as people age.

- They tend to be progressive, worsening over time.

Because chronic conditions cannot be cured, most rehabilitation/intervention plans aim to slow progression of the disorder and/or address the major symptoms that interfere with independent daily functioning. For instance, a client with osteoporosis (excessive loss of mineral content in bones) may become involved in an aquatic exercise program to retard the progression of bone loss (weight-bearing exercise slows the rate of loss of mineral content in bone).

Table 10.1   Leading Causes of Death Among Persons 65 and Older in the United States for 1998

Cause	Mortality Rate per 100,000 Persons
Heart Disease	1795
Cancer	1125
Stroke	414
Chronic Lung Disease	288
Pneumonia and Influenza	248
Diabetes	144

The causes of chronic conditions relate to three variables, including age, adverse environmental factors (e.g., excessive exposure to sunlight), and detrimental lifestyle habits (e.g., cigarette smoking). Researchers know that chronic conditions become more prevalent as people age. Where caution needs to be exercised is in the interpretation of age alone as a causative event. Although even normal aging is associated with biological changes (e.g., more difficulty hearing), it would be a mistake to say that age alone causes heart disease or any other chronic condition. What is correlated with the aging process is the cumulative exposure to negative environmental stimuli and poor lifestyle habits. Therefore, separating age effects from latent and manifest pathology is difficult.

Toxins and even excessive exposure to normally benign environmental stimuli may lead to an increased risk for a variety of chronic conditions. Some exposure to sunlight is fine—in fact, it is necessary to form Vitamin D. But most readers who have kept up with the popular media are aware that excessive exposure to sunlight is associated with an increased risk for skin cancer.

Negative lifestyle habits can be modified and usually result from conscious decisions. For example, most of the risk factors for heart disease are modifiable and represent several conscious decisions about health behavior. Cigarette smoking, sedentary lifestyle, high-fat diet, untreated high blood pressure, obesity, and stress are all subject to change in a favorable direction. Changing any or all of these habits can significantly reduce the risk of heart disease and other cardiovascular impairments.

In contrast, many of the leading causes of death among younger persons are *acute* afflictions or accidents. Acute conditions would include automobile accidents, motorcycle accidents, acute infections, or gunshot wounds. In the recent past, acute illnesses accounted for a large share of deaths, especially among the very young and very old—those most susceptible to opportunistic infections and contagious diseases. With the improvement in medications, especially ones designed to treat childhood diseases, the rate of mortality from acute conditions has dropped dramatically since World War II.

Another important point about chronic conditions is that usually the person has more than one affliction. It would not be unusual to find a person who had heart disease and high blood pressure and diabetes. Although heart disease may be the primary diagnosis, high blood pressure and diabetes exacerbate the heart disease, and are referred to as *comorbid* or *secondary* conditions.

Regardless of the impairment—acute or chronic—the patient today is more likely to be discharged sooner than later. Many clients are left to administer much of their rehabilitation on their own following a discharge planning process. With client education, the optimal goal is to teach the client to complete rehabilitation (e.g., exercise) on his or her own following discharge, without the aid a therapist. This practice is designed to reduce the length of hospital stays and thereby reduce healthcare costs. The problem is many people do not comply with their rehabilitation plan following discharge for a variety of reasons, ranging from lack of commitment and willpower, to inability to access the proper community-based resources.

The implications for TR, especially community-based TR, are significant. Community-based TR may assume a major role in outpatient and community-based care and follow-up by providing direct services, supportive environments for compliance with rehabilitation, preventive prescriptions, and maintenance of functional skills and abilities. As noted before, the problem with chronic conditions is they cannot be cured. This means the "new" patient will need ongoing, community-based follow-up to avoid further deterioration.

Quality of life is at risk when an individual is born with an impairment (congenital birth defect) or acquires an impairment (acute or chronic) through a gradual disease process or accident. Coyle and Kinney (1990) studied the effects of physical impairments on quality of life and leisure lifestyle among 790 persons with physical impairments living in the community. They discovered less than one in three were employed full-time or part-time and the average person with a physical impairment residing in the community was impoverished. Given the relative disadvantage that these individuals faced with respect to their vocational aspirations, one might conclude that they would seek satisfaction through leisure even more. However, this was not the case. The same subjects, on the average, described their leisure lifestyles as homebound, sedentary, and isolated. Their leisure was typically limited to television and reading. They were not able to leave their homes very often for a variety of reasons (e.g., lack of transportation, weather, inaccessible facilities). They were often alone at home all day while caretakers went to work or attended to other necessary tasks.

To the extent that most community-dwelling persons with disabilities will not find satisfaction through rewarding employment, augmentation and support of a satisfying leisure lifestyle is indicated. To do so, supportive and accessible facilities and programs will be needed. Instruction in the skills necessary to independent participation will have to be taught. Practice and adherence to exercise programs, skill acquisition, and inclusion to the greatest extent possible will be the future demands of persons with impairments. Community-based TR is well-positioned to deliver these services because such programs are most often affiliated with larger community recreation departments. In the United States, by law these services must be made accessible to all persons who reside in the community regardless of health or impairment. Furthermore, community recreation departments typically control a variety of enviable recreation resources the typical hospital or rehabilitation facility cannot afford (e.g., swimming pools, gymnasiums, parks). Community-based TR only needs to identify potential consumers, and then to follow through with services.

In this chapter we will introduce some of the most common acute and chronic conditions, although chronic conditions are far more prevalent. These are the conditions that the future TR specialist is most apt to see in practice. A description of each condition is provided, as well as some ideas for a TR response to patients who have those conditions. However, this chapter is not meant to substitute for a more advanced course that would explain the causes of the impairment and research-based treatment interventions for TR in more detail. Sections are organized according to systems. The language is intentionally kept user-friendly with the assumption the reader has not yet had a course in anatomy and physiology. Some information about normal functioning is included to the extent that it is necessary to the understanding of the impairments.

Skeletal and Joint Systems

The main functions of the skeletal system are

1. to provide protection (e.g., the brain is inside the skull and protected).

2. to provide support (e.g., the spine helps to put us in an upright posture).

3. to provide movement (when muscles are attached to bones and contract, movement occurs).

4. to store minerals (minerals are what make bones hard, they may be extracted from bone through physiologic processes mediated by hormones for use elsewhere).

5. to produce blood cells.

The skeletal system (see **Figure 10.1**, p. 262) is divided into two basic parts: the axial skeleton and the appendicular skeleton. The axial skeleton is composed of the skull, spine, sternum, and ribs and gets its name from its position on the central axis of the body. Its main job is to position the body into postures suited to specific tasks. The second part of the skeleton is the appendicular skeleton. It is associated with the appendages, the arms, shoulders, legs, and hips. The primary task of the appendicular skeleton is to enable movement and to allow for the manipulation of objects.

Where bones fit together, joints are formed. Not all joints allow for movement, but those formed by the appendicular skeleton allow for considerable movement. As a general rule, the more movement the joint allows the more at risk it is for injury or development of a chronic condition (e.g., arthritis). Also, the more weight a joint supports, the more likely it is to succumb to an injury or chronic condition (e.g., the lower part of the spine). There is a tradeoff—mobility and stability are the inverse of one another. Highly mobile joints make life more interesting and fun, but they are more apt to be hurt.

Disorders of the Skeletal and Joint Systems

One fairly common congenital disorder that affects the spine (and spinal cord) is *spina bifida*. Spina bifida is found in two types. The first is apt to go unnoticed; it is called the occulta (hidden) type. With the occulta type of spina bifida, some of the vertebrae are not completely formed, usually in the lower portion of the spine (lumbar region, lower back). Often this condition goes undetected and presents little in the way of a handicap to the individual. It is sometimes discovered later in life when the back is x-rayed for some other reason.

The more serious and debilitating type of spina bifida is known as the *cystica* variety. With the cystica type the spine is not completely formed, but

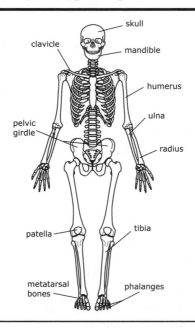

Figure 10.1   Anterior View of Skeleton

also the spinal cord (part of the nervous system) is not completely developed either. Again, the site of the disorder is usually in the lower back. But with involvement of the spinal cord in addition to the spine, spina bifida cystica becomes very handicapping. The child is usually paralyzed in both lower extremities (paraplegia). The child born with the more serious type of spina bifida is also at greater risk for hydrocephalus (water on the brain) and cognitive impairment. Early detection and medical intervention usually helps the patient avoid or minimize the risk of hydrocephalus and cognitive impairment. In addition, because of better medical care, patients with the severe form of spina bifida now live well into adulthood. As the patient ages, other conditions (comorbid or secondary) may become manifest, such as postural deformities or pressure sores (as a result of a prolonged seated position) and heart disease (from a sedentary lifestyle).

Arthritis is the most frequently occurring chronic condition in the United States and Canada, affecting a significant percentage of older adults. Statistics Canada (2001b) indicates that 39.9% of adults between the ages of 65–74 are affected by arthritis, and this increases to 47.5% after age 75. In Canada over a half a million older adults suffer from arthritis (National Health Forum, 2002, p. 126). Though not fatal, in its severe forms arthritis can impose marked mobility restrictions on the individual. Arthritis occurs in many different forms, but the two most common types are osteoarthritis and rheumatoid arthritis. *Osteoarthritis* is caused by wear and tear, or joint injury, and is characterized by a breakdown in the articular cartilage in a joint. Following deterioration of the articular cartilage, pain and restricted movement are the most common symptoms.

Rheumatoid arthritis is not as prevalent as osteoarthritis, but is more debilitating. In addition, rheumatoid arthritis tends to affect individuals at a younger age. Whereas osteoarthritis is typically seen in older adults, onset of rheumatoid arthritis occurs during middle adulthood, with a juvenile form manifesting during the teen years. Like osteoarthritis, the rheumatoid form is associated with pain and mobility limitation. But marked inflammation usually accompanies rheumatoid arthritis, further restricting movement.

Osteoporosis affects 1.4 million Canadians, affecting one in four women and one in eight men over the age of 50 (Osteoporosis Society of Canada, 2004). Osteoporosis refers to the loss in mineral content from the skeletal system. The mineral content in bone is what gives the skeletal system its ability to support the body's weight and to withstand external forces exerted on the skeleton during ambulation and weight-bearing exercises. Although men can get osteoporosis, its onset is usually associated with the menopause, the cessation of ovulation in the female. Hormones secreted by the female's ovaries seem to have a protective effect on the skeletal system but once those hormones are no longer secreted in adequate amounts, the protective effect disappears and there is a net loss in mineral content in bone. The biggest problem with osteoporosis is that the bones become weaker. Eventually the person may experience small fractures in weight-bearing bones, such as the spine. Furthermore, all bones become more susceptible to injury. Therefore, any sort of trauma may result in a fracture because of the loss of mineral content in bone tissue.

Fractures, of course, may occur at any age, but are far more serious in older adults. Fractures are also more common among older adults, because they are more likely to have manifest or latent osteoporosis. Adding to the problem, their bones do not heal as well as a younger person's. The most serious fractures among older adults (hip, ankle, skull) result from falls. Either the bone breaks as a result of the trauma from the fall, or the bone is so weak from osteoporosis that it gives way and causes the person to fall.

Orthopedic impairments share symptoms in common, although these symptoms are not unique to persons with disorders that affect the skeletal or joint systems. Symptoms common to skeletal and joint impairments include pain, immobility, and depression (reactive). These symptoms form the basis of a TR response.

TR Response to Skeletal and Joint Impairments

Pain is frequently observed with skeletal disorders, in part because bones have an abundant nerve supply. In particular, persons with arthritis, osteoporosis, and fractures experience both acute and chronic pain. Both interfere with one's ability to carry on a normal, independent lifestyle. Strategies to address pain include various sensory modalities alone or in combination with exercise. Stimulation of the affected area with warm or cool temperatures, for example, can short-circuit the pain impulses to the brain and give temporary relief. Aquatic therapy is an excellent method for cooling the body and countering pain. In addition, the patient also receives the benefit of exercise while in the water.

Mild to moderate intensity exercise provides added benefits based on several potential factors. First, exercise will strengthen muscles around a joint, thereby adding to the stability of the joint. Exercise has been associated with an increase in secretion of the body's own natural analgesics (pain relievers), thus augmenting pain relief. Exercise and sensory stimulation also provide both physiological and psychological diversionary effects.

Most older adults fear loss of independence more than death. Mobility limitations that frequently result from skeletal and joint disorders pose a threat to independence. Fortunately, the use of mild to moderate intensity exercise programs with persons who have skeletal and joint impairments have yielded favorable results. For example, persons with osteoporosis have been shown to benefit from mild forms of weight-bearing exercise, such as walking or light weight training. In more severe cases of osteoporosis, the patient can exercise in the water to remove some of the weight from the skeleton and joints because of the water's buoyancy. Likewise, persons with arthritis can improve strength, range of motion, and flexibility through mild forms of exercise. The risk of a sedentary lifestyle, even after the affliction has manifested, is that pain and immobility will lead to further limitations and the person will become progressively less willing to move—creating a downward spiral of more and more immobility and pain.

Like pain, depression is a symptom common to many impairments. The type of depression seen most often in company with physical illnesses is known as reactive depression. The person is depressed in response to the limitations and life changes associated with the illness. In many respects, this is a natural reaction. TR can help the patient to address depressive symptoms through several means. First, since many recreation activities take place in a social situation, social support, especially from peers, helps the person to understand he or she is not alone—others like him or her face similar challenges. Second, the patient can enhance self-efficacy through participation in and learning of recreation activities. These encourage a sense of perceived control in the client. And when many aspects of the person's life seem to be out of control, knowing that control and competence can be experienced through leisure participation is very beneficial, thus countering depression.

Muscle System

The muscle system works with the skeletal and joint systems to produce movement. When muscles contract and pull on tendons attached to bones they produce movements at joints (where bones meet). Muscular effort also helps to regulate body temperature (e.g., shivering in cold weather, radiating heat as a result of muscular effort). Posture is regulated by static rather than dynamic muscle contractions. Muscular effort is required to maintain an upright posture (seated or standing) and to hold the head erect. The type of muscle associated with movement and posture are referred to as skeletal muscle because they move the skeleton. Major skeletal muscles of the body are illustrated in **Figure 10.2** (p. 266).

There are two other types of muscle: cardiac muscle and smooth muscle. Cardiac muscle is unique to the heart. It has the capacity to contract to produce the heartbeat continuously and rhythmically throughout life. Smooth muscle is found lining the many hollow tube systems throughout the body, such as the circulatory system and digestive system. The smooth muscle lining these tubes allows for constriction (narrowing) and dilation (expansion) of the tube for more or less passage of the substance carried by the system (e.g., blood, food).

Disorders of the Muscle System

The good news is few impairments affect the muscle system from within. That is, few disorders affect muscle tissue directly. Rather, most limitations that affect muscles have their origin in the nervous system. Accordingly most of those will be covered under the nervous system section. Here we will concentrate on the few impairments that directly arise in muscle tissue.

Muscular dystrophy is a disorder unique to the muscular system. The childhood form (Duchenne type) is the most common. It is ultimately fatal. The adult form (Facio-Scapulo-Humeral type) has a better prognosis because it progresses more slowly.

Duchenne type muscular dystrophy (D-MD) is genetically transmitted and congenital (present at birth), although symptoms do not normally manifest until the toddler and preschool years. Parents of children with D-MD usually notice that their child fails to progress normally—motor skills and abilities are delayed. Only after taking their child to a physician do they learn the diagnosis of D-MD. The natural history of D-MD is one of progressive and

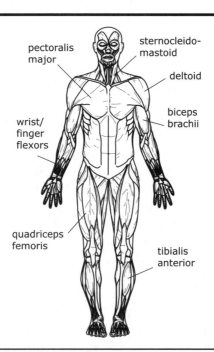

Figure 10.2   Anterior View of the Muscles of the Body

irreversible deterioration. The child is typically able to walk up until 12 years of age or so. After that, he or she requires a wheelchair. The Duchenne type of muscular dystrophy affects 1 in 3,500 worldwide (Kakulas & Mastaglia, 1990).

Muscle deterioration continues to progress during the teen years. With more of the muscle system involved, the adolescent may experience difficulty with breathing. Postural deformities may result from prolonged sitting and loss of muscle tone. By early adulthood the patient is in such a weakened state he or she often succumbs to an opportunistic infection, pneumonia, or weakened cardiac muscle.

Muscle deterioration in D-MD is caused by the replacement of healthy muscle tissue with fat and connective tissue. This may give the false appearance that the child or teen with D-MD is well-conditioned, but the opposite is the case. This false appearance of conditioning is known as pseudohypertrophy. D-MD tends to affect muscles of the trunk, shoulders, and hips initially, later progressing toward the extremities.

A second muscle system impairment is *myasthenia gravis*, caused by a blocked transmission of the impulse from a nerve to a muscle. The blockage is not complete, so muscles are partially stimulated. This leads to the characteristic signs of myasthenia gravis—muscle weakness and rapid fatigue. Unlike D-MD, myasthenia gravis is treatable and can be managed in most cases.

The final muscle disorder presented here is frailty. *Frailty* refers to low fitness of the muscle system as a whole. The usual cause of frailty is disuse and a sedentary lifestyle. This common problem of older adults is associated with many other more serious and debilitating disorders. One of the most common problems associated with frailty is a fall. In fact, the leading cause of falls in older adults is lower extremity weakness. Falls in older adults are very serious because seniors are also subject to osteoporosis. A frequent result of a fall in combination with osteoporosis is a significant fracture. Especially troublesome is a hip fracture that leads to immobility and institutionalization (nursing home). Frailty also threatens the older adult's ability to live independently because frailty is correlated with a loss of capability to take care of oneself.

Fortunately, most cases of frailty can be reversed. Because the leading cause of frailty is sustained inactivity, research has demonstrated that mild to moderate intensity strength training can reverse muscle frailty in older adults. Even in nursing home residents with muscle weakness so advanced that they can no longer walk or bear weight, strength training has shown remarkable results.

TR Response to Muscle System Impairments

The effectiveness of exercise for persons who have disorders of the muscle system depends on the impairment. Unfortunately, persons with D-MD do not respond well to exercise. Because of the advancement of the disease, the patient has progressively less effective muscle tissue. Some research demonstrates persons with D-MD can benefit from respiratory exercises, deep breathing, forced expiration (e.g., blowing up balloons), or exercises in the water (that force them to hold their breath or blow bubbles.) Other evidence suggests outcomes other than muscle strength and endurance may be possible with D-MD children and adolescents, such as improving range of motion, maintaining flexibility, and preventing contractures. The benefit is improved quality of life so that respiration is not as much of a struggle. The TR specialist should stress social outcomes (making friends) and social skills (learning how to interact with people in a mature and effective manner) with persons who have D-MD, because they will inevitably lose capacity and ability to complete motor tasks. Insofar as the distal extremities are not affected until later in the disease process, arts and crafts activities that require fine motor control of the small muscles in the hands will produce more satisfying results than exercise or sports.

The response to exercise of patients with myasthenia gravis is better than that of D-MD. Research has demonstrated significant improvements in muscles at the knee using weight training. However, the person with myasthenia gravis may need more rest periods during exercise as well as other activities because he or she will fatigue more rapidly.

Another issue for persons with myasthenia gravis, as well as the adult form of muscular dystrophy, is self-esteem. Because these individuals may not be able to work as long as an ordinary adult, they may have to seek support of their self-esteem from other, avocational sources. Leisure activities offer one alternative to work-related identification and may serve as an alternative source of self-esteem.

As suggested previously, the responsiveness of frail older adults to mild to moderate intensity strength training is heartening. Community-based and clinical strength training programs of mild to moderate intensity should therefore be strongly encouraged—with proper precautions (e.g., screening patients for eligibility, keeping program low intensity using light weights or resistance, teaching proper lifting techniques). With increases in strength, the frail older adult may become a candidate for other exercise activities, such as walking.

Nervous System

The fundamental unit of the nervous system is a nerve cell, known as a *neuron*. The basic function of the nervous system is to relay nervous impulses along the length of a neuron (see **Figure 10.3**) to stimulate a second structure (e.g., a muscle, another neuron). However, this basic function can be broken down into several specific parts. First, the nervous system orients the body to its external environment. It performs its orientation functions by sending sensory impulses from sensory receptors (e.g., the retina in the eye, touch receptors in the skin) to the brain for interpretation. Second, the nervous system coordinates the internal environment of the body to maintain normal functioning (homeostasis) at a subconscious level (e.g., maintains regular respiration, blood pressure, fluid volume). Learning is the third and most advanced function of the nervous system in humans, resulting in relatively permanent changes in behavior. Lastly, the nervous system is the home of instincts (e.g., survival emotions such as anger, sex drive).

The nervous system can be divided into two basic parts: the central nervous system and the peripheral nervous system. The central nervous system is composed of the brain and the spinal cord, and the peripheral nervous system is composed of nerves that travel to muscles to stimulate contraction and nerves that arise from various sensory receptors and take impulse back to the spinal cord and brain for processing an interpretation (see **Figure 10.4**, p. 270).

The control feature of the nervous system is exerted through nerve impulses and organized in a hierarchy. The brain controls the spinal cord. The spinal cord controls the muscle system. Sensory receptors send impulses back to the spinal cord, which then transmits those impulses to the brain for interpretation.

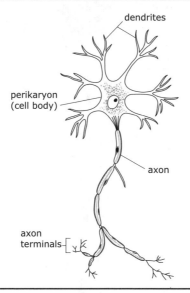

Figure 10.3   Typical Neuron

Disorders of the Nervous System

The reader will recall under the category of impairments of the muscle system we noted most motor impairments were actually caused by disorders of the nervous system. In fact, many serious disorders have their focal point in the nervous system. However, space limitations do not allow for a complete review of all neurological disorders. A representative set of the most frequent types of impairments is summarized here.

The peripheral nervous system represents all nerves that lead to muscles. If one of these nerves is damaged, then the muscle(s) the nerve innervates is paralyzed. However, the type of paralysis is quite specific—*flaccid paralysis*. With flaccid paralysis the muscle does receive any nervous impulse. As a result the muscle does not have the "tone" of a normal muscle. This is in contrast with the type of paralysis associated with damage to the spinal cord—*spastic paralysis*. Furthermore, injuries to peripheral nerves tend to have only a local effect, with impairment limited to only the muscles innervated by the

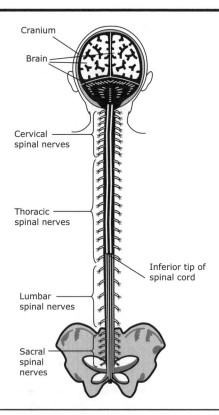

Figure 10.4   Brain, Spinal Cord, and Peripheral Nerves

injured nerve. Also, the prospects for recovery from a peripheral nerve injury are fairly good (in contrast to damage to the spinal cord).

As has been implied, damage to the spinal cord is a more serious matter. Depending on the location of the damage, a spinal cord injury may result in paraplegia (paralysis of both lower extremities) or quadriplegia (involvement of all four extremities). Hence, the extent of impairment is far greater than that resulting from damage to an individual peripheral nerve. Furthermore, the type of paralysis associated with spinal cord injuries is spastic paralysis. This mean that the person cannot voluntarily move the limbs involved *and* the muscles of the affected extremity have excessive tone, leaving them in a rigid and tightly contracted state.

Unfortunately, both spinal cord injuries and head injuries are more frequent among young people. This is because both are associated with risk-taking behaviors and accidents. Automobile accidents, motorcycle accidents, and other types of trauma are the most common causes of spinal cord injuries and head injuries.

Head injuries can be either closed or open. With *open head injuries*, the skull that houses the brain is actually penetrated by some sort of wound, puncture, or fracture. The added problem for a person with an open head injury is that the wound offers an opportunity for infections to enter and affect the brain, further exacerbating the extent of impairment. *Closed head injuries* result from sudden and violent movements of the head, as in a whiplash type of movement. The brain is "bounced" around inside the skull. Damage from a closed head injury result from the brain being traumatized by bony processes inside the skull.

Regardless of the type of head injury, a particular pattern of deficits is associated with head injuries. People who sustain head injuries present with one or more of the following symptoms:

1. difficulty processing information and maintaining attention.

2. learning and memory deficits.

3. problems with social appropriateness and labile emotions (i.e., emotional swings).

The memory device MAPE is sometimes used to help the student remember the major deficits associated with head injuries: *m*emory, *a*ttention, *p*rocessing, and *e*motional instability.

Multiple sclerosis (MS) is a disorder of the central nervous system that results in demyelination of nerve fibers. Myelin is a lipid coating that surrounds many nerve fibers and speeds up the conduction of a nervous impulse along the length of the fiber. With demyelination the patient with MS may experience intermittent periods of exacerbated symptoms and periods of remission. The patient usually has problems with slurred speech, balance, blurred vision, difficulty walking, and tremors. Hypersensitivity to heat and humidity are sometimes evident with MS clients. The condition is progressive and ultimately weakens the person to the extent that he or she becomes more susceptible to other disorders (e.g., pneumonia, kidney failure, heart disease). Onset is typically during young to middle adulthood. The cause of MS is not known, but like several other disorders, it may be an autoimmune disease.

Cerebral palsy (CP) is a congenital disorder of the nervous system caused by a variety of problems associated with gestation or the birth process (e.g., exposure to toxins, insufficient oxygen supply, some viruses). The symptoms of CP vary according to the area of the brain affected. The most common type of CP is the spastic type. The patient presents in a very contracted condition most of the time, which may deteriorate into contractures (permanent shortening of muscle and connective tissue). In its severe form, the client will have difficulty executing precise movements. All forms of CP are at increased risk for multiple handicaps. Mental retardation and learning problems are common as are difficulties with speech. Less frequently, persons with CP manifest problems with vision, hearing, and seizure disorders. Although these accompanying disorders are common, they are not inevitable—some persons with CP do not have other disabilities.

Seizure disorders can be caused by multiple factors, including head injuries, metabolic disorders, and substance abuse. A *seizure* is a random, transitory discharge of neurons that may cause a person to experience a temporary euphoric state or may cause a loss of consciousness, depending on severity. The seizure may involve one or both cerebral hemispheres in the brain. If the patient does have a significant seizure, the most important task for all personnel is to keep the person safe. For example, obstacles that might present a surface for the patient to strike with his or her head should be removed and medical personnel should be contacted immediately.

TR Response to Nervous System Impairments

The typical person with an SCI or head injury is a young male. The higher incidence among young males is probably attributable to more risk-taking behaviors. Regardless of the underlying social causes, the person with an SCI or head injury is apt to have a considerable portion of their identity invested in "embodied" (physically strenuous or demanding) activities. This makes SCIs or head injury psychologically devastating as well as physically limiting.

Research on rehabilitation of persons with SCIs indicates leisure may play an important role in adjusting to the associated impairment. Lee, Dattilo, Kleiber, and Caldwell (1996) found leisure was used by SCI patients to explore continuity between preinjury and postinjury lifestyle. Successful adjustment was thought to be a function of how and if the patient negotiated the continuity between preinjury and postinjury lifestyle. After sustaining an SCI, Lee hypothesized, patients are faced with the prospects that their future is much more provisional and uncertain—the imagined future that each person had was now in doubt. Accordingly, the SCI patient has to make adjustments in his or her life story (imagined future).

Lee et al. (1996) discovered three styles of adjustment:

1. *Seeking continuity*. These SCI patients expressed the desire to return to their preinjury lifestyle. It was an emerging awareness, a recognition of the situation. Seeking continuity served the purpose of acting as a motivational force—something to energize the person to take action.

2. *Establishing continuity*. With this style, the patient actually tried some of his or her preinjury leisure activities. Participation was seen as an approximation to preinjury leisure participation. The patient may secure the same psychological rewards from the activity, but the nature of the participation changed.

3. *Accommodating for continuity*. Here the patient made repeated attempts to participate in preinjury activities, with some mixed degree of success and failure. As a result of the participation experiences, he or she then made some accommodations to sustain or to improve participation. Either the patient came to recognize that successful participation would require some adaptations (e.g., adaptive equipment) or he or she recognized that satisfaction from previous activities was not sustainable and new activities would have to be adopted.

Practically speaking, the TRS will likely find himself or herself involved with prevention of secondary conditions as a major part of the rehabilitation and lifelong maintenance effort for persons with SCIs. The SCI patient is at risk for skin lesions because of prolonged seated posture. He or she is susceptible to bladder infections because of incontinence. Depression and boredom are also common among persons with SCIs, especially after discharge back into the community following rehabilitation.

The more contemporary approach to head injury rehabilitation assumes the brain takes a long time to repair itself. In the recent past, rehabilitation efforts would only be sustained for a few months after injury, but recent research has discovered persons with brain injuries can continue to improve for up to two years following trauma. Of course, the extended rehabilitation for persons with head injuries does not mean that they will recover completely. But to maximize the return, persons with head injuries now receive intensive and sustained rehabilitation from an allied team of therapists. Some research using TR and exercise has shown that interventions can promote return of function if sustained (usually over several months) and intensive (usually three or more hours of rehabilitation per day).

Stumbo and Bloom (1990) proposed several goals for TR intervention (primarily leisure education) with persons who sustained head injuries. Improving problem-solving ability, improving memory skills, and increasing attention span were thought to be supported by TR efforts. For example, Stumbo and Bloom proposed "leisure scenarios"—problems locating and accessing leisure resources in the community—as a problem-solving activity. They suggested leisure experience diaries as a method for improving and training memory skills. Asking questions at the end of a discussion group served as a method for assessing and improving attention span.

In the past, the medical community was very reluctant to recommend exercise or most kinds of physical activity for persons with MS. However, opinions changed considerably over the last 20 years. Some research indicated persons in the early stages of MS benefit significantly from exercise, particularly from strength training and aerobic exercise. Some efforts in the area of aquatic therapy with MS patients also showed good results. However, the TRS must be cautious because people with MS sometimes have adverse cardiac responses to exercise, and in some cases they are sensitive to heat and humidity. The best course to follow when the TRS and MS patient wish to pursue a program of exercise or aquatic therapy is to obtain clearance from the patient's physician before beginning a program. Once the program has started, the TRS should begin with mild intensity exercises and activities, only later progressing to moderate forms of activity.

Although CP is a lifelong disability, it does not usually require continuous institutionalization, except in very severe cases where the patient presents with multiple handicapping conditions. Persons with CP need to work on motor skills in a manner that does not precipitate adverse primitive reflexes (i.e., reflexes present at birth that the child with CP does not integrate like his able-bodied peers). Rhythmic games and activities tend to work best. Basic movement patterns (e.g., walking, throwing) should be emphasized through use of motor gyms and obstacle courses. Object control in craft, toy play, and other fine motor activities may prove to be useful as well. Proper positioning is very important to working with the CP patient. The TRS should work closely with other allied practitioners to assure that the CP client is returned to the wheelchair in proper position, for example. Some research has demonstrated that community dwelling persons with CP can benefit from a regular program of exercise. Exercise for persons with CP who are capable is of added importance, because many work at jobs that are manual in nature. Maintaining fitness can add years to the person's working career.

Sensory Systems

Sensory systems of the body are responsible for detecting various stimuli external to the body as well as inside the body. We will restrict our discussion to three sensory systems responsible for detecting external stimuli. The *visual system* detects light in the environment. The *auditory system* identifies vibrations in the air that we know as sounds. The *skin* detects a variety of sensory modalities because of several sensory receptors found there.

Visual stimuli enter the eye through an opening called the pupil. The lens of the eye then bends the light rays so they strike the sensory receptor for light at the back of the eye—the retina. Visual impairments represent more than various types of blindness, although legal blindness is certainly an important limitation. *Legal blindness* is also known as *functional blindness* because it affects a person's ability to negotiate and control his or her environment, making it difficult to function independently. Legal blindness is defined as 20/200 (the person can see at 20 feet what the normally sighted person can see at 200 feet). Very few individuals with legal blindness or less are totally blind (i.e., unable to detect even light). Approximately 15% to 20% of the population has some type of visual impairment (Canadian National Institute for the Blind, 2004).

Some other common visual impairments have to do with the lens. With age the lens loses some of its flexibility and therefore can no longer bend light rays enough to strike the retina (presbyopia). In other cases the lens has difficultly bending light rays that are close (hyperopia, farsightedness) or distant (myopia, nearsightedness). Clouding of the lens (cataract) is not uncommon among older adults, but corrective surgery is usually successful. Sometimes pressure can build up inside the eye (glaucoma) and damage the optic nerve or retina. *Glaucoma* is dangerous because it is often undetected. However, if detected early, glaucoma can be treated and visual impairment may be avoided. Finally, visual impairment may manifest as a comorbid condition, caused by some other primary disorder. One of the most common causes of visual impairment in middle to later life is diabetes. Diabetes may cause a deterioration of the blood vessels that supply the retina and optic nerve. This condition is known as *diabetic retinopathy*.

The auditory system consists of the outer, middle, and inner ear and the vestibulocochlear nerve. The outer ear is a canal from the external environment to the eardrum (tympanic membrane). The middle ear consists of three small bones (auditory ossicles) that move in response to vibrations in the air (sound). The inner ear contains the sensory receptor for hearing—the cochlea. Finally, the vestibulocochlear nerve transmits the auditory information detected by the cochlea to the brain for interpretation.

According to Statistics Canada (2001a) 2.9 million Canadian experience hearing loss, and approximately 1 in 10 Canadians are affected by hearing loss. Hearing losses can be of two types: conductive or sensory–neural. *Conductive hearing losses* are restricted to the outer and middle ear. Conductive losses may be caused by chronic middle ear infections (otitis media), herniation of the external ear into the middle ear (cholesteatoma), or otosclerosis (which causes immobilization of the auditory ossicles). *Sensory–neural hearing losses* are caused by damage to the cochlea or interruption of the pathway taken by the vestibulocochlear nerve. Conductive hearing losses respond to hearing aids (that amplify sound), sensory–neural losses do not.

Other auditory impairments relate to the aging process. *Meniere's disease* causes the older adult to experience hearing difficulties along with balance problems. The balance mechanism is located near the cochlea of the inner ear, and it is not unusual for an older adult with a hearing loss to also have problems with balance. Meniere's disease is often accompanied by ringing in the ears (tinnitis).

The skin serves many functions. One vital function is to act as a sensory detector for a variety of stimuli in the external environment. The skin is organized into three layers: an external *epidermis*, a middle layer called the *dermis*, and a inner layer known as the *subcutaneous layer*. Most of the sensory receptors in the skin are embedded in the second of its three layers (the dermis). The receptors in the skin are capable of detecting touch, pressure, pain, and temperature. These sensations are then transmitted by the spinal cord to the brain for interpretation.

The primary threat for the skin is thermal injury. Burns are classified according to how many of the three layers of the skin are affected. If the burn is restricted to the epidermis, it is a *first-degree burn*. A *second-degree burn* damages the epidermis and the dermis. A *third-degree burn* extends into the subcutaneous layer. Second and third degree burns require hospitalization, and sometimes (depending on the amount of tissue damaged) extensive rehabilitation. Besides grading burns according to the depth of injury, they are also described in terms of the percentage of surface area of the skin affected. The "rule of nines" is a method used to describe the extent of surface area involved in a thermal injury. The head and each upper extremity represent about 9% of the surface area of the body. The trunk represents 18% on the front and 18% on the back. Each lower extremity is 18%. For example, a burn that affect the right arm and leg would involve 27% of the body's surface area.

The short-term problem for the burn victim is shock. Shock is the adverse response of the body to excessive fluid loss. If the burn is severe (second or third degree) and a considerable percentage of surface area is involved, then fluid loss may be significant. The long-term/chronic problem for the burn patient is infection. Severe burns take a long time to heal and may require cosmetic surgery and skin grafts to close the wound. While the wound is open germs have direct access to the inside of the body and the risk of infection through the burn area is great.

TR Response to Sensory Impairments

It is unlikely the TRS will work with a person whose only problem is a visual or auditory impairment. In most clinical settings the person who has a visual or auditory deficit has other comorbid conditions. Frequently, they present with multiple handicapping conditions, such as severe or profound mental retardation, cerebral palsy, or diabetes. In community settings, the TRS is more likely to serve clients with visual or auditory impairments exclusively. In this case, the client may be a child or teen still in the public school system, or an adult resident of the community. One problem common among persons with either a visual or an auditory impairment is poor fitness. The low level of fitness characteristic of many sensory impaired clients may be traced to the lack of opportunities for exercise, sports and physical activity participation during the developmental years. Low levels of fitness are then perpetuated into adulthood and it becomes a difficult pattern to correct. The poor fitness levels of persons with sensory impairments is magnified because obesity often accompanies the low fitness.

Therefore, preventive and remedial fitness programs may be offered by TR in community settings to correct the low fitness of people with sensory impairments. These programs may be likewise offered on a contractual basis to the local school system to correct the problem early and to prevent weight and fitness problems among adults. Research has indicated no good reason for persons with auditory or visual impairments to present with low levels of fitness. Studies have aptly demonstrated they respond favorably to exercise programs and their physiology adapts in a manner identical to that of a non-impaired peer (e.g., endurance training improves the cardiovascular and respiratory systems). Hence, it is the lack of opportunity that caused the fitness and weight control problems among these individuals, and TR can correct this oversight by providing appropriate, supervised opportunities. (As with any exercise program, screening and physician approval for exercise should be secured before the client begins exercising.)

Another problem common to persons with congenital (present at birth) visual or auditory impairment are unusual behavioral displays, called blind-isms or deafisms. These behaviors, such as rocking, eye rubbing, waving the fingers in front of the eyes, vocalizations, and the like are thought to be the person's attempts to self-stimulate. In and of themselves, blindisms and deafisms are usually harmless, but they do present an obstacle if the intent is to include the person in regular recreation and exercise groups. The unusual behaviors may discourage involvement or create anxiety among sighted or hearing peers, thus blocking successful integration into a regular exercise group. Working with a treatment team (especially a counselor or psychologist) is usually required to correct or to minimize blindisms and deafisms. Correction often involves some sort of reinforcement schedule, modeling, and prompts from the TRS to alert the person to their behavior.

A problem unique to the hearing-impaired person relates to accompanying balance difficulties. Especially among older adults with hearing impairments, the balance mechanisms are also disrupted, although research has shown that school-age children with hearing impairments also frequently present with associated balance difficulties. TR interventions can assist with balance problems. With older adults, balance training can be easily integrated into a regular exercise program. Both static (stationary) and dynamic (while moving) balance should be challenged. With teens and children, a variety of recreational activities provide ample opportunity to exercise and improve balance. Activities such as gymnastics, dance, martial arts, tai chi, and yoga provide stimuli to both static and dynamic balance mechanisms.

Two problems with which burn patients must contend are pain and negative self-concept. Research has demonstrated pain can be managed in part through the use of recreational activities during painful treatments (e.g., hydrotherapy for children with burns). Opinion varies about why this technique is successful in helping the child manage pain, but the leading explanations are: a diversionary effect and/or a competing response (i.e., instead of exhibiting pain-related behaviors the child exhibits recreational behaviors which compete with the pain-related behaviors). Regardless of the reason, recreational activities used alone or in combination with positive reinforcers during painful treatments are useful pain management tools, especially with children.

The second common problem with which TR may be involved when working with patients who sustain a thermal injury is self-concept—more specifically the diminished self-concept associated with disfigurement from the thermal injury. Several techniques for improving self-concept are available through TR services. All of the methods to improve self-concept have one thing in common—empowerment. Leisure education may be used to help the person to acquire new skills or to improve preinjury skills in leisure activities. If the person continues to participate after injury, then it is likely he or she will come to perceive himself or herself as competent actors in their chosen recreational pursuits. Empowerment through learning, in turn, is correlated with improved self-concept. Improved skills in leisure activities and improved social skills can also lead to a successful inclusion experience when efforts to integrate the person into activities with peers are eventually attempted.

Cardiopulmonary Systems

The cardiopulmonary system is really two different systems, but they are often put together because of their shared responsibilities in respiration. The cardiovascular system is responsible for transporting oxygen-containing blood to tissues where the oxygen can be transferred to cells (e.g., muscle tissue) to do work. The cardiovascular system then returns deoxygenated blood to the lungs for reoxygenation. The pulmonary or respiratory system is responsible for delivering oxygen-containing air into the lungs through ventilation (breathing). There the oxygen enters the vascular system by way of air sacs (alveoli).

Besides the shared responsibility of respiration, the cardiovascular and respiratory systems have several unique functions. The cardiovascular system also transports hormones, nutrients, and waste products. Protection is another function performed by the cardiovascular system. Protection is conferred through production of white blood cells that recognize and destroy germs and foreign invaders. Protection is also afforded through prevention of excess blood loss—clotting is a function of blood-borne platelets and some plasma proteins.

Besides respiration, the pulmonary system also performs a major role in voice production when air is passed through an opening (glottis) in the trachea ("windpipe"). Also, protective reflexes, such as sneezing and coughing, are mediated by respiratory structures.

The anatomy of the cardiovascular system includes a pump (the heart), a tube system (blood vessels), and a fluid (plasma) with formed elements (red blood cells and white blood cells) suspended in it. The respiratory system includes a tube system (the bronchiole tubes, trachea, and nasal cavity) to deliver air to the organs of gas exchange—the lungs.

Disorders of the Cardiopulmonary Systems

The most frequent cardiovascular disorders range from heart disease to stroke, from hypertension (high blood pressure) to arrhythmias. The Heart and Stroke Foundation of Canada (2004) estimates that one in four Canadians are affected by stroke or heart disease. The causes of these disorders are similar. The causes of cardiovascular disease can be classified into two groups: (a) fixed or static risk factors and (b) modifiable or lifestyle risk factors.

Static risk factors are not subject to change and include gender (men are at greater risk than women), age (older people are more at risk than younger people), and heredity (people with immediate relatives with cardiovascular disease are more at risk themselves). *Modifiable risk factors* attract more interest from the healthcare community, because they can be changed in a favorable manner, thus reducing the risk of a variety of cardiovascular impairments. In particular, the health promotion/disease prevention movement has been embraced by several healthcare fields (e.g., physical therapy, medicine, nursing), including TR. Two recent models of TR include health promotion as part of service provision: Van Andel's [1998] Service Delivery Model and Austin's [1998] Health Protection/Health Promotion Model.

Health promotion programs often target modifiable risk factors. Loss of weight or prevention of obesity, adoption of a regular exercise habit, and smoking cessation/avoidance of smoking are risk factors that have been addressed by TR practitioners through health promotion. Though more difficult to document, stress is another area susceptible to modification in a favorable direction. Other lifestyle risk factors can be changed through compliance with medication (e.g., high blood pressure), or a combination of diet and medication (e.g., diabetes, elevated blood lipids).

In combination, risk factors make the person susceptible to heart disease, stroke, and other cardiovascular impairments because they promote atherosclerosis—the build-up of fats and scar tissues on the inside of blood vessel walls. The problem with atherosclerosis is the accumulation of material on the inside of a blood vessel may obstruct blood flow to a vital organ (e.g., heart, brain) through occlusion, or it may break free and float down to a smaller vessel and obstruct blood flow to a organ at a more distant location. Lastly, risk factors may eventually cause a blood vessel to rupture and deny blood supply to a vital organ.

Pulmonary disorders can be related to problems with ventilation (getting enough air into and out of the lungs through the bronchiole tube network), or disorders that interfere with the gas exchange in the air sacs in the lungs themselves. Asthma and emphysema are common impairments that interfere with the flow of air into and out of the lungs.

Asthma is caused by an excessive response to an allergen in the environment, causing interference with ventilation. *Emphysema* is almost always caused by smoking and results in difficulty moving air out of the lungs (because of a loss in the natural elastic capability of the lungs).

Cystic fibrosis is another problem with the bronchiole tube system, but unlike asthma, it is congenital. It also involves production of thicker than normal mucous. In turn, the mucous interferes with ventilation, and in some cases digestion.

Lung cancer may involve either interference with gas exchange in the lungs or interruption of normal ventilation. Chronic smoking is the most common cause. Cells inside the bronchiole tubes begin to divide uncontrollably, often producing abnormal cells as well. The cancer cells may put pressure on vital organs and interfere with function. Or, the cancer cells may compete with healthy tissue for a limited blood supply. Lung cancer is especially lethal because it often goes undiagnosed and symptom free until it has metastasized (i.e., spread to other organs and systems).

TR Response to Cardiopulmonary Impairments

TR goals for persons with various cardiovascular impairments include exercise, stress management, and diet. Indeed, these goals are likely shared by any number of allied health professionals who work with patients afflicted with cardiovascular disorders. The difference with TR interventions for this group is a matter of degree, not type of intervention.

Exercise, for instance, should be monitored primarily by the cardiac rehabilitation team, which normally includes physicians, nurses, and physical therapists specialized in such programs. Any allied health practitioner must be vigilant for complications and crises associated with placing the cardiac patient in an exercise-induced stress situation. Patients undergoing acute rehabilitation for a heart attack are closely monitored and ascribe to a specific protocol during rehabilitation. Clearly, recreational therapists are not trained for this type of intervention. In fact, the American Heart Association has a classification index for persons who have had a heart attack to set functional limitations. The limitations range from Class I (no limitations) to Class IV (unable to carry on any physical activity).

Nevertheless, TR may become increasingly involved as more time passes following the cardiac event. After near-term rehabilitation, the patient will likely return to as normal a lifestyle as possible (e.g., reside at home, resume work, return to routine tasks around the house). The problem facing the cardiac patient is lifestyle changes that were part of acute rehabilitation process need to be adopted for the long-term. Hence, the TR specialist practicing in a community setting or a clinical setting offering outpatient services may become involved with the cardiac patient in ongoing lifestyle modification. Exercise programs usually met with enthusiasm among patients recovering from a heart attack become boring and difficult to adhere to following completion of the formal rehabilitation process. But long-term compliance with a prudent program of mild to moderate exercise is the key to preventing another heart attack. Dietary changes closely monitored through prescribed meals in the hospital are now up to the discharged patient. Fast food becomes a tempting and expedient option. Smoking cessation is made easier in a facility that does not allow smoking. But what happens the first time the smoker is exposed to cigarette smoke at the local bowling alley?

During the time after formal rehabilitation, the TR specialist can be most effective, especially in areas of compliance and stress control. Facilities needed for exercise are often part of the community recreation department. Smart cooking classes and prudent shopping can also be a leisure education class offered to cardiac patients following discharge. Smoking cessation programs offered through the community recreation department will also assist with long-term compliance. Lifestyle changes can reduce the risk of a second heart attack, but only if ascribed to with some degree of discipline. This is the role for the TR specialist in cardiac rehabilitation. When patients are discharged from cardiac rehabilitation, they are taught how to exercise, how to watch their diet, and how to refrain from smoking. But compliance does become a problem once discharged back into the same environment that encouraged the negative lifestyle habits in the first place.

Stress management is another program supported by TR. It consists of educating the person to detect situations that cause excess stress and how to cope with the stress. A sound leisure education program can include both topics by introducing the patient to some self-screening questionnaires, by raising consciousness about situations that lead to stress, and by teaching strategies for reducing stress, such as exercise, progressive relaxation, tai chi, and guided imagery.

Like recovering cardiac patients, persons with chronic respiratory disorders must overcome fear and apprehension associated with their disorder and exercise. During rehabilitation, the person with a chronic respiratory disorder must learn to recognize the difference between respiratory distress and the shortness of breath that naturally comes with exercise. Following cessation of formal rehabilitation, the individual will need ongoing community-based or outpatient support to continue to exercise on a regular basis, and this again is where the community-based TR specialist comes in to play. By offering support and encouragement through creative programs, venues for exercise and social support, the TR specialist can add measurably to the person's ability to comply with lessons learned during inpatient education (e.g., regular exercise, abstinence from smoking).

In addition, some patients with respiratory disorders may benefit from programs designed to strengthen muscles of respiration. Any program that incorporates deep breathing, forced expiration, and repeated ventilation will be of benefit. For instance, activities as simple as blowing up balloons for a party, blowing bubbles during a recreational swim, or holding one's breath during aquatic exercise should all prove to be useful for some chronic respiratory disorders.

Because of fear, apprehension, and discomfort, many patients with cardiopulmonary disorders are difficult to motivate, especially for mild to moderate exercise. The TR specialist may perform a major role in motivating discharged clients to exercise or to comply with smoking cessation. Several techniques exist. For example, a decision balance sheet may be used. With this technique the consumer lists reasons for complying with an exercise program and reasons for not complying. If reason prevails, then the balance sheet should reinforce the wise choice—that continuing to exercise is the best decision. The TR specialist may also elect to start support groups for each important life style behavior—matching people with partners for exercise, having several people go shopping together to make nutritional purchases, and providing a hotline to call if one feels the urge to smoke.

Terminal Illnesses

Cancer, HIV/AIDS, and congestive heart failure all suggest terminal illness. But it would be a mistake to assume that persons with these illnesses should be treated as if they were terminally ill. The facts surrounding the progression of these disorders are often grim. But the facts may also reveal considerable hope as well. The five-year survival rates for many types of cancer are increasing: 95% diagnosed with testicular cancer survive, 40% with ovarian cancer survive, and 78% with breast cancer survive. The ten-year survival rate for prostate cancer is now 85%. Survival rates for HIV/AIDS are improving rapidly too. And breakthroughs in drug interventions, transplants, and stint and valve replacements have given the cardiac patient reason for hope.

Therefore, avoid the trap of defining terminal illness by the disease process alone. Certainly, no one would deny all of these are serious illnesses and often number among the leading causes of mortality. But it takes more than acquiring a specific illness to be considered terminally ill. When the person admits himself or herself to hospice center for persons with terminal illnesses, or when he or she chooses palliative interventions instead of curative treatments, then one may begin to assume the person is terminally ill.

Once the individual has made choices based on the assumption that the illness has little hope of being corrected, then interventions turn to new priorities. In place of curative interventions, treatments designed to advance the quality of life of the patient take precedence. Quality of life goals for the terminally ill patient include pain management, personal/perceived control, and self-expression.

Pain management is primarily the charge of the medical personnel involved in the case. Although TR may be indirectly involved through palliative treatment, it is primarily the medical support staff that actively treats pain.

Some successful TR interventions for dealing with pain were reviewed in the section pertaining to burn patients. But the idea behind treating pain with recreation remains the same—diversion and distraction with pleasant or enjoyable stimuli to redirect attention away from the pain. Meaningful activities may be used to support the patient's pharmacological pain management program.

Perceived control and self-expression are more promising areas for TR involvement with the terminally ill patient. To the greatest extent possible, the TR specialist should facilitate choice among patients with terminal illnesses. This may be implemented through offering a variety of recreational activity options, acting as an advocate for choices the patient makes (e.g., a final trip to a favorite destination, or to visit a friend or family member), or providing opportunities for control through induced responsibility (e.g., caring for a small garden or flower, choosing movies to watch, or participating in patient/family support groups).

Lastly, end-of-life care may include provision of opportunities for self-expression. Some experts believe many terminally ill patients want to leave a remembrance behind for their families and loved ones. The remembrance may take the form of an art or craft project, a poem or short story, a videotape, a song, a quilt, or any other token of remembrance. These activities appear to represent a very important step in terms of bringing closure to life, and for taking responsibility for sending a final message to family members.

The other manner in which a TR specialist may become involved with terminal illness is through the grieving process experienced by family and other persons close to deceased individual. It may be as simple as forming support groups for family and significant others. More challenging interventions may be directed at young children having difficulty understanding the death of the family member as well as having problems addressing the anger and depression that follow. In this situation, play may be a medium for expression of concerns, apprehension, and depression associated with the death.

Summary

Commonly encountered chronic conditions were reviewed in this chapter, with particular emphasis placed on the role of TR with each of the impairments. Some modalities for intervention cut across various impairments, so much so that they may be almost universally indicated (e.g., mild to moderate exercise). In other cases, interventions were specific to the problem, such as the use of games and reinforcement with children undergoing painful treatments for burns. With more research, especially as the TR discipline begins to accumulate case studies on impairments, future editions of this book should be able to give more specific guidance regarding useful interventions with specific impairment groups.

This chapter should not be considered comprehensive and representative of all possible physical impairments. And certainly, mental illness and most developmental disabilities have been left out. The purpose of the chapter was to give the student a "taste" of what TR is able to do with respect to some of the most frequently encountered disorders in clinical and community practice.

References

Austin, D. R. (1998). The health protection/health promotion model. *Therapeutic Recreation Journal, 32*, 109–117.

Canadian National Institute for the Blind. (2004). Retrieved from http://www.cnib.ca

Coyle, C. P. and Kinney, W. B. (1990). Leisure characteristics of adults with physical disabilities. *Therapeutic Recreation Journal, 24*, 64–73.

Heart and Stroke Foundation. (2004). Retrieved from http://www.heartandstroke.ca

Kakulas, B. and Mastaglia, F. (1990*). Pathogenesis and therapy of Duchenne and Becker muscular dystrophy*. New York, NY: Raven Press.

Lee, Y, Dattilo, J., Kleiber, D., and Caldwell, L. (1996). Exploring the meaning of continuity of recreation activity in the early stages of adjustment for people with spinal cord injury. *Leisure Sciences, 18*, 209–225.

National Health Forum. (2002). *Canada health action: Building on the legacy. Volume 2: Adults and Seniors*. Retrieved from http://www.hc-sc.gc.ca

Osteoporosis Society of Canada. (2004). Retrieved from http://www.osteoporosis.ca

Statistics Canada. (2001a). *International classification of diseases* (ICD-9). Ottawa, Canada: Minister of Supply and Services. Retrieved from http://www.statcan.ca

Statistics Canada. (2001b). CANSIM, Table 104-0002, Table 105-0002, and Catalogue # 82-221-XIE. Ottawa, Canada: Minister of Supply and Services. Retrieved from http://www.statcan.ca

Stumbo, N. J. and Bloom, C. W. (1990). The implications of traumatic brain injury for therapeutic recreation services in rehabilitation settings. *Therapeutic Recreation Journal, 24*, 64–79.

Van Andel, G. E. (1998). TR service delivery and TR outcome models. *Therapeutic Recreation Journal, 32*, 180–193.

Chapter 11

Case Studies in the Practice of TR

Learning Objectives

1. Summarize the usefulness and value of case studies for students and practitioners in therapeutic recreation.

2. Research spinal cord injuries in Chapter 10 and develop a fictitious case study client, describing probable impairments, comorbid conditions, prognosis, and background information.

3. For the case you created in #2, develop intervention plans using each of the therapeutic recreation practice models described in Chapter 9: Leisure Ability, Self-Determination, and Optimizing Lifelong Health.

The purpose of this chapter is to merge information about the nature of disabilities (Chapter 10), to apply the models of practice (Chapter 9), and to demonstrate the therapeutic recreation (TR) process with several hypothetical cases that may be encountered in TR practice. Since the early 1990s *Therapeutic Recreation Journal* has regularly published case studies in TR practice. What began as an experiment evolved into one of the most popular sections of the journal. In 1995, one issue of *Therapeutic Recreation Journal* was dedicated entirely to case studies.

Case studies are valuable because they serve as a means of sharing practice, innovation, and new ideas. Case studies are not held to the same scientific rigor as research articles insofar as the intent of a case study is not as ambitious. Case studies are suggestive rather than definitive, tentative rather than certain. Nevertheless, case studies are valued by practitioners who work with individuals similar to those documented in a case report. While no two cases are ever identical, the insights used by one practitioner may illuminate other possibilities to the reader.

Case studies are more adept at illustrating the complexities of practice, where clients do not typically have only one malady, but rather a collection of problems—some primary conditions and some secondary or comorbid conditions. Conversely, quantitative research articles tend to simplify the study of interventions, because the optimal study seeks to make two conditions (experimental and control) as alike as possible, save one difference: the intervention. In reality, of course, one cannot pick and choose clients, nor does one have the capacity to randomly assign subjects to groups as in some research studies. Practitioners must come to terms with and account for all confounding variables that amount to individual differences.

In this chapter we also add models of practice to each case. Normally, models are not part of case reports. However, in this book we wanted to give the reader a sense of the environment to further understand and appreciate the interventions used and why some interventions were implemented instead of others. This will serve to demonstrate the usefulness and influence models have in practice and make for interesting comparisons between the models and approaches each suggests. However, the reader must be cautious, because it is indeed rare to find a clinical or community setting based solely on one model of practice. In reality, most situations call for an eclectic approach that either combines several models or generates a "grassroots" model influenced by current models of practice. Subscribing exclusively to one model as the final word is a mistake because it leads to narrowed practice, oversimplifies the complexities of modern healthcare service, and ultimately limits the quality of service that may be provided. Staking the future on one model also suggests the condition of healthcare service provision will remain the same for the foreseeable future, a situation unlikely to be true.

It is with these assumptions we present three cases. We hope to stimulate the reader to think about the practice of TR, and to seek out other case reports and case studies. Knowledge is not attained in a single event, but rather accumulated slowly over time, one small piece at a time.

Case One

SV is an 82-year-old female living in the community in a condominium. She has osteoarthritis, osteoporosis, and marked sarcopenia (loss of muscle mass). She is referred to the local senior center for assistance in beginning an exercise program. She goes to church every Sunday and bingo at the church every Wednesday night. Friends from church provide transportation to both church and bingo. Her husband of 53 years died suddenly five years ago. They had many mutual friends, mostly couples formed through work friendships. (He was an accountant; she was an elementary school teacher.) Her two children reside quite some distance from her community (population: 200,000). They call regularly and visit about twice a year. Her condominium is one level and maintenance is provided as part of the monthly condominium fee. She does only a little cooking for herself, warming up soup for lunch along with a sandwich. Sweets (candy, cookies) make up a large part of her daily nutritional intake. She has been offered "meals-on-wheels" but has declined the service. She is 5 feet 2 inches tall and weighs 98 pounds.

The TR specialist in this case is employed by the city's recreation department and spends about 10 hours a week planning and implementing programs at the senior center, which is part of the same municipality. Existing programs include PACE (an Arthritis Foundation exercise program, *Persons With Arthritis Can Exercise*), bridge/pinochle club, cooking class, and a literary discussion group.

Leisure Ability Approach

Clearly the immediate concern is for SV is to improve function and to avoid or to postpone the development of secondary conditions and problems that would make independent living less probable (e.g., hip fracture). Using the Leisure Ability approach (Stumbo & Peterson, 1998) with this case, however, would give the TR specialist cause to think about the quality of SV's leisure lifestyle.

Assessments would naturally involve an appraisal of SVs functional status with respect to her balance, strength, and functional capability. But the practitioner would also be concerned with improvement in functional fitness, which might result from participation in the PACE program, as a point of departure for building a more diversified repertoire of leisure abilities. SV's problem from a leisure ability point of view is that her borderline functional status interferes with leading a more satisfying leisure lifestyle and attaining a higher quality of life in general. In conjunction with enhancing SV's leisure lifestyle, helping her to build new friendships or to reconstruct former ones would enhance socialization opportunities. SV is at risk not only for a hip fracture, but also for depression, loneliness, and isolation. The practitioner would therefore assess SV's current and past leisure preferences and her evaluation (e.g., intrinsically or extrinsically motivated, psychological need satisfied by each activity) of each of the activities.

Planning influenced by the Leisure Ability Model might result in the TR practitioner concluding SV needs to improve her functional ability before she is physically capable of expanding her leisure interests. But because the PACE program is a group activity, opportunities to socialize and to begin building affiliations and friendships seem likely. The practitioner may encourage socialization with the PACE group by introducing SV to the rest of the group members, by identifying common interests, and by pointing out people who live near SV.

Walking may also be advised, as research suggests weight-bearing exercise is useful in slowing the progress of osteoporosis or even reversing the porotic deterioration of bone. As with PACE, the practitioner would be interested not only in improving SV's functional status and reducing her risk of a fall, but also in using the walking activity as a stepping stone to building meaningful social relationships to counteract her isolation and to improve her leisure lifestyle. Hence, the practitioner may use the initial PACE meeting to survey the group and to discover who else is a walker, who would like a partner to walk with, and where possible matches exist (e.g., same neighborhood, same church).

Planning should also involve speculating about programs SV might transition into after completing the PACE program and improving her functional capacity. Since the card group already exists at the senior center, the practitioner should identify (a) whether SV played cards in the past or is interested in playing cards in the future and (b) whether someone in the PACE program also participates in the card group. If someone does participate in both groups, then they could act as SV's sponsor, mentor, and advocate with the existing group to help ease SVs inclusion.

Also during planning, the TR specialist might anticipate SV would be interested in finding other locations in the community to exercise, to play bingo, or to participate in any new interests she may have acquired. Leisure resource identification may then form the basis of a leisure education intervention in the near future. Better if the leisure education session could be coordinated in such a manner as to include new or current friends to enlarge the group and enhance efficiency of the TR specialist's effort.

Implementation would begin with motivating SV to attend the PACE group. Hopefully, the motivation to attend the PACE program would grow into more intrinsic motivation as socialization increases and some of the benefits of the exercise start to accrue. Periodic reassessment (e.g., every two weeks) of functional fitness would provide for monitoring of progress and gains in functional status. In a best-case scenario, SV's participation in PACE would be supplemented by regular walking with a partner from the senior center. Initially SV may be able to rely on friends or church members to provide transportation. Later public or subsidized transportation options may have to be identified.

Self-Determination Approach

Although the ultimate activities used in this case may be the same or similar, the underlying objective of the intervention is somewhat different using the Self-Determination Model. The Self-Determination Model is based on intra-psychological phenomena that occur within the psyche of the individual. With this approach the practitioner is concerned about SV's perceptions of recreation situations, her sense of control over the situation, and her level of intrinsic motivation.

Assessment using the Self-Determination approach would begin with a thorough evaluation of functional fitness. Many of the same assessments used under the leisure ability approach would be equally suited to functional assessment here. However, instead of looking to SV's leisure lifestyle in the broad sense suggested under the Leisure Ability paradigm, the TR specialist using the Self-Determination approach would question SV about her motivation to participate. Attendance becomes a very important marker for initial and sustained motivation.

Further evaluation of motivation and perception of motivation may be completed using a formal assessment, such as the Leisure Diagnostic Battery (Ellis & Witt, 1986). Or, the therapist may elect to use a shorter device, such as the Leisure Attitude Scale (Crandall & Slivken, 1980). Or, the assessment of intrinsic motivation may be based on conversations with SV and/or her daughters and friends, SV's rating of enjoyment of the activity, or through development of a "home-grown" assessment by the practitioner. The therapist needs to know not only where SV stands with respect to functional fitness, but also where she sees herself with respect to her motivation to participate and her sense of enjoyment.

Planning within a Self-Determination framework must be rather deliberate and calculated, because functional improvement alone is not enough. In this sense both the Leisure Ability approach and the Self-Determination approach have the same goal: to help SV to learn how to enjoy her free time and to enrich her life (and indirectly to sustain her fitness and to reduce her risk of a fall). The TR specialist would need to anticipate SV's reluctance to participate initially and determine whether that reluctance centers on the perception that she cannot perform the exercises, the perception that she cannot benefit from the exercises, or even an embedded cultural bias that older women should not exercise.

Flow theory (Csikszentmihalyi, 1975) and effectance motivation (Bandura, 1977; see Chapter 9) suggest that certain manipulations (i.e., changes in the environment to bring about desirable changes in the client, such as regular participation in the PACE program and the confidence that comes with attaining a sense of competence) may be needed to induce initial participation and later sustain participation. The goal of the therapist using the Self-Determination approach is to manipulate the environment and SV's perceptions in ways that cause her to perceive the activities as enjoyable (intrinsically motivated) and rewarding (leading to a sense of accomplishment, a perception of competence). To accomplish these ambitious aims, the therapist may anticipate the use of techniques that would skew SV's participation and perceptions in a favorable direction (e.g., active and regular participation, perceptions of competence).

Fortunately, effectance motivation theory specifies several techniques for motivating participation of a reluctant consumer (Bandura, 1977). When people appraise their competence and ability to execute a task (in this case a recreational activity), they may base that appraisal on any or all of four sources of information: participation-related feedback, vicarious observation, verbal persuasion, and/or visceral feedback (see **Table 11.1**).

Dattilo, Kleiber, and Williams (1998) recommended several other strategies specific to TR. One important belief within the Self-Determination framework is the perception of manageable change: changing an "I can't" personal affirmation into "I can" personal affirmation. The practitioner needs to help SV to appraise the challenge realistically. This may be done by daily or even moment-to-moment verbal feedback while SV is participating in the activity (e.g., "I see that you [SV] are doing the squats so that your knees are not stressed too much—that's something we should all keep in mind when doing this exercise.").

A second strategy that may be used to encourage a perception of manageable challenge in SV is the development of activity skills. In this case, teaching participants to do the exercises correctly will maximize benefits and minimize the chances of injury and soreness. When supplemented with verbal feedback from the practitioner during implementation of the PACE group, SV will begin to perceive that participation in a regular program of exercise is accessible to her, that she can successfully participate in the exercise, and that she can reap significant benefits from the exercise. The bottom line with the Self-Determination approach compared to the Leisure Ability approach is the former is much more focused on the immediate experiencing of the activity the client selected and less concerned with a global approach to leisure lifestyle.

Follow up with SV may focus on compliance as a long-term goal, because exercise must be continued for it to produce lasting benefit (reducing the risk of a fall, improving or maintaining functional fitness). Specifically, the therapist should be very concerned with continuity of exercise after SV's initial experience with PACE and walking. While initial participation often rides a wave of enthusiasm stimulated by apprehension (of the consequences of not exercising with respect the risk of a fall, osteoporosis), long-term commitment to a program of exercise is more problematic. SV may well participate with great energy at first after her physician and others she trusts convince her to participate. Good attendance may be the result of seeing improvements in functional fitness during the two- to three-month exercise program. Long-term compliance is more likely to result from social support from other members of the exercise group and/or SV's walking partner. After the initial enthusiasm wanes, SV must discipline herself enough to participate even if the PACE group membership changes, if there is an interim period when the PACE program is not offered, or if her walking partner leaves to spend winter in a warmer climate.

Table 11.1   Sources of Motivational Information

Participation
Nothing succeeds like success. If SV is willing to give participation a try without encouragement from the therapist, then the therapist should concentrate on providing SV with positive affirmations related to her participation ("You did a great job today. I noticed that you were completing the exercises using slow and steady movements. That will really help you to improve quickly.")

Vicarious Observation
In this case, SV is initially reluctant to participate, but consents to attend one exercise session after you invite her to watch. The therapist should emphasize that the other people participating in the group are very much like her (role models). Several women have similar problems and are about the same age as SV.

Verbal Persuasion
If SV trusts or values the therapist as an information source, then verbal encouragement from the therapist will be very persuasive. Alternatively, if SV does not know the therapist well enough to have any basis to trust verbal messages from the therapist, then the practitioner may be able to identify another person whose opinion is valued enough to be persuasive (e.g., studies have aptly demonstrated that physicians are very persuasive when it comes to recommendations they make to their patients). After all, someone must have persuaded SV to make an initial inquiry about the exercise program in the first place.

Visceral Feedback
This performance-related feedback results from participation. It is likely SV has not participated in a regular program of exercise at all, or not for a long time. Hence, SV's initial participation may produce some uncomfortable markers (e.g., sweating, shortness of breath, muscle soreness). The therapist must be prepared to counteract the possibility that these visceral symptoms may discourage her future participation. Effective therapist strategies would include suggesting to SV that sweating and hard breathing mean she is completing the exercises correctly and that muscle soreness is normal for a short time after starting an exercise program and should go away in a week or two.

After three months of participation, SV will have to rely on the perceptions of competence she acquired during exercise (the confidence to do the exercises correctly), self-confidence (the confidence to do the exercises on her own: "I can do this on my own because I know how to do the exercises and I have the equipment I need."), and positive affirmations (she tells herself she is competent in conducting her own program). The educational experiences provided by the TR specialist are critical to compliance, because skill acquisition leads to perceptions of competence: "I know how to exercise safely and in a way that is beneficial." The therapist may have to periodically reinforce SV's efforts by reminding her of the competence she has acquired in the exercise activities (PACE, fitness walking). Furthermore, occasional "boosters" from the TR specialist may be needed to support SV's confidence in her own capacity to manage her own exercise program. Realistically, keeping SV informed of opportunities to retake the PACE course and identifying and referring her to other walking partners will serve to prevent a failure of compliance with her chosen exercise preferences.

Optimizing Lifelong Health (OLH) Approach

The OLH Model (Wilhite, Keller & Caldwell, 1999) combines aspects of both the Leisure Ability Model and the Self-Determination Model. It emphasizes attaining and maintaining a healthy leisure lifestyle, similar to the Leisure Ability Model. And it places considerable importance on empowerment and personal control, similar to the Self-Determination Model. The OLH Model departs from these themes, however, insofar as it takes a life course perspective. According to a life course approach, life is a process of continuous adaptation and accommodation. When these adaptations and accommodations include leisure (and health), TR may be involved. Furthermore, from the OLH perspective, potential clients include anyone with an adaptive challenge to their leisure lifestyle who has a manifest (e.g., arthritis, osteoporosis) or latent problem (e.g., risk of a fall).

Compared to the Leisure Ability Model and especially the Self-Determination Model, the TR specialist plays a less directive role within the context of the OLH Model. Alternatively, education and facilitation are featured intervention techniques. These techniques are preferred with the OLH approach, because of the model's emphasis on independence and interdependence (shared responsibility between the client and the therapist). This places a significant burden on the TR professional to implement creative methods for helping clients to develop and to maintain their own healthy leisure lifestyle by inducing client empowerment and personal control.

Life requires ongoing adaptation and adjustment, oscillating between better adjustment (more personal control) and worse adjustment (less personal control) to health challenges. The OLH Model sees maintenance of a healthy leisure lifestyle as ongoing, requiring periodic adjustment in the best-case or significant adaptation and accommodation in cases where chronic conditions are manifest.

Four elements of the OLH Model represent the TR process. The first is *selecting*, where the client focuses on a goal that helps to achieve a healthy leisure lifestyle. It also includes active planning on the part of clients insofar as they identify activities that will satisfy their healthy leisure lifestyle goals. In the case of SV, she may need some consciousness-raising, because she may not even recognize the significant risk profile under which she operates. This may come from conversations with her friends and family, recommendations from her physician, or discussions with the TR specialist. For instance, since the TR specialist in this scenario is contracting with a senior center, he or she could accurately deduce many of the persons attending the center present the same or a similar risk profile. Because one of the major roles for the therapist under the OLH system is educator, she could arrange for periodic presentations, workshops, and conferences on health and quality of life concerns for older adults. Topics might include avoiding falls, maintaining an independent lifestyle, the importance of continuous social contact, getting around without a car, or proper nutrition on a fixed income. If SV were to attend one or more of these sessions, then she might come to recognize she is at risk of losing her independence as a result of several lifestyle risk factors.

Once SV recognizes she has a concern, she would visit with the therapist to work on developing goals and selecting activities for reaching those goals. Of the three models, using the OLH approach would rely the most on client input and allow more time for the client to process and to problem solve because it is the least directive. But for now, let us suppose SV recognizes she is at risk of losing her preferred independent lifestyle and believes she must do something to narrow the window of risk. Working interdependently with the TR specialist, SV should discover exercise programs specifically developed for older adults and focused on the problems of older adults. The TR professional may then present an array of options for attaining the goal of maintaining independence. Likely activity options would include many of those already mentioned, such as PACE, aquatic exercise, walking, and light weight training. Additionally, the professional may be able to raise the client's awareness of several other potential problem areas, including transportation, maintaining an independent household, and maintaining or augmenting social contact with people.

The second step in the OLH process is *optimizing*. This refers to the active engagement in the chosen activity or activities. SV might start slowly and experiment with one activity, say PACE. The TR specialist might assist by debriefing SV about the ease/difficulty of participation, whether participation was making a difference, friendships formed as a result of participation (and how to make the most of those new friendships), and whether there were any other things SV could do to supplement the PACE program.

The third part of the OLH process is *compensation*. It occurs concurrently with optimization and involves making adaptations and accommodations to activity selection and participation as needed. At this point in our discussion we have not indicated that SV would have any constraints to her participation in the sampling of activities mentioned. Perhaps we have skipped a step—we could speculate that SV recognized her risk profile and tried walking for exercise. But walking may have proven to be too painful (because of arthritis), too strenuous (because of frailty), and/or too risky (because of osteoporosis and the danger of slipping during inclement weather). If these or any concerns were recognized and articulated to the professional by SV, then adaptation and accommodation would be indicated. In effect, by directing SV to PACE or aquatic exercise in earlier model applications, we have skipped the compensation phase of the OLH process.

Lastly, the OLH process has an evaluation component. Evaluation of the activity—whether it is useful in reaching the goals identified during the selecting phase and whether compensation has proven to be adequate— occurs in this phase. SV may find that even PACE is too tiring and she must find a less strenuous alternative. The therapist and SV together may conclude that a non-weight-bearing form of exercise would be better (e.g., buoyancy in aquatic exercise is less stressful). They may further conclude if SV makes progress with aquatic exercise, then she may transition into a more strenuous form of exercise within two months. The *evaluating* part of the OLH Model is positioned on the diagram (see Figure 9.3, p. 238) in a manner that suggests its role in providing a feedback function. Judgments about the effectiveness of the PACE program are used to speculate about the next step to take, the next activity to attempt to enhance SV's healthy leisure lifestyle.

Hence, even though the process used in each of the models was different, the results were similar. Focus with each model ranged from a satisfying leisure lifestyle, to enjoyment, to a healthy leisure lifestyle. Each model was able to recognize that SV has a significant functional problem that stood in the way of her quality of life. But methods used by the therapist differed, with the therapist fairly directive with the leisure ability approach (because SV's problems stood in the way of her leisure lifestyle), to manipulative with the Self-Determination Model (altering the environment to produce perceptions of control and intrinsic motivation), to the OLH methods (that patiently wait for the client to come to the realization she needs help to attain a healthy leisure lifestyle). Each approach is unique; each has strengths and weaknesses. Only the practitioner is in a position to judge which approach they prefer, which approach works best in a particular context, and which approach he or she can live with from a philosophical point of view.

Case Two

AV is a 49-year-old male who sustained a stroke (cerebrovascular accident; CVA) two months ago. The CVA was on the nondominant hemisphere and he has a small amount of motor impairment on his left side (some difficulty with fine motor control in his left hand and sometimes drags his left foot when walking, especially when he is fatigued). AV's case history profile reveals he is married (a third marriage) and he has one child from a previous marriage. He works for a large computer company in a management-level job. He smoked a pack of cigarettes a day for almost 30 years, a habit he picked up during military service. At discharge from his rehabilitation program AV started to smoke again despite advice to the contrary from his physician. He typically has a couple of drinks at business lunches, which he has practically every day. He also has a couple of cocktails before supper at home. He tends to work about 60 hours per week, normally working at night after he arrives home, and he usually goes in to work at least one day on the weekend. His free time is spent with his family and getting together with his extended family, who reside locally. He also plays golf regularly, and his 14-year-old son frequently accompanies him. Following a month of rehabilitation as an inpatient and later as an outpatient, he has convalesced at home for the last two weeks. He is anxious to return to work. A psychological evaluation of AV prior to discharge revealed a highly competitive personality that staked his identity and self-esteem in his work role.

The TR specialist in the rehabilitation facility has been assigned to follow up with AV to assist with his transition from discharge back into his home, work, and community. The therapist has worked with several clients who had strokes before, but all of them have been older (age 60–70) and did not wish to return to work. The therapist also kept up with the stroke literature and learned that quality of life following discharge frequently suffers and often does not return to that of prestroke quality of life (Niemi, Laaksonen, Kotila & Waltimo, 1988). All of the patients in the Niemi et al. study were under 65 with a mean age of 48 years at the time of the event, but only 54% returned to work. Family relationships deteriorated for more than one half (54%) of the subjects in the four years subsequent to their strokes, as did leisure activities outside the home for 80% of the subjects in the study. There was also a strong correlation between coordination deficits and deterioration of quality of life and between tendency toward depression and deterioration of quality of life. Along with depressive tendency, difficulty with ambulation was also a significant predictor of deterioration in quality of life during the four-year follow-up interval. Niemi and her colleagues concluded if stroke patients received needed support and education, they may improve the probability of successful (and realistic) adjustment to life following their CVA event.

Leisure Ability Approach

AV clearly has to confront the real problems he faces in his leisure lifestyle and the risk of deterioration of his leisure lifestyle subsequent to his recovery and rehabilitation from his stroke. Casual assessment from a Leisure Ability perspective suggests the quality of AV's leisure lifestyle even before his stroke was suspect. After consulting the literature, the practitioner learns of several management techniques that may be included in the treatment plan for AV (Feinberg et al., 1994): treating high blood lipid levels, beginning a program of regular physical activity, controlling blood pressure, quitting smoking, treating cardiac disorders, and limiting alcohol use to moderate consumption. Depending on the breadth of assessment, several functional problems standing in the way of a satisfying leisure lifestyle may be identified. Those identified as management techniques and functional problems related to leisure lifestyle would be legitimate grounds for TR intervention.

Assuming a liberal interpretation of functional problems related to leisure, the practitioner identifies lack of adequate exercise, smoking, and excessive alcohol consumption as areas in need of intervention. AV is likely susceptible to stress related to his job and possibly his personal life (e.g., previous marriages). His leisure seems to be at least limited and at worst impoverished, as he reports working 60 hours per week, and golf and family-based socialization as the only leisure activities in his repertoire. Based on the literature, the professional may also want to attend to AV's risk for deterioration of quality of life (e.g., his prospects for returning to his job and the risky lifestyle associated with it present significant health risks). The assistance of a psychologist or a professional counselor may be indicated, because his lifestyle habits may stem from his basic personality makeup, which is resistant to change. One thing is certain: unless AV changes some aspects of his lifestyle, he is at great risk for another stroke.

Consultation with the TR literature identifies one article published on TR programming for persons who have sustained a stroke (MacNeil & Pringnitz, 1982). The article may be used as a stimulus for program possibilities, because the authors report on a Leisure Ability approach: "preparing the client to continue his involvement in social and leisure experiences in his home environment is the goal of therapeutic recreation..." (MacNeil & Pringnitz, 1982, p. 29). The authors reported the use of six different programs with stroke patients: individual recreational therapy, aquatics, unilateral skills, group evening activity, community integration, and family education. Of these, community integration and family education seem appropriate to AV. Because AV has been discharged, some of the other interventions are less feasible because of their clinical and rehabilitation orientation. Also, the article is dated insofar as rehabilitation of persons with brain injuries has advanced considerably beyond what was available in the 1982. Hence, while not discarding useful work conducted in the past, the practitioner must be alert to the fact that rehabilitative approaches change over time.

The practitioner using the Leisure Ability approach should identify leisure education as an appropriate intervention technique for several reasons. AV probably did not have an appreciation for leisure before his CVA, and he has expressed the wish to return to work as soon as possible. Although this is likely because his residual handicap is not pronounced, he remains at high risk for subsequent CVAs if he does not alter his lifestyle. Smoking, excess alcohol consumption, stress, and a sedentary lifestyle are all risk factors for subsequent strokes following an initial event. Hence, leisure education in the areas of leisure awareness and leisure skills may be indicated. Leisure awareness would help AV to develop a greater appreciation for leisure and its (potential) importance in his life as a source for life satisfaction and part of the basis for his identity. Part of this leisure awareness may include topics such as enjoying free time without alcohol, and the TR specialist may refer AV to a smoking cessation program.

Leisure skill development is indicated because AV has a very limited leisure repertoire. He may not be able to continue golfing at a skill level acceptable to himself because of motor involvement in his hand. Certainly, he would likely need to use an electric golf cart if he did continue to golf, and this would be contrary to getting at least some exercise to decrease his risk of another stroke (and also to cope with his stress). Teaching AV about the various options for exercise, in consultation with his physician, would provide AV with a sampling of exercise choices.

Exercise is a modality with which the TR specialist should be cautious whenever working with patients who sustained a cardiovascular event, such as a stroke or a heart attack. While mild to moderate exercise (e.g., walking, light weight training, yoga, stretching, aquatic exercise) can be offered safely through a TR program, more aggressive cardiovascular exercise should be delivered on a referral basis by a cardiac or stroke rehabilitation unit. Once AV has adopted a program of regular exercise, however, the community-based TR specialist may act as a referral agent, directing AV toward existing opportunities within the community for the type of exercise he seeks.

Second—and this is the "intervention point" for the TR specialist adopting the Leisure Ability approach—AV's lifestyle problem may be viewed as largely a leisure problem. He abuses substances (alcohol, tobacco) during at least part of his free time. He seems quite driven at work to the detriment of his free time. Although he reports he spends his free time with his family, one wonders how much time he really had in the past. Including family in the leisure education process and focusing on family activities may be motivational, because AV stated he values his time with his family.

Third, we may also inquire how much his leisure activities contribute to his satisfaction with life because of the significant emphasis he seems to place on his work role. Again, expanding his horizons with respect to the potential for leisure to be a source of satisfaction and directly or indirectly helping him to accrue the leisure skills needed to capitalize on his new appreciation for free time hold promise for a more satisfying leisure lifestyle.

Collectively, the focus of the practitioner seeing a patient like AV is to enrich his free time experiences, because the literature suggests quality of life is at risk for patients such as AV. If successful, AV may indirectly benefit, because a more satisfactory leisure lifestyle should be manifest in the absence of several detrimental risk factors for another stroke—smoking, excessive drinking, lack of adequate exercise, stress. Additionally, AV would likely need ongoing support to sustain his altered leisure lifestyle, because adherence to the modified lifestyle would deteriorate as time passed. For example, exercise compliance is known to falter around six months after initiating an exercise program. The community-based practitioner must be available for follow-up and to administer a leisure "booster shot" when needed. The community-based practitioner should view TR as an ongoing process that is always available. This is especially critical for the majority of individuals in the community who have chronic conditions—conditions that will never be "cured."

Self-Determination Approach

As with the previous case, the Self-Determination approach would focus on whether AV was enjoying leisure through intrinsically rewarding activity that was also challenging. In the latest version of the model (Dattilo et al., 1998), functional improvement is seen as a benefit that results from enjoyable leisure participation. However, with the Self-Determination Model, functional improvement is not the point of departure for intervention by TR.

Similar to the approach used with the Leisure Ability Model, a practitioner taking a Self-Determination approach to AV's problems may view at least some of his risk factors as leisure-related difficulties. Although not made explicit in his case description, the TR practitioner may suspect AV has trouble using his free time in rewarding ways. Despite claims he is anxious to spend time with his family, the main contributor to his identity and self-esteem is his job. He has not stated he wants to spend more time with his family, but rather, he wants to return to work as soon as possible. Certainly, in a real case these speculations could be validated via several sources: AV himself, his relatives and friends, and his healthcare staff while in rehabilitation (e.g., nursing staff, physical therapy staff, physician). A psychological evaluation of a person following a stroke is not unusual, and the attending psychologist may have some insights to confirm or to refute the therapist's hypothesis about AV's ability to enjoy free time.

Since AV did not sustain significant motor impairment as a result of his stroke, golf may be used as a starting point for TR programming. Capitalizing on a prestroke leisure interest (especially because he golfed with another family member) may ease the transition from preinjury to postinjury lifestyle (see Lee, Dattilo, Kleiber & Caldwell, 1996, for transition from preinjury to postinjury leisure applied to persons with spinal cord injuries). Supposing AV did secure some intrinsic rewards and enjoyment from participation in golf prior to his brain injury, the TR specialist may elect to assess AV's potential to play golf to a level of competence that is personally rewarding. However, AV may well have to negotiate with his own psyche to determine whether he can play at a preinjury level of proficiency. If he could not, then his potential for securing enjoyment through leisure would be diminished. At that point AV and the therapist could work together to problem solve.

With the assistance of the TR professional in the community, AV could learn to be satisfied with his postinjury level of performance, acknowledging that postinjury golf is similar to preinjury golf but not exactly the same. Then AV would have to work through the impact the lowered level of proficiency would have on his enjoyment of the activity. This might take at least two different paths of resolution. AV might recognize the seriousness of his stroke and be thankful to return to his preinjury leisure, even though he is not as proficient as he was before his stroke. Or, AV may quickly learn he may never golf at the same level he could before his stroke. The latter scenario might result in a quick cessation of the activity and rapid discouragement. That discouragement could be doubly harmful because it could generalize to the few other activities AV pursues in his free time, or may even generalize to nonleisure activities (e.g., "I can't even golf, so how can I expect to be effective at work?"). Or, AV may need the assistance of the TR professional to relearn how to become proficient enough at golf to reach a level of competence in the activity similar to his preinjury level.

In the latter scenario he would need to fight discouragement during early attempts at returning to golf, because his initial attempts would probably not be as successful as his preinjury level of performance. The TR specialist may intervene with several adaptations and environmental manipulations to address AV's discouragement with his performance. By helping AV to appraise the challenge realistically ("Golf is a difficult sport, even without the stroke, the length of time you have not played would have affected your performance.") and by teaching adapted skills ("Your follow-through is naturally going to change because your hand is not as strong as it once was.") the TR practitioner helps AV to adapt and to adjust to his postinjury level of performance. Additionally, if the TR professional cannot provide instruction and adaptive strategies directly, he or she could consult with a local golf professional for assistance.

Regardless of whether AV is successful at golf and continues to enjoy the activity, another problem looms large: his impoverished leisure repertoire. He claims to work 60 hours per week, so the therapist may conclude he has few if any other leisure activities he could use to substitute for golf or to pursue as something new and stimulating in his free time. Hence, as with the Leisure Ability approach, teaching as a modality seems to be indicated. Diversifying AV's leisure interests would serve to accomplish several things important to his enjoyment of free time (and quality of life): (a) he will develop alternatives to golf for use during inclement weather, or if golf becomes less intrinsically rewarding in the future; (b) he will develop an appreciation for the potential for leisure to serve as a source of intrinsic reward in life (as we suspect that work provides not only material rewards to AV, but also intrinsic rewards); and (c) he may be able to secure a secondary benefit as a result of improving his leisure experiences—coping with stress associated with work (although stress is not explicit in the case description, it is another problem that may prove to be latent).

Specific to work-related stress, assuming the TR specialist is able to confirm stress is a problem for AV, the Self-Determination Model does illustrate functional improvement (in this case coping with stress) may result from participating in intrinsically rewarding leisure activities. Some evidence in the literature suggests leisure activities are effective in coping with stress (Coleman & Iso-Ahola, 1993). The second point to be made with respect to work (and its resulting stress) is the practitioner must be careful to respect AV's partiality toward his work. Indeed, research on the transition into retirement suggests that work and leisure are not necessarily seen as antithetical to one another (Atchley, 1971). Therefore, it is not necessary to suggest AV needs to decrease the importance he places on work and the self-esteem he secures as a result. He may come to discover he needs to do this himself, but the TR professional should be more interested that AV instead increase the value he places on his leisure. (Recall that quality of life diminishes among many persons who have sustained a stroke.)

Several aspects of the Self-Determination approach contrast markedly with the Leisure Ability approach. The Self-Determination approach would have even more difficulty addressing the risk factors for another stroke that AV must change (e.g., smoking, excessive drinking, insufficient exercise). We argued previously a more diversified and rewarding blend of leisure activities might indirectly help AV to cope with stress, but the Self-Determination Model is hard pressed to take on AV's other risk factors directly. (Recall that the Leisure Ability Model provides a justification for doing so under the guise of the risk factors being constraints on a satisfying leisure lifestyle.) The advantage of a microapproach, such as the one suggested by the Self-Determination Model, is it provides a clear mechanism for change, facilitating intrinsic motivation and enjoyment by manipulating environmental factors (see Dattilo et al., 1998, for specific examples). However, starting TR intervention with the intent of reducing risk exposure for a subsequent stroke is not consistent with the main theme of the model.

OLH Approach

Recall that the OLH Model is designed to promote a healthy leisure lifestyle. Because a healthy leisure lifestyle reduces the prospects for development of problems secondary to a primary disability (e.g., stroke), the OLH approach can take on AV's risk factors for a second stroke directly. Using the OLH approach means AV's risk behaviors, such as smoking, excessive drinking, and sedentary lifestyle, become available as goals for TR. During the initial selection phase, the TR professional should be judicious with goal development. Trying to develop plans to alter all of AV's risk behaviors at once could prove discouraging. Anyone who has tried to stop smoking, start and adhere to a regular program of exercise, or curb alcohol consumption knows it is difficult to change one of these behaviors, much less all three at the same time.

Selecting smoking, for instance, as a behavior to modify would likely require a multidisciplinary approach. Nicotine is a very addicting substance, making a long history of smoking difficult to stop. Furthermore, the prospects for relapse and restarting smoking are very real, even after months of compliance. Unless the TR specialist has received training specific to smoking cessation, he or she would be of most service to AV by acting as a coordinator, putting together a team of professionals necessary for effecting behavioral change—in this case smoking cessation. That team may include a physician (AV's family MD would work best, as patients tend to view physician's recommendations with more credibility than others), a psychologist or counselor (someone from the rehabilitation center where AV completed his acute rehabilitation would be best, as he or she has a history with AV that serves to establish familiarity and credibility), and possibly family members (who would help by supporting AV's attempt to stop smoking and should also stop smoking themselves if they are current smokers).

AV should be assessed during the selecting phase to determine his willingness to quit smoking, his awareness of the dangers smoking presents as a detrimental health behavior, and his tendency to rely on substance abuse as a leisure activity. Hopefully, assessment activities will also raise AV's consciousness about the serious health threat that smoking presents. If we view assessment as a process, we hope this sort of awareness will emerge as AV is confronted with the facts about smoking, especially as it elevates his risk for another stroke. This emerging awareness is a necessary step with the OLH approach, because client autonomy and self-determination are prerequisite to the success of any intervention. (Recall that the OLH Model calls for mostly independent or interdependent decision making on the part of the client.)

The planning process may include activities the TR specialist facilitates directly, such as identification of leisure activities that present a health risk and how to reduce the health risk. For example, if AV plays golf in a league or with friends who also smoke and drink, or if AV sees smoking and drinking as part of the golf culture to which he is committed, then AV and the therapist together need to identify ways for AV to pursue golf in settings that reduce or eliminate temptations to smoke and drink. Perhaps the local municipal course does not allow smoking or drinking, similar to many public facilities. This may also require some drastic changes in AV's behavior, such as altering his friendship and support network. If AV cannot alter his leisure lifestyle in a healthy manner, then the therapist and AV will have to confront the fact that golf may not be a leisure activity he can pursue in a healthy manner. Throughout the selecting phase, the TR professional assists in a variety of ways under an OLH approach.

Once plans and goals are developed in the selecting phase, AV would begin participation in the activities he and therapist have selected: golf, smoking cessation program at a local hospital, identification of leisure resources in the community that avoid substance abuse, continued planning to address other risk behaviors (e.g., alcohol consumption, lack of exercise), and expanding the diversity of his leisure interests. This would correspond to the optimization phase of the OLH Model.

The compensation phase is also part of implementation and may occur after only one trial, or AV and the therapist may recognize that adaptation and accommodation are in order after several attempts at the selected activities. The latter scenario is more likely because initial participation is based on a known, preinjury leisure activity and several trials would be needed to determine whether AV is able to participate at his preinjury level or is satisfied with a lower level of performance. Suppose that after several golf outings that AV expresses his dissatisfaction with his golf experience and has trouble quitting smoking. Hence, adaptation and accommodation seem necessary in this case.

After several attempts at golf, in consultation with the recreational therapist, AV would debrief about his perceptions of his participation. Topics would include a realistic self-appraisal of whether he can participate at a level of proficiency comparable to his preinjury level of competence. If not, then he would have to appraise his alternatives: (a) continue the activity at the present level of performance and recognize his stroke may have affected his level of competence, (b) determine he is not satisfied with his level of performance and seek adaptations to configure golf in an acceptable manner, (c) determine he is not satisfied with his level of performance and seek to accommodate by changing his expectations of how well he can perform the activity, or (d) seek other activities that may replace the intrinsic motivation and perceived competence he previously associated with golf.

In the event that b, c, or d occur, then adaptation and accommodation may be indicated. For example, in scenario b the therapist and AV would work together to make adaptations to golf, perhaps by using assistive devices. For scenario c AV may have to alter his level of expectation for his performance in golf by playing shorter tees, taking an allowable handicap when determining his score, or deciding to take golf less seriously and decrease his expected level of performance in golf. Which of these options or which combination of these options AV chooses will determine how much adaptation or accommodation AV will experience.

After repeated attempts at golf following his stroke, AV needs to decide whether long-term continued participation in golf is in his best interests. Can he participate in golf and avoid smoking and drinking to excess? Can he play golf and manage to get enough exercise (one adaptation that may be made is to walk instead of riding a golf cart)? And even if he can adapt and accommodate to postinjury golf, he must weigh the costs versus benefits of continuing to play golf in the future. Through the evaluation process costs and benefits are analyzed and fed back into each stage of the OLH Model (see Wilhite et al., 1999). If AV decides he cannot return to an acceptable level of golf performance, then the role of the TR specialist is to assist AV in his search for other leisure activities that may substitute for golf. The bias the therapist brings to the interaction is that alternatives should be healthy leisure activities. In AV's case, he should look to substitutes that avoid social pressure to smoke and to drink to excess. This might be a good point to open a dialogue about beginning a regular program of exercise, too.

Case Three

JM is a 31-year-old female diagnosed as HIV positive a year ago. She has two children, ages five and three, and has been divorced for three years. She continues to work at her full-time accounting job with a prominent firm, but has not told anyone of her diagnosis. She has been referred to you, a community-based TR specialist, by her physician, who recommended she get help starting a regular exercise program (some research studies have indicated exercise may be useful in decreasing stress and helping people to manage HIV/AIDS better). She breaks down crying in your office, telling you that you are the first person other than her doctor who knows of her diagnosis. She is afraid to tell others of her diagnosis for several reasons:

- stigma associated with the disorder, with people making assumptions about her character and lifestyle.

- causing (irrational) fear among her coworkers, friends, and family.

- potential for discrimination at work (a job she cannot afford to lose because of her children).

- embarrassment on the part of family members once they learn of her affliction.

She seems well-informed about HIV/AIDS, its progression, and her prognosis. She knows that the HIV virus (a virus is similar to a parasite) invades some white blood cells, called T-lymphocytes, and causes them to dysfunction. The T-lymphocytes are responsible for recognizing germs and stimulating other white blood cells to proliferate and attack those germs. When the body is unable to recognize and destroy germs, a person becomes more susceptible to opportunistic infections and some forms of cancer that the body would normally fight off with a healthy immune system. As the HIV virus destroys more T-lymphocytes over time, the person becomes more susceptible until they are classified as having full-blown AIDS.

Under the supervision of her physician, she is taking a combination of medications designed to retard the progression of the disease. Her white blood cell count is near normal currently, and she has not recently experienced any of the flu-like symptoms that first caused to see her doctor. She has learned that some people have lived symptom free, healthy, and productive lives for many years after being diagnosed with the virus. But she also knows there is no cure for HIV/AIDS, and most people with HIV eventually convert to AIDS.

She is understandably worried about many aspects of her disorder. And even though she was initially referred to you for some advice about starting an exercise program, it has turned into something more complex. (It is sometimes easier to talk to a complete stranger about problems because they are "safe" and without any emotional ties to the situation.) She has abstained from sex since learning of her diagnosis and was told to have a checkup for the virus by the only sexual partner she has had since her divorce (after he was diagnosed). She worries about losing her job. She worries about losing custody of her children. She does know who will support them when she is gone. She comes home after work exhausted, stressed about keeping her diagnosis hidden, and anxious about what the future holds for her and her children. She feels guilty about being exhausted because she thinks she should be spending as much quality time with her children as she can while she is still healthy. She states that she feels like she is living on borrowed time, that she is living a provisional life that may end at any moment. She feels foolish and irresponsible about the circumstances that led to her HIV infection. She sees the future for herself as grim, and sees nothing but even more stress and more anxiety because the risk of an exacerbation becomes more likely as time passes.

Currently, to cope with this stress and to relieve that psychological strain, JM has developed a habit of having a cocktail or two after work. She even admits to you that one or two drinks have become two or three drinks almost every day. She has also started bumming a cigarette or two a day at work. Both the alcohol and the cigarettes, she says, give her temporary relief from the stress, anxiety, and uncertainty associated with her disease. They provide a temporary respite from the almost constant stress and exhaustion she experiences. She says she cannot sleep very well at night, but before her diagnosis she was a very sound sleeper. "I'll bet you can't guess how much sleep I am getting by on? Three or fours hours a day, that's it, and I'm really tired of it. If I don't do something soon I think I will explode." Others (Caroleo, 2001) reported stress is associated with the effort required to hide the HIV diagnosis from coworkers and family, to "bear the burden" of HIV with a stoic attitude. This leads to isolation and loneliness, which research suggests is contrary to successful adjustment to a HIV diagnosis.

So, what started as a simple request developed into a complex challenge for the recreational therapist. Each of the TR models has something different to offer to JM in terms of the approach taken and the goals of the TR intervention. Regardless of the approach, however, JM needs assistance from a team of professionals representing several disciplines—psychology and/or counseling, medicine and/or nursing, financial planning, and law. (Neither the planner nor the attorney are typical members of an allied health team, but certainly people who could assist JM considerably in planning for the future and addressing some of its uncertainty.) This means the TR specialist will have to perform a significant facilitator role, identifying and expediting support services for JM. Case Three reminds the professional he or she must be prepared for anything as clients are apt to share more when they are in a relaxed, nondemanding, recreational environment. The therapist must be prepared to deal with multiple demands and problems and must be knowledgeable enough to know which other team members should be consulted.

Leisure Ability Approach

Grossman and Caroleo (1996) detailed a leisure ability approach to working with a HIV/AIDS client. They suggested several goals for TR when working with an individual with HIV/AIDS:

- decreasing stress.

- improving self-esteem.

- reducing stigmatization.

- promoting satisfying leisure.

- empowering clients.

- enhancing opportunities for expression.

- facilitating meaningful leisure experiences.

Although these goals are somewhat redundant, they do provide direction to TR intervention under the Leisure Ability approach. The rationale for intervention with symptoms, such as stress, is they stand in the way of a satisfying leisure lifestyle. According to the Leisure Ability perspective, problems like stress and excessive anxiety are functional deficits that constrain a favorable quality of life. In Case Three, JM has a considerable number of psychological functional deficits that prevent her from experiencing a satisfying leisure lifestyle. In concert with other professionals the recreational therapist has contacted to help with JM, working on coping with stress strategies and anxiety, developing a prudent exercise program, and augmenting socialization and social support stand to improve quality of life for JM. The initial conversation with JM provides a wealth of assessment data that may be harnessed to programs designed by the TR specialist.

The importance of the planning phase cannot be overstated. Owing to JM's perceived lack of control over her own life, empowerment may be a function of active involvement by JM in planning not only which activities will satisfy her leisure needs, but also the amount of influence she exerts over the planning process. In this case, and under the Leisure Ability approach, the therapist should permit JM to have significant influence over which activities are selected. After all, it does not matter which of an array of exercise modalities that JM selects, only that JM pursues some exercise in preference to no exercise. What is the difference if JM chooses to participate in walking instead of aerobics or biking on a stationary cycle? So long as the TR professional observed proper precautions in consultation with JM's doctor, any of these physical activities would achieve the goal of ascribing to a regular program of exercise. This does not mean the therapist should overlook opportunities to bias JM's willingness to participate in regular exercise by reinforcing the physician's advice to exercise to reduce stress and possibly buffer JM's immune system. Reminding JM of the importance of exercise should provide enough momentum to keep JM on task and to avoid procrastination about exercise.

Taking charge of her own leisure lifestyle is part (perhaps a small but initial part) of taking charge of her overall lifestyle—her quality of life in general. The fact is no one can say precisely whether JM will succumb to HIV/AIDS in the next year, or 5 years, or 10 years, or ever. Research holds hope for discovering methods and medicines for dealing with the virus, or at least for managing the disorder so that symptoms and secondary problems are minimal (Caroleo, 2001).

Another role for the therapist is to alert JM to coping strategies, one of which is exercise. But others exist, although alternative coping strategies should be influenced by JM's preferences to subtly but unmistakably support empowerment of JM. The task for the TR specialist is to marry JM's quest for an improved leisure lifestyle (and quality of life in general) with the leisure activity choices she makes. Furthermore, it is obvious JM is using substance abuse to cope with stress at work and at home. It is incumbent on the recreational therapist to suggest healthy leisure alternatives for coping and to refer her to appropriate resources to address her substance abuse risk profile before it gets out of hand.

During the planning phase, leisure activity awareness may be indicated because many leisure activities are consistent with improving or maintaining JM's health status. Better nutrition may result from cooking groups or group activities that incorporate food. HIV/AIDS support groups may be identified (it would be JM's choice to attend or not) to help with the psychological trauma JM is obviously experiencing as a result of being diagnosed with the disease. Through interaction with others who have HIV/AIDS she may discover coping strategies and techniques successful in allying apprehension about work peers and family members should either of the groups find out JM's diagnosis.

Even financial planning and legal counsel (though obviously not the primary responsibility of the TR professional) would serve to reduce uncertainty about the future. This is especially true since JM expressed significant concern over what would happen to her children in the event of her death or her inability to continue work. In conjunction with legal counsel, the community TR professional may include educational sessions about the Americans With Disabilities Act and what JM's rights are with respect to work and public accommodations (e.g., government and private recreation facilities). In this case study, we suggest the TR specialist may cut a broad path by addressing aspects of JM's situation beyond the traditional realm of TR intervention, especially while operating under a Leisure Ability approach with its emphasis on a satisfying leisure lifestyle.

After implementation of the plan, JM may learn some forms of exercise do not appeal to her. In this event, the recreational therapist needs to be ready to suggest alternatives. JM may find it difficult to confront some or all aspects of her HIV/AIDS prognosis. Although it is not the therapist's role to force JM to confront the implications of her disease for her vocation and family relations, JM will eventually have to do so (assuming a cure or treatment to alter the ultimate consequence of HIV/AIDS is not discovered). Acting in JM's best interest means constantly pushing her and motivating her to take charge and to take control of her life—empowerment is the most crucial goal. If leisure activity, and the favorable perceptions of control associated with it, contribute to JM's empowerment, then all the better.

Evaluation of the leisure experiences that JM selected initially is a matter of her assessing the extent to which her leisure satisfaction and quality of life have improved as a result. Usually the planning/implementation/evaluation processes are repeated until the client discovers the best combination of leisure and support experiences that enhance quality of life. The professional's role during the repeated bouts of planning/implementation/evaluation is to serve as a sounding board for new alternatives JM suggests (e.g., for exercise, coping with stress) and/or to suggest alternatives in the event JM cannot come up with them on her own.

After a time, the need for the TR professional should diminish and the client (optimally) will take charge of her own leisure lifestyle (and life in general). This does not mean the therapist abandons JM, but rather stands by to provide support, guidance, and suggestions when JM encounters obstacles and constraints. In the case of HIV/AIDS, because the disease process is progressive and cumulative, there is a high probability JM will eventually experience an exacerbation or deterioration that will necessitate adjustments to the manner in which JM pursues her leisure lifestyle. Hence, intermittent contact between JM and the TR specialist in the future is likely to make adaptations and adjustments, in consultation with JM.

Self-Determination Approach

Regardless of the approach used, the TR specialist will have to be mindful of issues with JM that require the assistance of other allied health professionals. One hallmark of sound practice in any profession is to recognize when certain problems lie outside one's expertise, and JM's substance abuse as a coping device is one such example. Certainly, acquiring a sense of control through leisure experiences can help JM with the restoration of her sense of control over her own life. The literature indicates gaining a sense of control seems important to people with HIV/AIDS (Caroleo, 2001). Therefore, JM is not exceptional in this regard. On the other hand, to suggest leisure competence alone will assure JM will be empowered enough to stop abusing substances is naïve.

Having said that, if perception of control is important when using a Leisure Ability approach to JM's HIV/AIDS related challenges, then it is even more crucial when assuming a Self-Determination orientation to JM's need for empowerment. And lack of control/empowerment may be at the source of several of her other problems—anxiety, stress, and sleep deprivation. As with the preceding two cases, the Self-Determination approach is very adept at configuring the environment so the client attains a sense of control and competence, at least in his or her leisure activities.

A likely scenario using the Self-Determination approach would involve initial assessment and follow-up conversations designed to prioritize her leisure activities from most important to less important relative to the needs and challenges she expressed in conversation. The modalities used under the Self-Determination approach are manipulations by the professional designed to enhance the enjoyment by the client. Recall that in the case of this approach, enjoyment amounts to attaining a personally satisfying level of competence in one or more activities—being able to master the skills and competencies required to experience success in the chosen activity. Also, functional improvement may result from the acquisition of competence in the selected activities.

Suppose JM shared the same information with you using the Self-Determination approach as she did using the Leisure Ability approach. You, as the therapist, then know she is experiencing a pronounced sense of helplessness, isolation, and loneliness. She does not sense she can share her problems with anyone for fear of alienating that employer, coworker, or family member. She desperately needs to take charge of her life and to restore her own sense of control over as many aspects of her life she still can.

You might begin the planning sessions by reminding her even though she has been diagnosed with HIV/AIDS there are new medications being discovered every year, she is asymptomatic now, she still has a job, and she still has her children. These facts about her life and condition mean new treatments may extend the number of asymptomatic years she has, or even cause the virus to remain dormant for an indefinite period. After all, only a short time ago few thought survival would be extended by aggressive treatment using a drug mixture/cocktail that combines several medications and is more effective than any one treatment alone (Caroleo, 2001; Grossman & Caroleo, 1996). Further, you might suggest she should be motivated to retain control over several aspects of her life for as long as possible (e.g., children, job, independent living).

At the same time, JM will need to come to terms with stress for the short and long term. For the short term, she seems to have an overwhelming amount of stress associated with "keeping a secret" when she needs to share with others in the hope she will secure some support and empathy from those around her. Her concern is well-grounded. Unfortunately, as other have observed, "coming out" as HIV positive has a tendency to result in stigmatizing the person with the virus. Loss of her job, loss of custody of her children, and loss of family support hang in the balance. In the long term, progression of the disorder may produce symptoms that are so marked that she cannot keep her secret any longer. Preparing for that eventuality will prove to be a future stressor she will have to find a solution for. Your role as a recreational therapist is to help her find that solution by referring her to the appropriate resources and support she will need (counseling services and others).

For now, JM and you decide together beginning an exercise program will be the most productive use of leisure that will both help her physically and help her with stress. Some studies have shown exercise is useful in buffering the immune system of those with a HIV positive diagnosis, while other studies have shown exercise is associated with decreased levels of stress (Caroleo, 2001). But the underlying agenda for the TR specialist in this case is to facilitate an activity that will result in JM making personal attributions of control and competence as a result of participation—that is, to empower JM to reassert control over her own life.

Because the Self-Determination approach focuses more on altering the client's perceptions of control and competence (and promoting enjoyment through successful participation), it usually addresses one or only a few activities at one time. This in contrast to the more global lifestyle orientation characteristic of the Leisure Ability approach or the OLH method. Hence, suppose JM and the therapist agree an exercise program that combines walking with light weightlifting is an appropriate place to begin. Both of you hope for additional benefit (functional improvements) in terms of health and stress management as a result (and consistent with the Self-Determination Model predictions).

At this point it is important to assure the activity identification and selection process is perceived by JM as self-determined. Actively exploring and researching exercise activity options and ultimately making a decision on one exercise program must be perceived by JM as being under her control. The therapist may guide JM's search, make suggestions, and run interference by obtaining physician approval of the exercise choices JM made. But JM must be convinced her actions resulted in the exercise program she has chosen. The first step to feeling like one is in control of an activity or situation is a result of being able to choose and to carry out your preferences—being able to make a choice and to act on that choice. From the therapist's point of view, the exercise chosen by JM (within reason) hardly matters. What is more vital is that JM sees the decision as hers and takes responsibility for that decision. That way JM will feel empowered.

Once planning is complete and JM embarks on her initial attempts at exercise, the therapist's job is to configure the environment to increase the probability JM will perceive herself as competent and therefore in control of her exercise activity. Implementation of the exercise activity program means the TR specialist's job has just begun. First of all, JM has to be convinced the activity (exercise) can be intrinsically rewarding. Accordingly, the therapist could suggest adding some features to the exercise program that might enhance intrinsic motivation (e.g., suggesting partners to exercise with to enhance socialization through exercise, appreciating the pleasantly tired feeling of accomplishment one has following completion of the exercise program, recognizing successful completion of the exercise program each week, listening to music while exercising). And even if JM does achieve some of these examples of intrinsic motivation, she may need the therapist to point out these attributes to appreciate the intrinsically valuable aspects of the activity. Hence, the therapist is standing by to make sure that JM is getting everything (psychologically) she should from the exercise activity.

As JM persists in her exercise activity she may gradually come to see the activity as too difficult, because after the initial enthusiasm wears off exercise can be seen as simply a lot of hard work. Excuses and procrastination take over as one missed session become three and three becomes five and so on. These are the "dog days" of exercise compliance. JM may see the challenge of exercise compliance as insurmountable.

Persistence during this time of boredom, fatigue, and repetitiveness will reap rewards, but sometimes participants needs a reminder of the long-term rewards they will attain (e.g., better health, coping with stress). To accomplish this, the therapist may simply have to remind JM of the long-term goals she has set for herself. Or, the practitioner may have to intervene on a day-to-day basis to help JM fulfill her exercise promise to herself. For instance, the TR specialist may have to walk or lift weights with JM for a few days to set a good example and provide an exercise partner for JM. Showing JM daily or regular exercise is an achievable goal will help JM to appraise the challenge of exercise realistically—as a challenge that can be met. The net reward that awaits those willing to persist is a great sense of accomplishment and achievement. Of course, such perceptions of accomplishment are vital to JM's physical and mental health. Clearly, the manipulations performed by the therapist can play an important role in helping JM come to rest on an enjoyable (mastering a manageable challenge) leisure (exercise in this case) experience. The endpoint is JM will come to perceive herself in control of her leisure activity, enhancing a sense of empowerment. Ideally, this would generalize to JM's entire lifestyle and improve her quality of life.

Because the Self-Determination Model is a closed system that naturally feeds back into itself, it is well-suited to situations that require intermittent adjustments. This is certainly the case with HIV/AIDS, as the literature (Caroleo, 2001) suggests, because of the progressive and idiosyncratic nature of HIV/AIDS. That is, everyone responds to HIV/AIDS differently, both physically and psychologically. As the years pass, the risk for exacerbations of the disease and/or conversion to full-blown AIDS increases. The TR specialist must be prepared to assist JM in adjusting to the demands necessitated by helping JM to identify and to act on adaptations to her activity repertoire. For instance, if JM finds she has difficulty with fatigue as the disease progresses, she can alter her exercise demand by changing to a slightly less demanding type of exercise (e.g., water walking). Of course, continuation of exercise, even an adapted version, is contingent on the continued approval and endorsement of JM's physician.

As JM experiences success with her exercise program, her therapist may suggest increasing the breadth of her leisure repertoire to include other useful activities to enhance her sense of control and empowerment. Caroleo (2001) identified other activities useful in coping with stress and enhancing health among persons who are HIV positive, including tai chi, relaxation techniques, and massage. Therefore, despite the fact JM attains a sense of competence in one exercise pursuit, JM (and the TR specialist) would be wise to add activities now that may serve as substitutes in the future if JM's condition deteriorates.

OLH Approach

The case of JM is similar to the case of AV (stroke client), because like AV she reported an array of health risk behaviors directly or indirectly related to leisure. These leisure-related health problems are associated with substance abuse during free time (cigarettes and alcohol) as coping methods, an impoverished free time activity profile (especially physical activity that serves to promote her health), and apprehension about family (social) interactions because of her "secret." As with AV's case, the OLH Model has the advantage over the other two models because one of its basic principles is to promote healthy leisure to reduce the risk of secondary impairments. The Leisure Ability and Self-Determination approaches can address health risk factors, too, but only indirectly through advancing a satisfying leisure lifestyle (which one assumes is also consistent with good health) or empowering the client by advancing competence (and enjoyment) in one or more leisure activities (which leads to associated functional improvements according to the Self-Determination Model).

The first step with JM will be goal setting that evolves during assessment. With the OLH approach, the client plays an active role in the process of goal setting. The TR specialist provides guidance and serves as an information source for JM to facilitate goal setting. JM may want to focus on one or a few achievable goals initially. Because the OLH Model feeds back into itself, JM can add more goals and/or modify goals following early participation. Later, JM may need to adjust her goals as a result of exacerbations, complications, or conversion to AIDS. The professional serves JM best when he or she points out that as JM's life course plays out it may mean some goals will change, and some goals will be incompatible with other goals (e.g., advocating for her rights to leisure opportunities vs. keeping her secret).

As part of the selection phase of the OLH approach, JM and the practitioner will plan one or more activities for JM's participation. During this time the TR specialist plays a very important role as an educator. This is not simply a matter of leisure education, although instruction or arranging for instruction is important. Education during the early part of the TR process within the OLH approach includes educating the client about restricting and expanding activities. Owing to its life course approach, the therapist must orient JM to the potential impact of health status (an exacerbation of acute infection) and environmental variables (her family learns of her diagnosis) on her leisure goals. Speculating and thinking about the consequences or various scenarios will help JM to anticipate adjustments that may need to be made in the future.

The optimizing phase of the model refers to actual participation that results from implementation of the plan devised in the selecting phase. With both AV and JM, and especially during initial attempts at participation, activity engagement should be viewed as a learning process. JM will learn if the exercise program she has selected blends with her overall lifestyle (her work and family obligations). As time passes, she will also learn about other aspects of her overall lifestyle she may alter to enhance her pursuit of health and coping with stress through exercise. For example, she may ask the community-based TR practitioner how to adjust her diet to have more energy to exercise and to lose weight or to stabilize her current weight. (Case Three does not indicate that JM has a weight problem, however.) Capitalizing on JM's heightened awareness of her health and willingness to make adjustments in her lifestyle to enhance her health, the therapist may suggest that JM look at other health-enhancing adjustments (e.g., seeking help with her sleep deprivation problem by consulting a psychologist or her physician).

Continued engagement in leisure activities should be instructive, insofar as JM may learn adjustments to her approach to exercise and stress control. During the compensation phase, JM may learn, for instance, that walking is difficult during inclement weather. The therapist may recommend an indoor treadmill located at the city recreation center or the local mall during bad weather. JM may be bored with walking all the time and want some variety. The therapist may recommend yoga, water walking (in the recreation center pool), stationary biking (at the local recreation center), as well as other alternatives. JM may also experiment with other exercise options on her own as well, such as free weights, medicine balls, and Therabands, to improve strength.

JM may need an exercise partner. The therapist could contact the local HIV/AIDS support group to inquire about others seeking an exercise companion and in need of social support. Or, the therapist may recommend that she identify someone at work who also exercises as a potential partner.

Prolonged participation may cause a shift in JM's motivation for exercise. Initial participation will likely be based on health motives. ("Medical authorities have told me if I exercise it will improve my immune system, help me to sleep better, and improve my ability to cope with stress.") Later, as exercise is (hopefully) incorporated into JM's daily routine and becomes something she looks forward to, her motivation will shift to intrinsic motivation. She learns that exercise is fun, it makes her feel like she accomplishes something each day, and it is a time just for her to reflect and to think clearly.

Gradually, evaluation will evolve from continued participation. Resources (actual and emotional) are compared to the rewards of participation. Evaluation and reflection on participation in JM's case should probably not occur immediately, but only after sustained participation has elapsed. A preestablished timeline should not drive evaluation; rather, evaluation should emerge from conversations between JM and the professionals on the treatment team. Once JM is ready, however, during evaluation goals and activities may be reexamined. Evaluation does not necessarily mean that a decision to discontinue an activity and its related goal is the only course. Rather, JM may find walking becomes too easy. Instead, she looks for an exercise that challenges her capacity more. Jogging, swimming, or cycling may be ways to augment her exercise program and in pursuit of a more ambitious goal of fitness necessary to participate in 5K races or to complete marathons, or triathlons. Regardless of whether JM's evaluation of her goals and leisure lifestyle is provoked by illness exacerbation, discouragement, abatement of symptoms, or improvement, the TR specialist should help JM to explore the consequences of any decision she might make.

For example, if JM complains she is sore from exercise and wants to quit, the therapist may remind her that to continue to secure the benefits of exercise she will have to continue exercising. At this point, JM should be reminded that the soreness associated with beginning an exercise program usually subsides after the person's physiology has adapted to the exercise. She may conclude that, although she likes exercise and thinks it is beneficial, she feels guilty over not spending that same time with her children. You could suggest she try to incorporate exercise into work time. For instance, she could walk to work or part of the way to work. She may be able to take part of her lunch hour to exercise, or take advantage of employer sponsored exercise programs. (Some employers encourage exercise among employees because exercise has been associated with less absenteeism and greater productivity.)

The evaluation stage, like all other phases of the OLH process, is ultimately driven by client interest and motivation in consultation with the therapist. Perhaps the most vital role for the therapist operating under the OLH approach is to avoid the temptation to be paternalistic with the client. Even though most therapists would undoubtedly make decisions in the client's best interest, with the OLH approach the client manages his or her own leisure independently or interdependently with the TR specialist.

Summary

The present chapter endeavored to apply information on several disabilities and to join it with several different TR approaches. Clearly, the approach one takes does make a difference. Goals vary, the latitude the TR specialist has for working with the client and how much direction he or she gives differs, and the fit between service setting and approach marks a distinction as well. Although many cases, such as the ones reviewed here, can be very complex, struggling with case studies is well worth the effort because it will ultimately translate into better practice.

References

Atchley, R. (1971). Retirement and leisure participation: Continuity or crisis. *The Gerontologist, 11*, 13–17.

Bandura, A. (1977). Self-efficacy: Toward a unifying theory of behavioral change. *Psychological Review, 84*, 191–215.

Caroleo, O. (2001). An ethnographic study examining the impact of a therapeutic recreation program on people with AIDS: In their own words. *Therapeutic Recreation Journal, 35*, 155–169.

Coleman, D. and Iso-Ahola, S. E. (1993). Leisure and health: The role of social support and self-determination. *Journal of Leisure Research, 25*, 111–128.

Crandall, R. and Slivken, K. (1980). Leisure attitudes and their measurement. In S. E. Iso-Ahola (Ed.), *Social psychological perspectives on leisure and recreation* (pp. 261–284). Springfield, IL: Thomas.

Csikszentmihalyi, M. (1975). *Flow: Beyond boredom and anxiety*. San Francisco, CA: Jossey-Bass.

Dattilo, J., Kleiber, D., and Williams, R. (1998). Self-determination and enjoyment enhancement: A psychologically based service delivery model for therapeutic recreation. *Therapeutic Recreation Journal, 32*, 258–271.

Ellis, G. D. and Witt, P. A. (1986). The leisure diagnostic battery: Past, present, and future. *Therapeutic Recreation Journal, 20*, 31–47.

Feinberg, W. M., Albers, G. W., Barnett, H. J. M., Biller, J., Caplan, L. R., Carter, L. P., et al. (1994). Guidelines for management of transient ischemic attacks. *Circulation, 89*, 2950–2965.

Grossman, A. H. and Caroleo, O. (1996). Acquired immunodeficiency syndrome (AIDS). In D. R. Austin and M. E. Crawford (Eds.), *Therapeutic recreation: An introduction*. Boston, MA: Allyn & Bacon.

Lee, Y., Dattilo, J., Kleiber, D., and Caldwell, L. (1996). Exploring the meaning of continuity of recreation activity in the early stage of adjustment for people with spinal cord injury. *Leisure Sciences, 18*, 209–225.

MacNeil, R. D. and Pringnitz, T. D. (1982). The role of therapeutic recreation in stroke rehabilitation. *Therapeutic Recreation Journal, 16*(4), 26–34.

Niemi, M., Laaksonen, R., Kotila, M., and Waltimo, O. (1988). Quality of life 4 years after stroke. *Stroke, 19*, 1101–1107.

Stumbo, N. J. and Peterson, C. A. (1998). The leisure ability model. *Therapeutic Recreation Journal, 32*, 82–96.

Wilhite, B., Keller, M. J., and Caldwell, L. (1999). Optimizing lifelong health and well-being: A health enhancing model of therapeutic recreation. *Therapeutic Recreation Journal, 33*, 98–108.

Chapter 12

International TR

Learning Objectives

1. Develop an awareness of recreation services and approaches to people with disabilities in different parts of the world.

2. Identify resources and links to TR-related services across the globe.

3. Understand variances in titles and training for individuals working in TR-related services outside Canada and the United States.

4. Develop an appreciation for the importance of understanding TR in a global way.

5. Develop an awareness of TR outside the United States, to enhance services by including different perspectives.

6. Create an awareness of the various groups that represent the international interests of people with disabilities.

This final chapter looks at therapeutic recreation and recreation service provision for people with disabilities in countries outside Canada and the United States. The term "therapeutic recreation" is not universal; however, the search for information revealed many approaches to services related to the delivery of recreation services for disadvantaged populations.

The purpose of this chapter is to expose students to a variety of different sources of information and terminology available internationally. Many countries make reference to recreation service delivery for disadvantaged populations. However, these references are not organized systematically and are difficult to classify because they are written in different languages, classified under different professional affiliations, and use different terminology related to job titles and responsibilities. Yet the clientele, settings, programs, and services closely align with the traditional notions of TR in North America.

While the term "therapeutic recreation" does not appear often, one can learn unique and practical approaches to issues such as integration, inclusion, social barriers to community participation, community development, and the focus of recreation in specific areas, such as the arts, culture, and physical activity for people with disabilities. Language and cultural differences make locating and summarizing TR services across the globe a difficult task. It may not be realistic to assess TR in a culture where there is no word for leisure. In some languages, the word leisure may exist but not in the same context of free choice and self-expression.

Examining different practices in other countries can enhance understanding of our own behavior and may improve our approach to services. It can also lead to an attitude of "here is what I found and here is why our way is better." There is a tendency to compare services abroad to what we know in North America, yet this is much like comparing apples and oranges, since economic and social values are different, and services for people with disabilities vary, with radical differences in terms of access to programs and emphasis on leisure and recreation.

Anecdotal reports suggest parts of the world emphasize different aspects of recreation with a greater focus on community support and a distinction between physical and social recreational activities for people with disabilities. There is a huge international movement supporting people with disabilities. A wealth of networks address the delivery of TR services directly or indirectly.

This chapter is divided into three sections. The first section introduces the complexities of international TR and the importance of studying TR globally. The second section discusses TR-related services with examples of organizations, services and associations in different parts of the world. The final section highlights links and websites to world disability sites, with information on recreation, leisure, community support, rehabilitation, and advocacy for the rights of people with disabilities.

Importance of Studying TR
From an International Perspective

Most of the coursework in TR curriculums in Canada and the United States address the TR planning process, understanding disability, adapting equipment and programs, assessment and evaluation, and issues related to service delivery. Very few programs address specifically what other approaches to recreation services have been developed for people with disabilities outside North America.

Multicultural issues have received little attention in the TR literature (Calloway, 1992; Peregoy & Dieser, 1997). The majority of full-time faculty teaching in TR programs studied in North America do not necessarily represent international approaches to providing leisure services for people with disabilities. This has resulted in TR practice models being criticized for being "American" with a focus on individual health and not reflective of values in other countries. According to Sheldon and Dattilo (1997) a review of professional journals and textbooks in TR yielded few references to ethnic, racial, religious, or other cultural diversity. If TR professionals are to provide services in a society that values numerous backgrounds we can no longer focus on "traditional white male, middle class able bodied heterosexual perspectives" (Henderson, 1995, p. 2).

TR professionals need to design and to develop services to meet the diverse needs of clients. This chapter identifies a variety of resources and links for people with disabilities in different areas of the world. While not all focus on recreation, there is useful information on how disability organizations are structured globally and provide contacts and links to many networks and services.

Challenges in Understanding TR Internationally

No single international professional association represents TR. This is not a surprise, because even in the United States, where there is seemingly common ground on what TR is about, there is no single association representing the profession and there are still significant differences in philosophy and beliefs and services.

Most of what has been written on international TR has been compiled by Americans who have traveled abroad or by researchers in privileged and powerful locations (White, financially secure, highly educated, and from a democratic political structure). The quest for accurate, reliable information is a challenge, because there are many different titles, languages, and sources of information. From scholarly journals to agency reports to client testimonials, the information is varied and often inconsistent.

In searching for information, a wide net was cast to include services for people with disabilities and recreation and leisure for people with disabilities. Information was carried out through direct contact with people in various countries and through web-based searches. In the discussion of findings on the search for international TR, any attempt to provide an overview runs the risk of making sweeping generalizations that will not be practically helpful, and may even reinforce stereotypical assumptions about situations in specific countries or in different cultures. There is a caution that the information in this chapter is limited, and it does not reflect the practices of a whole country.

Since we are most familiar with TR in North America, it is easy to criticize other countries for not being as "advanced" in the profession. Yet many factors need to be considered, such as healthcare; financial, economic, and political stability; and attitudes toward providing services. Just as other countries can learn from approaches in Canada and the United States, North American TR practitioners can develop an awareness of other approaches to services, and other structures that might be more effective. There is also a need to understand that the notion of TR service is really a privileged service of a developed healthcare and economic and political system of beliefs and attitudes, which is not the case in developing countries.

International Therapeutic Recreation

People with disabilities live, work, and play in every part of the world. Anyone can acquire a disability at any time, and as the world population ages, disability will be the experience of an increasing percentage of every society. Yet universally people with disabilities have been denied access to basic human rights. Across the globe, people with disabilities are marginalized, discriminated against, and excluded.

The impact of people with disabilities is overwhelming on an international scale. According to Werner (1986) approximately 10% of the world's population has a disability. These numbers are underestimated, because it depends on how disability is recognized and it may not include the 100 million people who have disabilities as a result of malnutrition. In poorer countries, people with mild impairments may be severely disabled because of lack of opportunities to rectifiable services, such as access to eyeglasses, cleft palate operations, and other minor surgeries. As a result mild impairments are more significant and common. People with severe medical conditions are not as likely to survive. Conditions such as HIV/AIDS, mental health problems, tuberculosis, chronic malaria, psychological trauma as a result of conflict, or refugee situations can give rise to permanent impairments that result in exclusion and discrimination. These people are not included in the estimated 10%, so the numbers of people in the world with disabilities is significant.

Many people with disabilities live in poor countries where the primary human rights issues concern the right to life, food, water, and shelter. Because poverty is both a cause and consequence of disability, some estimate as many as 1 in 5 poor people are disabled (Christian Aid, 2001). This would mean that practically every family in a poor community would be directly affected by disability (Nordic Development Cooperation, 2000). Given that basic needs are not met in poorer or less developed countries, it is understandable that access to recreation and leisure services is not seen as a priority. In economically deprived countries, people with disabilities usually remain excluded from community activities and are often seen as burdens on already struggling social support systems.

Many people living in developing countries are illiterate and struggle for access to social services. Many live in small rural villages with limited resources. Attitudes toward people with disabilities vary greatly around the globe. According to Oka (1988), in Bangladesh a common misconception is that "disability" is God's desire and nothing can be done. This belief condemns a person born with a disability to a state of dependency. In Bhutan, disability is linked to manifestations of evil spirits in this or a previous life. Negative perceptions, beliefs, and attitudes greatly influence the availability and nature of services for people with disabilities.

Even when there is an awareness of the need to include people with disabilities in recreational and community activities, there are still misunderstandings and ignorance about what this means in practice. Many decision makers in communities assume it is a highly specialized area requiring significant specialist resources. Yet the inclusion of people with disabilities could be easily be facilitated if people with disabilities were consulted and an effort was made to decrease barriers to participation.

Over the last two decades, there has been a vast amount of experience gained and knowledge shared between communities, local and international nongovernment organizations, disability organizations, governments, and international agencies who have offered a wide range of strategies to address the issue of disability in developing countries. In an effort to standardize information sharing related to supporting people with disabilities, The United Nations (UN; 1994) created a universal definition of disability. The term *disability* summarizes a great number of functional limitations occurring in any population in any country of the world. People with disabilities may have physical or intellectual limitations, sensory impairments, medical conditions, or mental illnesses, which may be permanent or transitional in nature.

The UN distinguishes between disability and the term *handicap*, which means the loss or limitation of opportunities to take part in life of the community on an equal level with others. It describes the encounter between a person with a disability and the environment. The purpose of the term is to emphasize shortcomings in the environment and in many organized activities in society. (For further discussion of these terms see Chapter 5.) The term *handicapped* is now considered stigmatizing and is not readily used in the English speaking world; however, the term is still commonly used in other languages.

World definitions of disability can be divided into two models. The *individual* model of disability incorporates both the charity and medical models. It perceives the person with a disability as a problem and aims to alleviate the problem on an individual level rather than fix the society. The model is prevalent in developing countries and agencies looking for a quick solution such as building an institution or special school but it does not address the system that creates inequality. The *social* model of disability is perceived as a relationship between the individual and society. It is consistent with the human rights approach. In development cooperation, it provides a sound basis for analysis and planning. The focus is on addressing and removing barriers, creating positive inclusive environments, and stakeholders rather than on specific limitations of an individual. The social model does not deny the need for rehabilitation and medical treatment of the individual but implies the system should adapt to the person, not the person to the system.

An example of the social model of disability in practice can be found at the Rowan Organization (RO) in Warwickshire in the United Kingdom (http://www.rowanorganization.com). The RO is an organization of disabled people that provides access to information, services, and resources to increase their opportunities for independence and to enable freedom of choice. RO services follow four guiding principles:

1. Services offered should support people with disabilities to have increased choices, independence, and control over their lives.

2. Support provided should be based on and directed by the aims, objectives, and needs of clients.

3. The same range of activities and opportunities should be available to people with disabilities as are available to other members of the community.

4. People with disabilities should not be segregated against because of their impairment.

RO rejects the medical or individual model of disability that emphasizes the problem as lying with an individual and seeks to change the person so they are better able to cope with their situation. Instead, RO addresses the social model of disability and predominant social attitudes that exist and perpetuate a dependent stereotypical image of people with disabilities. RO provides a service, which focuses on providing access to a full range of activities people with disabilities want to pursue. The day service works with clients to access activities, which include sports, recreation, education, the arts, and other leisure activities. The focus of services is on skill development, support transportation, discussion and debate, and specific leisure programs.

Most developed nations acknowledge inclusion of disadvantaged populations in community activities is both a goal and a process. In creating opportunities for people with disabilities, a *twin track* approach is adopted, giving disability (individual) specific strategies, such as rehabilitation, prevention from impairments worsening, providing basic assistive aids and equipment, and building grass roots organization of people with disabilities to develop life skills, self-esteem, and an understanding of how to be their best resource.

The twin track approach used in most commonwealth countries can be linked directly with both the "therapy" and "recreation" aspects of therapeutic recreation. The twin track approach provides a distinction between the therapy (or individual services related specifically to disability) and community involvement (social support and recreation participation).

International Associations, Organizations, and Websites

In the search for international information on therapeutic recreation, a number of valuable websites and associations were identified. This section gives a brief overview of some of the links useful to TR practitioners.

The *World Leisure Association* (http://www.worldleisure.org) offers information and links to leisure in all parts of the world. The organization includes a charter of leisure, information on international conferences, and a commission on access and inclusion. The purpose of the commission is

- to promote and develop initiatives that assure the equitable participation and inclusion of all members of the community to play, recreation, and leisure services.

- to serve as a mechanism to advocate for policies and programs within world leisure that focus on access and inclusion.

- to foster basic and applied research that examines the meaning and impact of leisure and recreation in the lives of people with disabilities.

- to serve as a vehicle to ensure that the needs and issues of access and inclusion are addressed throughout the work of world leisure and its various commissions, committees, and projects.

The *Global Therapeutic Recreation Collection* (http://www.lin.ca/resource) offers a collection of essays organized from six international TR symposiums providing research and specific program information in a variety of countries.

The *World Alliance of YMCA* website (http://www.ymcainternational) gives an overview of YMCA history and provides links to YMCA programs and organizations and services worldwide. The focus is on programs for youth and youth development.

Rehabilitation International (RI; http://www.rehab-international.org) is a worldwide network of people with disabilities, service providers, and government agencies working together to improve the quality of life for people with disabilities and their families. The agency, founded in 1922, includes 200 member organizations from 90 countries, and the main office is housed in New York.

RI is a federation of national and international organizations and agencies. It develops and promotes initiatives to protect the rights of people with disabilities, and to improve rehabilitation and other crucial services for people with disabilities and their families. Specifically the organization provides

- an open exchange of experience and information on research and practice.

- advocacy tools for policy and legislation, recognizing the rights of people with disabilities and their families.

- initiatives to promote change of public attitudes to encourage equal participation for people with disabilities in education, employment, and the cultural and social life of their communities.

Some projects organized by RI include originating the international symbols of accessibility, hosting the first world conference on community-based rehabilitation, social barriers of integration, legislation concerning people with disabilities, barrier free design environments, economics of disability, and the media and disability. RI is currently working on providing practical support to the disability focus of UNICEF and promoting the UN standards for equalization of opportunities for people with disabilities.

RI is a valuable resource for anyone in the TR field. The organization publishes periodicals and reports on disability in *International Rehab Review* and *One in Ten*. It also hosts an online international magazine addressing disability issues.

Disability World (http://www.disabilityworld.org) is a free online magazine with a variety of articles related to issues and disability. The online magazine is nonrefereed, but contains many articles on children, women, and community support of people with disabilities. It also includes innovative programs to address disability issues and creates a social awareness, and gives valuable information links.

Therapeutic Recreation Directory (http://www.recreationtherapy.com) dedicated to sharing information from different countries. The website provides links to a variety of countries practicing or delivering TR service.

TR-Related Services Across the Globe

This section examines therapeutic recreation services for people with disabilities and support services for people with disabilities in different parts of the world. Not all areas are represented. Countries reflected were selected based on access to information, language, and knowledge of contact people in a specific area. Some agencies have direct recreation applications and some information refers to information on approach or organizations that represent disadvantaged populations.

This section offers approaches and examples of programs and services, educational and professional requirements, professional associations, job titles, and positions. The information related to TR was found under a number of different professional associations, titles, and terms, because programs and services varied considerably within and between countries.

Diversion Therapy

In Australia, New Zealand, and parts of the United Kingdom, recreation services for people with disabilities was identified as *diversional therapy*. According the New Zealand Society of Diversional Therapists (NZSDT), diversional therapy (DT) is "a professional practice which recognizes and facilitates purposeful recreation, leisure, and pleasure activities with individual client choice to increase the physical, intellectual, spiritual, and emotional well-being of older people in supportive environments." DT is client centered and recognizes that leisure and recreation experiences are the right of all individuals and should be positive and valuable. DT involves designing programs for resident needs to support or to maintain dignity, independence, and self-esteem. DT practitioners work with people of all ages and abilities to design leisure and recreation programs. Activities are designed to support, challenge, and enhance the psychological, spiritual, social, emotional, and physical well-being of individuals.

The Australian Diversion Therapy Association operates in all areas of Australia (http://www.diversion therapy.com.au). The professional association of DT represents those employed as diversion therapists, and recreation activity officers, as well as those employed in the recreation and leisure industry working with people with disabilities. Employment settings include rehabilitation and hospital units, community centers, day and respite services, aged care residential facilities, ethnic specific services, palliative care units, outreach programs, mental health services, specialist organizations, consultancy, and private practice and management.

The Diversion Therapist Association of Australia identifies specific areas of skills and knowledge for the profession. The specialized skills are applicable in health community and leisure settings and include the following:

- leisure counseling and education.

- assessment of leisure-related needs and abilities.

- development of individual personal programs.

- facilitating client choices and decision making.

- lifestyle management.

- creative and expressive recreation.

- activity analysis and modification.

- documentation of professional practice and client care.

- continuous quality improvement and evaluation.

- teaching and facilitation.

- health promotion.

- management.

- team and group work.

According to the NZSDT, diversional recreation programs are diverse and focus on many elements, including self-esteem, free choice, use of visual and hand skills, creative activities with a worthwhile outcome, communication, expression, socialization, reminiscence, giving hope and meaning to life, strategies to improve individual and group time, and development of relationships.

Diversional Therapists in New Zealand are recognized by a national certification program through the organization of community support services industry training. The DT associations in Australia and New Zealand have a code of professional ethics and a list of responsibilities related to positions. Typical roles of a diversion therapist include the following:

- assessing client preferences and capabilities.

- developing individualized activity profiles.

- providing opportunities for choice.

- offering individual and group activities.

- developing community facilities and community links of clients.

- creating and maintaining written plans of ongoing progress.

- participating in multidiscipline resident reviews.

- planning weekly activities.

Occupational Therapy

The European Network of Occupational Therapy in Higher Education (ENOTHE) indirectly represents the recreational interests of people with disabilities in Europe. ENOTHE is a nonprofit organization founded in 1995 representing each EU country except Luxembourg. Supported by the European Commission, the aim of the network is to develop, to harmonize, to improve standards of professional practice and education, and advance the body of knowledge of OT throughout Europe.

In Canada and the United States clear distinctions are made between occupational therapy (OT) and therapeutic recreation (TR). In Europe the emphasis on OT is on occupation, which has two meanings. The first is the focus on "work"-related skills, such as tasks of daily living, a particular strength, adaptation, or competence related to something specific on the job. The second emphasis is on keeping "occupied" or active as opposed to doing very little. It is the second focus that includes recreation or broadly defined therapeutic recreation. The focus on "occupation" involves promoting diversional activities to promote boredom, creating challenging and meaningful uses of free time, and developing skills related to hobbies and leisure interests.

The mission and goals of the association support broadly the goals of therapeutic recreation. Recreation is included as part of the mandate of OT education. The focus of ENOTHE is

- to exchange ideas, theory, and language.

- to set curriculum.

- to give program support.

- to facilitate interaction between members.

- to support programs that move away from the medical model.

- to focus on both work and free time client issues.

Adapted Physical Activity and Adapted Sport

Adapted physical activity and adapted sport emphasis was significant in countries in the European Union and in Australia. Adapted physical activity (APA) is an interdisciplinary/multidisciplinary area of expertise, including rehabilitation and therapy; physical education; sport, leisure, and recreation; and competitive sport at all levels. APA combines information and research findings from sport and movement sciences (e.g., biomechanics, physiology) and other science areas (e.g., medicine, rehabilitation sciences, psychology) dealing with physical activity and sport in relation to persons with diverse needs, especially individuals with disabilities (DePauw & Sherrill, 1994)

Health sports are defined as physical activities designed to improve physical abilities and to foster higher levels of mental, physical, and spiritual well-being. Adapted physical activities are used in preventive healthcare and in rehabilitation of people with chronic or temporary disabilities. The term "health sports" is a national variant of the international term adapted physical activity. The academic study "Physical Activity and Disability" varies from a four-year undergraduate degree (Australia) to a is a one-year full-time study at the undergraduate level (Norway). Graduate programs in APA are also available at 30 European universities and are organized by the University of Leuven in Belgium.

There are many links to international sport specific agencies. APA focuses on physical health development through involvement in sport and recreation. The Beitostølen Health Sports Center in Norway provides an example of APA approach. Active Australia is an example of the APA emphasis on physical recreation.

Beitostølen Health Sports Center (BHSC) was opened as a Norwegian national center on November 7, 1970. During a typical year, about 1000 clients, ranging in age from 6 to 70 with different disabilities, stay at the center. BHSC includes physical training, environmental activities and treatment, education and information, and research and development activities. A stay at the center, usually four weeks for adults and two and a half weeks for children, is paid for by the Norwegian Social Security System.

Besides residential facilities, BHSC consists of several buildings, including a large sports hall that can be divided in three rooms, a therapy pool and a swimming pool, a room with training apparatus, testing laboratories, indoor riding hall, horse stable, dog kennel, and rooms for different hobby activities. There is a sports stadium, a lake for water sports and fishing, nature paths, campfires, cabins, cross-country skiing trails, and an alpine ski hill. The center is recognized as an official part of the national specialist health service system, and as such, a part of the rehabilitation services in Norway. The staff at BHSC are divided into four rehabilitation teams. The daily practical work in the teams is cross-disciplinary, with the activities jointly organized mainly by the APA instructors and the physiotherapists, in cooperation also with the environmental activity staff.

The clients are admitted to the center by applications from a medical professional, a rehabilitation team, special pedagogues, or another relevant education or rehabilitation professional. The goal of the center is to help persons with disabilities to achieve a better quality of life by means of physical, social, and cultural activities. This can be reached through experiences, learning, and mastery of skills that give increased physical and mental competencies in coping with the daily life in the individuals' local community. The programs are carried out in close cooperation with the users themselves, and strive toward optimal functional independence for the user.

The programs at the center are a supplement and an alternative to other forms of rehabilitation. Health sports are considered by the health authorities an important part of a comprehensive rehabilitation "chain." A stay at the center is a short-term stay in relation to a total rehabilitation process, and might serve as one important part of a rehabilitation chain. The main focus is providing a wide spectrum of activities—to "focus on the potential." In addition the facility offers a range of services that in some cases can be a precondition for participating in activities, and in other cases might be necessary to obtain full effect of the activity programs. These services are related to the professional background of the staff. The activities offered to some extent reflect the Norwegian activity culture, with great emphasis on outdoor activities.

With the long winter in Norway, it is natural to have a variety of winter activities available, like different ice and snow activities (e.g. cross-country and alpine skiing [sitting, standing, with mono-skis, or with other types of equipment and helping devices], biathlon, sledding activities by means of poles and/or dogs). Other examples of sport activities are gymnastics, ball games, activities in the two pools, horseback riding (10 horses), cycling, athletics, orienteering, rowing, paddling, archery, air-gun shooting, hiking, and outdoor life.

Environmental and hobby activities might include stone work (gem polishing), leather work, handicrafts (e.g., weaving, knitting, silk painting), informal games and plays, entertainment and dance, biology lessons, dance lessons, tours, and several outdoor activities.

Specific, individual treatment is also offered to eliminate or relieve pain, to correct disturbances in the circulatory system, to normalize functions in the muscles and joints, and as ADL training.

Active Australia (http://www.ausport.gov.au) encourages more Australians to participate in sport and physical activity and to improve the places where sport and physical activity occur. A key part of Active Australia is the promotion of physically active lifestyles, including Australians with disabilities. This promotion is done through the Disability Education Program, which provides training and resources for teachers, coaches, and community leaders to overcome the barriers people with disabilities face in taking part in physical activity and sport. Within Active Australia, three networks have been developed to improve the delivery of sport and physical activity in the community:

- Clubs and organizations provide opportunities for sport and physical activity for members of the community.

- Local councils provide programs, services, and facilities within the community, and many have sport and recreation officers who work with clubs and schools in their council regions.

- Schools provide the opportunities for young Australians to develop positive attitudes and behaviors to be active for life.

Chyrio Recreation

The term "chiryo" means therapeutic. In Korea *chiryo recreation* is the closest to North American defined TR. Chiryo recreation takes place in settings similar to North America, including long-term care facilities, hospitals, rehabilitation centers, and social welfare agencies.

Since the Paralympics in 1988, there has been an increasing awareness of the recreation needs of people with disabilities. In Korea, there is no formal credentialing process for people working in the field. Emphasis is currently on highlighting the unique professional training of Chiryo recreation workers.

In Korea, the Leisure Ability Model (see Chapter 9) has been adopted as the approach to service, and continuing education is offered several times a year with the focus on impacts and benefits of programs, assessment, case studies, and leisure education. The Daehan TR association (2003) reports an attempt to create a TR movement in Korea. Current Chiryo recreation workers are primarily volunteers and not seen as central to the treatment team. For more information written in the Korean language contact http://www.tr4u.co.kr.

Fukushi Recreation

According to Chino (1997) TR in Japan is closely linked to *fukushi recreation*. Although both terms are quite dissimilar, concepts between *fukushi recreation* and therapeutic recreation are quite similar. "Fukushi" means welfare. So *fukushi recreation* means recreation as a process carried out in social welfare settings, such as nursing homes, senior citizen centers, mental health hospitals, and rehabilitations centers.

In 1987 the Japanese government started to issue a national license for care workers for secondary care of various people with disabling conditions and older adults. To obtain a license there was a recognition that there was a formal plan of study needed, including taking such subjects as social welfare, psychology, medical care, disabilities, and senility, as well as recreation and its services. Programs of study related to *fukushi recreation* address basic concepts of recreation, leisure and play, and a history of the recreation movement and TR. Most fukushi recreation workers are organized by the National Recreation Association of Japan. The largest employer is with older adults in nursing homes, which has been a rapidly expanding service as the population of Japan ages.

According to Chino, the first Fukushi Recreation forum was held in 1997, which helped to launch the TR movement in Japan. Although there is a comprehensive team for each client in medical settings, nursing homes, and rehabilitations settings, generally fukushi recreation workers are not included. This may change in coming years since many fukushi recreation workers (most are volunteers) have client-centered programs, and offer results-oriented recreation services.

Nani-Tr (http://www.uwlax.edu/rmtr/tr/nanitr) is a website designed to promote TR Japan. This site was initially developed because of some issues and concerns from students in Japan studying TR in the United States. The site promotes discussion on such issues as current trends in Japan, activity ideas, facilitation techniques, assessments, documentation, TR career opportunities, and promoting TR in Japan.

According to Inclusion Japan (Suzuki, 2003), there are currently about 150 groups of self-advocates in Japan. Activities are diverse, including recreational and educational events such as bowling, karaoke, one-day sightseeing trips, cooking classes, as well as studying activities and advocacy where clients learn about social welfare systems and their rights, or have meetings with administrative representatives. Thus people with intellectual disabilities work with colleagues in their own way, are able to think about the relationship between themselves and society, and can start the integration process. The number of members and the structure of self-advocate groups differ widely but a group called "People First" is preparing to establish a national organization.

Grassroots Development

There are many examples of grassroots recreation and leisure services in developing countries on various websites. While leisure and recreation services are not main priorities in developing countries, a number of community initiatives support the rights of people with disabilities to access leisure services. This section highlights one example in grassroots development to show how strategies are being used to promote services and awareness for the needs of services.

Georgia and Armenia

A project titled *Facilitating Participation of People With Disabilities in Armenia and Georgia* outlined strategies for increasing opportunities for people with disabilities in these countries. The project was created in an effort to work toward creating comparable health systems and standards. Initiatives were developed with an emphasis on social protection of people with disabilities and rehabilitation. The long-term goal is to create a system that enables participation of children and adults with physical and mental disabilities into society. The introduction of allied health professionals into the healthcare system have played an important role in the process.

To begin to create services in undeveloped areas can be a daunting task. There are examples of programs set up by importing professionals to train others until professional formal training in the areas have evolved. The project identified two areas of developmental need. First there was a need to create opportunities for education and training in universities. Second there needed to be opportunities and support in healthcare institutions to facilitate the participation of people with disabilities in Armenian and Georgian society. To address the need for continuing education, intensive coursework was developed to allow for training in a shorter period of time, and existing courses were adapted or modified with different topics or approaches. To increase opportunities for people with disabilities, target groups were identified and comprehensive lists of service needs were developed.

Resources and Web Links for TR-Related Services Worldwide

The amount of information and Web links related to TR is overwhelming. A variety of websites have been organized to develop an awareness of disability issues in recreation across the globe. These websites provide information on different approaches to services, programming, and other relevant links.

Europe

European Network on Disability Studies (http://www.disability-europe.info). The site of the European Network on Disability Studies hopes to create new opportunities to promote the social inclusion and citizenship of disabled people through communication, meetings, publications, collaborative research, and an online knowledge bank. The site offers links to various reports of research.

European Year of Persons With Disabilities 2003 (http://www. eypd2003.org). This website describes activities to promote the European year designated to create an awareness of the rights of people with disabilities. The theme "nothing about us without us" was promoted in all countries in the European Union. Examples of promotional activities by country are found on the website.

The purpose of the special designated year was to raise an awareness of the rights of people with disabilities to full equality and participation in all areas. The objectives of the European year of people with disabilities are

- to encourage reflection on and discussion of the measures needed to promote equal opportunities for people with disabilities in Europe.

- to promote the exchange of experience of good practice and effective strategies devised at local, national, and European level.

- to reinforce the cooperation between all parties concerned (government, social partners, nongovernment organizations, nonprofit organizations, social services, private sector, communities, voluntary sector groups, and people with disabilities and their families).

- to pay special attention to awareness of the rights of children with disabilities to equality education, to encourage and support full integration in societies.

Autism Europe (http://www.autismeurope.org). The website of a well-developed European network of organizations and research groups involved with autism. The main objective of the organization is to advance the rights of people with autism and their families and help to improve lives. The organization represents 77 national and regional associations of parents of children with autism and offers services to 30 countries. The site provides Web links specific to associations by country in Europe.

Disability and Media Society (http://www.abm-median.de). The website of Germany's Disability and Media Society includes information in English and German about international disability short film festival, held in Munich every three years.

DisabilityNOW (http://www.disabilitynow.org.uk). The site of a monthly newspaper reporting on disability issues in Britain. Selected news and features are available for free, or entire site is available by subscription. The site includes links to papers and gives news, articles, advice, and chat forum. Mostly opinions, and nonrefereed information.

Eucrea International (http://www.Eucrea-international.org). A site for a nongovernmental organization for the promotion of equal opportunities for people with disabilities (all disabilities, all ages) in the areas of art, culture, and media.

European Disability Forum (http://www.edf-feph.org). Website of the European Disability Forum, which promotes equal opportunities for disabled people and ensures disabled citizens' full access to fundamental and human rights by representing disabled people in dialogue with the European Union and other European authorities. EDF is a European umbrella organization that represents 37 million people with disabilities in Europe.

The mission of the organization is to ensure citizens with disabilities have full access to fundamental and human rights through active involvement in policy development and implementation in the European Union. The website contains useful information on people with disabilities living in institutions and provides links to other disability organizations. The current priorities of the EDF are nondiscrimination, human rights, employment, public procurement, transportation, sharing information and technology, development and cooperation, and social inclusion and policy.

Inclusion International (http://www.inclusion-international.org). A global organization of family-based organizations advocating for human rights of people with intellectual disabilities worldwide, supported by the Canadian International Development Agency.

The mission of the organization is to address four principles affecting the lives of people with disabilities: (a) inclusion in all aspects of society, (b) full citizenship, which respects individual human rights responsibilities, (c) self-determination to have control over the decisions affecting one's life, and (d) family support through adequate services and support networks to families with a disabled member. There are links to specific countries and links to papers on support and intellectual disability.

Institute on Independent Living (http://www.independentliving.org). A Swedish site with a comprehensive library of articles, information exchange bulletin boards, and lots of international links. There are resources for those working with people with extensive disabilities. The organization aims to develop consumer-driven policies aimed at self-determination, self-respect, and dignity.

Irish National Disability Authority (http://www.nda.ie). The site of the Irish National Disability Authority, established as a policy advisory and research body by the Department of Justice, Equality & Law Reform. The site gives information on exploring advocacy, accessible buildings, and disability facts.

Nordic Cooperation on Disability (http://www.nsh.se). A Swedish-based website of Nordic Cooperation on Disability, featuring reports in Swedish and English of collaborative projects promoting accessibility of environment and transport and a newsletter, *Society for All*.

Parents for Inclusion (http://www.parentsforinclusion.org). The website for a UK organization of "parents helping parents so that disabled children can learn, make friends, and have a voice in ordinary school and throughout life."

The organization was started in 1994 to create tools for inclusion. The organization places the child's views and wishes at the center of the action and fully supports the social (systemic) model of disability. The site provides useful links to education sites addressing inclusion strategies and offers training sessions for parents.

Spanish Disability Information Service (http://sid.usal.esl). The website of Spanish Disability Information Service (SID), offering tools and documents on disability and is sponsored by the University of Salamanca, in Spain.

The Russia Journal (http://www.russiajournal.com). An English-language business weekly with news coverage of disability issues in Russia. A great tool for discussion of news in Russian with clients.

What's on in Spain (http://www.polibea.com). Site providing information on meetings, seminars, courses and any subject of interest to and about the disabled. Accessible travel section featuring a magazine, Polibea Turismo, with actual information about accessible accommodation, museums, beaches, and more. The site is renewed every week.

World Blind Union (http://umc.once.esl). Information about the WBU and The World Blind magazine. The World Blind union represents 600 different organizations in 158 countries. It is a nonprofit organization that distributes pictograms of blindness for public use and identifies rehabilitation through sport and leisure activities as part of their mission.

Africa

All Africa (http://www.allafrica.com). A site providing news and information on Africa, including coverage of disability issues. A resource to discuss African news with clients from Africa. Information can be found to add to cultural programming.

Epic Enabled (http://www.epic-enabled.com). An overland tour company committed to opening up Africa to enable the disabled traveler through interactive participation tours. The company offers accessible overland camping and adventure safaris in South Africa for adults with physical disabilities. The company aims to promote knowledge and awareness of South Africa and leisure interest of travelers. The site provides detailed travel schedules and shows pictures of adapted transportation and accommodation.

Action and Disability Development (http://www.add.org.uk). UK-based Association for Disability and Development, working with disabled people's organizations in 12 of the poorest countries in Africa and Asia "to produce positive change." The site provides new from a variety of countries with photos on a notice board.

Australia and New Zealand

Disability Information, Communication, and Exchange (http://www.dice.org.au). An Australian site offering regular news from several organizations, including the National Council on Intellectual Disability. DICE identifies nine areas of policy development, including access to quality education for people with disabilities, access to employment, access to accommodation, family skill development, health human rights, aging, retirement, unmet needs, and developing leadership in people with disabilities.

Disability Rights (http://www.humanrights.gov.au). The site of the Australian Human Rights and Equal Opportunity Commission featuring "a range of resources and links on disability rights and discrimination issues." Recognizes arts and culture and recreation as basic human rights. There are links to sport and recreation sites in Australia.

Disability Information Resource (http://www.accessbility.com.au/sport.htm). A government website outlining a number of links for children and accessibility issues.

Australian Capital Territory (ACT) and Disabled Sports and Recreation Association (ADSRA) (http://dmoz.org/regional/oceania/australia/recreation_and_sports). ADSRA provides opportunities in sport, recreation and fitness for all people with disabilities including physical, intellectual, and mental health.

Disabled Person Assembly (http://www.dpa.nz). Explains the disabled persons assembly in New Zealand and has a number of links to different disabling conditions.

New Zealand Society of Diversional Therapists, Inc. (http://www.diversiontherapy.org.nz). A website representing the New Zealand Society of Diversion Therapists. The site lists definitions, sample job titles, roles, and a professional code of ethics. It also offers strategies for diversion therapists and information on professional certification.

Victorian Network on Recreation and Disability (http://www.vicnord. org). VICNORD is a statewide information and advocacy network for people with disabilities and recreation.

NICAN (http://www.nican.com.au). Nican provides an Australia-wide information service on recreation and tourism, sports and the arts for people with disabilities. It has information on both specialist and mainstream organizations.

Latin America

El Cisne (http://www.elcisne.org). A monthly publication for all those connected to disability issues.

Paso a Paso (http://www.pasoapaso.com.ve). The website of the Paso a Paso Foundation, formed in 1991 by a group of parents in Venezuela. The site offers a great amount of information in Spanish concerning the improvement of lives of children with special needs and their families. It also offers services and publications, as well as a bimonthly bulletin.

Rede Saci (http://www.saci.org). The site of Saci Network (Rede Saci), created in Sao Paulo, Brazil to promote citizenship and social integration of all disabled people. The site provides a dynamic space for information exchange among disabled people, their families, the public sector, and businesses.

The Office of the President of Mexico (www.presidencia.gob.mx). A site of the Office of the President of Mexico, where documentation on disability policies are introduced.

Asia

Asia–Pacific Development Center for Disability (http://www.apcdproject. org). Founded in 2002, the Asia Pacific Development Center on Disability, based in Thailand, is a technical assistance project of the government of Japan and the government of Thailand. Site features news, training courses, and information resources.

The goal is the empowerment of people with disabilities and a barrier-free society in developing countries in Asia and Pacific region. The organization implements training in independent living, community based rehabilitation, building self-help organizations of people with disabilities and the design of barrier-free environments.

Asia Disability Institute (http://member.nifty.ne.jp). Site posting comprehensive reports, primarily on independent living and disability rights activities in Japan. This site provides access to a number of articles on accessibility and independent living in Japan.

Asian Pacific Decade of Disabled Persons (http://unescape.org). A site run by the UN Economic and Social Council for Asia and Pacific, describing initiatives on behalf of the Asia and Pacific Decade of Disabled Persons. Many links to other countries best practices.

Japanese Society for Rehabilitation of Persons with Disabilities (http://www.jsrd.or.jpl). JSRPD promotes activities for persons with disabilities in every way possible within and outside Japan. The organization provides surveys, disseminates research, provides information and cooperates with disability organizations. Supports research linked to quality of life, arts and culture and provides free online publications.

The Japan Times (http://www.japan times.com). An online English language newspaper with coverage of disability issues in Japan.

Disability India Network (http://www.disabilityindia.org). An activist site with links to journals and other organizations in India. Includes links to inclusion sites and provides links to *Disability India Journal.*

India's National Center for Promotion of Employment of Disabled Persons (http://www.ncpedp.org). India's National Center for Promotion of Employment of Disabled Persons is updated every two weeks with various information about activities and policies and provides valuable national time-line of disability related developments.

Summary

This final chapter introduced a variety of resources for therapeutic recreation-related services around the globe. In the search for information on different parts of the world, it became clear a significant number of services and approaches are offered to people with disabilities to enhance leisure opportunities. The challenge to understanding the different approaches is in how the information is organized. Therapeutic recreation is a term common only in North America. Because TR practitioners work with a diverse clientele, it is important to examine how leisure is viewed in different cultures and how it translates into services and opportunities in so many varied settings. This chapter provided an introduction to Web resources related to understanding international TR. Future work is needed to develop a comprehensive understanding of global TR-related services.

References

Calloway, J. (1992). Organizational and management styles in therapeutic recreation. In R. M. Winslow and K. J. Halberg (Eds.), *The management of therapeutic recreation service* (pp. 1–24). Arlington, VA: National Recreation and Parks Association.

Chino, H. (1997, August 19). Fukushi recreation: TR in Japan. Retrieved from http://www.recreationtherapy.com/articles

Christian Aid. (2001, November). *Master or servant: How global trade can work to the benefit of poor people.* Retrieved from http:www.christian-aid.org.uk

Daehan TR Association. (2003). Retrieved from http://www.tr4u.co.kr

DePauw, K. and Sherrill, C. (1994). Adapted physical activity: Present and future. *Physical Education Review, 17*(1), 6–13.

Henderson, K. (1995). Leisure in a diverse society: Designing a course. *Schole: A Journal of Leisure Studies and Recreation Education, 10,* 1–15.

Oka, Y. (1988). *Self reliance in interdependent communities: Independent living of disabled persons in Asia Pacific region.* Paper presented at the post congress seminar on social rehabilitation by rehabilitation international, Hamamatsu, Japan.

Nordic Development Cooperation. (2000). *Copenhagen conference report: Inclusion of the disability dimension in Nordic Development Cooperation.* Denmark: DSI.

Peregoy, J. and Dieser, R. (1997). Multicultural awareness in therapeutic recreation: Hamlet living. *Therapeutic Recreation Journal, 8,* 174–189.

Sheldon, K. and Dattilo, J. (1997). Multiculturalism in therapeutic recreation: Terminology clarification and practical suggestions. *Therapeutic Recreation Journal, 31*(3), 148–158.

Suzuki, K (2003). *A cry is sounded at Asian Conference on mental retardation and self advocate activities in Japan.* Paper presented at the 16th annual Conference on MR, Tsukuba City, Ibaraki, Japan.

United Nations. (1994) *The standard rules on equalization of opportunities for personnel with disabilities.* New York, NY: Author.

Werner, D. (1986). *Arguments for including disabled children in primary health care.* Paper presented at the CBR conference in Kenya.

Other Books by Venture Publishing

The A•B•Cs of Behavior Change: Skills for Working With Behavior Problems in Nursing Homes
by Margaret D. Cohn, Michael A. Smyer, and Ann L. Horgas

Activity Experiences and Programming within Long-Term Care
by Ted Tedrick and Elaine R. Green

The Activity Gourmet
by Peggy Powers

Advanced Concepts for Geriatric Nursing Assistants
by Carolyn A. McDonald

Adventure Programming
edited by John C. Miles and Simon Priest

Assessment: The Cornerstone of Activity Programs
by Ruth Perschbacher

Behavior Modification in Therapeutic Recreation: An Introductory Manual
by John Dattilo and William D. Murphy

Benefits of Leisure
edited by B. L. Driver, Perry J. Brown, and George L. Peterson

Benefits of Recreation Research Update
by Judy M. Sefton and W. Kerry Mummery

Beyond Baskets and Beads: Activities for Older Adults With Functional Impairments
by Mary Hart, Karen Primm, and Kathy Cranisky

Beyond Bingo: Innovative Programs for the New Senior
by Sal Arrigo, Jr., Ann Lewis, and Hank Mattimore

Beyond Bingo 2: More Innovative Programs for the New Senior
by Sal Arrigo, Jr.

Both Gains and Gaps: Feminist Perspectives on Women's Leisure
by Karla Henderson, M. Deborah Bialeschki, Susan M. Shaw, and Valeria J. Freysinger

Client Assessment in Therapeutic Recreation Services
by Norma J. Stumbo

Client Outcomes in Therapeutic Recreation Services
edited by Norma J. Stumbo

Conceptual Foundations for Therapeutic Recreation
edited by David R. Austin, John Dattilo, and Bryan P. McCormick

Dimensions of Choice: A Qualitative Approach to Recreation, Parks, and Leisure Research
by Karla A. Henderson

Dementia Care Programming: An Identity-Focused Approach
By Rosemary Dunne

Diversity and the Recreation Profession: Organizational Perspectives
edited by Maria T. Allison and Ingrid E. Schneider

Effective Management in Therapeutic Recreation Service
by Gerald S. O'Morrow and Marcia Jean Carter

Evaluating Leisure Services: Making Enlightened Decisions, Second Edition
by Karla A. Henderson and M. Deborah Bialeschki

Everything From A to Y: The Zest Is up to You! Older Adult Activities for Every Day of the Year
by Nancy R. Cheshire and Martha L. Kenney

The Evolution of Leisure: Historical and Philosophical Perspectives
by Thomas Goodale and Geoffrey Godbey

Experience Marketing: Strategies for the New Millennium
by Ellen L. O'Sullivan and Kathy J. Spangler

Facilitation Techniques in Therapeutic Recreation
by John Dattilo

File o' Fun: A Recreation Planner for Games & Activities, Third Edition
by Jane Harris Ericson and Diane Ruth Albright

Functional Interdisciplinary–Transdisciplinary Therapy Manual
by Deborah M. Schott, Judy D. Burdett, Beverly J. Cook, Karren S. Ford, and Kathleen M. Orban

The Game and Play Leader's Handbook: Facilitating Fun and Positive Interaction, Revised Edition
by Bill Michaelis and John M. O'Connell

The Game Finder—A Leader's Guide to Great Activities
by Annette C. Moore

Getting People Involved in Life and Activities: Effective Motivating Techniques
by Jeanne Adams

Glossary of Recreation Therapy and Occupational Therapy
by David R. Austin

Great Special Events and Activities
by Annie Morton, Angie Prosser, and Sue Spangler

Group Games & Activity Leadership
by Kenneth J. Bulik

Growing With Care: Using Greenery, Gardens, and Nature With Aging and Special Populations
by Betsy Kreidler

Hands on! Children's Activities for Fairs, Festivals, and Special Events
by Karen L. Ramey

Inclusion: Including People With Disabilities in Parks and Recreation Opportunities
by Lynn Anderson and Carla Brown Kress

Inclusive Leisure Services: Responding to the Rights of People with Disabilities, Second Edition
by John Dattilo

Innovations: A Recreation Therapy Approach to Restorative Programs
by Dawn R. De Vries and Julie M. Lake

In Search of the Starfish: Creating a Caring Environment
by Mary Hart, Karen Primm, and Kathy Cranisky

Internships in Recreation and Leisure Services: A Practical Guide for Students, Third Edition
by Edward E. Seagle, Jr. and Ralph W. Smith

Interpretation of Cultural and Natural Resources, Second Edition
by Douglas M. Knudson, Ted T. Cable, and Larry Beck

Intervention Activities for At-Risk Youth
by Norma J. Stumbo

Introduction to Recreation and Leisure Services, Eighth Edition
by Karla A. Henderson, M. Deborah Bialeschki, John L. Hemingway, Jan S. Hodges, Beth D. Kivel, and H. Douglas Sessoms

Introduction to Writing Goals and Objectives: A Manual for Recreation Therapy Students and Entry-Level Professionals
by Suzanne Melcher

Leadership and Administration of Outdoor Pursuits, Second Edition
by Phyllis Ford and James Blanchard

Leadership in Leisure Services: Making a Difference, Second Edition
by Debra J. Jordan

Leisure and Leisure Services in the 21st Century
by Geoffrey Godbey

The Leisure Diagnostic Battery: Users Manual and Sample Forms
by Peter A. Witt and Gary Ellis

Leisure Education I: A Manual of Activities and Resources, Second Edition
by Norma J. Stumbo

Leisure Education II: More Activities and Resources, Second Edition
by Norma J. Stumbo

Leisure Education III: More Goal-Oriented Activities
by Norma J. Stumbo

Leisure Education IV: Activities for Individuals with Substance Addictions
by Norma J. Stumbo

Leisure Education Program Planning: A Systematic Approach, Second Edition
by John Dattilo

Leisure Education Specific Programs
by John Dattilo

Leisure in Your Life: An Exploration, Sixth Edition
by Geoffrey Godbey

Leisure Services in Canada: An Introduction, Second Edition
by Mark S. Searle and Russell E. Brayley

Leisure Studies: Prospects for the Twenty-First Century
edited by Edgar L. Jackson and Thomas L. Burton

The Lifestory Re-Play Circle: A Manual of Activities and Techniques
by Rosilyn Wilder

Models of Change in Municipal Parks and Recreation: A Book of Innovative Case Studies
edited by Mark E. Havitz

More Than a Game: A New Focus on Senior Activity Services
by Brenda Corbett

Nature and the Human Spirit: Toward an Expanded Land Management Ethic
edited by B. L. Driver, Daniel Dustin, Tony Baltic, Gary Elsner, and George Peterson

The Organizational Basis of Leisure Participation: A Motivational Exploration
by Robert A. Stebbins

Outdoor Recreation for 21st Century America
by H. Ken Cordell, principal author

Outdoor Recreation Management: Theory and Application, Third Edition
by Alan Jubenville and Ben Twight

Therapeutic Recreation in the Nursing Home
by Linda Buettner and Shelley L. Martin

Therapeutic Recreation Protocol for Treatment of Substance Addictions
by Rozanne W. Faulkner

Tourism and Society: A Guide to Problems and Issues
by Robert W. Wyllie

A Training Manual for Americans with Disabilities Act Compliance in Parks and Recreation Settings
by Carol Stensrud